The One Book

for

Every Opera Lover

MILTON CROSS, whose name is synonymous with opera in America, has compiled in this one volume everything that any listener needs to get true pleasure from the greatest operas.

Whether you are an opera fan or an occasional listener, *Stories of the Great Operas* will multiply many times the enjoyment you get from great music.

Written with lucid wit and acknowledged authority, this is a book every cultured person should own.

Stories of the Great Operas was originally published by Doubleday & Company, Inc. For this edition, the author has retained 36 of the 72 operas in the original edition, rewritten Part II, brought Part III and the Selected Reading Guide up to date and added a guide to opera recordings.

MILTON CROSS

STORIES OF THE
GREAT
OPERAS

WASHINGTON SQUARE PRESS, INC. • NEW YORK

STORIES OF THE GREAT OPERAS

(Original title:
Milton Cross' Complete Stories of the Great Operas)

A *Washington Square Press* Edition

1st printing....................November, 1955
4th printing......................January, 1967

This WASHINGTON SQUARE PRESS edition contains 36 of the 72 operas which appeared in the original, hardcover book. Sections of this book have been revised and updated with new material added by the author.

L

Published by
Washington Square Press, Inc., 630 Fifth Avenue, New York, N.Y.

WASHINGTON SQUARE PRESS editions are distributed in the U.S. by Simon & Schuster, Inc., 630 Fifth Avenue, New York, N.Y. 10020 and in Canada by Simon & Schuster of Canada, Ltd., Richmond Hill, Ontario, Canada.

Copyright, 1947, 1952, ©, 1955, by Milton J. Cross. All rights reserved. Library of Congress Catalog Card Number: 55-8723. This WASHINGTON SQUARE PRESS *edition is published by arrangement with Doubleday & Company, Inc. Printed in the U.S.A.*

Contents

FOREWORD vii

PART I. STORIES OF THE GREAT OPERAS 1
- Aïda, *Verdi* 1
- Un Ballo in Maschera, *Verdi* 10
- Il Barbiere di Siviglia, *Rossini* 25
- La Bohème, *Puccini* 42
- Boris Godunof, *Moussorgsky* 60
- Carmen, *Bizet* 76
- Cavalleria Rusticana, *Mascagni* 94
- Così Fan Tutte, *Mozart* 102
- Don Giovanni, *Mozart* 114
- Faust, *Gounod* 128
- La Forza del Destino, *Verdi* 139
- Gianni Schicchi, *Puccini* 155
- Hänsel und Gretel, *Humperdinck* 161
- Lohengrin, *Wagner* 169
- Lucia di Lammermoor, *Donizetti* 183
- Madama Butterfly, *Puccini* 191
- Die Meistersinger von Nürnberg, *Wagner* . . . 199
- Mignon, *Thomas* . . . . 21?

CONTENTS

Norma, *Bellini* 222

Le Nozze di Figaro, *Mozart* 232

Otello, *Verdi* 245

Pagliacci, *Leoncavallo* 259

Parsifal, *Wagner* 265

Rigoletto, *Verdi* 279

Der Ring des Nibelungen, *Wagner* 290

    Das Rheingold 290

    Die Walküre 299

    Siegfried 307

    Die Götterdämmerung 318

Der Rosenkavalier, *Strauss* 328

Salome, *Strauss* 352

Tannhäuser, *Wagner* 358

Tosca, *Puccini* 368

La Traviata, *Verdi* 378

Tristan und Isolde, *Wagner* 392

Il Trovatore, *Verdi* 401

Die Zauberflöte, *Mozart* 413

PART II. How TO ENJOY AN OPERA 427

PART III. A BRIEF HISTORY OF OPERA 435

SELECTED READING GUIDE 461

SELECTED OPERA RECORDINGS 464

INDEX 469

Foreword

THIS is a book of stories—the stories of the great and enduring operas. Most of them I have told on the air many times in the twenty-odd years that I've been privileged to work with opera broadcasts. Some of them have become so familiar that I return to them each year almost as one returns each season to the Christmas story.

To me the stories in this volume are never old, never timeworn. I've enjoyed retelling them here as I have on the air. Indeed, this book has in a sense grown out of the broadcasts, for through the years nothing has given me more pleasure, I think, than the letters from listeners, newcomers, and seasoned operagoers alike, telling me how important the stories had been in the appreciation and enjoyment of the music. A disturbing element, however, has been the number of people who told me that they wanted to know the stories in greater detail than we could tell them. I can't say how many thousands of times I have explained that the synopses preceding the broadcasts were brief only because of the limitation of time. I do know, though, with what pleasure I have tried to work into the stories in the book the color and flavor and detail that I have never had the opportunity to use on the air. I have retold them here as fully, as clearly, and as carefully as I could. Whatever faults there may be this time are mine alone.

This book then is an attempt to fill a need—to tell the stories of the best-known operas completely and accurately, with every bit of essential action described, with every important musical section indicated, with the relationship between action and music clearly defined. In later sections of the book the study of the libretti and the scores themselves is recommended. But I am fully aware, of course, that frequently the libretti and scores are not available and that, even when they are, many readers are not yet ready to study the operas in such detail. Then, too, even the most ardent opera enthusiast must admit that libretti in English translation are too often both inaccurate and dull. I hope that as the stories are retold here, with all of the distinctive passages—such as the opening lines of each aria—given in the language in which the opera is sung, they will provide all of the essential landmarks so necessary to a true understanding of the operas.

To preserve the utmost accuracy and to avoid the errors which have crept into many of the translations, the stories in this volume have been taken from the scores and the libretti in the original languages. There is, however, an element of risk even in complete accuracy, for many performances today abbreviate or deviate from the script. In many cases these deviations have become traditional, so that throughout this book it has been necessary to indicate the exact plot of the opera not only as it is written, but also as it is normally produced. This situation has been further complicated by the fact that the variations are not always uniform, and considerable effort has frequently been necessary to trace the pattern of the stories as they are actually produced in the important opera houses of the world.

Needless to say, there are many and varied opinions as to what constitutes "standard" or "favorite" repertoire. Some will consider many of the thirty-six operas in this volume too infrequently performed to be worthy of inclusion. Others will surely think the list too short and will point to one or several operas which they rate as worthy as others included here. It is worth stressing that the list has not been compiled on the basis of personal preference. It is based fundamentally on an analysis of actual frequency-of-performance statistics of leading opera houses for the last fifty years. Obviously such a method is, in itself, not completely satisfactory, and to prevent the list from becoming a mere mathematical computation, a group of people closely associated with the opera were queried and the benefits of their knowledge superimposed on the statistical results. I have tried—and, I hope, successfully—

FOREWORD

to keep my own personal preferences from interfering with a more desirable system.

The reasons for including in a book of opera stories sections on the history of the opera and on how to enjoy an opera must be obvious. In them are embodied answers to the questions most frequently asked by those anxious to create a richer background for the enjoyment of operatic music. Actually each section is intended to serve a dual purpose: to provide at least a minimum foundation for the more casual reader and to indicate the more important fields of study for those serious students who wish to go further.

The writing and compilation of this book represents the work of five years, and without the aid, advice, and encouragement of many persons, it would almost certainly never have been completed. Inadequate though my thanks may be, I want to express my gratitude to a few of those who have helped.

First, to Karl Kohrs, whose assistance has been invaluable. The burden of research was his, and his careful checking and rechecking of doubtful points insure the accuracy of this book. In addition, much of the credit for final rewriting goes to him, because his choice of word and phrase has frequently made possible the logical clarification of a scene which the librettist had left only half told, half implied.

To Ralph Beebe and Mel Evans, who believed in this book from the start. Their ideas and their encouragement gave the book its broad plan and purpose, and they guided it through difficult periods.

To Miss Gladys E. Chamberlain, librarian of the Music Branch, New York Public Library, and to her assistants Mary Lee Daniels, Elsa Hollister, Louise Howe, Eleanor Chasan, Lily Goldberg, and Hilda Stolov, for their co-operation in making available scores, libretti, books, and other research sources.

To Paul Weiss, of Boosey & Hawkes, Inc., and to Alfred Mapleson of the Mapleson Music Library, for their understanding kindness in allowing the use of materials otherwise difficult to obtain.

To Goddard Lieberson, of Columbia Recording Corporation, and to music critic Irving Kolodin, of the *Saturday Review of Literature,* for their aid in selecting the operas to be included.

To Madame Zinaïda Lisichkina for her transliterations of arias from the Russian to the Latin alphabet.

To Nelson Lansdale, of Columbia Concerts, Inc., for his generous advice on opera décor.

To Richard Crooks, who made the initial contact between author and publisher that brought this book into being.

To Mark Woods, Charles Barry, Helen Guy, Harold Strickland, Ruth Crawford, Ruth Smith, and numerous other associates at American Broadcasting Company who have helped in many ways to ease the progress of this book. Also to my many friends at the National Broadcasting Company, the Metropolitan Opera Association, and others associated with the opera broadcasts over the years, because the knowledge and the help I obtained in working with them have contributed both directly and indirectly to this book.

And finally to my wife. Her assistance was no passive encouragement from the side lines. Not only did she read and listen to the stories hour upon hour; she participated in the work directly, and many of the most felicitous words and phrases are hers. Her patience and competence have frequently rescued a scene or an act from my hands and given it new life.

M. J. C.

PART I

STORIES OF THE GREAT OPERAS

Aïda

by GIUSEPPE VERDI
[1813-1901]

Libretto by
ANTONIO GHISLANZONI

Based on a sketch by Mariette Bey which was later used as a basis for a prose drama written by Camille du Locle in collaboration with Verdi

CHARACTERS

The King of Egypt	Bass
Amneris, his daughter	Mezzo-soprano
Aïda, an Ethiopian girl and slave to Amneris	Soprano
Radames, an Egyptian captain of the guard	Tenor
Ramfis, a high priest of Isis	Bass
Amonasro, King of Ethiopia and father of Aïda	Baritone
Messenger	Tenor
Priestess	Soprano

Priests and priestesses, guards, slaves, dancers, soldiers, Egyptians, prisoners

Place: Memphis and Thebes in ancient Egypt
Time: The dynasty of the Pharaohs
First performance: Cairo Opera House, Cairo, Egypt, December 24, 1871
Original language: Italian

VERDI was nearing sixty when he composed *Aïda* at the invitation of the Khedive of Egypt, who had asked him to write an opera on an Egyptian subject for the opening of the Italian Opera House in Cairo in 1869 as part of the celebration in honor of the dedication of the Suez Canal. The opera, however, was not completed in time for the festivities.

The composer had become interested in a scenario by the French Egyptologist, Mariette Bey, who, it is said, based it on an incident in ancient Egyptian history disclosed during his archaeological excavations at Memphis. Verdi and the dramatist, Du Locle, expanded the scenario into a prose drama, and the composer also collaborated with Ghislanzoni in turning the drama into a libretto.

The prelude begins with the violins softly stating the theme associated with Aïda throughout the opera. This gives way to the somber motive of the priests of Isis, foreshadowing the final doom pronounced by those priests on Aïda and Radames. The Aïda theme then recurs briefly.

ACT ONE

[*Scene One*] A great hall in the palace of the Egyptian King at Memphis. Ramfis and Radames are seen in conversation. The High Priest reveals that the Ethiopians are again challenging Egypt's power in the Nile Valley and are threatening Thebes. He expects word from messengers shortly. Radames inquires if the goddess Isis has been consulted. Isis has named the man who is to lead the Egyptians, Ramfis replies, looking significantly at Radames. He then leaves to report the sacred decree to the King.

Radames exclaims that perhaps now he will realize his greatest ambition—to lead Egypt's army to victory. Then he will return in triumph to Memphis—and to his beloved Aïda. In the aria, "Celeste Aïda, forma divina," he reveals his secret love for the captive Ethiopian girl who is the slave of Amneris. He envisions her in the homeland she longs for, reigning as a beautiful queen on a throne near the sun. Radames concludes the aria on a high ringing note of exaltation.

At the conclusion of the number Amneris enters, and Radames tells her that today he has achieved his proudest desire. She asks pointedly if no other feeling touches his heart—thoughts of someone in Memphis, perhaps. As the theme of Amneris's jealousy stirs in the orchestra, Radames, in an aside, wonders if in his enthusiasm he has betrayed his love for Aïda. Amneris, also to herself, voices her haunting suspicion that Aïda is her rival.

Aïda appears as her characteristic theme is heard. Amneris asks her why she is sad ("Vieni, O diletta, appressati"), and these words introduce an impressive trio. The talk of war frightens her, Aïda replies, and she is distressed by the country's danger. By this subterfuge Aïda successfully conceals her grief for her own country. Her Egyptian captors do not suspect that she is the daughter of Amonasro, King of Ethiopia. Over the jealousy theme Amneris fumes in an aside that Aïda's efforts to deceive her are in vain. Aïda expresses her foreboding, while Radames frets over Amneris's malevolent look, fearing that her suspicions will ruin all his plans.

Suddenly there is a fanfare of trumpets. The King enters, preceded by his guards and followed by Ramfis, ministers, priests, and officers. A courier reports that the Ethiopians have invaded Egypt and are marching on Thebes. The enemy troops are under the command of Amonasro, their King. The throng shouts in anger, while Aïda cries out in fear and alarm as she hears her father's name. Turning to Radames, the King announces that Isis has decreed that he is to lead the attack, then bids him enter the Temple of Vulcan to be vested with the sacred armor. In a martial strain, "Su! del Nilo al sacro lido!" he calls on his people to fight. Singing a chorus of triumph, the throng leaves the great hall, acclaiming Radames with the shout, "Ritorna vincitor!" Aïda, left alone, repeats the phrase, "Ritorna vincitor!" which introduces the aria thus familiarly titled. Wondering how she can say, "Return victorious," she describes how she is torn between devotion to her father and love for Radames. Bitterly she reproaches herself for daring to utter the unholy words which mean the conquest of her own father. She visions the conqueror, stained with the blood of her brothers, riding triumphantly in his chariot—and behind his chariot her father in chains. In poignant phrases ("O Numi, sperdete") she implores the gods to give her father the victory. Then, recalling her love for Radames, she wails that she can pray neither for father nor lover without blaspheming one or the other. Again her voice soars in an eloquent prayer ("Numi, pietà"). At the end of the aria her voice dies away in a mournful sigh. The curtain falls.

[*Scene Two*] The Temple of Vulcan in Memphis. In the center of the stage is an altar carved with sacred emblems. Clouds of incense rise from the great golden tripods. Ramfis stands at the foot of the altar with priests and priestesses around him. The priestesses chant an invocation to the god Phtha ("Possente, Phtha!"), to which the priests respond. The ritual dance of the priestesses then begins. Radames enters and proceeds to the altar. A silver veil is draped over his head, and in his outstretched hands Ramfis places the sacred sword. The High Priest invokes the aid of the gods in protecting Egypt ("Nume, custode e vindice"). Radames repeats the prayer. The chorus breaks out into a tremendous cry to the great Phtha ("Immenso Phtha!") as the curtain falls.

Act Two

[*Scene One*] An open court outside the palace apartments of Amneris. Her serving-women are attiring her for the victory festival in honor of the returning armies. Moorish slave boys dance for her, while slave girls sing of the delights of love that await the victor ("Chi mai fra gli inni e i plausi"). The voice of Amneris rises above the chorus as she bids her hero hasten to her arms ("Vieni, amor mio").

Suddenly she sees Aïda approaching. She dismisses her slaves, resolving to wring from Aïda the confession of her love for Radames. A powerfully dramatic duet ensues ("Fu la sorte dell' armi"). Amneris first tells Aïda that Radames has been slain. When Aïda's deep grief betrays her love, Amneris says that she has trapped her with a lie—Radames is alive! Overcome with joy, Aïda thanks the gods. Amneris furiously commands her slave to look upon the one whom she dares oppose in love—a daughter of the Pharaohs. Aïda is about to disclose that she, too, is of royal blood, but she checks herself. Falling to her knees, she pleads for mercy and confesses her love. From outside comes a blare of trumpets, followed by the shouts of the crowd hailing the conqueror. Amneris tells Aïda that in the victory festival she shall play her true role—a slave groveling in the dust. She herself will be seated on the throne in triumph at the King's side. Aïda implores once again for mercy. The curtain falls.

[*Scene Two*] A great palm-bordered avenue at an entrance to the city of Memphis. On one side is the Temple of Ammon, on the other a canopied throne. At the rear is a triumphal arch. The scene is crowded with people. The King enters with his vast retinue. Followed by Aïda and her other slaves, Amneris appears and takes her place on the throne at the King's side. A massive chorus ("Gloria all' Egitto") bursts forth, acclaiming the glory of Egypt. Then the priests thunder a chorus of thanksgiving ("Della vittoria agli arbitri") for the deliverance of the nation.

Led by a phalanx of trumpeters playing the *Grand March*, the Egyptian troops enter in a glittering pageant of banners, arms, chariots, sacred vessels, and statues of the gods. The warriors arrange themselves on either side. Dancing girls, carrying the spoils of victory, perform a ballet symbolic of the Egyptian triumph. The chorus rises to a great crescendo as Radames rides up in his chariot.

As the theme of Amneris's infatuation for Radames vibrates in the orchestra, she bestows upon him the victor's crown. In response to his request the Ethiopian captives are led forth in chains, the last prisoner being Amonasro, dressed as an officer. Aïda gasps that he is her father. All exclaim in surprise. When she embraces him he warns her not to disclose his kingly identity. Amonasro tells the King that as an officer he fought for his sovereign, who was slain in battle. In the melody of noble dignity ("Ma tu, o Re, tu possente") he beseeches the King to be merciful to the defeated.

Amonasro is joined in his entreaty by Aïda, the other slaves, and the captives. In a great ensemble ("Struggi, o Re, queste ciurme feroci"), the priests grimly demand revenge, while the people urge the King to heed the pleas of the conquered. As Radames expresses his love for Aïda, Amneris, watching them both, cries out for revenge. The King mourns that he must bow to the will of the gods. This ensemble is interrupted when Radames requests the King to free the Ethiopian captives. Ramfis, however, objects, saying he will consent to their release only if Aïda's father is held as hostage. The King agrees. Turning to Radames, he declares that his reward for winning the victory will be the hand of Amneris. Another triumphal chorus concludes the act.

Act Three

The banks of the Nile. Granite rocks, partially hidden by palm trees, rise from its edge. Near the top of the ramparts is the Temple of Isis. From within come the voices of the priests chanting a hymn to Isis. Amneris and Ramfis, followed by a group of heavily veiled women, step from a boat which has glided to the shore. Ramfis invites Amneris to the temple, where she may invoke the blessing of the goddess on her wedding eve. All then enter the sanctuary.

With her face veiled, Aïda now appears and sings the famous aria which is familiarly known as "O patria mia." Beginning with the phrase, "Ocieli azzuri," Aïda poignantly expresses her hopeless longing for her homeland. As she stands bowed in sorrow Amonasro suddenly enters. Sternly he says that he has learned that she is in love with Radames, the

conqueror of her people. He angrily reminds her that the
Egyptian hordes have devastated her homeland and commands
her to forget her love in thoughts of revenge. The
Ethiopians are now poised to strike back, Amonasro says, but
they must first know the name of the pass through which the
Egyptians will march. Aïda herself must betray Radames into
revealing that secret, Amonasro declares. When her protests
prove useless Aïda yields and promises to obey. Amonasro
hides among the palms as Radames approaches.

Radames greets Aïda with an ecstatic cry. She responds
coldly, reminding him that he is soon to wed Amneris. He
swears that he loves Aïda alone and will never forsake her.
Yielding at length to his fervent declarations, Aïda says that
only one course remains—they must flee from this inhospitable
country to her native land, where they can share the
bliss of love ("Fuggiam gli ardori inospiti"). Radames at first
hesitates but finally resolves to go with her ("Ah! no! fuggiamo!").
Together they sing of the joys that await them. Aïda
then asks Radames what route they will take to avoid the
opposing armies. Through the pass, he answers, where the
Egyptians have planned to ambush the Ethiopians—it will
be unguarded until morning. Deliberately Aïda asks him to
name it. The pass of Napata, he replies.

Scarcely has he spoken when Amonasro springs from his
hiding place, reveals himself as King of the Ethiopians, and
exclaims that he will order his troops to the pass at once.
Radames cries that for Aïda's sake he has unwittingly become
a traitor ("Io son disonorato!"). Amonasro and Aïda
try to calm him, saying that he is guiltless and that his actions
were decreed by destiny. At that moment Amneris
rushes from the temple, shouting "Traitor!" She is followed
by Ramfis, the priests, and the temple guards. Amonasro,
dagger in hand, lunges at Amneris but is restrained by
Radames, who urges him to flee with Aïda. Ramfis orders his
guards to follow the fleeing pair. With a cry of surrender
("Sacerdote, io resto a te") Radames hands his sword to the
High Priest. The curtain falls.

STORIES OF THE GREAT OPERAS

ACT FOUR

[*Scene One*] A hall in the palace of the Egyptian King. At right is the portal of the prison where Radames is waiting to hear the traitor's doom from the lips of the priests. At left is the entrance to the subterranean hall of judgment. Before it stands Amneris in an attitude of dejection. In recitative she expresses her conflicting emotions of jealousy and love. Resolving to make one final attempt to save Radames, she orders the soldiers to bring him before her.

An intensely dramatic duet follows ("Già i sacerdoti adunansi"). Amneris entreats him to confess his guilt, throw himself on the mercy of the priests, and clear his name. Radames scorns her pleas. She has robbed him of Aïda, he says—perhaps even caused her death—and now nothing is left him but infamy. Aïda lives, Amneris answers. She tells Radames that only Amonasro was killed, while Aïda escaped. Amneris offers to save him if he will promise to forget Aïda, but Radames calmly refuses to bargain, saying he is prepared to die.

Radames is returned to his cell by the guards as the grim theme of the priests sounds in the orchestra. Amneris sings that in her jealous fury she has condemned Radames to death and herself to unending woe ("Ohimè! morir mi sento"). She cowers in terror as the priests cross the stage to the entrance of the judgment hall. Below, in an unaccompanied chorus ("Spirito del Nume sovra noi discendi!"), they call upon the gods to witness the justice of their sentence.

Now Radames, between guards, crosses the stage and descends to the judgment hall. We hear the voice of Ramfis stating the charge of treason. The priests command him to defend himself ("Discolpati!"). There is no answer. Three times Ramfis calls, "Radames"; three times the priests exhort him to reply. He remains silent. During the pauses Amneris implores the gods for mercy.

Suddenly, in a powerful chorus, the sentence is pronounced: Radames is to be buried alive in a tomb under the altar of the god whose wrath he has provoked ("Radames, è deciso il tuo fato"). The priests emerge from the hall, chanting that justice has been done. Amneris rages that in their lust for revenge they have condemned an innocent man. In answer they intone that the traitor must die ("È traditor! morrà!"). As they slowly move off, Amneris screams a curse after them. The curtain falls.

[*Scene Two*] This is the famous double scene. The upper part is the Temple of Vulcan, flooded with light. The lower portion is a tomb, deep in shadow. Radames is seated on the steps leading down from above. Two priests move a great stone slab into place over the tomb. Radames sings that the stone has now closed over him ("La fatal pietra") and laments that he will never see Aïda again. Suddenly a figure emerges from the shadows. Recognizing Aïda, he cries out in astonishment at seeing her in the tomb ("Tu—in questa tomba!"). Now begins the moving duet which dominates the opera's great closing scene. Aïda tells Radames that she stole unseen into the tomb to share death with him ("Presago il core della tua condanna"). Radames protests that she must not thus doom herself.

Meanwhile the ritual dance begins in the temple above and we hear the voices of the priests in the death chant. In a last frenzied effort Radames tries to move the stone. Then he clasps Aïda in his arms, and together they sing their farewell to earth ("O terra, addio"). Amneris appears above and flings herself on the stone of the vault, sobbing a prayer to Isis. Her voice and the chanting of the priests blend with the final phrases of the lovers' duet. Aïda dies in the arms of Radames. As the curtain slowly descends we hear the prayer of Amneris imploring peace ("Pace t'imploro") and the priests' final invocation to Phtha.

Un Ballo in Maschera

(The Masked Ball)

by GIUSEPPE VERDI
[1813–1901]

Libretto by
ANTONIO SOMMA

Based on the libretto written by the French dramatist Scribe for
the opera Gustavus III, ou Le Bal Masqué
by Daniel Auber

CHARACTERS

Samuele ⎱ conspirators .... *Bass*
Tommaso ⎰
Edgardo, page to King Riccardo .... *Soprano*
Riccardo, King of Sweden .... *Tenor*
Renato, secretary to King Riccardo .... *Baritone*
Ulrica, a sorceress .... *Contralto*
Adelia, wife of Renato .... *Soprano*
Silvano, a sailor in King Riccardo's service .... *Bass*
A judge, townspeople, courtiers, maskers, dancers

Place: Sweden
Time: Eighteenth century
First performance: Teatro Apollo, Rome, February 17, 1859
Original language: Italian

Un ballo in maschera, like several other Verdi operas, had the distinction of being the center of a political tempest at the time of its scheduled première. It was to have been presented in 1858 under its original title, *Gustavus III*, the plot being based on the events surrounding the assassination of King Gustavus III of Sweden at a court ball in 1792.

Un Ballo in Maschera

While the opera was in rehearsal, Italian revolutionists attempted to assassinate Napoleon III in Paris. In view of the fact that Verdi's opera had to do with a successful conspiracy against royalty, it was promptly banned by the authorities. They suggested to Verdi that he adapt his music to a new libretto, but this he flatly refused to do.

When the controversy came to the attention of the public it touched off vociferous demonstrations in behalf of the composer. Crowds marched through the streets shouting, "Viva Verdi!" Actually his name was being used as a political battle cry by those factions which sought to unite Italy under the leadership of King Victor Emmanuel. Someone had discovered that the letters V E R D I might well represent the slogan "Vittorio Emmanuele, Re D'Italia" (Victor Emmanuel, King of Italy).

The problem was finally solved in a rather remarkable way. For the opera's presentation in 1859, Verdi made several changes. The title was changed to *Un Ballo in Maschera*, the locale was shifted from Sweden to Puritan New England, and King Gustavus became Riccardo (or Richard), Earl of Warwick and Governor of Boston. The conspirators Samuele and Tommaso were cast as Negroes, the secretary Renato (or Reinhart) as a Creole, and Ulrica, the sorceress, as a Negress.

In later years it became customary to present the opera with a European setting, usually Naples. Although today the work is frequently performed either with the Naples or the Boston locale, in many opera houses it is given in its original setting: the court of the King of Sweden.

Act One

The palatial audience chamber of King Riccardo. After a brief prelude, a group of officials and gentlemen of the court sing the praises of the King and pledge their loyalty. Samuele and Tommaso, standing at one side with their followers, assert in a sinister undertone that those whom the King has wronged are burning for revenge. He need not think, they warn, that his victims lie forgotten in their graves.

Edgardo,[1] the page, announces the King. Riccardo enters and greets the assemblage, then receives various petitions. He promises that all will receive justice, adding that it is the first duty of those in power to give aid and comfort to their subjects. The page then gives him, for his approval, the list of guests for the forthcoming masked ball. Riccardo says he hopes that none of the court beauties have been overlooked. Seeing the name of Adelia,[2] he exclaims that she is the fairest of the fair, and that her very name fills his heart with joy. These phrases introduce the ecstatic romanza, "La rivedro nell' estasi," in which Riccardo rhapsodizes over his love for Adelia.

An impressive ensemble follows as various persons in the chamber express their sentiments. The conspirators sing that this is not the propitious moment for their plot, as the King is surrounded by his friends. Edgardo and the courtiers observe the look of happiness on the King's face.

Riccardo dismisses the page, who, on leaving, announces Renato. As Renato enters, the courtiers withdraw. The secretary remarks that the King seems troubled. The latter, in an aside, expresses the disturbing thought that this man is the husband of his beloved. The honest Renato wonders why the King seems sad while the city rings with his praises. Riccardo says he is oppressed by a secret woe. When Renato declares he knows the source of the King's concern, Riccardo utters an exclamation of guilty fear. Each, of course, is unaware of the other's real meaning. Renato warns the King that he is no longer safe in his own palace because a certain faction is plotting his death. Relieved, but still concerned, Riccardo asks for further details. When Renato offers to reveal names, the King avers that the matter is, after all, unimportant. Were he to know, he adds, he would have to shed blood, and that he will not do, for God and his loyal subjects will protect him.

[1] Sometimes Oscar.

[2] Sometimes Amelia.

In a dramatic aria, "Alla vita che t'arride," Renato reminds the King that the destiny of thousands depends upon him, and if he were to perish, the pride and glory of the fatherland would perish with him. But Riccardo brushes aside his secretary's warning. Edgardo enters with a judge, who presents a decree of exile for the King's signature. As he peruses it, Riccardo demands the name of the woman who is to be exiled. Her name is Ulrica, a woman of a foreign race, the judge replies. Edgardo interrupts to say that people from near and far—even renowned sages and soothsayers—come to her for advice. The judge declares that this crone's lair is a rendezvous for outlaws and malefactors and insists that the sentence be carried out. When Riccardo, somewhat amused, asks Edgardo for his opinion, the page implores him to intercede. In a florid aria, "Volta la terrea," the page vividly portrays Ulrica as a mighty prophetess who can read good or evil fortunes in the stars and who undoubtedly is in league with the devil himself.

As the aria ends, the judge reiterates that Ulrica must be condemned. Edgardo again implores mercy for her. Riccardo now prepares to announce his decision to the assemblage. When the courtiers have re-entered, he declares that he himself intends to visit Ulrica's hut in disguise and invites his court to accompany him. Renato endeavors to dissuade the King, pointing out that someone may recognize him, but Riccardo deprecates his warning. Edgardo enthuses over the adventure. The King tells the page to make ready a sailor's costume for his disguise. Samuele and Tommaso sneer at Renato's cautious counsel, then gloat over the fact that the King's whim may further their plot.

Riccardo gaily bids all to make the most of this amusing adventure and tells them he will be at the sorceress's den at the hour of three in the morning. Renato promises to keep a watchful eye on the proceedings, while Edgardo jubilantly declares that he proposes to have his own fortune told. Samuele and Tommaso, in a somber undercurrent, utter dire threats. The courtiers express their pleasure over the exciting diversion in store for them, and a tremendous chorus brings the act to a close.

Act Two

Ulrica's dwelling, a large hut of rough-hewn timbers.[3] At the left is a steaming cauldron hung on a tripod over a fire. At the rear is a staircase leading above, and at its base a secret door. The hut is crowded with people intently watching Ulrica as she stands before the cauldron. After a weird and somber introduction, the onlookers sing of the evil genie that is soon to appear. Ulrica, stirring her witch's brew, begins the great incantation aria, "Re dell' abisso affretati." Dramatically she bids the monarch of the underworld to appear before her. Three times, she chants, the owl has screeched, three times the salamander has leaped through the fire, three times the dead have groaned from the tomb.

Suddenly Riccardo strides in, announcing that he is first to arrive. The women in the crowd, horrified at the interruption, order him away, while Ulrica glares at him. With a careless laugh he walks to the rear and stands in the shadows. A flash of light illumines the hut, and the women gasp in terror. Resuming her incantation, Ulrica sings in primitive ecstasy that the evil genie has come at her bidding, bringing her the terrible power of sorcery that will give her command over human destiny. Her voice now sinks to a hoarse whisper as she demands silence. The effect is one of extraordinary dramatic power.

There is a stir as Silvano, a sailor, shoulders his way through the cowering throng and demands that Ulrica tell his fortune. He relates that as a seaman in the service of the King he has served faithfully and has more than once saved his sovereign's life. After fifteen years, he complains, he has received neither promotion nor increase in pay. What is his reward to be? he asks. Riccardo, in an aside, commends his

[3] The opera was originally written in three acts, this being Scene Two, Act One.

Un Ballo in Maschera

forthrightness. Ulrica takes the sailor's hand and tells him that he will soon be amply recompensed. Silvano is skeptical, but Ulrica reassures him. Riccardo surreptitiously scribbles a note and slips it, with some money, into the sailor's pocket, stating that he will make *this* prophecy come true. Declaring that Ulrica's optimistic prediction must not go unrewarded, Silvano puts his hand into his pocket. He exclaims in joy when he discovers the money and note of promotion. Ulrica is hailed as a great prophetess.

At that moment there is a knock at the secret door. To Riccardo's surprise, Adelia's servant enters. He tells Ulrica that his mistress is waiting outside and wishes to consult her secretly. Ulrica answers that she must first dismiss the people. She advises her visitors that in order to reveal their fortunes it will be necessary to speak to the oracle alone. After all but Riccardo withdraw, Adelia enters in great agitation. The sorceress asks what troubles her. The torment of secret love, Adelia replies, and then implores Ulrica to pluck from her heart the love of one whom destiny has placed on the throne.

Hearing this, Riccardo is overjoyed. In somber tones Ulrica tells Adelia of a plant possessing the power to control the heart's impulses. Whoever desires this plant must gather it alone at midnight from the fearsome spot in which it grows. Eagerly Adelia asks where she must go, saying that nothing will daunt her. In dramatic, sonorous phrases, Ulrica describes the gallows tree which stands near the west gate of the city ("Della città all' occaso"). At its base grows the evil plant, flourishing in soil shadowed by the bodies of criminals who have atoned for their sins at the rope's end.

Adelia recoils in horror. Ulrica takes note of her terrified mien, while Riccardo pities her distress. When Adelia vows that she will not shirk her duty, the sorceress directs her to gather the plant this very night. In an aside, Riccardo declares that she shall not go alone. An impressive trio follows. Adelia prays for strength to face the ordeal and implores Heaven to cleanse her heart of its illicit passion ("Consentimi, O Signore"). Ulrica assures her that she will be restored by the magic of the herb. Riccardo passionately avows his love and swears that he will protect Adelia. They are interrupted by the voices of courtiers outside, demanding admittance. Adelia hurries out.

Samuele and Tommaso, Edgardo, and the courtiers, all in disguise, crowd into the hut followed by the townspeople. They urge Ulrica to continue her prophecies. Edgardo inquires about the King, and Riccardo warns the page not to betray his identity. Approaching Ulrica, he asks her to reveal what the future has in store for him. In character with the nautical role he is playing, Riccardo sings the famous *Barcarolle* ("Di' tu se fidele"). Like any sailor, he wonders if his sweetheart is true to him, saying he fears neither wind nor waves, but thinks only of the welcome that awaits him when his ship comes safely back to harbor. The crowd makes a spirited response as he declares that, whatever Ulrica's prophecy, he will hear it unafraid.

The sorceress turns on him with a grim warning that the man who dares mock his destiny may bitterly repent such folly. After a moment's parley as to who will be the first to learn his fate, Riccardo disdainfully holds forth his hand. The sorceress proclaims it the hand of a nobleman and a warrior. True enough, Edgardo remarks impudently. Riccardo silences the page. Suddenly Ulrica lets go his hand and curtly bids him leave and ask no more questions. The others urge her to go on, and as she hesitates, Riccardo commands her to speak.

Thereupon Ulrica cries out that his doom is near. If it is to be a soldier's death, says Riccardo carelessly, he will be grateful. He will die by the hand of a friend—thus it is decreed, Ulrica intones. The crowd exclaims in horror. But Riccardo derides the grim prophecy as idle folly in a mocking strain beginning with the words "E scherzo od e follia." This serves to introduce a quintet which is considered one of Verdi's finest operatic ensemble numbers. Edgardo expresses his fears as Ulrica, glaring at Samuele and Tommaso, repeats her warning of doom, as though reading their thoughts. The conspirators now fear their plot has been discovered.

The ensemble is interrupted when Riccardo asks Ulrica

Un Ballo in Maschera

who is destined to slay him. The first man who shakes his hand, she replies. Riccardo promptly holds out his hand to the courtiers, defiantly urging someone to fulfill the prophecy then and there. All shrink back in terror. At that moment Renato enters. The King strides over to him and grasps his hand as the crowd thunders out Renato's name. Samuele and Tommaso, to their great relief, are still beyond suspicion. The crowd proclaims that the prophecy has failed as Riccardo informs Ulrica that the man whose hand he holds is his most trusted friend. Renato then reveals the King's identity. With good-natured sarcasm, Riccardo tells Ulrica that the omniscient genie she conjured up not only failed to inform her of the King's presence but neglected to tell her that she had been put under a decree of banishment that very day. As Ulrica gasps in terror, Riccardo reassures her and gives her a purse. Humbly grateful, Ulrica warns him again that a traitor hovers near. Perhaps more than one, she adds significantly. Samuele and Tommaso, overhearing, are alarmed.

Then from outside come voices hailing Riccardo. Silvano enters with a large group of friends. Pointing to Riccardo, he announces that the King is present and bids all to do him homage. They do so in a ringing chorus, "O figlio d' Inghilterra." All join in the tribute except Ulrica and the conspirators—Ulrica reiterating her dire predictions and Samuele and Tommaso fuming over the fact that the King, thus surrounded by his fawning subjects, is safe from their designs.

ACT THREE

A snow-covered plain, dominated by a gallows.[4] To the accompaniment of the prelude, Adelia appears on the scene and walks hesitantly toward the gibbet. In recitative she says that the sight of the fearful gallows, with the baleful plant at its base, makes her blood run cold. The very sound of her own footsteps frightens her. But she vows that not even the threat of death will deter her from this ghastly errand.

[4] Act Two in the original.

Adelia then sings the dramatic aria, "Ma dall' arido," in which she laments that the glorious love in her heart is about to be destroyed by the evil power of the herb. And when that love is gone, nothing remains, she sighs in despair. Dolefully she bids her heart harden like the very stones in its resolve, then cries out for the surcease that death can bring. Suddenly she gasps in terror as she spies a figure approaching through the gloom. In her panic she imagines that it is an apparition with fiery eyes and grisly countenance. Adelia feverishly prays for protection and then, as the figure draws closer, sinks fear-stricken to her knees.

Riccardo rushes up and takes her in his arms. Distractedly Adelia tries to repulse him, begging him to go. Riccardo ardently replies that he will never leave her because his heart is aflame with love. She tells the King that she must be faithful to another—to the man who would die for his sovereign. Alas, the bitter truth, Riccardo cries. With passionate intensity he tells Adelia that though he is tormented by remorse, he has struggled in vain against his overpowering love for her. In anguish she pleads for death to save her from dishonor. Again she implores Riccardo to go, but he ignores her protests and begs for one word of love.

Yielding to his ardor, Adelia confesses her love for him. Riccardo ecstatically responds. Tenderly Adelia sings that now he must answer both for her honor and her heart, to which Riccardo replies that for her love he will disdain all thoughts of guilt and sacrifice every friendship. In a long, melodious duet, "O qual soave brivido," they pour out their devotion for each other.

Suddenly someone is heard approaching. The King asks who dares come to this place of doom. In the next moment he recognizes Renato. Gasping that it is her husband, Adelia quickly lowers her veil. Renato tells Riccardo that he has come to protect him from traitors who are at this moment in pursuit. The secretary goes on to say that, with his face hidden by his cloak, he had come upon the plotters and had been taken for one of them. He had overheard one say that he had seen the King on his way to a rendezvous with a

Un Ballo in Maschera

mysterious woman; another replied that he intended to interrupt the King's trysting with a sword stroke.

Renato throws his mantle around Riccardo to hide his royal garb, then tells him to flee by a certain pathway. The King protests that he cannot leave his companion, but in an aside Adelia begs him to go at once. Renato, misunderstanding her entreaty, reproachfully asks her if she would deliver the King into the hands of his would-be murderers merely for the sake of her love. Adelia implores Riccardo to make his escape while the way is still clear, but the King vows that he will die before he will leave her. In desperation, Adelia threatens to tear aside her veil. This threat has an immediate effect, and Riccardo turns to speak to Renato, while, in a dramatic aside, Adelia declares that she would gladly die to save her royal lover from the evil fate that stalks him.

Riccardo asks Renato to swear that he will escort his lady safely to the city, that he will not attempt to speak to her or to ascertain her identity, and that he will never try to see her again. The loyal Renato promises unhesitatingly. A spirited trio follows. Renato and Adelia warn of the impending danger and urge the King to flight. Riccardo, fuming against the conspirators, confesses that he too is a traitor. For an illicit love he has shamefully betrayed his truest friend. Were it not for his guilt he would stay and face his enemies.

As Riccardo rushes off, Renato assures Adelia that he will protect her. In the next instant Samuele and Tommaso, with their fellow conspirators, burst upon the scene shouting for vengeance. Renato calls out to them. The conspirators halt in their tracks, exclaiming in baffled fury that he is not the King. The secretary defiantly informs them that the King is safely away, then makes himself known. Samuele ironically remarks that Renato is indeed fortunate to be in the company of so fair a lady. Tommaso adds that he feels obliged to unveil the beauty. Angrily Renato draws his sword. The conspirators are about to attack when Adelia rushes forward to shield Renato. Her veil falls from her face. Horror-stricken, Renato cries out her name. The conspirators are astounded.

Samuele sneers about the guileless husband who unwittingly makes love to his own wife at a secret tryst in the moonlight. He and the others break into sardonic laughter, gloating over how they will regale the whole town with this delectable morsel of court scandal. A powerfully dramatic chorus ensues. Adelia, overwhelmed with grief and shame, laments her wretched fate, while Renato, burning with rage and humiliation, cries that the King has rewarded his devotion with infamy and dishonor. The conspirators, with malicious glee, describe how the gossip will spread through the town.

Interrupting, Renato grimly asks Samuele and Tommaso to come to his home in the morning. When Samuele hints at planning revenge, Renato curtly replies that he will explain purpose when they meet. Renato coldly tells Adelia that he will keep his promise to escort her to the city, but his words sound to her like a judgment of doom. As the conspirators withdraw, their voices die away to insinuating whispers. The curtain falls.

Act Four

The library of Renato's home.[5] On one wall hangs a great oil painting, a portrait of King Riccardo. After a few measures of introduction the curtain rises to reveal Adelia and Renato. In cold anger he tells his wife that she can expect no mercy—only death. Adelia tries desperately to convince him that what he saw was only the appearance of guilt, not guilt itself. Her protests only goad Renato to greater fury, and he wildly repeats that her doom is sealed. In anguish Adelia kneels before him, begging for one last favor in a moving refrain, "Morro, ma prima in grazia." She asks to see their son once more, so that in her last hour of life she may embrace him.

Renato, moved despite his anger, roughly orders Adelia to her chamber. There in the gloomy silence, he says, she may see her son and think upon her dishonor. Alone, he muses

[5]Act Three in the original.

Un Ballo in Maschera

that he will spare his wife and son the consequences of his vengeance. Facing Riccardo's portrait, he cries out in bitter wrath that there is the one whose blood will flow to blot out this disgrace. Then Renato sings the famous aria, "Eri tu che macchiavi," in which he pours out his grief over the treachery of the man whose friendship he had cherished. He recalls his happiness with Adelia when their love was unsullied. In an eloquent, profoundly moving climax, he sings that hope and love are gone forever.

Crushed by despair, Renato stands with bowed head before the portrait. Suddenly Samuele and Tommaso enter. Renato, showing them an official report, abruptly informs them that he has known of their plot against Riccardo. Samuele comments that now Renato will, of course, inform the King. On the contrary, Renato retorts, he wishes to join the conspiracy.

Samuele and Tommaso are dumbfounded, but Renato says he will give them a token of good faith. Not only will he aid them in carrying out their bloody plan, he declares, but he will offer his son's life as forfeit if he fails to do his part. To the conspirators this sudden about-face is beyond belief. Renato asks them not to question his motives and repeats that he will join their cause, with his son as hostage. In a brief but dramatic trio the plotters swear that they will stand united in one single purpose: revenge.

At this point Renato asks that he be allowed to strike the fatal blow. Samuele objects, as his father was deprived of his home by Riccardo, and for this he must have his revenge. Tommaso demands the privilege, saying that for ten years he has waited to settle accounts with Riccardo for murdering his brother. Renato finally suggests they draw lots. The three then write their names on separate slips of paper and place them in a vase.

At this tense moment Adelia enters to announce that Edgardo is waiting with an invitation to Riccardo's masked ball. Although surprised, Renato grimly observes that fate must have sent Adelia to him at this moment. Fear-stricken, Adelia voices her premonition of disaster. Renato tells Samuele and

Tommaso that Adelia will decide the fateful issue. With sardonic gallantry, he leads her to the vase and invites her to draw one name from it with her innocent hand. She asks why. Angrily he orders her to obey without further question. In an aside, Adelia murmurs that destiny has forced her hand to a bloody deed.

Dark, somber chords vibrate in the orchestra as Adelia tremblingly takes a slip of paper from the vase and hands it to Renato, who gives it to Samuele. Excitedly Renato asks whom fate has chosen. When Samuele reads his name, Renato exults in vengeful triumph. Adelia cries that the King will fall defenseless before the conspirators' weapons. The four voices join in a dramatic quartet—Adelia voicing her despair over the King's fate, the men rejoicing that their revenge is near.

Renato then admits Edgardo, who presents the King's invitation to the ball. The page assures him that Riccardo will be present, adding that the ball will be an affair of unusual magnificence. Looking sharply at Adelia, Renato promises he will attend with his wife. Samuele and Tommaso, in an aside, note that the masked ball will greatly expedite their plans. Edgardo begins a spirited refrain, "Ah, di che fulgor," introducing the brilliant quintet which closes the act. The page sings of the gaiety and splendor in store for the guests; Adelia bewails the fact that she has become an unwitting accomplice in the plot against the King; Renato, Samuele, and Tommaso exult in the prospect of perpetrating their revenge in mask and domino.

Act Five

A private audience chamber in the King's palace.[6] Riccardo is seated at his writing desk. The orchestra softly plays the melody of his aria in Act One, in which he revealed his love for Adelia. In recitative, the King sings that he will renounce

[6] Originally written as Scene Two of Act Three. Sometimes this is played as Scene One of Act Five and takes place at the front of the stage before the curtain.

the woman he loves and send Renato back to England, the land of his birth. Adelia shall accompany him. Thus, Riccardo sighs, an ocean will forever separate him from his beloved. Firmly he signs the document, then laments that he has sealed his fate.

In the ensuing aria, "Ma se m'è forza perderti," Riccardo gives vent to his sorrow and despair. He is haunted by the premonition that when Adelia departs not only love but life itself will depart with her. He then prepares to leave for the ball, cheered by the thought that he may see Adelia for at least one more brief moment. Edgardo enters and hands him a note, saying that it is a secret message from a mysterious masked woman. It informs the King that someone is plotting to kill him during the ball. Riccardo pauses, then resolutely declares that he will attend despite all threats. Expressing his happiness at the prospect of seeing Adelia, he quickly leaves.

The curtains part to reveal the final scene—the great ballroom. The guests sing gaily of the joys of the dance. Samuele, Tommaso, Renato, and their followers appear wearing blue domino costumes set off by a red ribbon. Renato, in conversation with Samuele, expresses doubt that Riccardo will appear, whereupon Samuele fumes that once more they may be cheated of their prey. The secretary warns that they are being watched, indicating the masked figure of Edgardo. He approaches the page, and after some banter they unmask each other. Craftily Renato suggests that perhaps Edgardo has slipped away to enjoy the dancing while the King is asleep. The page replies that Riccardo is present, then coolly tells Renato to seek out the King for himself. Renato entreats the page at least to describe the King's costume. In a sprightly aria, "Saper vorreste," Edgardo mocks Renato's questioning. He sings that though he knows well enough where the King is, he will never tell. Renato persists in his efforts to trick Edgardo into betraying the King's whereabouts. Finally he tells the page that before the night is out he must speak to the King on urgent business, implying that Edgardo will be held to account if the meeting is not arranged.

Thus tricked, Edgardo reveals that the King is wearing a

black domino with a red rosette. Renato says he has one more question, but Edgardo cuts him short and leaves. Dancers and merrymakers again dominate the scene. Riccardo suddenly appears, thoughtfully watching the throng. In a moment Adelia, dressed in a white costume, hurries to his side. Disguising her voice, she urgently advises him to leave. He asks her if she wrote the warning letter. In answer she tells him that he is in mortal danger and must flee at once. Riccardo asks who she is and why she is so concerned. Adelia, no longer able to control herself, speaks in her natural voice, whereupon Riccardo fervently exclaims that her disguise has been in vain.

To the accompaniment of the graceful rhythm of a mazurka, the two sing an impassioned duet of farewell ("T'amo, si, t'amo, e in lagrime"). Again and again Adelia beseeches Riccardo to escape before it is too late. Ignoring her desperate entreaties, the King reveals that he is going to send her back to England with her husband, then ardently avows his love for her. Passionately they sing their last farewell.

At that instant Renato lunges toward the King, crying out, "And here is *my* farewell!" He fires his pistol at close range, and Riccardo falls.[7] With shouts of rage the crowd closes in on Renato. The dying King, raising himself, commands them to release the assassin. Slowly he draws from his pocket the document assigning Renato to his duties in England and hands it to his secretary. Quietly he assures him that Adelia is innocent. Though he loved her, the King declares, he did nothing to dishonor her name. Renato and Adelia cry out in the anguish of remorse, and the people join in voicing their grief over this tragic denouement.

As Renato bitterly condemns himself, the King forgives all who conspired against him. Summoning his ebbing strength in one last supreme effort, Riccardo utters a ringing phrase of farewell, then falls back dead. As the chorus rises to a powerful climax, the curtain slowly falls.

[7] As originally written, the action calls for Renato to stab Riccardo with a knife, but it has become customary in some opera houses to substitute shooting with a pistol.

Il Barbiere di Siviglia

(The Barber of Seville)

by GIOACHINO ANTONIO ROSSINI

[1792–1868]

Libretto by
CESARE STERBINI

Based on the comedy
LE BARBIER DE SÉVILLE
by the French dramatist Beaumarchais

CHARACTERS

Fiorello, Count Almaviva's servant	Bass
Count Almaviva	Tenor
Figaro, a barber	Baritone
Rosina, ward of Dr. Bartolo	Soprano
Dr. Bartolo	Bass
Don Basilio, a music teacher	Bass
Bertha, Dr. Bartolo's housemaid	Soprano
Ambrosius, Dr. Bartolo's servant	Bass

A magistrate, a notary, an officer, musicians, and soldiers

Place: Seville
Time: Seventeenth century
First performance: Teatro Argentina, Rome, February 5, 1816
Original language: Italian

THE STORY of *Il Barbiere di Siviglia* is based on the first of a series of three comedies by the eighteenth-century playwright Beaumarchais. The three plays—*Le Barbier de Séville, Le Mariage de Figaro,* and *La Mère Coupable*—are sometimes known as the "Figaro trilogy" because they have as their hero Figaro, barber and jack-of-all-trades in Seville. The second play formed the basis of Mozart's *The Marriage of Figaro*. Several characters in Mozart's opera appear in Rossini's work. Rossini was not the first to set Beaumarchais's *Le Barbier* to music. Giovanni Paisiello, another Italian composer, had already written an opera, *Il Barbiere di Siviglia* (1776), based on the French comedy.

The impresario of the Teatro Argentina, Duke Cesarini, commissioned Rossini to write two operas for the carnival season of 1816. The first, *Torvaldo e Doliska*, was produced on December 26, 1815. That same day Rossini agreed to have the first act of the second opera—destined to become *The Barber of Seville*—ready on January 20. Time was short, and it was decided to adapt the plot used by Paisiello. Some historians say that Rossini completed the opera in thirteen days; others, in fifteen. In any case, it was written between December 26, 1815, and February 5, 1816.

In view of the continued popularity of Paisiello's work, Rossini realized that his own use of the same plot might incur not only the venerable composer's disfavor but that of the public as well. He wrote Paisiello, requesting permission to use the story and pointing out that the title had been changed to *Almaviva, ossia l'inutile Precauzione* (*Almaviva, or the Useless Precaution*). He also stated that he had required the librettist to make an entirely new versification of the Beaumarchais comedy.

Though Paisiello granted Rossini's request, it did not prevent a fiasco. The entire first act was sung over a bedlam of whistles, catcalls, shrieks, and howls. No one could hear the music except the singers themselves and the players in the orchestra, led by Rossini himself, at the piano. The second performance, however, was well received, and within a week the opera achieved the popularity it has maintained for more than 125 years.

The overture to *The Barber* has an interesting history. The one played at the first performance is said to be identical with that which had served for two earlier Rossini operas—*Il Turco in Italia* (*The Turk in Italy*) and *Sigismondo*. When

Il Barbiere di Siviglia

for some strange reason the music disappeared Rossini calmly substituted an overture he had used for at least two other operas—*Aureliano in Palmira* (*Aurelian in Palmyra*) and *Elisabetta, Regina d'Inghilterra* (*Elizabeth, Queen of England*). This one has endured as the opera's overture.

ACT ONE

[*Scene One*]   A square in Seville. Facing it is the house of Dr. Bartolo. There is a second-floor balcony with shuttered windows. As the music softly begins Fiorello enters carrying a lantern and leading a group of musicians. He cautions them to be quiet and they repeat the admonition in chorus. Count Almaviva appears and quietly calls to Fiorello, who assures him that the musicians are ready. The Count commends them, then warns all to be silent. There is a pause while the musicians tune their instruments. In a moment the orchestra begins the air of the Count's serenade to Rosina, "Ecco ridente in cielo."[1]

The Count sings that the dawn's glow is driving away the gloom of night. He bids his loved one rise and fill his heart with joy. He rhapsodizes over the blissful moment of her appearance and of the enchantment she brings to his heart. The aria ends in a florid climax, but Rosina does not appear. Almaviva asks Fiorello if he sees Rosina, then voices his disappointment. The servant reminds the Count that the morning is getting on, whereupon the latter calls to the musicians. Almaviva gives his purse to Fiorello, who starts paying off the players. They are so profuse and long-winded in their thanks that both Almaviva and Fiorello impatiently tell them to be off. All voices blend in a spirited chorus.

A recitative follows. The Count and his servant fret over the noisy musicians, grumbling that they have awakened the whole neighborhood. Almaviva vows he will not leave until

[1] Rossini inserted this cavatina for the second performance to replace the ill-fated "Spanish serenade" that Manuel Garcia had insisted on singing on the opening night. The composer had used the cavatina previously in his *Aurelian in Palmyra* and *Cyrus in Babylon*.

he can speak with Rosina, whom he has been secretly watching from afar every morning. He tells Fiorello to leave. He assures himself that he needs only a word with Rosina—and he wants no witnesses. Rosina must have discovered his purpose by this time, he adds, and realizes that he loves her. He resolves to make her his Countess.

Suddenly from the distance comes the rollicking voice of Figaro. The Count wonders who the intruder might be, then decides to hide in a doorway. Figaro appears and begins the famous aria, "Largo al factotum della città." Make way for the town's most useful citizen, he sings. He is Figaro the barber—a gentleman of parts at the top of his profession. In a word, Fortune's favorite.

He is at everyone's service—anywhere, any time. Ready with scissors, combs, and razors, he awaits his customers. Observe his resourcefulness! He advises lovelorn maidens and ardent swains. Everyone demands and commands—young and old, matron and belle: "My wig! Hurry, a shave! What a headache! Quick—post this letter!" No rest day or night! It is always Figaro-Figaro-Figaro, until he can bear it no longer. Have pity! One at a time, please! It's Figaro here—there, high—low, come—go! Yes, the most illustrious citizen of the town. Bravo, Figaro! The most favored of men! Thus the barber brings his aria to a spectacular close.

In recitative Figaro goes on bragging about himself. It's a great life, he declares—lots of fun and plenty of money. As the result of his distinguished position, not a maid in all Seville can find a husband without his aid, and all the pretty widows give him alluring glances. By day he wields the tools of his trade, by night he strums his guitar. And so he is welcome everywhere.

The Count, meanwhile, wonders where he has seen Figaro before. The barber, catching sight of Almaviva, likewise speculates. Then they greet in mutual recognition. The Count explains that he has come to town incognito and does not wish his presence known. Anyone as clever as Figaro can easily understand why. Figaro instantly agrees, then asks the Count what he is doing in Seville. Almaviva tells him that while strolling along the Prado one evening he saw a very beautiful girl. He discovered that she is the daughter of an old codger of a doctor who lives in this very house. Since he saw her he has spent most of his time beneath her balcony.

Well, says Figaro, that is a rare stroke of luck for the Count. In that very doctor's house, he, Figaro himself, is barber, hairdresser, consultant, and confidant extraordinary. And what is more, that beautiful girl is not the doctor's daughter, but his ward. The Count is overjoyed. Suddenly Figaro cautions silence. The window opens and Rosina steps out on the balcony. Almaviva exclaims in rapture.

If she could only give "him" the letter she holds in her hand, Rosina sighs to herself. Just as she catches sight of the Count and Figaro below, Dr. Bartolo comes bustling out and asks to see the note. Rosina assures him that she has written down the words of a song from *The Vain Precaution*. The Count and Figaro marvel at her clever ruse. Bartolo asks the meaning of *Vain Precaution*, and the girl explains that it is a new and popular opera. The doctor scoffs at current musical productions, at the stupid public which goes to see them, and the detestable artists who perform them.

Suddenly Rosina exclaims that she has dropped the note and asks Bartolo to get it for her. In an aside she signals the Count, who snatches up the letter and hides in the doorway. Bartolo grumbles that he cannot find the paper. Rosina says that the wind has probably blown it away. Bartolo mutters his suspicions and then roughly orders his ward to go into the house. Rosina laments her misfortune, and Bartolo growls out that the balcony will be walled off tomorrow.

Almaviva exclaims that this turn of events will only strengthen his resolve. Figaro urges him to read Rosina's note. It tells the Count that his visits have been noticed. The doctor is going out, and as soon as he is gone the unknown admirer must somehow identify himself. Although it is impossible to appear on the balcony without her tyrannical guardian, Rosina will make every effort to escape.

Highly pleased with the contents of the note, the Count asks Figaro more about the doctor. Figaro answers that the man is mad, to begin with, and an ill-tempered old skinflint. He is over sixty, yet he is conceited enough to think he can persuade Rosina to marry him—for her money, of course. He tells everyone he is Rosina's future spouse.

Figaro suddenly notices that the door of the house is opening. Out comes Dr. Bartolo, loudly ordering that if Don Basilio arrives he is to wait. He will now arrange his marriage, he mutters to himself as he leaves. Once that is done, there will be no need for Rosina's seclusion.

The Count scornfully observes that if the old fool thinks he will marry Rosina he must be drunk. He asks Figaro about Don Basilio. The barber informs him that Basilio is a crafty, conniving rascal, an unscrupulous matchmaker, and an inveterate chiseler. Yet he is the man, Figaro adds sardonically, who has been hired to teach Rosina the high art of music. The Count remarks that he will make use of him.

The barber now suggests that the Count give his attention to Rosina's wishes as stated in the note. Almaviva decides that he will not disclose his royal identity until he is sure that Rosina loves him for himself alone, not for his rank and money. When he asks Figaro to help him in his campaign the barber tells him he will need no assistance because Rosina is at this very moment standing at her window. All he has to do is to sing a serenade of his own devising, one which will reveal his name and his sentiments.

Almaviva forthwith begins a charming song ("Se il mio nome"), a musical reply to Rosina's letter. He sings that he is Lindoro, who loves her ardently and begs her to say that she loves him in return. Rosina answers him in a tender phrase. Almaviva is in ecstasy over her reply, and Figaro urges him to continue. The second stanza tells Rosina that her Lindoro can offer her neither wealth nor fame but only boundless devotion. He implores her not to scorn what he seeks to give her.

Rosina begins a phrase in answer, then abruptly disappears within. The Count is vexed, but Figaro warns him that someone apparently has entered the house. Impatiently the Count declares that he must see Rosina today at any cost

Il Barbiere di Siviglia

and again asks Figaro to help him. He tells the barber to put his genius to work contriving an entree to the doctor's home. Almaviva says he will pay Figaro well for his trouble—any amount he needs—and bids him get busy. The barber replies that "Signor Lindoro" cannot realize what a magical effect the offer of gold has on his inventive genius.

In a delightfully mock-serious air ("All' idea di quel metallo"), Figaro proclaims that gold stirs his mighty brain into volcanic action. The Count interrupts the barber, advising him to reveal his stupendous thoughts before they overburden his mind. Then, in a brilliant vocal passage, he tells Figaro that if he can successfully carry off this intrigue he will be hailed as the greatest of all barbers.

Figaro suggests that the Count disguise himself as a soldier, reminding him that troops are expected in the town today. The Count approves, remarking that the colonel is a friend of his. What luck! says Figaro. It will be easy to demand quarters at the doctor's house, he explains, because nobody will dare refuse a soldier with good connections. He asks the Count's opinion of his scheme, and Almaviva compliments him on his sagacity. In an amusing duet ("Che invenzione") Figaro joins the Count in praise of himself. The barber interrupts to say that the gold has inspired another brilliant idea. The soldier, he explains, must give the impression that he is drunk. Obviously, anybody in his cups will never be suspected of being a spy. Triumphantly Figaro sings again of his inventive genius, with the Count joining in a continuation of the duet.

They are about to part when the Count asks Figaro where he lives. Figaro answers that there is no mistaking his home —it is the barbershop. Then, in an engaging aria ("Numero quindici a mano manca"), he sings that his shop is at "number fifteen," the left side of the street, four steps up, the door painted white. In the window are displayed five magnificent wigs, as well as wonderful beauty preparations.

You can't miss it, Figaro declares. Keep to the left—remember the five wigs. There he will be. The Count assures the barber that he will be able to find his shop and thanks him for all he has done. Figaro answers that he considers the Count's success as his first duty. Almaviva promises to return with plenty of money. Then the two begin an exultant duet. The Count sings of the bliss of love which this day's planning will bring, while Figaro hails the gold that will soon be clinking in his pockets. As they continue, Figaro reiterates the instructions on how to find his shop, and the Count in his amorous excitement repeats them after him. At the end of the duet the Count leaves and Figaro goes into Dr. Bartolo's house. Fiorello appears and in a brief recitative grumbles that he has been waiting for his master for two solid hours, only to find that he has gone somewhere else. And all because he is in love, Fiorello mutters, going on his way.[2] The curtain falls.

[*Scene Two*] A drawing room in Dr. Bartolo's home.[3] Large arched french windows lead to a balcony. The curtain rises to reveal Rosina alone in the room. She holds a letter. After a few bars of music suggesting her trembling heart, she begins the brilliant "Una voce poco fa," one of the best-known arias in the coloratura soprano repertoire.[4] A secret voice is enshrined in her heart—the voice of Lindoro, she sings, and vows that he shall be her love. She will thwart her guardian's plans and will never disclose her love until she has given her hand.

Then Rosina goes on to say that she is by nature very sweet and reasonable—until she is crossed. If she does not get her way she will turn like a serpent, resorting to any kind of trickery to get what she wants. This is a lesson, she warns, that everybody had better learn.

In recitative she wonders where she can find a messenger to deliver her letter, lamenting that she has no one she can trust—always under the eye of that awful ogre, she pouts.

[2] Sometimes omitted.

[3] This is sometimes played as Act Two.

[4] This aria was originally sung in the contralto key because the role was written for low voice. Through the years it gradually became the property of coloraturas.

Il Barbiere di Siviglia

Then, while sealing the letter, she recalls that she saw Figaro and the Count talking together. The barber is a decent, accommodating person—he surely will help her. At that moment he enters. He notices her troubled expression and observes that a beautiful girl should always be lighthearted and gay. Of what use is it to be gay, Rosina remarks, when she is hidden away from the world? She might as well be dead, she sighs.

At that Figaro takes her aside and is about to tell her something when the doctor is heard approaching. Figaro quickly hides behind the draperies. Bartolo comes in roaring that Figaro, the villain, has made everybody in his household ill with his potions and medicines. He asks Rosina if she has seen the barber, and she replies that she has just had a very pleasant conversation with him on a number of interesting topics. Bartolo, his suspicions immediately aroused, calls Bertha and Ambrosius and tries to find out from them what Figaro and Rosina have been talking about. He gets nowhere, because Bertha, under the influence of a potion, sneezes helplessly, while Ambrosius, drugged, yawns in the doctor's face.

Bartolo swears vengeance on the barber for this trick. At that moment Don Basilio enters. The doctor tells him that he is determined to marry Rosina tomorrow, fairly or otherwise. Basilio says he understands, then takes Bartolo aside and informs him that he has seen Count Almaviva in the neighborhood. He implies that it is the Count who is wooing Rosina. Bartolo storms at this, but Basilio tells him that he has a foolproof plan for disposing of the Count as a rival. The key to his scheme, says Basilio triumphantly, is slander.

Then Basilio sings the great aria, "La calunnia,"[5] in which he traces the fatal course of slander from the merest sigh of suspicion to the storm of accusation which destroys its victim. The music rises with overpowering effect from the first insinuating notes to its tremendous climax.

Bartolo, however, expresses doubt as to Basilio's scheme

---

[5] This aria has been cited as another example of Rossini's "borrowing." It is said to have been adapted from *Sigismondo*.

and then decides that his own strategy is safer. He asks Basilio to help him draw up the marriage contract immediately. Once he is married, he says, he will put an end to Rosina's intrigue. In an aside Basilio sneers that he is a conceited old fool. As they leave the room Figaro emerges, chuckling at the absurdity of Dr. Bartolo's efforts to marry Rosina. As she reappears he tells her that he has astonishing news: Her noble mentor has decided to make himself her adoring spouse! He and Basilio are even now inscribing the marriage papers. Rosina casually remarks that she will have a proper answer for them, then asks the barber whom he met earlier under her window.

Figaro informs her that the stranger is his cousin Lindoro, a personable young man who is studying hard to make a success. Unfortunately he has one sad failing, Figaro goes on gravely. He is hopelessly in love. Rosina expresses great interest and inquires if the young man's ladylove is far away. Nearby, Figaro answers. Then he describes her, enumerating Rosina's own charms and revealing the lady's name by coyly spelling out "Rosina."

Rosina joyously sings that she can scarcely believe that the stranger really loves her—observing, however, that she suspected it all along. Figaro comments admiringly on the girl's cleverness. Excitedly Rosina asks how she may meet her Lindoro at once. Figaro advises her to send him some token —perhaps a short letter. At that Rosina takes a paper from her pocket, saying that the necessary letter has already been written. A duet follows ("Fortunati affetti miei") in which Rosina expresses her rapture over the prospect of meeting her lover, while Figaro comments with amused cynicism on woman's inborn genius for intrigue. The barber leaves as Rosina thanks him for his aid.

Dr. Bartolo returns and with suspicious gentleness asks Rosina what the barber had to say. Warily she answers that it was nothing of importance—Paris fashions, the illness of his daughter Marcellina, and so on. Bartolo suggests that perhaps Figaro brought her an answer to the letter which was "posted" at the window this morning—the "aria" that the wind

Il Barbiere di Siviglia

blew from the balcony. Suddenly he demands to know why her fingers are stained with ink. The girl replies that she burned her finger and applied ink to cure it. Bartolo asks why one sheet of paper is missing from the six that were on the table. Rosina explains that she used one sheet to wrap up candy for Marcellina. Clever! Bartolo sneers, then points out that the pen still has ink on the point. Innocently Rosina says she used it to trace a design on her embroidery.

Bartolo now loses his temper completely and roars at Rosina to be quiet. He bursts into a florid aria ("A un dottor della mia sorte"), berating Rosina for daring to practice her deceptions on a man of his exalted importance. He storms and rants at great length, warning that henceforth he will keep her under lock and key. At the end of the number Bartolo strides furiously from the room. Rosina quietly follows, pausing to remark that the more he objects to her behavior the more she is determined to have her own way.

Bertha now enters, wondering at the uproar. There is a knock at the door and the Count calls from without. Bertha goes to admit him. She is still sneezing. Calling loudly, the Count appears in the uniform of a soldier, pretending to be quite drunk. When Bartolo comes in, the Count takes a piece of paper from his pocket and tries to read Bartolo's name. He repeats it with ridiculous mispronunciations, utterly ignoring Bartolo's shouted efforts to set him right. Drunkenly trying to embrace the old gentleman, the Count says that he is the regimental physician and is to be billeted in Bartolo's house. The doctor splutters in exasperation, while the Count hails him as a true comrade.

At this moment Rosina enters, and an uproarious trio follows. Bartolo desperately protests that he has a paper exempting him from billeting. The Count, managing to reveal his identity to Rosina, declares that he wishes to go at once to his room. Bartolo finally finds the exemption paper and shows it to the Count, who scornfully tosses it aside. The doctor threatens him with his stick, whereupon the Count challenges him to a duel. He takes a stance, calling to Rosina to throw down her handkerchief as a signal for battle.

Deftly he drops a letter as Rosina lets her handkerchief fall. Feigning surprise at seeing the letter, the Count pauses to hand both it and the handkerchief to Rosina. Furiously Bartolo demands that Rosina give him the letter. At that point the Count diverts Bartolo's attention, giving Rosina time to substitute a laundry list for the letter. She assures the doctor that it is only a laundry list. Bartolo discovers that it actually *is* a laundry list and is more confused than ever. At this point Bertha and Basilio enter. The din continues in quintet form.

There is a pause in the ensemble as Rosina, resorting to tears, reproaches Bartolo for his cruel suspicions. The doctor moans his remorse as the Count draws his sword. The uproar breaks out again as Rosina restrains the Count from attacking Bartolo. Then in comes Figaro, carrying his barber's basin. He exclaims at the bedlam, saying that it has attracted a crowd outside. In an aside he warns the Count to be careful. But the Count and Bartolo continue to call each other names until Figaro, in mock severity, rebukes Almaviva, at the same time trying to warn him that the guard has been called. Nothing avails, however, and the pandemonium continues.

It ceases abruptly as a thunderous knock is heard. From without come the voice of the officer of the guard and a chorus of soldiers. All in the room express their consternation in a short but dramatic ensemble. Then a guard enters and demands to know who is involved in this fracas. With that the bedlam breaks out afresh as everyone in the room either makes accusations or attempts to explain matters.

They are stopped by the officer, who steps up to Almaviva and tells him he is under arrest. The Count takes the officer aside and reveals to him his rank. Amazed, the officer steps back and salutes. In a short trio ("Fredda ed immobile") Rosina and Bartolo express their bewilderment, while the Count gloats over his coup. The others, voicing their consternation, join in the brilliant ensemble which concludes the act.

Il Barbiere di Siviglia

Act Two

The scene is the same as Scene Two.[6] When the curtain rises Bartolo is alone, musing about the drunken soldier. He concludes that the fellow was sent by Almaviva to find out everything he can about Rosina. There is a knock. Hesitantly Bartolo goes to the door. The Count enters in the guise of a music teacher. He greets the doctor with elaborate politeness, and an amusing duet follows ("Pace e gioia sia con voi"). Bartolo becomes so annoyed with the visitor's flowery salutations that he implores him to desist and get to the point. Then he loses his temper altogether and storms that every meddling scoundrel in the world somehow manages to get into his house. The Count, meanwhile, exults that his plan is drawing closer to a successful conclusion.

The Count finally introduces himself as "Don Alonzo," professor of music and pupil of Don Basilio. To add to the deception the supposed pupil is dressed in the same garb as that of his teacher. Basilio, who is ill, has sent him to give Rosina her music lesson. When Bartolo expresses alarm and says he will go to see Basilio, the Count hastily assures him that the music teacher is not seriously ill. Bartolo is instantly suspicious, whereupon the Count whispers that he has just come from Almaviva's apartment. There in the Count's absence he came upon a letter from Rosina addressed to the Count. He lets Bartolo see the letter and suggests that if he could show it to Rosina he could easily convince her that the Count is involved with another woman. That will surely turn her against the Count, he reminds the doctor. Bartolo observes that the scheme is a masterpiece of slander and compliments Don Alonzo on being indeed a worthy pupil of Don Basilio. At that point Bartolo pockets the letter.

As Bartolo leaves to summon Rosina the Count ruefully reflects that he has outsmarted himself by telling the doctor about the letter. He is confident, however, that he will be able to explain everything to his adored one. Rosina then enters and is introduced to the Count—"Don Alonzo"—who

[6]Sometimes played as Act Three.

tells her that he is substituting for Don Basilio. Now begins the famous lesson scene, in which singers in the role of Rosina customarily interpolate arias of their own choosing.[1] At some point during the scene Rosina and the Count manage to make their plotting known to each other.

As the lesson ends, the Count praises Rosina's voice. Bartolo interrupts to tell them about an aria sung by a famous opera singer of his day, then proceeds to sing it himself ("Quando mi sei vicina"). Figaro enters and imitates the doctor behind his back. The barber then announces that he has come to shave Bartolo and that it must be done today. Tomorrow will not do, he says over Bartolo's protests, because he will be much too busy with his other customers.

Bartolo finally assents, and after some hesitation gives the barber his bunch of keys so that he can get the shaving utensils. Figaro surreptitiously finds out from Rosina which key fits the balcony entrance and removes it. He leaves the room, and a few moments later there is a terrific crash of broken crockery. Bartolo rushes out in great excitement, while Rosina and her "Lindoro" make the most of his absence to pledge their devotion to each other. Figaro returns with the infuriated Bartolo, who fumes that the clumsy barber has broken six plates, eight goblets, and a tureen.

Bartolo no sooner seats himself to be shaved than in walks Don Basilio. The two gasp in astonishment. Rosina, Figaro, and the Count voice their dismay, fearing that Basilio will expose the Count's identity by denying that he knows this substitute music teacher, "Don Alonzo." But the Count saves the situation by convincing Dr. Bartolo, in an aside, that as Basilio knows nothing of the letter which is to poison Rosina's mind it will be well to get him out of the house at once.

Thereupon Bartolo suggests that Basilio has a high fever and should never have left his house. The Count and Figaro add their warnings, telling Basilio first that he looks like a corpse and in the next breath that he surely must have scarlet

---

[1] It is said that the trio which Rossini composed for this scene was lost after the première. Instead of writing another he left the number to the discretion of the prima donna.

Il Barbiere di Siviglia

fever. Basilio, completely bewildered, becomes even more so when the Count presses a purseful of money into his hand. Then follows an ingenious ensemble, beginning with a short duet by the Count and Rosina—"Buona sera, mio signore." The others join to bid Basilio good night and good health.

Figaro once more prepares to shave Bartolo, while Rosina and the Count seat themselves at the harpsichord. The barber contrives to stand so that he hides the lovers from Bartolo's view. Presumably engrossed in the music lesson, Rosina and Almaviva plan their elopement at midnight. Figaro diverts Bartolo's attention by spattering soap in his eyes. Unfortunately the Count raises his voice in trying to explain to Rosina how he had to make use of her letter. The suspicious Bartolo overhears, leaps from the chair, and shouts accusations at the conspirators. The three merely mock at his rage, then quickly make their exit, leaving the doctor purple with rage.

Bartolo calls in Bertha and Ambrosius. He sends the manservant off to summon Basilio and orders Bertha to go downstairs and see to it that no one enters the house. The next moment he decides to take care of that himself. Bertha, left alone, sings an aria in which she expresses a number of uncomplimentary opinions about marriage, among which is the observation that every old fool in the world seems determined to wed ("Il vecchietto cerca moglie").

Bartolo re-enters with Basilio, arguing about the "Alonzo" deception. The doctor is sure that Alonzo is the Count's spy, while Basilio is convinced that the man is Almaviva himself. Bartolo insists that the marriage contract be arranged that very evening and sends Basilio off to fetch a lawyer. Rosina enters, and Bartolo suddenly decides on a way to trick his rival. He shows his ward the letter given him by Alonzo, citing it as proof that her lover is unfaithful, that everybody is in league against her, and that she is being betrayed into the hands of Almaviva. Recognizing the letter as her own, Rosina is convinced. Determined to have her revenge, she consents then and there to marry Bartolo.

Rosina reveals that Figaro and "Lindoro" have planned to

steal into the house at midnight. She and the doctor plot to capture the intruders, then both leave. With the room momentarily deserted, the orchestra plays a dramatic interlude depicting a thunderstorm. In the half darkness two figures enter from the balcony—the Count and Figaro. They have gained access by means of the key which Figaro took from Bartolo's key ring. Rosina is waiting, and she answers the Count's greeting with scorn and fury. At that point her lover reveals that he is not Lindoro, an emissary of Count Almaviva, but the Count himself. The two then express their rapture in a brilliant duet, "Ah, qual colpo." Figaro urges them to postpone their love-making for the moment because time is short.

As prelude to the elopement, the three sing the delightful trio, "Zitti, zitti, piano, piano," a warning of the need for caution and silence. As they are about to leave Figaro cries out that the ladder has been taken away from the window. At that moment Basilio enters with the notary who is to draw up the marriage contract between Count Almaviva and Rosina. The Count takes Basilio aside and offers him a ring as a bribe, emphasizing his offer by flourishing a pistol. The contract is signed, with Figaro and Basilio as witnesses.

The general rejoicing is interrupted by the entrance of Bartolo with a group of soldiers. He orders the Count's arrest, whereupon the latter reveals that not only is Rosina his wife but that he himself is Count Almaviva. In a dramatic aria he sings that Rosina is now out of the doctor's clutches and that all protests are in vain ("Cessa di piu resistere"). Then he expresses his joy at being united with Rosina as the assembled company add their congratulations.

As the ensemble ends, Bartolo turns on Basilio and accuses him of betrayal because he witnessed the marriage contract. Basilio merely replies that the Count's money was too strong an argument. Ruefully the doctor confesses that he unwittingly helped the marriage along by taking the ladder away from the window. That brings from Figaro the ironical comment that it was a "vain precaution." The doctor is consoled, however, when Almaviva tells him he may keep Rosina's dowry. Bartolo philosophically makes the best of the situation and bestows his blessing on the couple. All express their happiness in a short but brilliant chorus which ends the opera.

La Bohème

by GIACOMO PUCCINI

[1858–1924]

Libretto by
GIUSEPPE GIACOSA *and* LUIGI ILLICA

Based on Henri Murger's novel
Scènes de la Vie de Bohème

CHARACTERS

Marcello, a painter	*Baritone*
Rodolpho, a poet	*Tenor*
Colline, a philosopher	*Bass*
Schaunard, a musician	*Baritone*
Benoit, a landlord	*Bass*
Mimi, a seamstress	*Soprano*
Parpignol, a vendor of toys	*Tenor*
Musetta, a girl of the Latin Quarter	*Soprano*
Alcindoro, an admirer of Musetta	*Bass*
Customs guard	*Bass*

Habitués of the Latin Quarter, merchants, shopgirls, students, vendors, soldiers, waiters

Place: Latin Quarter of Paris
Time: About 1830
First performance: Teatro Reggio, Turin, February 1, 1896
Original language: Italian

When puccini wrote *La Bohème* he had already achieved renown as the composer of *Manon Lescaut,* which scored a sensational success. *La Bohème,* the composer's fourth opera, won him even greater fame, and he was hailed by many as the successor to Verdi.

La Bohème

The characters of *La Bohème* are said to be fairly accurate portraits of artists and habitués of the Latin Quarter who were friends of Henri Murger during his youthful days as a struggling writer.

Act One

An attic studio in Paris. At right is a large window, giving a view of snow-covered roofs. Next to the window is an empty fireplace. In the center of the room, a table and some chairs. At right, a bed. The curtain rises as the music begins, and we see Marcello at work at his easel, while Rodolpho stands looking out of the window. Both men occasionally draw their coats closer around them, blow on their fingers, and stamp their feet in an effort to keep warm. The music begins brightly and vivaciously and sustains this mood throughout most of the scene. After a brief prelude Marcello stops work on his masterpiece, "The Passage through the Red Sea," to remark that the chilly waters of the Red Sea seem to be running down the back of his neck. Just for that, he adds in mock anger, he will drown a Pharaoh. He makes a few vigorous strokes with his brush, then addresses Rodolpho.

The poet, gazing out of the window, observes that all the chimneys in the neighborhood are dutifully emitting smoke. Meanwhile, their own stove is idling like a lazy scoundrel who is too good to work and fancies himself one of the aristocracy. Marcello reminds him that the stove has had no legitimate payment for a long time. Well, sighs Rodolpho, forests are of little use under snow. Marcello declares that one fact is certain: He is very cold. Rodolpho concurs. It seems, Marcello complains, as though his fingers had been frozen by contact with the stone-cold heart of the perfidious Musetta. The two then briefly philosophize about love, comparing it to a furnace in which man is consumed, while woman—who lighted the fire in the first place—watches the process.

All of which, they conclude, does not obviate the fact that they are freezing to death and starving. Marcello impulsively seizes a chair and prepares to smash it up for kindling. At that moment Rodolpho has an inspiration. He picks up a thick manuscript from the table, saying that genius has fostered a brilliant idea. Marcello enthusiastically suggests burning up his "Red Sea," but Rodolpho objects because it probably would smell too badly. His great play, he says, will warm them. Pretending to be horrified, Marcello exclaims that reading the play will only make them colder.

Rodolpho explains that he is going to feed his play to the flames and thus send its soul back whence it came. The world will somehow have to bear up under the stupendous loss. With that, the two stuff some pages of the manuscript into the grate, light a fire, then bask gleefully in its warmth.

Suddenly the door bursts open and Colline stamps in. Tossing a bundle of books on the table, he grumbles that the pawnshops are closed on Christmas Eve. When he exclaims over the fire Rodolpho informs him in mock grief that his play is feeding the flames. Colline ironically comments that the play is certainly scintillating, while Marcello offers a few harsh words about the entr'actes. As Rodolpho casually tosses Act Two into the fire, however, Marcello is loud in his praises of its profound sentiments. The poet mourns the immolation of its passionate declarations of love. That crackling sound? Kisses burning, Rodolpho sighs sadly. He heaves the rest of the manuscript into the fireplace, saying he wishes to see all three remaining acts at once. The three applaud as the flames soar, then mutter gloomily as the fire dies down. When it becomes only a glow, Colline and Marcello, in mock anger, cry down the author.

Without warning, the door again flies open and two errand boys enter laden with firewood, food, and wine. Rodolpho, Marcello, and Colline gape for a moment in amazement, then make a rush for the food, jubilantly exclaiming that now they will be able to enjoy a holiday feast. Schaunard comes striding in and with a lordly gesture tosses a handful of coins on the floor. More than all the money in the Bank of France, he announces. The others, dumfounded, pick up the coins, believing them to be medallions. When Rodolpho discovers that the coins are stamped with the image of King Louis Philippe, all four ceremoniously acclaim the King.

Schaunard now tells the story of how he came by all this good fortune ("Or vi dirò: quest'oro"), but the others ignore him completely. They set the table, unwrap the food, and stoke up the fire. Schaunard persists in spite of their inattention, explaining that he had learned that a certain Englishman—Lord Somebody-or-other—was looking for a music teacher. He applied, was instantly hired, then inquired when the lessons were to begin. Immediately, the Englishman replied. Then, pointing to a parrot sitting in its cage in the house of a neighbor, he bade Schaunard to play and sing until the bird dropped dead.

For three days, Schaunard goes on, he thumped and shouted to no avail. Suddenly he had an inspiration. With his irresistible charm he won the confidence of the servant girl. At this point there is an amusing interplay of musical dialogue. Rodolpho, Marcello, and Colline, still utterly oblivious of Schaunard's babbling, look about for a tablecloth. They finally decide to use a copy of *The Constitutional*, Rodolpho remarking that they can thus digest food and news at the same time. While they finish setting the table, Schaunard, still at his story, explains that he persuaded the maid to secure a sprig of parsley. And that, he finished triumphantly, had the same effect on the parrot that hemlock had on Socrates.

At that point Schaunard becomes aware that so far as the others are concerned he has been talking to nobody but himself. Highly indignant, he consigns them all to the devil. When they begin wolfing down the food he quickly takes it from the table, declaring that it is to be saved for the gloomy tomorrow. Nobody would think of dining at home on Christmas Eve, he adds, when the Latin Quarter offers its festive delights on every hand. Already the streets are fragrant with appetizing odors. Then there are other tempting attractions, such as the pretty girls. Schaunard's suggestion wins unanimous approval. Tonight, then, he proclaims, they will bow to sacred custom: Drink at home, dine abroad.

With a great flourish, they pour out the wine. At that moment there is a knock at the door. It is Benoit, the landlord. After much excited consultation Schaunard lets him in. The four blithely ignore the rent slip in Benoit's hand and greet him with effusive hospitality. Rodolpho immediately plies him with wine. When Benoit says he has come for the rent, his hosts toast his health. Deliberately Marcello shows him the money on the table. Rodolpho and Schaunard are thunderstruck, but Marcello craftily suggests to the landlord that as he has seen the money with his own eyes he may as well relax and enjoy himself.

Taking care to keep Benoit's wineglass filled to the brim, they flatteringly ask him if he is not about the same age as themselves. As Benoit beams at the compliment, Marcello slyly remarks that he saw him making love to a very pretty girl at the Café Mabille one evening. Thereupon the others lustily hail him as a gay dog and a devil of a fellow with the ladies and compliment him on his gallant love-making. Thoroughly befuddled, Benoit brags that, though he was timid when a boy, now in his old age he is at his best. He confesses a weakness for gay young maidens—those who are neither too plump nor—heaven forbid!—too thin. Thin women, he declares, are likely to be catty and ill-tempered. Anyway, they remind him of his wife.

At that the four pretend to be outraged at Benoit's shameless conduct in wantonly deceiving his poor wife. The room must be aired out at once, they exclaim, lest they be contaminated by such immorality. Together they steer the reeling landlord out of the door, melodramatically telling him to be off. In unison they bid him an ironic good night. Roaring with laughter, Marcello announces that now he has paid the last installment on the rent.

Schaunard then reminds his friends that revelry awaits them outside and begins to divide the money. When each pockets his share Marcello holds a battered mirror up to Colline. Now that he has the money, Marcello tells him, he owes it to humanity to get himself a haircut. Colline promises to look for a barber immediately. In an amusing bur-

La Bohème

lesque of "grand opera" exits, Marcello, Colline, and Schaunard announce that they are leaving. Rodolpho, however, says that he must remain behind to complete an article for his magazine, *The Beaver*. It will be a matter of only five minutes, he adds. Schaunard puns that he had better cut the *Beaver's* tale short.

As the three start down the stairs Rodolpho stands at the landing outside the door to light their way with a candle. They descend, good-naturedly cursing the darkness. Suddenly there is a resounding crash, and Colline groans that he has fallen. Rodolpho calls to Colline, asking him if he has managed to kill himself. Colline replies that he is safe. The voices fade.

Rodolpho closes the door, sets the candle on the table, and starts to write. After a few lines he impatiently crumples up the page, throws it on the floor, and murmurs that he is not in the mood. There is a gentle knock at the door, and as Rodolpho rises to answer, the tender "Mimi" theme sounds in the orchestra. Mimi, on her way up the stairs to her room, is heard calling that her candle has blown out. Rodolpho finds her at the door, candle and key in hand. As she hesitates, he urges her to come in. Distressed by her painful coughing, Rodolpho asks if she is ill and exclaims in alarm at her pallor. Mimi gasps that climbing the stairs has taken her breath, then faints in Rodolpho's arms. Her key and candle drop to the floor. Rodolpho places her gently on a chair, sprinkles water on her face, remarks again about her paleness, and gazes at her long and thoughtfully. Slowly she revives. The poet, offering her a glass of wine, invites her to sit closer to the fire. In an aside he marvels at her beauty. Mimi sips the wine, rises, and asks if she may light her candle. After Rodolpho relights it for her they bid each other good night.

As Mimi reaches the door she finds that she has dropped her key. Rodolpho warns her that the draft in the doorway will again blow out her candle, and in the next moment it flickers out. She asks him to light it once more, but as he tries to do so the wind blows out his own light, plunging the room into darkness. Mimi wonders where the key can be, while Rodolpho, unobserved, latches the door. She asks his forgiveness for being such a bothersome neighbor, meanwhile feeling about the floor. Rodolpho gallantly tries to put her at her ease, then drops to his knees to join in the search.

Suddenly he comes upon the key and, with a suppressed exclamation, pockets it. Still pretending to search, he comes closer to Mimi, and in the next moment their hands touch. Mimi exclaims softly. Clasping her hand, Rodolpho begins his great aria, "Che gelida manina." Her hand is cold, he sings softly, and asks her leave to restore its warmth. There is no need to search further in the darkness. Soon the moonlight will flood the room to help them find the key. Meanwhile he will tell her about himself. Mimi, greatly moved, sinks into the chair, and Rodolpho gently lets go her hand. He sings that he is a poet and that he makes his living—such as it is— by writing. Riches he has none, but the beauty of women transports him into a world of fantasy in which he is wealthy beyond the dreams of avarice.

Passionately he tells Mimi that her eyes have stolen away all the priceless jewels of his fancy and the brightest of his dreams. But the loss is nothing, he sings exultantly, for now he has found love. Then quietly he asks Mimi to tell her own story.

They call her Mimi, she begins ("Mi chiamano Mimi"), although her name is Lucia. Her story is brief: She does embroidery to earn her living. The roses and lilies which she stitches are symbols of love and springtime—they are the stuff of dreams and poetry. But why they call her Mimi, she muses, she does not know. She continues that she eats her frugal meals alone, goes to church infrequently but prays often. She spends most of her time in her lonely attic room. But when spring comes, she sings ecstatically, her life then is flooded with sunshine and fragrance. These poor flowers of hers, she adds as an afterthought, have no aroma of their own. There is no more to tell, she concludes simply. For the rest, she is only a bothersome neighbor.

The tender mood of the scene is interrupted by the shouts of Rodolpho's companions urging him to join them. He goes

La Bohème

to the window, calls down that he has only three lines still to write, then explains to Mimi that his friends are waiting below. He informs the three that someone is with him in the room and asks them to reserve two places at the Café Momus. The voices of Marcello, Colline, and Schaunard, chanting of Momus, die away.

Mimi and Rodolpho stand alone at the window in a flood of moonlight, and in a rapturous duet ("O soave fanciulla") declare their love for each other. Passionately they kiss. Mimi, freeing herself, reminds Rodolpho that his friends are waiting, then with charming naïveté asks him if she may accompany him. Rodolpho exclaims in delight, then pointedly suggests remaining in the room instead. Fervently Mimi cries that she will stay with him always. When he hints at returning later, however, she is charmingly evasive. Arm in arm, they slowly walk out of the room, singing of their love in ecstatic, soaring phrases. The curtain slowly falls.

Act Two

A square surrounded by shops. At one corner is the Café Momus. It is Christmas Eve, and the square is crowded with people. Rodolpho and Mimi are seen strolling. Colline is talking to a clothes mender; Schaunard, before another shop, is bargaining for a pipe and a horn, while Marcello is in the middle of the throng flirting with the pretty girls. Vendors, students, and townspeople sing a spirited chorus urging everyone to buy ("Aranci datteril"). Schaunard is heard complaining about the sour notes that the horn gives forth. Mimi says she wants to shop for a hat. Colline expresses satisfaction with his newly mended coat, puts it on, and promptly stuffs the pockets full of books. Marcello invites every girl he meets to make love.

The friends rendezvous in front of the Café Momus. First comes Schaunard, philosophically commenting on the crowd's feverish pursuit of pleasure. Colline joins him, holding up a book and happily proclaiming that he has found a collector's item. A little later Marcello appears. Rodolpho and Mimi arrive, Mimi in transports of delight over her new hat. When Marcello, Colline, and Schaunard are unsuccessful in finding a table out of doors they go inside, while Rodolpho and Mimi continue window shopping. Mimi admires a necklace on display. Rodolpho tells her that he has a rich old aunt, and if the Lord decides to end her days he will be able to buy a much more beautiful necklace.

Shouting and singing, the crowd gradually withdraws from the square. Marcello, Schaunard, and Colline emerge from the café, carrying a table. They seat themselves around it, Colline loftily remarking that, like Horace, he cannot bear rubbing elbows with the masses. Rodolpho and Mimi approach, discussing the pros and cons of jealousy. Phrases of Rodolpho's aria in Act One soar through the music as he talks of his love for Mimi. Schaunard demands privacy while he is dining. Marcello calls for the best of everything. From the distance comes the voice of Parpignol crying his wares.

Rodolpho presents Mimi to his friends. In phrases of striking lyric beauty he tells them her name, saying that she is the Muse who inspires him to his most magnificent expressions of love ("Questa è Mimi"). This soulful peroration brings a burst of cynical laughter from his companions, but they salute Mimi with true gallantry.

A colorful interlude follows as Parpignol appears with his cart, surrounded by a noisy crowd of mothers and children. The urchins pester their mothers for toys—one demands a drum, another a horse. Parpignol moves out of sight with his chattering customers. Marcello asks Mimi if she has received a gift from Rodolpho. Proudly she exhibits her new hat. She has wanted a hat like that for ever so long, she says, and marvels that Rodolpho chose it for her. She declares that the man who can so accurately read a woman's heart is indeed an extraordinary person. A savant, undoubtedly, Schaunard agrees with gentle irony. Colline remarks that Rodolpho is already a poet laureate of love. Oddly enough, Schaunard observes, everything the fellow prates about sounds very convincing. Marcello adds that all you need to do is believe, and the most fantastic dreams come true.

La Bohème

Love, Rodolpho proclaims, is the poet's highest inspiration. Mimi remarks that love can be either honey or vinegar—it is a matter of personal taste. Then in charming distress she exclaims that now she has offended Rodolpho. The others cut short the poet's sentimental protest by calling for a toast. And let the drink be poison, Marcello adds sourly, thinking of Musetta.

In the next moment Musetta imperiously sweeps in, followed by Alcindoro, her wealthy and aging admirer. Those at the table acclaim her beauty. Alcindoro, prancing after her, fumes that he must jump at her bidding like a servant. Musetta confirms this by contemptuously calling to him as though he were a dog. She orders him to secure a table near the others, then sits down facing the other party. Colline comments amusedly about Alcindoro, while Marcello mutters sardonically about the old duffer's "virtuous" companion. When Mimi asks who she is Marcello starts off on a bitter tirade. A brief duet follows between Musetta and Marcello ("Marcello mi vide"). She gives way to her anger at being snubbed by her erstwhile lover and his friends. Marcello describes her to Mimi as a fickle temptress, an insatiable bird of prey which feeds on human hearts. That is why, he declares acidly, he now has no heart—and will someone please pass the ragout!

Furious at Marcello's indifference, Musetta shouts for the waiter, scolds about the food, then hurls her plate to the ground. Alcindoro's efforts to calm her only increase her rage, and the two quarrel violently, to the unalloyed amusement not only of the group at the other table but a passing crowd of shopgirls. The quarrel suddenly sputters out. Musetta, her eyes fixed on Marcello, begins her brilliant aria ("Quando me'n vo'soletta"), in which she describes how everyone turns to marvel at her beauty as she passes by. Marcello can scarcely control himself as she sings that the ardent glances of the men prove that she has ensnared their hearts. In dramatic phrases she exults in her triumphs. Alcindoro rants helplessly. Musetta tauntingly reminds Marcello that he once lost his heart to her. But now, she sings with passionate intensity, he would rather die than admit that she has hurt him.

Mimi remarks that now it is clear that these two are lovers. Rodolpho explains that Musetta spurned Marcello for another. Schaunard and Colline, highly amused, comment cynically on the situation. Stung to fury, Marcello starts to leave but pauses as if transfixed as Musetta cries out that she has conquered him. The voices of the others blend with hers in a melodious quintet. Musetta alternately gibes at Marcello and berates Alcindoro. Mimi and Rodolpho express their sympathy for the unhappy lovers, while Schaunard and Colline continue their flippant comments.

Musetta suddenly screams that her shoe is causing her unbearable pain, makes Alcindoro take it off, and orders him to buy her a new pair immediately. As he distractedly leaves, Marcello realizes the purpose of Musetta's ruse and sings to her ecstatically. They rush into each other's arms as the ensemble comes to a brilliant climax. A moment later the waiter appears with the check. The men look at each other in comic distress, exclaiming that they have no money. Musetta ingeniously solves the problem by telling the waiter that her escort will pay the entire amount when he returns.

From the distance comes the beating of a drum, and the crowd gathers excitedly in the square. In a moment the patrol enters, led by a giant drum major twirling his baton. The crowd hails the marchers in a stirring chorus ("Ecco il tambur maggiore"), and as they go on their way everyone follows. When Musetta, minus her shoe, comically tries to hop along, Marcello and Colline gallantly carry her off on their shoulders. Rodolpho and Mimi follow, arm in arm. Schaunard goes next, merrily blowing his horn. When the square is deserted, Alcindoro rushes in, clutching the neatly wrapped package of shoes. Silently the waiter hands him the check. Alcindoro looks at it, groans, and collapses in a chair. The curtain falls.

ACT THREE

An open space before one of the gates of Paris. At the left is a tavern. Over the door hangs Marcello's "Red Sea" master-

La Bohème

piece, now a tavern sign. A brief prelude in a striking minor mood reflects the gloomy chill of a winter dawn. A group of shivering scavengers rattle the gate, demanding admittance. The sleepy guard finally lets them in. From the tavern come voices of late revelers singing a drinking song ("Chi nel ber trovò il piacer"). Musetta's voice is heard in a merry tune. Carters and farm women, laden with produce, are checked through the toll gate.

As the characteristic theme from Mimi's aria in Act One echoes softly in the orchestra, Mimi herself appears. She pauses a moment, racked by coughing, then asks a guard if there is an inn nearby at which an artist is staying. The guard points to the tavern. At that moment a woman comes out, and Mimi implores her to look for an artist named Marcello and tell him that Mimi wishes to see him. The woman complies. Marcello appears, and Mimi greets him eagerly. He tells her that he and Musetta are staying at the tavern. To pay their lodging, he goes on, Musetta gives singing lessons while he himself now paints tavern signs instead of masterpieces.

Marcello invites Mimi in. When she learns that Rodolpho is there she sobs that she must not enter. In despair she begs Marcello to help her ("Oh, buon Marcello, aiuto!"). Rodolpho, though he adores her madly, refuses to come back to her, she cries. His unreasonable jealousy had made their life together unbearable, Mimi continues bitterly, and she is at a loss for an answer to his cruel accusations. Marcello observes that under the circumstances they would be wise to separate. Mimi sadly agrees and entreats Marcello to help them bring about a parting. Marcello observes that he and Musetta are happy with each other because they can laugh and sing together. Mimi's voice blends briefly with his as she heartbrokenly sings that parting is inevitable.

Marcello says he will go to waken Rodolpho, who, worn out, has dropped off to sleep on a bench. He points him out to Mimi through a window. Marcello expresses alarm at her constant coughing. Mimi gasps that it is unending torture—and now Rodolpho chooses to leave her with the explanation that everything is at an end. At that moment Rodolpho is heard calling Marcello. The painter advises Mimi to conceal herself. Rodolpho comes striding out of the inn. Excitedly he declares that he must part from Mimi. Marcello dryly asks him if that is his latest caprice. Rodolpho dramatically answers that his ardor for Mimi was cooling ("Già un'altra volta credetti"), but one look into her eyes rekindled his passion—to his sorrow. Marcello observes that when love brings tears it is not worth cherishing—with love there must be laughter. He then bluntly reminds Rodolpho that he is unreasonably jealous, ill-tempered, and obstinate.

In an aside Mimi ponders over Rodolpho's rising anger. The poet protests that Mimi is an unfeeling coquette who tries out her charms on every man she sees. Marcello sharply says he does not believe it. Contritely Rodolpho retracts his bitter words. In dramatic, moving phrases he declares that despite his torments he realizes that Mimi is dearer to him than anything else in the world. But there is something more serious, he adds. Mimi is very ill, and he fears she is doomed.

Seeing Mimi approaching, Marcello tries to maneuver Rodolpho away so that she will not overhear. Rodolpho admits that while the terrible cough was slowly destroying her she was forced to share his poverty in his cold, cheerless rooms. Yet she bore everything uncomplainingly. Privation has desolated this fragile flower, he cries out, and now not even his love can save her. Marcello vainly tries to quiet him. Mimi, having overheard, sobs that her doom is sealed.

Weeping, shaken by her cough, Mimi no longer troubles to conceal herself. Wildly calling her name, Rodolpho takes her in his arms. Marcello regrets that she has heard Rodolpho's fateful words. Rodolpho asks Mimi to go into the tavern, but she refuses. Suddenly Musetta's laughter rings out. Marcello, angrily accusing her of playing him false again, rushes inside.

Mimi softly bids Rodolpho good-by ("Addio, senza rancor"). She must go back to the lonely attic room she left at his bidding, she sings, for now love and life are at an end. She asks him to wrap up her belongings—her gold bracelet, her prayer book—and put them aside for her, but tells him he may keep her treasured hat as a remembrance. Then the two join in a profoundly moving duet ("Addio, o dolce svegliare") expressing the anguish of hopeless love and inevitable parting.

The mood of the scene is shattered by the crashing of crockery, and in the next moment Musetta and Marcello come storming out of the tavern. There follows a quartet in which two sharply contrasting moods are combined with striking effect ("Soli l'inverno è cosa da morire!"). Mimi and Rodolpho passionately declare their love for each other and vow that they will wait for another spring before they part. Musetta and Marcello rant furiously at each other. Marcello rages that he will no longer tolerate her incorrigible flirting, while she defies him to stop her. Violently shouting his good-by, Marcello dashes back into the tavern. Musetta, screaming a final imprecation, rushes away. Rodolpho and Mimi slowly walk off. From the distance comes the rapturous ending of their duet. The curtain falls.

Act Four

The attic studio, as in Act One. When the curtain rises Marcello is seen at his easel, Rodolpho at the table. Both are making obvious efforts to appear absorbed in their work. Actually, their thoughts are on Mimi and Musetta. Rodolpho says he saw Musetta riding in a fine carriage. When he asked her about the state of her heart she told him that the lovely velvet she was wearing prevented her from knowing whether it was beating or not. Marcello, with a forced laugh, remarks that he is very happy about it. Rodolpho, in an aside, mutters that Marcello is a faker—he's really raging. Marcello snaps that if "it" is not beating, well and good, and then begins painting furiously. After a moment he reverses the situation by casually mentioning that he saw Mimi riding about like a queen. Rodolpho declares he is overjoyed. Marcello brands him a love-smitten liar.

After another desperate attempt at working, both give up in disgust and stare glumly into space. Marcello turns his back on Rodolpho, takes a rosette from his pocket, and presses it to his lips. The two then sing a melodious duet ("Ah, Mimi, tu più non torni"). Rodolpho grieves over Mimi's perfidy and recalls his lost happiness with her. Marcello sings that his brush refuses to paint anything but two alluring eyes and a laughing mouth. Rodolpho takes Mimi's hat from the table drawer and clutches it to his breast. He and Marcello express their heartbreak in a melodramatic outburst of song.

After a moment Rodolpho, trying to cloak his feelings, asks the time. Marcello jokingly replies that it is the hour for yesterday's dinner. Suddenly Schaunard and Colline enter. Schaunard has four rolls, and Colline has a herring in a paper bag. They place the food on the table and then the four ceremoniously seat themselves as though they were taking their places at a formal banquet. Schaunard places the water carafe in Colline's upturned hat and announces that he has put the champagne on ice. Rodolpho, offering "Baron" Marcello a roll, asks him if he prefers salmon or flounder. Marcello recommends to "Duke" Schaunard a dish of delicious fowl—another roll. Schaunard says he must refuse because he is performing in a ballet this evening. They sip water from a solitary tumbler as though it were rare wine.

Colline rises and pompously informs the others that he has an appointment with the King. The others feign great interest, but Colline declines to divulge the nature of his business at the palace. Schaunard leaps up on a chair, raises the tumbler of water, and proposes a toast. He says he feels a poetic inspiration coming on, but the others shout him down. Undaunted, Schaunard suggests a dance, and they decide it shall be a quadrille. Rodolpho and Marcello pair off, with Marcello playing the damsel. Schaunard and Colline pretend to quarrel, challenge each other, then begin a furious duel with fire tongs and poker. The other two decide to dance a fandango while the duelists are slaying each other.

When the fun is at its height, Musetta suddenly appears, greatly concerned. She says that she has brought Mimi, who was barely able to climb the stairs. Rodolpho and Marcello see Mimi on the landing, help her into the room, and place her on the bed. Mimi begs Rodolpho to let her stay, and he fervently assures her that she may remain forever. Musetta tells the others that she learned Mimi had left her rich friend and had gone away to die alone. She finally found her, more dead than alive. Mimi had whispered that she was dying and implored Musetta to take her to Rodolpho.

Phrases from Mimi's aria in Act One come softly from the orchestra as she sings of her happiness in this reunion. Rodolpho voices his happiness in her return. The others reveal that there is neither food nor medicine for the stricken girl. Schaunard, looking at Mimi, whispers that the end is near. Between spells of coughing Mimi murmurs that her hands are cold and laments that she does not have her muff. Rodolpho sings that he will warm her hands in his. With a pathetic attempt at gaiety Mimi says that she is getting accustomed to her cough, then greets the others. They urge her not to speak. Gently she tells Marcello that he must believe in Musetta's goodness. In answer Marcello quietly takes Musetta's hand.

Leading Marcello to one side, Musetta takes off her earrings and tells the painter to sell them, buy medicine, and find a doctor. Rodolpho seats himself at the bedside. Mimi begs him not to leave her, then closes her eyes. Musetta whispers to Marcello that poor Mimi's requests will probably be her last, and then leaves with Marcello to bring back Mimi's muff.

Meanwhile Colline slowly takes off his beloved coat, holds it out before him, and sings to it a touching farewell ("Vecchia zimarra, senti"). It has served him long and faithfully, he says, and recalls how its pockets have held the treasures of philosophy and poetry. He puts the coat under his arm and starts to leave. He pauses to tell Schaunard that although they have often clashed over their opinions they can at this moment agree on two acts of mercy: to sell the coat and to leave the two lovers to themselves. Deeply moved, Schaunard agrees. As an excuse to leave he picks up the water carafe and then follows Colline.

No sooner has the door closed than Mimi tells Rodolpho

("Sono andati?") that she was only pretending to be asleep because she wanted to be alone with him. There are so many things to say, she goes on. One thought, above all, is as deep and limitless as the ocean: He is her beloved, her very life. She asks Rodolpho if he still thinks her beautiful. Beautiful as the dawn, he replies. Mimi says the simile is wrong—he should have compared her to the sunset. Then, as if in a dream, she sings the poignant phrase from her Act One aria—they call her Mimi, but she does not know why.

In answer Rodolpho sings another phrase of her song, then brings Mimi her frivolous little hat. She exclaims in pleasure as he puts it on her head. As themes from the Act One love music echo through the orchestra they recall incidents of their happy past—how they fell in love, how they looked for the key that night in the darkened attic room. Mimi reminds Rodolpho that he contrived to find it very quickly. Rodolpho gently answers that Destiny guided him. Softly she sings the opening phrases of Rodolpho's song as he held her hand in the darkness. Suddenly she is racked by a paroxysm of coughing. As Rodolpho cries out frantically, Schaunard hurries in and rushes to the bedside. Recovering momentarily, Mimi reassures them. Musetta and Marcello return, bringing Mimi's muff and a bottle of medicine. Marcello tells Rodolpho that a doctor is on the way. Musetta gives Mimi the muff. Mimi exclaims over it in childlike delight, saying that now her hands will no longer be cold. When she pretends to chide Rodolpho for his extravagance in buying the muff for her, he sobs bitterly. Tenderly she comforts him, saying she will always be near. Then, clasping her hands in her muff, she sighs that now she will sleep.

Rodolpho tiptoes away from the bed and whispers to his companions. Musetta sings a prayer for Mimi, breaking off to ask Marcello to shield Mimi's eyes from the light of the lamp. Rodolpho anxiously consults her about Mimi, and she tries to reassure him. In the next moment Schaunard, who has tiptoed over to the bed, whispers in a voice choked with grief that Mimi is dead. Unseen by Rodolpho, who is draping Musetta's cloak over the window to keep the first rays of the sun from Mimi's eyes, Schaunard gestures to the others.

Rodolpho turns and sees the terror and despair in the faces of his friends. In fear-stricken tones he implores them to tell him what is wrong. Then, as Marcello brokenly bids him have courage, the terrible realization dawns upon him. Frantically he rushes over to the bed and takes Mimi's lifeless form in his arms. In an agony of grief he cries out her name. Somber, powerful chords thunder forth as the orchestra intones, in minor key, the phrase in which Mimi sang to Rodolpho that she was only pretending sleep.

Boris Godunof

by MODEST PETROVICH MOUSSORGSKY
[1839–1881]

Libretto by the Composer

Based on the drama of the same name by Aleksandr Pushkin

CHARACTERS

Police officer	*Bass*
Mitiukha, a Russian peasant	*Bass*
Prince Vassili Ivanovich Shuisky, court adviser to Boris Godunof	*Tenor*
Andrei Shchelkalof, Secretary of the Duma	*Baritone*
Pimen, a monk and historian	*Bass*
Grigory, a novice (later Dimitri the Pretender)	*Tenor*
Boris Godunof	*Bass*
Hostess of the inn	*Mezzo-soprano*
Missail } mendicant friars	*Tenor*
Varlaam	*Bass*
Xenia, daughter of Boris	*Soprano*
Feodor, son of Boris	*Mezzo-soprano*
Nurse to Xenia	*Contralto*
Marina Mnishek, daughter of a Polish landowner	*Mezzo-soprano*
Rangoni, a Jesuit priest	*Bass*
Khrushchof, a boyar	*Tenor*
The Simpleton	*Tenor*
Lavitsky } Jesuit priests	*Tenor*
Chernikofsky	*Baritone*

Russian people, soldiers, guards, boyars, pilgrims, children, ladies and gentlemen of the Polish court

Place: Russia and Poland
Time: 1598–1605
First performance: Marinsky Theater, St. Petersburg, January 24, 1874
Original language: Russian

Boris Godunof

Boris godunof is essentially an opera about the Russian people. Although the action centers around certain individuals, it is the spirit of a struggling people that dominates the stage. This spirit finds dramatic expression in the opera's brilliant pageantry and its magnificent choruses. There are few set arias in conventional operatic fashion. The action is carried forward through the medium of recitative and musical dialogue, supported by a complex orchestral accompaniment.

The opera is based on an actual episode in Russian history. Boris Godunof was a minister in the court of Czar Feodor, son of Ivan the Terrible. According to Moussorgsky's plot, Boris contrived the murder of Dimitri, younger brother of Feodor and successor to the throne. When Feodor died, Boris forced the people to demand that he become czar, then took the throne as if in response to the will of the Russians.

Meanwhile Grigory, a young novice, fled to Poland, announced himself as the Czarevich Dimitri, and fomented a revolutionary movement which hastened the downfall and death of Boris. It is interesting to note that historians subsequently absolved Boris of any blame in the death of the boy Dimitri.

Boris Godunof is usually performed from the score prepared by Nikolai Rimsky-Korsakov, who revised the opera in 1896 and again in 1908. The score as Moussorgsky wrote it was published by the Soviet Government in 1928. In this country the opera is usually sung in Russian or Italian.

Act One

[*Scene One*] The courtyard in front of the Novodievichy monastery near Moscow.[1] Boris has gone into retirement here following the death of Czar Feodor. Crowds of people are milling about the courtyard in sullen obedience to the harsh

[1] In the original score the opera begins with a Prologue, which has two scenes—the scene at the Novodievichy monastery and the *Coronation Scene*. It is customary, however, to present the opera in either three or four acts without a prologue.

commands of a police officer. The voice of Mitiukha, apparently a minor leader among the people, is heard briefly as he tries to explain why they are being forced to appeal to Boris. The people are leaderless, says Mitiukha, and only Boris can save Russia from ruin. Led by Prince Shuisky, the boyars' cross the courtyard and enter the monastery. The people, threatened by the clubs of the police, reluctantly kneel facing the monastery and break into a noisy chorus of entreaty.

Shchelkalof appears at the entrance of the monastery and informs the crowd that Boris refuses to accept the throne. Russia is doomed, he adds in solemn tones, then unctuously prays that Heaven may enlighten the soul of Boris. From behind the scenes comes the chanting of pilgrims approaching the monastery. They enter in a slow procession, exhorting the crowd to hail Boris as their leader. Moving through the kneeling throng, the pilgrims present sacred tokens to the people. When the holy men have disappeared, the police roughly order the people to reassemble at the Kremlin for further demonstrations. The crowd moves off as the curtain falls.

[*Scene Two*] The cell of the monk Pimen in the Chudof monastery.[3] Pimen is writing at a table, while on a nearby cot the novice Grigory lies asleep. The monk pauses in reflection as he sings ("Yesho odno poslednje skazanje"—*Pimen's Narrative*), musing that soon his great work of recording the history of Russia will be completed. A murmuring accompaniment seems to follow the movement of his pen as he writes. From behind the scenes comes the soft chanting of the monks.

Suddenly Grigory awakes and sits bolt upright, exclaiming, "Vsje tot-je son" ("Forever that dream"). He frets that he is haunted by a nightmare. Gazing at Pimen, he notes to himself the monk's calm and quiet air as he sits writing his endless chronicles. Grigory then tells Pimen of his dream—how he climbed a long stairway to a high tower and looked down

[2] Privileged members of the Russian aristocracy, next to the ruling princes. The class was abolished by Peter the Great (1682–1725).

[3] Act One, Scene One, in the original score.

upon a gesticulating throng. The people cursed and derided him. Terror-stricken, he fell, and thus awoke.

Pimen tells the novice that his troubled dreams are but the sign of his youthful restlessness and counsels him to ease his mind with prayer and meditation. But Grigory replies that he chafes at the restrictions of monastic life and longs to escape to the outside world—to savor the thrill of combat and the delights of feasting. The monk answers that the world offers only shallow and illusory pleasures, which are as nothing compared with the holy calm of the cell. Deep in thought, Pimen recalls the days of Czar Ivan the Terrible and his son Feodor—how they lived devoutly and reigned in peace. But now, he concludes in somber tones, Russia is groaning under the heel of a ruthless assassin.

Grigory, fascinated by Pimen's words, says he has been told that the monk witnessed the murder of the Czarevich Dimitri. Pimen thereupon describes how three conspirators slew the boy at the instigation of Boris. The novice asks how old the boy was at the time of his murder. After a moment's thought the monk replies that, had the boy lived, he would be approximately Grigory's own age—and on the throne of Russia. At these words Grigory leaps to his feet in great excitement, but in the next instant controls himself and again assumes the humble mien of a novice.

Pimen, oblivious to his movements, charges Grigory with continuing his chronicles, then slowly leaves the cell. Bells tolling in the monastery summon the monks to matins. Grigory, going to the door, pauses, and then cries out that now all grovel in fear before Boris ("Boris, Boris! Vsje pred toboy trepeshed!"). But the deeds that are being recorded in this lonely cell, he declares gloatingly, will bring down terrible judgment upon the head of the murderous tyrant. The curtain falls.

[*Scene Three*] A square before the Kremlin in Moscow. At one side is the Cathedral of the Assumption. Opposite is the Cathedral of the Archangels. At the rear is the façade of the imperial palace. Now ensues the famous *Coronation Scene* in which Boris is crowned czar. A surging orchestral accompaniment mingles with the reverberation of great bells as a stately procession emerges from the palace and moves toward the Cathedral of the Assumption.

Prince Shuisky and Shchelkalof are seen in the van of the pageant, which includes boyars, palace guards, and dignitaries of church and state. At the steps of the cathedral Prince Shuisky pauses to bid the kneeling throng hail the new czar. The people answer in a thunderous chorus hailing Boris ("Givi i sdravstvuy tsar nash batushka"). As the music rises to a dazzling climax, Boris comes out of the church with his two children. Unheard by the throng that bows before him, he voices the haunting terror of his conscience ("Skorbit doosha"). Feverishly he prays for aid and guidance. Recovering himself, he imperiously bids the people pay homage to the memory of the czars of Russia, then invites all to the royal feast of coronation. Led by Boris, the procession moves across the square to the Cathedral of the Archangels and then proceeds to the palace. The chorus of acclaim rises to a tremendous fortissimo as the curtain falls.

Act Two

[*Scene One*] An inn at the border of Lithuania.[4] After a brief, lively introduction the curtain rises to disclose the hostess of the inn busily engaged in household tasks. She sings to herself a gay, nonsensical little song about a duckling ("Poymala ja siza seleznya"). Her singing is interrupted by the sound of loud laughter and talking outside. She listens and hears two voices unsteadily chanting an appeal for alms to build a church ("Lud christianskiy"). The hostess peers excitedly out of the window and mentions that two holy men are approaching. Opening the door, she bows and scrapes as Varlaam and Missail enter. The two disreputable-looking friars are followed by Grigory, who is disguised in peasant's clothing. He is fleeing Russia because a warrant has been

[4] Scene Two of Act One in the original score.

issued for his arrest. The police have learned of his activities in spreading the report that the supposedly slain Dimitri is still alive and should be placed on the throne instead of Boris.

With practiced humility the two friars ask the hostess for wine, and she leaves hurriedly to fetch it. Grigory seats himself at a table and stares into space with an apprehensive and preoccupied air. Varlaam tries to cheer him, but Grigory says he is greatly concerned about reaching the Lithuanian border. When the hostess returns with the wine, Varlaam and Missail greedily fill their glasses. Grigory ignores an invitation to join them.

After a few moments of drinking, Varlaam, waving a bottle, gets to his feet and launches into the famous song about the town of Kazan ("Kack vo gorode beelo vo Kazani"). He tells the story of how Czar Ivan laid siege to the Tartar fortress of Kazan. With great relish he relates how the czar had his engineers dig tunnels under the walls and then roll casks of powder, with fuses sputtering, down the apertures. When the casks exploded, some forty-three thousand Tartars were blown to bits. And that is how Kazan met its fate, Varlaam concludes, taking a long drink from the bottle.

When he notices that Grigory is not drinking, he twits him for remaining sober. Bellowing that he has no use for sobriety, Varlaam proceeds to drink himself into a stupor and finally sinks down at the table, muttering drunkenly as he falls asleep. Missail lurches over to a wooden bench and also drops off to sleep.

Grigory now quietly approaches the hostess and, pointing out of the window, asks where the road leads. To Lithuania, she answers. The border is not far away, but one must be careful of the frontier guards. They are questioning closely all who seek to cross, the hostess says, because they are hunting a fugitive. Varlaam revives momentarily and tries to continue singing. Grigory fears that now he may not be able to get into Lithuania, then asks whom the authorities are looking for. Some thief or other, the hostess answers casually. But they'll never catch him, she adds, for he will undoubtedly make his escape by using the secret path. Obligingly the hostess describes the path in great detail.

She is interrupted by a knock at the door. Complaining that the soldiers are at their searching again, she goes to open it. Entering, the soldiers look sharply at the three visitors. Varlaam and Missail, roused out of their stupor and startled at the sight of the soldiers, immediately offer the information that they are only poor, innocent friars and that this peasant —indicating Grigory—is their companion. Grigory himself explains that he merely led the holy men to the inn and is now preparing to go on his way.

With a deceptive show of sympathy, the officer turns to Varlaam and asks him how he is faring with his almsgathering. Varlaam paints the situation as black as possible, squirming somewhat as the officer eyes him coldly. Suddenly his questioner produces an official document and reads that Czar Boris has ordered a search for a renegade monk, Grishka Otrepief, who has escaped from Moscow. If he is caught he is to be hanged. "Are you the man?" ("Sli-hal-li ti yeto?") the officer asks. Befuddled and frightened out of his wits, Varlaam stammers that he does not know.

The officer, whose ability to read is limited, asks who can read the particulars of the warrant. Grigory volunteers. After a moment's hesitation he begins reading the document, which explains that a traitorous monk, Grishka or Grigory Otrepief by name, has succumbed to the wiles of the devil, fled the Chudof monastery, and is now trying to make his way toward Lithuania. When Grigory reaches the official description of the fugitive, he slyly glances at Varlaam. Pretending to read, he describes the friar in detail. The officer, who has been watching Varlaam closely, promptly orders him seized. Sensing that he is being tricked, the friar fights off the soldiers. Snatching up the document, he shouts that even if he cannot read he can spell out the words letter by letter.

Painstakingly he makes out the description of Grigory, who meanwhile has moved stealthily over to a window. When Varlaam finishes, he stares at Grigory for a moment, then blurts out that *he* is the wanted man. In a flash Grigory whips out his knife and leaps through the window. The soldiers stand for a moment in openmouthed astonishment and then storm after him. There is momentary confusion and uproar as the curtain falls.

[*Scene Two*] The luxuriously furnished apartment of Czar Boris in the Kremlin in Moscow.[5] Xenia is seated at a table, looking at a picture of a young man. Near by is her nurse. At another table sits Feodor, absorbed in a book on geography. Xenia sings heartbrokenly of the death of her beloved ("Gdje ti genih moy!"). Feodor's voice now blends with her lamentations as he recites aloud the names of the countries, cities, and seas he is learning about. The nurse tries to console Xenia, telling her that she will soon find happiness with a new lover. When the girl does not respond, the nurse attempts to amuse her by singing a song about a flea.[6] It is a story about the flea's friend, the gnat, who labored on the farm of a sexton. One day a greedy cricket invaded the farm and devastated the hayfield. When the gnat tried to beat off the cricket with the handle of a rake, he succeeded only in mortally wounding himself. The flea, trying to carry him home, died of the strenuous effort—and so both the gnat and the flea perished.

Feodor objects to the sad ending of the song and says he will sing a jollier one about Mother Goose. He coaxes the nurse to join him in a game, and the two dance around in a circle, clapping hands and singing nursery rhymes. The game stops abruptly as Boris enters. Observing Xenia's grief, he seeks to comfort her, urging her to forget her sorrow in the companionship of her young friends. Xenia and the nurse leave. Turning his attention to Feodor, Boris listens attentively as the boy comes to his side and tells how he has studied the map of Russia.

With paternal pride the czar praises his son for learning his lessons well. He admonishes Feodor to be diligent, for some-

[5] Act Two in the original score.

[6] Not the same as the "Song of the Flea," composed by Moussorgsky as an individual vocal number.

day he himself will rule this great country. Feodor goes back to his book. Boris now gives voice to his gloomy forebodings in a dramatic soliloquy ("Dostig ya visshey vlasti"). For five years he has reigned supreme, he muses bitterly, but the success foretold by the soothsayers is only a mockery. All around him are treacherous conspirators. The people, in their blind hatred, heap upon him the blame for all the evils in the kingdom. His soul is torn by remorse and guilt, and he—the mighty czar—must grovel for mercy before God, seeking a moment's peace of mind. Distractedly he sings that the terrible sight of the murdered Dimitri relentlessly haunts his dreams. The drama of the scene is heightened at this point by a menacing, insistent rhythm in the orchestra that seems to suggest the inexorable ticking of the huge clock in one corner of the room. In a paroxysm of anguish, Boris leaps to his feet, then falls heavily into a chair, gasping a prayer for mercy ("O, gospodi, Boje moyl").

There is a commotion outside, with the voices of women rising shrilly. After a moment a court attendant (a boyar) enters to announce that Prince Shuisky desires an interview. The boyar furtively whispers that Shuisky and others have been plotting and have received a messenger from Cracow. Boris furiously orders the messenger's arrest. The boyar hurriedly leaves. Feodor approaches and looks timidly up at his father. Boris forgets his anger as the boy naïvely explains the cause of the disturbance outside. It was all because one of the nurses teased Polly the parrot, Feodor explains. Then Polly flew into a rage and tried to bite her. In compassion and tenderness, Boris embraces his son and thanks him for his story. He exclaims that if he could but live to see the boy succeed him as czar, he would gladly sacrifice the throne. Grimly he warns Feodor that, should he rule, he must guard himself well against wily traitors like Shuisky.

At that point Shuisky enters with a servile bow. Boris turns on him with a flood of contempt and vituperation. Shuisky, however, chooses to ignore the insults and informs Boris that a traitor is plotting a revolution against him and that this renegade has the support of both church and people. Boris demands the plotter's name. As Feodor comes closer to listen, Shuisky, with hypocritical concern, replies that he may well be using the name of Dimitri. That name, Shuisky adds craftily, is one the people well know. Horrified, Boris sends Feodor out of the room.

Confronting Shuisky, Boris commands him to close Russia's borders at once and to prepare for war. In rising excitement he asks the prince if it could be possible for slain children to rise from their graves to haunt a czar. A heaven-appointed Czar of Russia, he adds with a burst of frenzied laughter. Flinging himself upon Shuisky, he forces the prince to relate how he saw the body of the murdered czarevich at Uglich. With evil satisfaction, Shuisky describes the scene in every gory detail. Unable to control himself, Boris commands Shuisky to leave him. He falls into a chair as the prince slinks away. Then follows the intensely dramatic scene in which Boris gives way to the remorse and guilt which torment him.

Almost bereft of reason, he imagines he sees the apparition of the murdered Dimitri approaching. Wildly he denies his guilt and implores the child to spare him this horror. Shaken by his emotions, Boris abjectly prays for mercy as the curtain falls.

ACT THREE

[*Scene One*] The boudoir of Marina Mnishek in Sandomir Castle, Poland. Marina sits looking into the mirror of her dressing table. As a maid combs her hair, the ladies-in-waiting sing that their mistress's beauty enchants all her admirers. She stops them impatiently, saying that she is bored with songs of lovesick swains and longs to hear only of Poland's valiant heroes and their conquests.

Marina dismisses her attendants, then begins a melodious refrain in the characteristic rhythm of a Polish mazurka. She expresses her contempt for the crowds of suitors eternally fawning at her feet ("Kack tomitelno i vyalo"). But there is one, she muses, who has brought new interest and excitement into her life—the young Dimitri from Moscow. He is to play a part in her completely unscrupulous ambitions. She will rob him of his will through her feminine allurements, drive him to overthrow Boris and to proclaim himself czar. Then, as czarina, she will share the throne with him and thus finally have the power and glory she so fiercely craves. Marina ends her song in a burst of triumphant laughter.

At that moment she sees the Jesuit priest, Rangoni, standing in the doorway. With suave humility he asks permission to speak with her. Then follows a long and dramatic colloquy. Insinuatingly the Jesuit tells Marina that it is her holy duty to go to Moscow with Dimitri and help him strengthen the position of the church. To that end, Rangoni goes on, she must use all her womanly charm to make Dimitri a slave to her passion. Then, when he is helpless in her power, she must wring from him a pledge of loyalty to the church. When Marina recoils at the Jesuit's treacherous scheming, the priest violently threatens her with eternal damnation. Groveling in superstitious terror, Marina acquiesces. As Rangoni stands over her exultantly, the curtain falls.

[*Scene Two*] A fountain in the garden of Mnishek Castle.[7] A bright moonlit night. The monk Grigory, now in his guise of the Pretender Dimitri, enters from the castle in the background. Ecstatically he murmurs, "V polnoch v sadu u fontana," repeating Marina's words designating the fountain as their rendezvous. Passionately he sings of his longing for her. As he gazes toward the castle, softly repeating Marina's name, Rangoni steps out of the shadows and approaches him.

Dimitri angrily berates the Jesuit for dogging his footsteps. Rangoni answers that he has a message from Marina—she is burning with love for the czarevich and is coming to meet him here. Jubilantly Dimitri sings that she shall accompany him to Moscow in the hour of his triumph. Suddenly suspicious, he turns on Rangoni, warning him not to lie about

[7] Known as the Fountain Scene, this is sometimes played as Scene Three of Act Two, or Scene One of Act Three. The scene in Marina's boudoir is then omitted entirely.

Boris Godunof

Marina. The Jesuit assures him of his sincerity, then slyly asserts that Marina is constant in her love despite the jealous gossiping of the court.

Fervently Dimitri avows he is determined to make Marina his queen in defiance of all the courtiers and their slandering tongues. He begs Rangoni to help him win Marina, promising the Jesuit anything he asks in return for the favor. Rangoni unctuously replies that all he desires is to be allowed to remain at Dimitri's side as his friend and counselor. Impetuously Dimitri agrees.

Rangoni interrupts to warn that some of the guests are entering the garden from the castle, and advises Dimitri to conceal himself for the moment. Marina appears, escorted by an aging nobleman. She replies to his love-making with cynical banter. There is an interlude of brilliant polonaise music and choral phrases as the guests dance and then sing about the glorious battle in which Poland's heroes will dethrone the usurper Boris.

As Marina re-enters the castle, followed by the throng singing her praises, Dimitri hurries forward in great excitement. He exclaims in distaste at Rangoni's machinations, then gives vent to his jealousy over seeing Marina gazing fondly into the eyes of a doddering noble. He momentarily forswears love and vows to bend all his efforts toward marching to Moscow as a conqueror.

At the height of his heroic exultation Marina approaches and calls his name. Dimitri rushes to her with a passionate cry ("Sdyes moya golubka, krasavitza moya"), which introduces an ardent love duet. At first Marina deliberately jeers at his impassioned declarations of love and chides him for placing his emotions above his ambition. Dimitri, goaded to helpless fury, finally cries that he will conquer alone, and then all the world will laugh in scorn at the woman who spurned the destined Czar of Russia.

Instantly Marina's demeanor changes to one of tenderness and allure. She assures Dimitri that she wants only his love and solemnly pledges her eternal faith ("O, tsarevich, umolyau"). Their voices blend in the rapturous climax of the duet ("O povtori, povtori Marina!"). As they embrace, Rangoni stealthily emerges from his hiding place and joins his voice with those of the lovers in a phrase of evil triumph. The curtain falls.

Act Four

[*Scene One*] A clearing in the forest of Kromy, not far from Moscow.[8] It is night. After a brief introduction, the shouts of a crowd are heard. Then peasants rush in, dragging the Boyar Khrushchof, whom they have captured. His arms are bound and his clothing torn. The peasants torment him mercilessly. Czar Boris plundered the throne, they sing, and this rascal stole from the plunderer. They push a whimpering crone toward him, saying that so fine a nobleman must not be without a sweetheart. Dancing around their helpless captive, they hail him in mocking chorus ("Oh, oojh i slava-jh tebe boyarinu").

The attention of the mob is suddenly diverted by the appearance of the Simpleton, a sorry figure in rags, wearing a tin pot for a helmet. Fighting off a crowd of teasing children, he seats himself on a rock and begins singing a plaintive, meaningless refrain about the moon and a weeping cat ("Mesyatz yedet kotenok platched"). He takes a coin from his pocket, whereupon the children snatch it from him and run away.

As the Simpleton bewails the loss of his treasure, his cries merge with the voices of the approaching mendicants, Varlaam and Missail. They are heard sardonically chanting the praises of Czar Boris for desolating Russia and oppressing the people. Emboldened by the friars' defiant protest, the peasants join their voices in a fierce chorus in which they pledge their loyalty to Dimitri and swear revenge against Boris.

Now two more voices are heard, chanting in Latin. In a

[8] In the original score this is Scene Two of Act Four, and the final scene in the opera. When the opera is presented in three acts, however, it is sometimes Scene One of Act Three, or Scene Two of Act Three.

Boris Godunof

moment the Jesuits Lavitsky and Chernikofsky appear. Shouting furious epithets, the peasants surround the priests and tie their arms with ropes. Incited by Varlaam and Missail, the mob demands that the Jesuits be hanged at once. Still resolutely chanting, the two are dragged off into the forest.

From the distance comes the blare of trumpets. A troop of white-clad soldiers rides into the clearing and is greeted by a lusty chorus acclaiming the Czarevich Dimitri. Dimitri himself shortly appears. He pauses to address the crowd, exhorting all to march with him to Moscow and to victory. As he rides away with his soldiers, followed by the crowd, bells toll wildly from afar off.

Soon the grove is deserted except for the Simpleton. He gets to his feet and turns to stare at the glow of a great fire on the horizon. In wailing tones he sings of the terror and death that are being loosed upon Russia in this night of doom. The curtain falls.

[*Scene Two*] The council hall of the Kremlin in Moscow.[9] The Duma, or Council of Boyars, is in special session. Shchelkalof enters and reads the czar's message to the boyars. It proclaims that a betrayer who calls himself the czarevich is leading a revolt against Boris with the aid of certain traitorous boyars. At that the members of the council excitedly denounce the false czarevich and demand that he be executed immediately. Cooler heads observe that he must first be caught.

During the uproar Shuisky enters. With his usual obsequiousness, he apologizes for being late, saying that he is much concerned over the czar. Impelled by anxiety over Boris, Shuisky tells the council, he peered secretly into the royal chamber. There he saw the monarch in the grip of some terrible fear. He seemed to be seeing the apparition of the slain Dimitri and madly prayed for mercy. Over and over he begged the ghost to depart.

---

[9] Scene One of Act Four in the original score. When the opera is played in three acts, this is either Scene Two of Act Three or Scene Three of Act Three.

As the boyars exclaim in shocked surprise, Boris reels into the chamber. Beside himself with terror, he cowers as though trying to escape from a pursuer. In fear-stricken tones he protests that he is guiltless. Dimitri lives, he mutters, and Shuisky must be punished for spreading the vile lie about his murder.

Suddenly he recovers himself, greets the boyars with his accustomed dignity and authority, and then takes his seat on the throne. Shuisky hesitantly approaches and informs him that a venerable monk is waiting to speak to the czar on a matter of great importance. Boris orders him to be admitted, saying that this holy man may bring some peace to his troubled spirit.

Summoned by Shuisky, the monk Pimen enters. He pauses for a moment at the door, then slowly approaches Boris, who quietly bids him speak. In an impressive aria, "Odnajdi v vetcherniy tchass prishel ko mnye pastuh," Pimen tells his story. He relates that he was visited by an aged shepherd who told him of a miracle. The shepherd explained that he had been blind from childhood. All cures had failed, he said, and he was resigned to eternal darkness. Then in a dream he heard the voice of a young boy bidding him go to the cathedral at Uglich and kneel in prayer at his tomb. The child had said he was the Czarevich Dimitri. The shepherd went immediately to Uglich, and hardly had he prayed than his sight was restored. There before him stood Dimitri.

Boris suddenly clutches at his heart and cries out wildly for help. Great excitement prevails as the boyars crowd around him. Reviving somewhat, Boris calls for his son. Feodor is brought in. He runs to his father's arms, and Boris commands all to leave. Then ensues a moving scene of farewell as Boris sings, "Protshay moy sin."

To the accompaniment of a somber theme in the orchestra, Boris tells Feodor that he will soon take his place on the throne of Russia. He must never seek to learn how his father came to rule, and must guard himself well against traitors. He counsels the boy to pay heed to the will of the people and to rule honorably and justly. Gently he commits Xenia to

Feodor's care. Placing his hands upon the boy's head, Boris, in broken phrases, prays for a blessing on his son.

From the distance come the tolling of bells and the chanting of the people as they offer a prayer for their dying monarch. In his final agony Boris cries to Heaven for mercy as boyars and monks enter the council chamber in solemn procession. With a desperate effort the dying czar rises to his feet and commands them to halt. Pointing to his son, he gasps, "Vot vash Tsar!" ("There is your Czar!"). A prayer for mercy on his lips, Czar Boris topples from the dais. The curtain falls.

Carmen

by GEORGES BIZET
[1838–1875]

Libretto by

HENRI MEILHAC *and* LUDOVIC HALÉVY

Based on the story of the same name by the French novelist,
Prosper Mérimée

CHARACTERS

Morales, an officer	Bass
Micaela, a peasant girl	Soprano
Zuniga, a captain of dragoons	Bass
Don José, a corporal of dragoons	Tenor
Carmen, a gypsy girl	Soprano
Mercedes } gypsy companions of Carmen	Mezzo-soprano
Frasquita }	Mezzo-soprano
Escamillo, a toreador	Baritone
El Remendado } smugglers	Tenor
El Dancairo }	Baritone

Cigarette girls, dragoons, an innkeeper, smugglers, dancers

Place: In and near Seville
Time: About 1820
First performance: Opéra-Comique, Paris, March 3, 1875
Original language: French

CARMEN, which is often referred to as an outstanding example of *opéra-comique*, is one of the universal favorites of the operatic stage. In setting Mérimée's story to music, Bizet

Carmen

exploited to the fullest his talent for vivid musical characterization, brilliant orchestration, and dramatic use of "local color." *Carmen* rings true throughout to Spanish temperament and atmosphere.

It has been said that the opera was so dismal a failure that Bizet died not long afterward of sheer humiliation and disappointment. That story has been challenged. It is true that the composer succumbed some three months after the opening, but his death was attributed to physical causes aggravated by overwork.

Carmen was, in fact, moderately well received. Paris was rather cool to it for several reasons. It was not in the conventional operatic idiom of the day. Bizet's use of continuously flowing melody led critics to accuse him of "Wagnerianism," against which there was violent prejudice in Paris at the time. The opera also lacked a happy ending. Finally, Parisian audiences were said to have been shocked by the bohemian character of Carmen herself.

Although withdrawn from the stage of the Opéra-Comique, *Carmen* was enthusiastically acclaimed in other European capitals a few months after its première. Eventually it won not only the favor of Paris but of the entire operatic world.

The prelude begins with the vigorous rhythm reflecting the festive atmosphere of the bullfight in the last act. Then comes the stirring refrain of the *Toreador Song*. This is followed by the somber motive of Carmen's tragic destiny—the so-called "fate motive." Just as this builds up to a crescendo it is shattered by an explosive chord. There is a dramatic pause, and the curtain rises.

Act One

A public square in Seville. At the right is the entrance to the tobacco factory, at the left, a guardhouse. A bridge spans the rear of the scene. It is noon. Townspeople are crossing the square. Morales and a number of dragoons are lounging in front of the guardhouse. The soldiers sing about the passing throng. As the brief chorus ends, Micaela enters. Morales calls attention to the comely girl who is approaching, and the guards express lively interest.

Courteously Morales asks Micaela for whom she is looking. A corporal, she replies. Himself, perhaps, suggests the officer hopefully. Micaela explains that she is seeking Don José. Morales says they all know of him but that he does not belong to their company. He is expected soon, the officer continues, because there will shortly be a change of guard. Then he invites her to wait inside the guardhouse. Micaela thanks him but declines, whereupon Morales hastily assures her that she will be in no danger. Micaela answers that she is quite sure of that, but thinks it will be better if she returns later when the relief guard arrives. The soldiers, pressing around, entreat her to stay. She adroitly evades their attentions, gaily bids them good-by, and runs off. Morales remarks philosophically that the bird has escaped and that there is nothing to do but go on watching the crowd as before.

Then begins the bright, martial music of the changing of the guard. The relief detachment is led in by Zuniga and Don José, preceded by a group of street urchins marching along to a merry tune of their own. While the guard is changing, the youngsters march around singing of how they go forward like true soldiers, shoulders back and heads high. They imitate trumpets as they sing.

Morales tells Don José that a pretty girl, with braided hair and dressed in blue, came to the guardhouse looking for him. That must have been Micaela, Don José exclaims. The off-duty guard marches away, with the boys following and singing their gay, piping tune.

In recitative, Zuniga asks Don José if the cigarette girls work in the factory across the square. Don José tells him they do, and adds that they are known to be a flirtatious lot. When Zuniga asks if they are good-looking, Don José confesses that he has never paid any attention to them. Zuniga knowingly remarks that his thoughts are probably wrapped up in a pretty girl in blue, whose name is Micaela. The corporal admits that he loves her very much. He goes on to say that the

Carmen

cigarette girls will shortly appear, and then Zuniga can judge for himself if they are beautiful.

A bell rings and the workers stream out of the factory. First come the men, singing how they wait each noon to make love to the girls ("La cloche a sonné"). Then the girls, smoking cigarettes, stroll into the square. To the accompaniment of a gracefully flowing theme the men describe the alluring movements of the girls as they smoke and compare lovers' words and promises to smoke that ascends to the sky and is gone.

The men wonder why they have not seen Carmen. In the next instant the fate motive flashes in the orchestra and Carmen stands before them. The crowd hails her lustily, the men imploring her to tell when she will give them her heart. Darting a look at Don José, Carmen answers that she does not know—perhaps never, perhaps tomorrow. At any rate, it will not be today.

To a throbbing rhythm, Carmen now begins the well-known *Habanera*. Love is like a bird that will never be tamed, she sings ("L'amour est un oiseau rebelle"). If he does not find your heart to his fancy, all entreaties are in vain. One lover woos with ardent phrases, another with silent adoration —and it is the latter whom Carmen chooses. The chorus repeats her words in a rhythmic chant. Carmen continues that love is like a gypsy, lawless and free. If you do not love her, she will love you nevertheless—and if she loves you, be on your guard. Repeating the refrain, Carmen sings that love is like an elusive bird: just as you think you have caught it, the creature flies away. The *Habanera* ends with a defiant flourish, and the men again beg Carmen to answer their pleas.

As the fate motive again is heard, Carmen starts toward the factory, suddenly turns, and approaches Don José. With an impudent laugh, she takes a flower from her dress, throws it in his face, then runs away. A group of cigarette girls surround Don José and mockingly repeat a strain from the *Habanera*. In a moment the factory bell rings, calling the men and women back to their work.

Don José is left alone. Slowly he picks up the flower, commenting as he wonders about Carmen's brazen gesture. He recalls how the flower sped like a bullet from her hand. The perfume is heady and the flower beautiful, he muses. As for the woman herself, if there are such beings as sorceresses, she most certainly is one.

At that moment Micaela appears and calls his name. Joyously Don José greets her. When Micaela tells him she brings greetings from his mother, he excitedly asks for further news of her. His mother has sent him a letter and some money, Micaela says. Shyly she adds that she has been entrusted with something for him that is far more precious. Eagerly Don José asks her to explain. Micaela replies that whatever has been given her for José, she in turn will give him.

She tells Don José that his mother had kissed her when they left the chapel together and had told her to seek her son in Seville. She bade Micaela say to her son that his mother thinks of him day and night and forgives his erring ways. The parting kiss she gave Micaela was for her son. Don José voices his emotion in a dramatic phrase. Now, Micaela continues, she will give Don José the kiss his mother sent.

A lyrical duet follows in which the two lovers sing of their tender memories of home and childhood ("Ma mère, je la vois"). The refrain is interrupted by the sinister fate theme. Don José turns abruptly away from Micaela and, in recitative, recalls the evil that strangely menaced him only today. He muses that the kiss his mother sent him from afar has saved him from great danger. What evil? What danger? Thus Micaela anxiously questions him. Don José brushes aside her queries by asking when she plans to return home. She replies that she will see his mother on the morrow.

In a brief but moving air, Don José asks Micaela to give his mother this message: He repents his wrongdoings and hopes she will forgive him. In return for her kiss he sends her the one he now gives Micaela. The two then resume the music of the duet.[1]

---

[1] The recitative and Don José's following air are sometimes cut. In that case, the first and second parts of the duet are combined and sung without interruption.

As Don José prepares to read his mother's letter, Micaela says she will leave him so that he might be alone. With the music of the duet echoing softly in the orchestra, the corporal utters his thoughts as he reads. His mother need have no fear, he sings, because her prayers will be answered. He loves Micaela and will take her for his wife. He meditates a moment, then in sudden anger his mind reverts to Carmen, the "sorceress," and her flower. He is about to throw the flower away when there is a burst of excitement in the factory. Zuniga rushes out of the guardhouse and asks what has happened. The workers hurry into the square, the women crying for help. They crowd around Zuniga, all chattering at once, some accusing Carmen, others defending her. One group finally takes the bewildered officer aside and tells him the story. Manuelita, one of the cigarette girls, announced that she had decided to buy a donkey, whereupon Carmen remarked that she would be better off buying a broom. Manuelita retorted that Carmen, with all her fine airs, would look well riding on a donkey—with two grooms at her side to chase away the flies. That touched off a hair-pulling match, the women add breathlessly.

Zuniga tries to quiet the excited group, then orders Don José to take two soldiers and find out what happened in the factory. The women again begin pestering Zuniga with their noisy arguments. One faction declares that Carmen struck the first blow, the other blames Manuelita. The names are tossed back and forth in an amusing chorus.

Suddenly Carmen appears, escorted by Don José and the two soldiers. Don José tells Zuniga that the two women exchanged blows and that one has been wounded. When Zuniga asks who is to blame, Don José replies that Carmen can tell him. The captain demands an explanation. With deliberate insolence, Carmen begins singing to herself, then replies that even torture could not make her talk. She says that she will defy all his weapons and heaven itself. Zuniga brusquely tells her to save her singing for another time and answer the charges. Carmen retorts that the answer is her own secret—and she means to keep it. She adds that there is someone near by whom she loves well enough to die for. Angrily Zuniga warns that she will do her singing in jail. By way of an answer, Carmen cuffs the first woman within reach, then resumes her singing with more impudence than ever. Thereupon Zuniga declares that, as much as he regrets it, he is forced to bind the arms of this young and charming person. He does so, and puts her in Don José's charge.

As the captain leaves, Carmen asks Don José where he is going to take her. He replies that there is nothing he can do but obey orders and take her to jail. The gypsy calmly informs him that, on the contrary, he will not only help her but bow to her every whim because he loves her. When Don José protests, she declares that the flower she gave him has charmed him into her power. Angrily Don José orders her to be quiet. Instead of obeying, she begins the alluring *Seguidilla*.

To the accompaniment of its insinuating rhythm she sings that she is going to dance and drink *manzanilla* at the tavern of her good friend Lillas Pastia, just outside the walls of Seville ("Près des remparts de Séville"). As there is no pleasure in going alone, she will take a lover along. But her current lover is gone—the devil knows where—and now her poor heart is as free as air again. Swains there are by the dozen, but not one of them pleases. And yet her heart and her soul may be had for the asking.

Meaningfully she observes that Don José has come along at just the right moment—and so she will go dancing and drinking at Lillas Pastia's with her new love. Outraged, Don José commands her to be silent. Carmen innocently replies that she was only singing to herself and meant him no harm. She was just thinking of a certain soldier who is in love with her and knows she means to do him no wrong. He's not a captain, nor even a lieutenant, but a mere corporal—yet it's all the same to a poor gypsy girl. Yes, he will do, Carmen adds seductively.

Don José protests that he is going mad. In passionate excitement he demands to know if she will always be true to him and love him if he relents. As if hypnotized, he loosens her bonds, again and again demanding her promise to love him.

Deliberately Carmen continues to torment him with her song, which she ends in brazen triumph.

Zuniga comes out of the guardhouse and gives Don José his orders, warning him to watch Carmen closely. In an aside, Carmen tells the corporal her plans for escape: At a certain moment she will push him and he must pretend to fall, leaving her unguarded. She reminds him again of their rendezvous. Then, laughing insolently in Zuniga's face, she repeats the refrain of the *Habanera*. Don José and the soldiers march her off. As they reach the bridge, Carmen puts her trick into effect and runs away shouting with laughter. The curtain falls.

ACT TWO

There is a brief entr'acte, which has for its theme an air sung by Don José later in the act. The curtain rises on Lillas Pastia's tavern. Gypsies and smugglers are sitting at tables with officers and soldiers. Dancers whirl about to the rhythmic beat of gypsy music. They pause as Carmen begins a fiery gypsy song ("Les tringles des sistres tintaient"). As the music grows wilder and wilder, the dancing begins again in a frenzy of color and movement. Frasquita and Mercedes join Carmen in her song, and the number ends in a riotous outburst of singing and dancing.

Frasquita then announces that it is closing time. Zuniga suggests that she and Mercedes leave with him, but they refuse. He invites Carmen, and she likewise declines. Annoyed at her refusal, he remarks that she looks angry. When she asks why she should be angry, the jealous captain replies that it is probably because of that soldier who was imprisoned for allowing her to escape. Carmen caustically asks if he has been put to death for his crime. Zuniga reveals that Don José has been released, and Carmen exclaims in obvious delight. She and the two other girls bid the disgruntled Zuniga and the soldiers good night with mocking politeness.

Suddenly from outside the tavern come the shouts of a crowd hailing Escamillo. It is a torchlight procession, Zuniga announces from the door. He then invites Escamillo in for a drink, and soon the blustering hero enters. The people crowd into the tavern and toast the bullfighter in a lusty chorus. In response, he sings the famous *Toreador Song*. He describes the great arena, with its vast throng shouting for the hero of the day. The chorus takes up the refrain, singing of the toreador's reward—the hand of his ladylove. Escamillo, continuing his aria, portrays the mad rush of the bull and the agile thrusts of the daring toreador as he stalks his prey. Again the chorus joins him, bringing the number to a stirring climax.

As he ends his song, Escamillo swaggers over to Carmen. He asks her to tell him her name, so that he may repeat it the next time he is in danger. Carmen obliges, but parries his pointed questions about love. Zuniga interrupts to warn her that if she will not come with him now he will return for her later. That will be a waste of time, she replies. The captain scornfully retorts that he is willing to take a chance.

With a flourish of the toreador music, Escamillo struts out, followed by the crowd. Frasquita asks El Dancairo about the plans for a proposed smuggling raid. He replies that the chances for success are good, but that the smugglers will need the expert assistance of the women to carry it out. This is the cue for one of the most delightful numbers in the opera —the scintillating quintet sung by Frasquita, Mercedes, El Dancairo, El Remendado, and Carmen ("Nous avons en tête une affaire"). They expound the theory that in plotting any kind of conspiracy, thievery, or deception, one must first make sure to have the co-operation of women. Their natural gift for duplicity will insure success. Frasquita and Mercedes agree at once to join the smugglers, but Carmen refuses. El Dancairo and El Remendado ask her why, and after much entreaty she finally tells them that she is in love. But they are incredulous. Carmen repeats that she is out of her mind with love. With ingratiating irony, the two smugglers observe that Carmen heretofore has always managed to compromise gracefully between her obligations and affections. She still refuses, saying that this time there can be no compromise. The smugglers plead in vain. Then all resume the refrain of the quintet with its humorous, rapid-fire patter.

El Dancairo, noting Carmen's restless manner, asks if she is expecting someone. She answers that she awaits a soldier who went to prison for her sake. A touching matter, remarks El Remendado cynically, while El Dancairo reminds Carmen that her soldier may very well change his mind about coming.

At that moment the voice of Don José is heard in the distance. He sings a short unaccompanied air (heard previously in the entr'acte) in praise of the brave dragoons of Alcala ("Halte là, qui va là?"). Carmen voices her joy. Frasquita and Mercedes peer outside and comment approvingly, and the two smugglers urge Carmen to ask Don José to join their band. Don José sings another stanza about the dragoons of Alcala as he approaches and enters the tavern. Carmen greets him eagerly. Don José tells her he has been in jail for two months and would gladly have stayed longer for her sake. He ardently assures her of his love.

She teases him by saying that she has just danced for some of his comrades, then taunts him for showing jealousy. Don José admits he is jealous. In gay mockery, Carmen says that now she will sing and dance for Sir Soldier alone. Commanding his attention, she begins a sinuous dance, singing a rhythmic, wordless air to the clicking accompaniment of castanets. Suddenly bugles blare in the distance. Don José stops Carmen and tells her that the retreat is being sounded. She sarcastically remarks that Don José is evidently bored with her singing and dancing and welcomes this interruption. After a moment she resumes her alluring dance. Don José once more restrains her, trying to explain that he must obey the call of duty and go back to quarters.

Carmen turns on Don José in fury. Angrily she reproaches herself for being so stupid as to try to please him with her singing and dancing. She might even have fallen in love with him, she storms. No sooner does he hear the bugle call, Carmen rages as she scornfully parodies the notes, than off he must go. With that she picks up his saber and helmet from the table, flings them at him, and derisively advises him to scamper back to quarters.

Shocked and humiliated, Don José reproaches Carmen for her cruelty. He assures her that he is loath to go—that never has any woman so profoundly stirred his heart. Carmen's reply is again to mock the bugle call and jeer at him for running off the moment he hears the retreat. And *that* is how he loves, she taunts bitterly. As she continues to deride and insult him, Don José declares in ringing, dramatic phrases that he loves her and that she must listen to his words.

Taking her flower from his blouse, he begins the *Flower Song* ("La fleur que tu m'avais jetée") one of the most famous of tenor arias. This flower, he sings, was his solace in prison. Though withered, its perfume still lingered, and during the night it brought back the vision of her face. Then, tortured by his longing, he cursed the day he first saw her and the destiny that set her in his path. But that was blasphemy, for deep in his heart there was only one desire and one hope—to return to her. From the first moment of their meeting, at her very first glance, she claimed his soul. Don José vows that he had but one single thought: he loves her.

But Carmen sullenly replies that he does not love her, that if he really did he would come away with her at once to her native mountains. There they would be free to love—no commands to obey, no retreat to quarters to heed. Ignoring Don José's desperate protests, Carmen relentlessly continues, as though casting a spell over him. He must follow her to the mountains, she repeats, to freedom beyond the law.

Suddenly Don José tears himself from Carmen's arms, declaring that he will not stoop to the infamy of desertion. His refusal goads Carmen into wild fury. She pours out her hatred for him and bids him good-by forever. In utter despair, Don José sings his farewell and prepares to leave. At that moment there is a knock on the door, and Zuniga is heard calling Carmen's name. She warns Don José to be silent. Zuniga bursts in. Seeing Don José, he makes a sneering reference to Carmen's lack of taste, asking why she chooses a plain soldier when there are officers available. He angrily orders Don José to leave, but the corporal calmly refuses. The captain makes a threatening gesture, whereupon Don José impetuously draws his sword and dares him to fight. Carmen quickly steps between the two men and excitedly summons the gypsies, who pour into the room. El Dancairo and El Remendado swiftly disarm Zuniga. As he stands helplessly between the two, Carmen tauntingly remarks that love has tricked him into arriving at exactly the wrong moment.

She informs him that they will be forced to hold him prisoner for a while to assure their own safety. The two smugglers, sticking their pistols into Zuniga's ribs, suggest with elaborate irony that it is time for him to leave. Merely for a stroll, Carmen explains mockingly. Zuniga assents, remarking that there is no resisting certain methods of argument. Casually he reminds them that there will be a reckoning later. That means war, El Dancairo observes with a shrug, but as things stand now, the captain had better come along without any further talk. The gypsies jeer at Zuniga as he is led away.

Carmen turns to Don José and asks him if he is now willing to join the smugglers. When he resignedly replies that he has no other choice, she chides him for his lack of gallantry. Exultantly she again begins the theme of her song of freedom. The chorus takes up the refrain, closing the act with a stirring ensemble ("Suis-nous à travers la campagne").

Act Three

After the entr'acte, a meditative air of quiet charm, the curtain rises on the smugglers' rendezvous in a wild mountain glen near a pass. Some of the band are lying about wrapped in their cloaks. Others enter cautiously to the accompaniment of an impressive, marchlike tune. Then the smugglers begin a dramatic chorus in which they warn of the need for caution as they ply their dangerous trade ("Ecoute, écoute, compagnon"). Danger lurks everywhere, they sing stealthily, and every moment they must be on their guard. The last notes die away in somber silence.

Carmen comes upon Don José staring unhappily down into the valley and asks what he sees. Sorrowfully he answers that down there lives a good, brave woman who still believes him to be an upright man. Bitterly he adds that she is wrong. With cutting sarcasm, Carmen asks who this remarkable woman is. Don José protests at her tone and says he is speaking of his mother. Carmen scornfully advises him to go home at once because he certainly is not suited to the smugglers' trade. She warns that if he does not leave, he will regret it.

Don José is aghast at her callousness in suggesting that they part. As Carmen repeats that they must part, the fate motive is briefly intoned by the orchestra. In rising anger, Don José warns her not to talk thus. She retorts that he will probably kill her for it, then notes the sinister look on his face. When Don José makes no reply, Carmen says indifferently that nothing matters because Destiny is after all the master.

A little distance away Frasquita and Mercedes are playing cards. They sing a charming duet in which they beseech the cards to tell them who their lovers will be. Frasquita sees her lover as an ardent young man. Mercedes says her wooer is a rich old man who talks of marriage. Frasquita foretells that her young man is going to carry her off to the mountains on his dashing steed. There he will rule as a great chieftain, with hundreds of men to do his bidding. Mercedes boasts that she will have gold and diamonds galore, then triumphantly announces that her aged lover will die and leave her all his vast fortune.

Carmen saunters over and picks up the cards—first a diamond, then a spade. There is a sinister suggestion of the fate motive, followed by sustained descending notes, as Carmen reads her tragic fortune: death—first for her, then for him. To the accompaniment of brooding minor chords she sings of the fateful cards ("En vain pour éviter les réponses amères"). No one can ignore the answers they give. No use to shuffle them—they never lie. If your Destiny is a happy one, every card will foretell good fortune. But if you are fated to die, you may pick up twenty cards and each one will pitilessly repeat your doom. Twice Carmen turns up the cards as the harmonies harshly reverberate in the orchestra. Death—and again Death, Carmen murmurs hopelessly. Frasquita and Mercedes interrupt her as they begin their gay refrain. A striking trio follows, with the two girls singing lightly of their lovers and Carmen reiterating her prophecy of doom.

El Dancairo suddenly appears, announces that the smugglers will try to get through the pass with contraband, and asks Don José to remain behind to guard their stores. He adds that he saw three guards at the pass, and that they will have to be taken care of. Carmen, ordering the men to shoulder their booty, declares that they must and will get through.

A vigorous chorus follows, in which the smugglers explain how they will outwit the guards. As the soldiers are gallant gentlemen, they will not be able to resist the smiles of the women, and while they are thus diverted, the men will pass by with the contraband, unobserved. A moment after the smugglers have left, Micaela appears, searching for Don José. In recitative, she vows to conquer fear and carry out the task imposed on her by his mother. Then, in one of the best-known arias in the opera, "Je dis que rien ne m'épouvante," she voices her determination to accomplish her task. She admits that this wild mountain spot fills her with dread, but offers up a prayer for strength to face the ordeal. She resolves to confront the evil temptress who has lured Don José to his ruin. Her aria ends in a dramatic entreaty for divine guidance.

Suddenly Micaela sees Don José in the distance. She calls his name. Trembling with fear, she watches him take aim and fire at an unseen target, then conceals herself. A moment later Escamillo comes striding up through the pass, hat in hand. He inspects the bullet hole in the hat and jovially remarks that if the shot had struck a bit lower it would have finished him off. Don José rushes up and demands his name. Escamillo suavely identifies himself.

Don José bids him welcome, but adds that he risked his life coming through the pass alone. The other replies that he is too much in love to worry about such trifles, and that anyone who calls himself a man would certainly risk all to see his ladylove. Don José asks who she is. A gypsy girl, Escamillo tells him, Carmen by name. Don José starts in surprise. The toreador relates that Carmen was in love with a certain soldier who became a deserter in order to be near her. But that's all over now, Escamillo adds, because Carmen's affairs never last more than six months.

Don José sharply asks Escamillo if he is aware of the fact that whoever tries to take a gypsy's woman away must be prepared to pay the price. Escamillo coolly asks what that may be. The slash of a dagger, Don José retorts. Then it dawns upon the toreador that this angry renegade is Carmen's erstwhile lover. Mockingly he expresses his pleasure at meeting his rival. The challenge given, the two sing a dramatic duet as they prepare to duel with daggers ("Enfin ma colère"). They lunge at each other. Escamillo falls, and Don José is about to plunge his knife into his adversary's throat when Carmen rushes in and stops him.

Escamillo gallantly thanks Carmen for saving his life. Turning to Don José, he observes that the score is even—now—but the winner will be decided "in the next round." El Dancairo interrupts impatiently and tells Escamillo to be off. The toreador pauses to invite all to the bullfight in Seville—particularly those who love him. As he speaks he looks significantly at Carmen. Don José, seeing the glance, makes a threatening gesture, but Escamillo flippantly advises the corporal not to be hasty, then slowly makes his exit, deliberately keeping his eyes on Carmen. Don José lunges at the toreador but is restrained by the smugglers.

He turns on Carmen and warns her not to torment him. El Dancairo urges all to go on their way. Suddenly El Remendado discovers Micaela and drags her from her hiding place. Don José ignores her eager greeting and asks why she has come. To the music of the duet in Act One, Micaela tells him that down in the valley his mother tearfully prays that her son will return to her. She implores Don José to come with her. Sneeringly Carmen advises him to go at once. Stung to fury, Don José accuses her of wanting to get rid of him so that she may follow her new love, the toreador. Wildly he swears that he will never leave Carmen, that death alone can break the chain that binds them. In chorus the smugglers urge him to leave for his own good. Don José brushes Micaela aside and confronts Carmen. He rages that he will force her to bow to the destiny that brought them together and again vows never to leave her. The smugglers appeal to him to heed their warning.

Micaela steps forward, pleading for a final word. Grief-stricken, she tells Don José that his mother is near death and that she wishes to forgive him before she dies. Don José cries out in anguish and prepares to leave with Micaela. In terrible anger he whirls on Carmen, warning her that they will meet again. The fate motive underscores the threat in his words.

From the distance comes the voice of Escamillo singing a phrase of the *Toreador Song*. Carmen attempts to meet him, but Don José prevents her with a menacing gesture. The smugglers slowly move off to the marchlike music heard earlier. The curtain falls.

ACT FOUR

The entr'acte music, flashing with brilliant Spanish rhythms, builds up to the festive gaiety of the bullfight scene which opens the act. The curtain rises on a square before the bull ring in Seville. An excited throng is waiting for the procession into the arena. A shout goes up as the parade approaches, and the scene glitters with colorful pageantry. Dancers, picadors, banderilleros, officers, and soldiers march proudly by.

A thunderous burst of applause greets Escamillo as he enters with Carmen on his arm. There is a brief but melodramatic duet. The toreador sings that if Carmen really loves him, she may well be proud of him today ("Si tu m'aimes, Carmen"). Fervently she answers that she has never loved anyone as she loves him. Their impassioned song is interrupted by the entrance of the Alcalde, the highest official of Seville. Frasquita and Mercedes approach and warn Carmen that Don José is lurking in the crowd. Carmen scornfully replies that she is not afraid, and will stay and talk with him. The crowd surges into the arena. Frasquita and Mercedes follow, and in the next moment Carmen and Don José stand face to face—alone.

They greet each other curtly. Carmen says that friends have tried to convince her that Don José has come to the arena with the intention of killing her. Don José quietly replies that he is not here to harm her, only to plead for her love. He entreats her to forget all their past bitterness and come away with him to some distant place where they can start life anew. Carmen answers that she will not lie—her mind is made up. All is over between them.

In a passionate, moving appeal, Don José begs her to allow him to save her—and, in saving her, save himself. Carmen harshly replies that she knows he will probably kill her if she refuses, but even that will not break her will. Their voices blend in a short but intensely dramatic duet, Carmen relentlessly repeating her refusal, Don José frenziedly pleading.

In despair, Don José cries out for her love, but Carmen spurns him with cruel indifference. Wildly he promises that if she will love him he will join the smugglers again—will do anything she asks. In a dramatic plea he implores her not to leave him. Carmen's reply is that she was born free and she will die free.

There is a sudden fanfare from the bull ring as the shouting crowd hails the toreador. With an exclamation of pride and joy, Carmen attempts to rush into the arena. Don José seizes her, sardonically commenting on the applause for her new lover. Violently he asks is she is really in love with the toreador. Carmen defiantly answers that even in the face of death she will admit her love. Another fanfare sounds in the arena, and the throng sings excitedly about the progress of the bullfight.

Again Carmen tries to force her way past Don José. Beside himself with jealous fury, he cries out that he has not pawned his soul for her love only to be scornfully cast aside for his rival. Furiously Carmen tells him either to kill her or let her pass. More cheers come from the arena. Don José curses Carmen and shouts that for the last time he asks her to yield. In answer she takes from her finger the ring he had given her and hurls it away. Don José rushes at her with a terrible cry. As the crowd pours out of the arena singing phrases of the *Toreador Song*, Don José seizes Carmen and plunges his dagger into her heart.

The people draw back in horror as they see him kneeling beside Carmen's body. Then, as the fate motive thunders forth, Don José cries out that it was he who slew her—his own Carmen, whom he adored. The curtain falls.

Cavalleria Rusticana

by PIETRO MASCAGNI
[1863–1945]

Libretto by
GIOVANNI TARGIONI-TOZZETTI *and* GUIDO MENASCI

Based on a short story
CAVALLERIA RUSTICANA
written and later dramatized by the Italian novelist, Giovanni Verga

CHARACTERS

Santuzza, a beautiful peasant girl	*Soprano*
Lucia, mother of Turiddu	*Contralto*
Alfio, a village teamster	*Baritone*
Turiddu, a young soldier	*Tenor*
Lola, the young wife of Alfio	*Mezzo-soprano*

Villagers and peasants

Place: A Sicilian village
Time: Nineteenth century
First performance: Teatro Constanzi, Rome, May 17, 1890
Original language: Italian

CAVALLERIA RUSTICANA, Mascagni's first opera, scored a spectacular success at its very first performance and lifted its composer from obscurity to fame and fortune overnight. It has held its place since then as one of the most popular works on the operatic stage.

At the time Mascagni wrote his masterpiece he was a struggling music teacher in the small Italian town of Cerignola. He had learned, in 1888, that the music publisher Sonzogno was offering a prize for the best one-act opera. Mascagni entered the competition in the hope of securing

Cavalleria Rusticana

much-needed funds. He found his inspiration in the libretto by Targioni-Tozzetti and Menasci and forthwith started composing. Early in 1890 he presented his score to the contest judges in Rome, where it was awarded first prize. Its subsequent production made operatic history. The opera is usually presented on the same bill with other short works, such as *Pagliacci, Salome,* and *Hänsel und Gretel.*

Ironically titled "Rustic Chivalry," *Cavalleria* deals with anything *but* chivalry. It is a grim story of illicit love and revenge, and the fact that the events take place on an Easter morning adds still further to the dramatic effect.

Action centers around Turiddu, a young soldier, whose mother keeps a wineshop in the village square. When he went away to serve in the army he was betrothed to Lola, but on his return he found her married to Alfio, the teamster. Turiddu, having thus lost Lola, consoled himself by making love to another village girl, Santuzza. Before long he betrayed, then abandoned, her, transferring his affections back to Lola, who willingly took advantage of her husband's frequent absences to encourage Turiddu's secret love-making. This tangled state of affairs already exists when the curtain rises.

The orchestral prelude states several themes that are important to the development of the drama. After a quiet opening strain which symbolizes the peace of Easter Day there comes the theme of Santuzza's impassioned pleading for Turiddu's love. The prelude is suddenly interrupted by the voice of Turiddu behind the scenes. To a rhythmic harp accompaniment he sings the *Siciliana*,[1] an amorous serenade in traditional Sicilian style. Turiddu compares Lola's lips to ripe red berries, speaks of the glow of love in her eyes, and likens the color of her cheeks to wild cherries. The man who can win these treasures for himself is indeed lucky. Then in a sinister foreshadowing of disaster Turiddu envisions blood on Lola's doorstep. But even the prospect of dying before her eyes does not frighten him, he sings. Only if Lola were not in Paradise

---

[1] The *Siciliana* is sometimes sung in Sicilian dialect instead of the classic Italian.

to greet him would he abandon himself to grief. The serenade dies away on long, sustained notes, and the orchestra again takes up the intensely moving themes of the tragedy which is to follow.

The curtain rises to the chiming of bells. We see the deserted square of a village in Sicily. At the right is the entrance of a church; at the left is the tavern and home of Mamma Lucia. It is dawn. As the music becomes brighter and gayer, peasants and villagers cross the square, their voices rising above the orchestral accompaniment in short simple phrases. Some of the people enter the church, while others stroll down the street. Women's voices are heard singing of the joy of Easter Day—of how the caroling of birds and the fresh beauty of awakening spring mingle with tender avowals of love.

As the women slowly enter the scene, men's voices are heard in praise of women's diligence and of feminine charms which ensnare the heart. The men now appear, and all the voices mingle in a tuneful chorus hymning the joys of spring and love. The last notes are charmingly echoed from behind the scenes, as though coming from afar off. The people drift away until the square once more is empty.

Abruptly the mood of the music changes to a somber motif of impending tragedy. As it rises in intensity Santuzza appears and meets Mamma Lucia coming out of her wineshop. The girl inquires for Turiddu. When Lucia asks why she has come to see her son, Santuzza merely repeats her query. Lucia agitatedly replies that she does not know her son's whereabouts, adding she wants no trouble. Desperately Santuzza implores her to have pity—as Christ had pity on Magdalene. She beseeches Lucia to tell her where Turiddu is hiding.

He has gone to fetch wine from Francofonte, Lucia says at last. Santuzza declares that Turiddu was seen in the village only last night. Alarmed, Lucia demands to know who told her so, because Turiddu has not been home. Then, touched by the girl's distress, Lucia invites her to come into the house. Santuzza cries that she dare not enter because she has been excommunicated. Fearfully Lucia asks what Santuzza knows about her son, but Santuzza speaks only of the anguish in her heart.

At that moment the music breaks softly into a rhythmic staccato which swiftly grows louder. Whips crack sharply and bells jingle gaily as into the square comes Alfio, the jolly teamster, surrounded by his friends. He strikes up a lusty song about his fine horse, the jingling bells, and the cracking whip ("Il cavallo scalpita"). Rain or shine, he has no cares. The men join in, hailing the carter as a fine fellow who has a trade that none can rival. Joyously Alfio sings of the bliss that awaits him in his Easter reunion with his beautiful wife, Lola. More and more neighbors stop to listen, and soon they, too, join Alfio in a rousing chorus.

As the throng disperses, Lucia greets Alfio, who asks if she still has some of her good wine left. She tells him that Turiddu has gone to the neighboring town to replenish her supply. Again she is contradicted, the teamster stating that he had seen Turiddu that very morning near his cottage. When Lucia exclaims in surprise Santuzza warns her to be quiet. Alfio then goes on his way, exhorting his neighbors to go into church.

Within the church the choir begins the majestic "Regina Coeli." Townspeople in the square slowly assume prayerful attitudes as they answer the choir with Hallelujahs. Then all join in singing the deeply moving Resurrection hymn so appropriate to this Easter morning. Santuzza's voice soars above the chorus as she carries the melody in broad, sweeping phrases to its great climax.

Presently the people enter the church, and finally only two are left—Santuzza and Lucia. In recitative, Lucia asks why Santuzza bade her be silent during her talk with Alfio. Santuzza, in reply, begins the famous aria, "Voi lo sapete," in which she tells the older woman the whole bitter story. She sings that Turiddu, before leaving to serve in the army, was engaged to Lola. He returned only to find her married to another. To console himself, Santuzza goes on, he sought her love, and she loved him madly in return. But Lola, out of envy and jealousy, lured Turiddu to her own arms again. Now, sings Santuzza, nothing is left to her but weeping.

Lucia expresses horror at the evil story told on this holy day. Santuzza cries out that she is accursed and begs Lucia to pray for her soul. She will go once more to Turiddu, she says, and plead for his love. Breathing a prayer for Santuzza, Lucia slowly enters the church, leaving the girl alone in the square.

At that point Turiddu appears, exclaiming in surprise when he sees Santuzza ("Tu qui Santuzza"). He tries to parry her questions as to where he has been and swears that he has just come from Francofonte. Santuzza retorts that she herself saw him in the village. What is more, he had been seen near Lola's home only this morning. Angrily Turiddu accuses her of spying. Santuzza denies it, saying that Alfio himself told the story—and he will spread it through the village.

Trying to bluff his way out, Turiddu berates the girl for being suspicious and orders her away. He denies loving Lola. Santuzza, now beside herself, curses him, and as Turiddu recoils in horror she declares that Lola has lured him away. Then the furious accusations of the two merge in an intensely dramatic duet ("Bada, Santuzza, schiavo non sono"). Violently Turiddu orders Santuzza to be silent, protesting that he will not be enslaved by her jealousy. Unheeding, Santuzza cries that though he may beat and revile her she will still adore him.

Suddenly their words are interrupted by a woman's voice in the distance. With gay mockery she sings about her "king of roses" ("Fior di giaggiolo"), and soon Lola strolls in. Feigning surprise, she asks Turiddu if he has seen Alfio. She ignores Turiddu's embarrassed answer and adds carelessly that Alfio is probably talking with the blacksmith. With deliberate malice Lola asks Turiddu and Santuzza if they are attending services of their own in the square. Turiddu, now completely confused, tries to explain. Santuzza angrily retorts that it is Easter and that God sees all. Lola asks if she is going to Mass. Santuzza replies pointedly that only those should go who are without sin. In brazen irreverence Lola gives thanks to God

Cavalleria Rusticana

that she is sinless, whereupon Santuzza sardonically compliments her on her brave words. Turiddu interrupts impatiently and starts to follow Lola into the church. With a sneer she tells him to stay with Santuzza, who now renews her pleas to Turiddu. Blasphemously uttering a blessing on Santuzza, Lola enters the church.

Turiddu furiously turns on Santuzza and the quarrel breaks out afresh, merging once again in an impassioned duet. Santuzza desperately tries to restrain Turiddu from entering the church, imploring him not to leave her ("No, Turiddu, rimani"). Turiddu brutally asks why she persists in spying on him. The duet rises to a blazing climax as Santuzza beseeches Turiddu not to abandon her, while he wrathfully orders her to leave him. Suddenly in wild anger he hurls her to the ground and runs into the church. She screams a curse after him and calls him her betrayer.

Santuzza looks up to find Alfio approaching. Quickly she regains her composure and rises to her feet. The Lord himself sent him at this moment, she says to Alfio. The teamster asks her how far the Mass has progressed. She replies that it is almost over, then significantly adds that Lola and Turiddu are attending service together. Unsuspecting, Alfio asks what she means. In cold fury Santuzza tells him that while he was away making a living Lola was seeking her pleasure with another. Alfio, aghast, demands to know what she is saying. The truth, Santuzza answers simply. Turiddu abandoned her because he could not resist Lola's charms. Alfio threatens to cut out her heart if she is lying. Santuzza retorts that she is not in the habit of lying and then swears by her very dishonor and humiliation that what she says is true.

There is a long pause. Calmly, then, Alfio thanks Santuzza. She expresses shame for having spoken, but Alfio declares that the shame is on the guilty pair. They are caught in the net, and he will have his revenge before the day is out. A stormy duet follows in which Santuzza cries in agony of remorse at having betrayed Turiddu, while Alfio swears terrible revenge ("Infami loro"). At the end of the number both hurry away, leaving the scene completely deserted.

Then follows the famous *Intermezzo*, played by the orchestra while the square remains empty, and this calm, sweet music brings a moment of relief to the opera. But it is like the ominous calm before the storm. Tragedy is impending, and it is only because the lovers are at worship that they have sanctuary from Alfio's revenge.

When the *Intermezzo* ends the villagers and peasants leave the church. They are all in good spirits. A number of them assemble in front of Lucia's wineshop and fill their glasses. The men, singing softly, urge all to go home to the joys of the hearth after the day's religious duties. The women repeat the refrain, then all sing together. Lola and Turiddu now come from the church. Turiddu, indicating the throng, asks Lola gaily if she would pass up the chance to meet with old friends. Lola says she must go home because she has not yet seen Alfio. Turiddu carelessly replies that she will probably see her husband in the square.

He invites the people to have a drink, and then begins the *Brindisi*—the famous drinking song, "Viva il vino spumeggiante." As it ends in a spirited chorus Alfio suddenly appears. He sings a greeting, and his friends lustily respond. Turiddu offers him a glass. Alfio refuses, saying he would not trust a drink given him by Turiddu—it might be poisoned.

Turiddu acknowledges the insult and casually tosses out the wine. Lola utters an exclamation of terror, whereupon the other women persuade her to leave. They hurry away as the two men confront each other. Turiddu asks Alfio if he has anything to say. When the answer is no, Turiddu issues the traditional challenge, placing himself at Alfio's "service." Alfio accepts. Then, according to true Sicilian custom, the two embrace and Turiddu bites Alfio's ear. Alfio significantly remarks that they seem to understand each other.

In a sudden change of mood Turiddu admits he has wronged Alfio and agrees that he deserves to die like a dog. He laments that if he is killed in the duel his "poor Santuzza" will be left without her lover. But, he adds defiantly, he still means to plunge his dagger into Alfio's heart. The teamster coldly warns him to think carefully on what he is about to undertake. He says he will meet Turiddu behind the garden wall, then stalks away.

Turiddu, suddenly panic-stricken, calls his mother to him. He haltingly tells her that he has drunk too much wine, that he is going for a walk to clear his brain. Before he goes he wants her blessing—just as he did when he went away to be a soldier. Then in impassioned phrases he demands Lucia's promise to be a mother to Santuzza—whom he has sworn to cherish—if he should not return ("Voi dovrete fare").

Lucia excitedly asks him the meaning of his strange words. He replies that the wine has set his brain awhirl. Wildly he implores God's forgiveness and begs his mother for one last kiss of farewell. In a final, soaring musical phrase Turiddu again entreats his mother to take care of Santuzza, then rushes frantically away.

Terror-stricken, Lucia tries to follow him, calling his name. Santuzza rushes in and takes Lucia in her arms. People crowd nervously into the square. Suddenly a woman rushes in shrieking: "Turiddu has been murdered!" All cry out in horror; Santuzza and Lucia fall fainting to the ground. The curtain swiftly descends.

Così Fan Tutte

by WOLFGANG AMADEUS MOZART
[1756–1791]

Libretto by
LORENZO DA PONTE

CHARACTERS

Ferrando, a young officer in love with Dorabella	Tenor
Guglielmo, a young officer in love with Fiordiligi	Bass
Don Alfonso, an elderly bachelor	Baritone
Fiordiligi, a lady of Ferrara	Soprano
Dorabella, her sister	Mezzo-soprano
Despina, their maid	Soprano

Townspeople, soldiers, singers, musicians,
ladies and gentlemen, servants

Place: Naples
Time: Eighteenth century
First performance: Burgtheater, Vienna, January 26, 1790
Original language: Italian

Così fan tutte, which Mozart wrote on commission from Emperor Franz Josef II, is one of the composer's last three operas, having been followed by *La Clemenza di Tito* and *Die Zauberflöte*. Although the work was a comparative failure at its première—mainly due, it is said, to the weakness of the libretto—it contains some of Mozart's most delightful music. The full title of the opera is *Così fan tutte, ossia La Scuola degli Amanti* (*So Do They All, or School for Lovers*).

The sparkling overture prominently states one theme which will be heard near the end of the opera. It is sung by Don Alfonso, Ferrando, and Guglielmo as they express the underlying thought of the opera itself—"Così fan tutte."

Act One

[*Scene One*]   A café in Naples. Ferrando and Guglielmo are heatedly arguing with Don Alfonso as to whether or not women are capable of being faithful. The two officers cite their own ladyloves, Fiordiligi and Dorabella, as paragons of womanly virtue and constancy, while Don Alfonso derides their naïve trust in womankind. The argument ensues in the form of a spirited trio ("La mia Dorabella capace non è"). Finally Don Alfonso makes a bet of one hundred sequins that the two young ladies will prove unfaithful when put to the test, and the two lovers enthusiastically accept his challenge. At the end of the scene Ferrando and Guglielmo are already discussing plans for spending the money after they have won it.

[*Scene Two*]   The garden of the villa of Fiordiligi and Dorabella on the Bay of Naples. The sisters, gazing at miniatures of their lovers, sing their praises in a tuneful duet ("Ah guarda, sorella"). As they express impatience because the gentlemen have not yet appeared, Don Alfonso enters and tells them that Ferrando and Guglielmo have been ordered to join their regiment tomorrow. Although they wished to spare their fiancées the painful ordeal of farewell, he continues, they are waiting outside and will appear if the women so desire it. With that he calls in the two officers, and a delightful quintet ensues ("Sento, o Dio!"). Ferrando and Guglielmo pretend to be greatly distressed at this unfortunate turn of events, while the sisters moan that they would rather be slain than part from their lovers. In an aside to Don Alfonso, the two officers declare that such devotion is ample proof of unswerving fidelity, but the Don complacently observes that he still will collect his bet. Embracing the women, Ferrando and Guglielmo assure them of their undying love in a sentimental duet ("Al fato dan legge quegli occhi vezzosi"). Their good-bys are interrupted by the sound of drums in the distance, and Don Alfonso announces that the regiment is preparing to embark.

A troop of soldiers, followed by townspeople, marches in, and we hear a martial chorus. After this the quintet is continued as Ferrando and Guglielmo sing their farewells and the women urge them to write often—"At least two letters a day," as Dorabella says. There is a repetition of the chorus, and then the two men join the ranks and march away. Fiordiligi, Dorabella, and Don Alfonso sing a charming trio ("Soave sia il vento"), voicing the hope that the departing heroes will have fair winds and smooth sailing. When the sisters leave, Don Alfonso expresses satisfaction over the progress of his plot, adding the observation that putting one's trust in women is as futile as sweeping up the sea, planting seeds in sand, or catching the wind in a net.

[*Scene Three*]   A chamber adjoining the rooms of the sisters. Despina enters carrying a tray. In a brief air ("Che vita maledetta"), she complains over the lot of a maid who is kept busy trying to anticipate the whims of two capricious young ladies. Dorabella enters in a state of great emotion. Melodramatically she orders Despina to close the windows and draw the shades, saying that she no longer cares to see light nor to breathe since her lover has gone. Dismissing the maid, she goes on with her lamentations in a dramatic aria ("Smanie implacabili"). After its conclusion Despina returns with Fiordiligi, who expresses sympathy over her sister's distress.

Despina ventures the opinion that the ladies are taking the absence of their lovers much too seriously. Even if they are killed in battle, she observes philosophically, that would mean the loss of only two men, leaving the ladies free to choose from all the other men left in the world. She elaborates on these sentiments in the aria "In uomini, in soldati," after which Dorabella and Fiordiligi, shocked and indignant at such cynicism, stalk out of the room.

Don Alfonso enters and cautiously sounds out Despina as

Così Fan Tutte

to her views on the dilemmas of her mistresses. The maid agrees that they most certainly deserve the consolation of male companionship. Thereupon Don Alfonso bribes her into aiding him in his plan and forthwith presents two candidates for Despina's approval. They are, of course, Ferrando and Guglielmo, now disguised as Albanians with bushy beards. When Despina, giving no sign that she recognizes the two officers, expresses disapproval over their barbaric appearance, the three plotters conclude that they will be safe from detection by the ladies themselves. Hearing Dorabella and Fiordiligi approach, Don Alfonso conceals himself.

The sisters, aghast at the presence of men in the house, berate Despina for admitting strangers. To their further confusion and alarm, the "Albanians" kneel down before them and ardently declare their love. The dialogue builds up into an amusing ensemble. The outraged demeanor of the ladies reassures Ferrando and Guglielmo of their fidelity, while Despina marvels at the ability of her sex to summon up a convincing show of emotions at a moment's notice. Don Alfonso makes himself known and greets the two Albanians as friends of long standing, warning them in an aside to play their parts according to his cues. The two officers grow more fervent in their pleas. Fiordiligi, exasperated at their persistence, finally orders them out in a dramatic recitative ("Stelle! che dir!"). She then proclaims that her love is as firmly anchored as a rock in the ocean bed and rebukes the strangers for attempting to swerve her affections. These sentiments are expressed in the famous aria "Come scoglio," which is remarkable for its brilliant passages and the extent of its vocal range.

But Fiordiligi's protests only move the strangers to more ardent entreaties, while Don Alfonso intercedes for them as worthy cavaliers and esteemed personal friends. Guglielmo pleads their cause in a mock-serious air ("Non siate ritrosi"), in which he implores the ladies to inspect them carefully and suggest any improvement which would make them more acceptable as wooers. Fiordiligi and Dorabella, unmoved by his gallantry, haughtily sweep out of the room. A gay trio follows

("E voi ridete?"). Ferrando and Guglielmo, satisfied that they now have convincing proof of the ladies' constancy, laugh heartily at Don Alfonso and magnanimously offer to cancel half or even three quarters of the bet. Don Alfonso, dryly observing that the last laugh is the best, declares that the original bet still stands. The men accept his challenge and agree to proceed according to his orders until the next day. Don Alfonso directs them to go into the garden to await further instructions. Before they leave, Ferrando pauses to sing the aria "Un' aura amorosa," in which he discourses on the sustaining power of love.

After he and Guglielmo have gone, Don Alfonso cynically remarks that in a world in which he was certain no woman was ever constant he has actually found two. Despina enters and tells him that the ladies are mooning about in the garden. When he asks her opinion as to whether the two sisters will ever yield to temptation, she replies that it is only a matter of time. She informs him that she has a plan of her own which will break down the defenses of her mistresses and then asks Don Alfonso to have his two swains in readiness in the garden.

[Scene Four] The garden of the sisters' home. In a melodious duet Dorabella and Fiordiligi bemoan the absence of their lovers ("Ah! che tutta in un momento"). Their mournful reflections are interrupted by cries of distress, and in another moment Ferrando and Guglielmo—still in their disguises—rush in, followed by Don Alfonso, who appears to be trying to calm them. Declaring that they can no longer live if their love is unrequited, they drink the contents of small vials which they hold in their hands. Don Alfonso tells the horrified ladies that the Albanians have taken poison. Sinking to the ground, the men reproach Dorabella and Fiordiligi for their cruel indifference and then pretend to succumb to the effects of the poison.

Wringing their hands in helpless confusion, the women call for Despina, who, of course, has been looking on unobserved. After properly expressing her alarm, the maid tells the ladies to comfort the victims as best they can while she and Don Alfonso run to fetch a doctor. When they have gone, Dorabella and Fiordiligi kneel beside the men and gingerly feel their pulses and listen for sounds of heartbeats, exclaiming in great distress that signs of life are fading. In asides, Ferrando and Guglielmo express great satisfaction over their solicitude.

Despina, in the disguise of a doctor, returns with Don Alfonso. Muttering Latin phrases, she examines the two victims, feeling their pulses and their brows in a pompous, professional manner. Their condition, the "doctor" announces at length, is obviously the result of a potion they have swallowed. Dorabella and Fiordiligi inform "him" that the two men, distracted by love, drank arsenic. Thereupon the doctor brings forth a huge magnet and with an impressive flourish bids all witness the remarkable curative powers of his great new invention. Holding the magnet over the men's bodies, Despina sings, as though uttering an incarnation, "Questo e quel pezzo."

Ferrando and Guglielmo dutifully begin trembling and appear to revive. Staring wildly at Dorabella and Fiordiligi, they ask if they are gazing on angels or goddesses and then pretend to be overjoyed to discover that these are the fair ones for whom they sought to die. The sisters are somewhat taken aback by the enthusiasm of the resuscitated Albanians, and matters are not improved when they implore kisses to make their recovery complete.

Dorabella and Fiordiligi flare up at this impertinence, despite the exhortations of Despina and Don Alfonso that a kiss would be an act of mercy. Ferrando and Guglielmo sing that the ladies' refusal to grant them kisses is a comforting indication of their fidelity. These various sentiments are expressed in a brilliant ensemble which brings the act to a close.

Act Two

[*Scene One*] A room in the home of the sisters. Dorabella and Fiordiligi are in conversation with Despina. The maid tries to point out that the ladies are depriving themselves of a great deal of enjoyment by not responding to the wooing of the Albanians. After all, she avers, women are made for love, and men have been supplied by a kind providence to give them the opportunity of loving. She assures her mistresses that the strangers are gallant gentlemen, and that if they have been acting strangely it is due to the effects of the poison they have swallowed. Dorabella and Fiordiligi, evincing some interest, ask how they would be expected to behave toward the gentlemen once they have accepted their company.

Despina explains her theories about the art of love-making in a tuneful aria ("Una donna a quindici anni"). Even a maid of fifteen, she sings, must know the arts of love—the sly glances, coy refusals, tantalizing deceptions—which can make a man her slave. She concludes the aria with an offer to give further advice on these matters if it is desired. After she has left, Dorabella and Fiordiligi rationalize themselves into accepting the attentions of the two Albanians. In the ensuing duet, "Prendero quel brunettino," Dorabella declares that she prefers the "dark one," with his quiet, gentle demeanor, while Fiordiligi decides to take the other, who is blond and vivacious. They amuse themselves by describing how they will exchange sigh for sigh and glance for glance with their suitors.

Their conversation is interrupted by Don Alfonso, who hurries in to ask them to join him at the end of the garden. There at the seashore, he says, they will find entertainment which will be very much to their liking.

[*Scene Two*] A pleasant spot along the seashore, with a small harbor in the background. A flower-festooned boat is seen at anchor, and in the boat are Ferrando and Guglielmo (still as Albanians) with a company of musicians and guests. When Dorabella and Fiordiligi appear, accompanied by Despina and Don Alfonso, the two men sing a melodious serenade ("Secondate, aurette amiche"). They then come ashore and greet the ladies, who respond rather self-consciously. Impatient with the stilted and hesitant manner of the

Così Fan Tutte

would-be lovers, Despina and Don Alfonso enact for their benefit the meeting of a young lady and her swain, pointing out the niceties of courtship. They then leave the four to themselves.

Fiordiligi pairs off with Ferrando, Dorabella with Guglielmo, and the couples stroll about in the garden. As Fiordiligi and Ferrando disappear among the trees, Dorabella and Guglielmo continue their amorous conversation in the form of a duet ("Il core vi dono"). Guglielmo persuades Dorabella to accept, as a token of his affection, a pendant in the form of a heart. Quickly following up his advantage, he takes off her necklace, from which hangs the miniature of Ferrando, and clasps it about his own neck. With coy declarations of affection, the two stroll away.

Ferrando and Fiordiligi reappear. Ferrando, however, apparently has been unsuccessful in his wooing, for he is being roundly denounced as an evil monster who is trying to lure an innocent maiden into faithlessness and deceit. Fiordiligi scornfully orders him to leave her. He declares his devotion in an impassioned air ("Ah! io veggio quell' anima bella"), and then, with a great show of disappointment, takes his leave.

Fiordiligi reveals her mingled agitation and uncertainty in a dramatic recitative ("Ei parte! Senti! Ah! no!") and aria ("Per pietà, ben mio perdona"). First she expresses her relief over the fact that the stranger has left, thus removing the temptation to which she might otherwise have yielded. Then she confesses that she is torn by unworthy desires and passions and abandons herself to remorse and self-reproach, after which she rushes distractedly away.

The two men return to compare their respective conquests. Ferrando cheers Guglielmo with the information that Fiordiligi rebuffed his love-making at every turn, and congratulates his friend on having so constant a fiancée. Guglielmo, however, is forced to confess that Dorabella appeared receptive to his advances and even gave him Ferrando's miniature in token of her love. Ferrando flies into a rage. Vowing terrible revenge, he starts off, but Guglielmo restrains him, warning him not to commit a rash act that may ruin his life simply because of a woman. In the ensuing aria, "Donne mie, la fate a tanti e tanti," he comments bitterly on woman's fatal instinct for duplicity. At its conclusion he sadly walks away, leaving Ferrando to express his disillusionment and chagrin in the equally dramatic aria, "Tradito, schernito dal perfido cor." Though brokenhearted over Dorabella's perfidy, he confesses that he is still in love with her.

Don Alfonso enters in time to hear these noble sentiments and cynically congratulates the young man on his devotion. Ferrando turns on him angrily, saying he is partly responsible for this unfortunate situation. But Don Alfonso disclaims any responsibility, remarking that Ferrando's anger is only natural under the circumstances. Guglielmo returns at this point and somewhat condescendingly observes that it was only logical that Dorabella should yield to a man of his superior attractiveness. He also reminds Don Alfonso that Fiordiligi's refusal of Ferrando has cost him half his bet. Don Alfonso merely answers that the test is not yet over and warns him not to count his chickens before they are hatched.

[*Scene Three*] A room in the home of the sisters. Despina is telling Dorabella that she acted in a manner quite natural to a woman. Dorabella frets that she was unable to resist the Albanian's ardent wooing. Fiordiligi enters, highly indignant over the way things have been going. She confesses that she loves her new suitor, but laments that he is not, after all, her Guglielmo. Dorabella advises letting nature take its course, setting forth her reasons in the aria "E' Amore un ladroncello." She observes that the God of Love is very agreeable when one is obedient to his whims, but is a tyrant when crossed. After the aria she and Despina leave.

Left alone, Fiordiligi declares her resolve to remain true to her real lover. As she is musing over the situation, Ferrando, Guglielmo, and Don Alfonso are seen through the open door, watching her from the other room. Suddenly an idea occurs to her. Calling Despina, she tells her to bring from her wardrobe the two swords, helmets, and uniforms which she will find there. When the maid returns, Fiordiligi, after sending Despina away, reveals her plan: she and Dorabella will disguise themselves in the uniforms of their lovers and join them on the battlefield, there to accept whatever fate may be in store for them.

Putting on the uniform, Fiordiligi expresses her eagerness to be off on her adventure as she sings, "Fra gliamplessi, in pochi istanti." This introduces a dramatic duet which follows when Ferrando, seizing the opportunity to avenge himself on Dorabella and turn the tables on Guglielmo, begins making passionate love to Fiordiligi. When he threatens to end his life with the sword she holds, she finally yields. After ecstatically declaring their love, the two leave the room.

Guglielmo rushes in followed by Don Alfonso. The young man is furious over Fiordiligi's infidelity. Ferrando reappears and the two almost come to blows. Don Alfonso restrains them, however, advising them to marry the ladies at once, and thus take advantage of being in the good graces of two acceptable females. In a brief refrain ("Tutti accusan le donne") he sings that women are women and in matters of love they all behave unpredictably—"Così fan tutte" (so do they all). Ferrando and Guglielmo ruefully repeat the phrase with him.

[*Scene Four*] A banquet room, where the two couples are celebrating the approaching nuptials. They are hailed by Despina, Don Alfonso, and a chorus of servants. The lovers then sing to each other of their happiness, the ensemble taking the form of a canon, which Fiordiligi begins with the phrase "E nel tuo, nel mio bicchiero." Only Guglielmo, still smarting under the memory of Fiordiligi's betrayal, fumes that he wishes the others were drinking poison.

Don Alfonso announces that a notary has arrived to officiate at the signing of the marriage contracts. He brings in Despina, who has disguised herself as a notary. She reads the terms of the contract—to the effect that Fiordiligi is to be married to one Sempronio and Dorabella to one Tizio. Just as the contracts are signed, a soldiers' chorus is heard behind the scenes. Don Alfonso leaves to investigate and returns a moment later with the alarming news that the regiment of Ferrando and Guglielmo has returned.

Fiordiligi and Dorabella, panic-stricken, push their would-be husbands into another room, and Despina goes with them. Don Alfonso tries to calm the ladies, assuring them that everything will turn out satisfactorily. Ferrando and Guglielmo, having put aside their disguises in the other room, now appear and fervently greet their fiancées. They explain that their regiment suddenly received orders to return.

The officers feign great concern over the agitation of the ladies, while Don Alfonso notes with satisfaction that the sisters are victims of their own duplicity—as he predicted they would be. Pretending to go into the other room to put down his knapsack, Guglielmo exclaims that a notary is there. Despina thereupon comes forward with the explanation that she has just returned from a masked ball, which she attended in a notary's costume.

During expressions of general consternation, Don Alfonso, in an aside, tells the men to pick up the marriage contracts, which he will let fall. Ferrando snatches up the papers. He and Guglielmo scan them and then turn on the women with expressions of reproach and threats of vengeance on the betrayers. Fiordiligi and Dorabella, overcome with remorse, beg their lovers to kill them, admitting that they have been faithless.

Don Alfonso, gravely informing the officers that tragic proof awaits them in the next room, leads them away. After some moments he returns with the men, who are now again in their Albanian disguises. At this point matters are quickly cleared up. Ferrando explains his identity to Fiordiligi; Guglielmo gives Dorabella the miniature and asks her to return his pendant. Like the doctor and his fabulous magnet, the officers sing gaily, this "invention" was their own.

The women, however, blame Don Alfonso for most of their troubles. He good-naturedly replies that he merely endeavored to prove his contention that, in matters of love, women the world over are victims of their own frailty. He urges the four to forget past complications and put their trust in each other's love and affection. All six principals join in the joyous closing ensemble of the opera ("Fortunato l'uom"), the theme of which is that the happy man is he who does not allow himself to be distracted by his troubles, but seeks contentment within himself.

Don Giovanni

by WOLFGANG AMADEUS MOZART
[1756–1791]

Libretto by

LORENZO DA PONTE

CHARACTERS

Don Giovanni, a licentious young nobleman	*Baritone*
Don Pedro, Commendatore of Seville	*Bass*
Donna Anna, Don Pedro's daughter	*Soprano*
Don Ottavio, Donna Anna's fiancé	*Tenor*
Donna Elvira, a noble lady of Burgos	*Soprano*
Leporello, servant of Don Giovanni	*Bass*
Zerlina, a peasant girl	*Soprano*
Masetto, a peasant, Zerlina's fiancé	*Bass*

Peasants, dancers, musicians, and demons

Place: In and near Seville
Time: Eighteenth century
First performance: National Theater, Prague, October 29, 1787
Original language: Italian

THE OPERA is based on a literary classic that dates back to the Middle Ages—the story of the legendary Spanish lover, Don Giovanni (or, in Spanish, Don Juan), a gallant libertine whose ruthless pursuit of the ladies and whose blasphemous conduct deserve the dramatic punishment he receives.

The overture starts with foreboding chords symbolizing the avenging fate that is finally to overtake Giovanni—chords which are heard again in the last act and which represent the heavy tread of the stone statue as it appears at the door of the Don's home to punish him for his misdeeds. The music then changes to an impetuous characterization of the Don:

Don Giovanni

daring, dashing, pleasure-seeking, heedless of the sorrow he leaves in his wake and deaf to the warnings of retribution to come.

Act One

[*Scene One*] The square before the palace of the Commendatore Don Pedro in Seville. It is about midnight; the moonlight is bright. Leporello is waiting for Don Giovanni, who has secretly entered the house to seduce Donna Anna. The servant, obviously impatient and tired, complains that his master's activities keep him on the go night and day ("Notte e giorno faticar"): He must keep watch while his master makes love to still another lady. The pay is bad; the food is worse. He is too clever for such drudgery. He will leave the Don and become a gentleman himself. But as soon as he hears footsteps approaching his brave words end and he hides himself.

Don Giovanni rushes from the palace, a cloaked figure in the shadows, struggling with Donna Anna, dressed in her night robe. He tries to make his escape, but she clings to his arm, attempting to see his face, demanding to know his name. As she screams for help he threatens her. Meanwhile, the cowardly Leporello crouches in his hiding place, commenting on the fix his master is in but doing nothing about it.

Donna Anna's cries bring her white-haired father, the Commendatore, to the scene. Seeing him approach, she hastily re-enters the palace as her father rushes to her aid, a torch in his left hand and a drawn sword in his right. "Draw and defend yourself!" he commands the Don. Giovanni is reluctant to engage in a duel with so old an adversary, but the Commendatore insists. Nonchalantly knocking the torch from Don Pedro's hands, Don Giovanni calmly parries his thrusts. The fighting grows more serious. Finally Giovanni runs his sword through the old Commandant. Gasping a few words, Don Pedro dies. Leporello, who has been cringing in his hiding place, emerges now and directs some weak wit at his master, who is in no mood for it. "Well done," he comments, "first to seduce the daughter, then kill the father." "He insisted on fighting," Don Giovanni answers. "And did the lady insist too?" Leporello asks slyly. "Silence! breathe not a word," threatens Giovanni, raising his hand to strike. As lights come on in the palace and sounds of commotion are heard Giovanni hurries Leporello away.

Donna Anna rushes from the palace, accompanied by her fiancé, Don Ottavio, sword in hand, and servants carrying torches. They find the slain Don Pedro. "My father!" cries Donna Anna, throwing herself across his body. Ottavio tries to raise her as she cries out her grief in a tragic recitative. At last he leads her away and orders the servants to remove the body of the Commandant. The scene closes with a duet in which Donna Anna, insane with grief, repulses Ottavio ("Fuggi, crudele, fuggi") as he tenderly attempts to console her ("Senti cor mio, deh senti"). He swears he will find the murderer, and together they vow vengeance and call for heaven's aid. The curtain falls as Ottavio leads Anna into the palace.

[*Scene Two*] A desolate road outside the city. It is early the following morning. Leporello is protesting against Giovanni's manner of living and tells him he is a rascal but again assumes his groveling manner when the Don threatens him. Giovanni, the events of the night already gone from his mind, begins to tell Leporello of a new beauty he is pursuing. He is to meet her tonight. Suddenly the Don sniffs the air. "Ah! I detect the odor of femininity." "What a perfect sense of smell," says Leporello. "And a beauty, too, I would say," continues Giovanni. "And what eyesight, too," says Leporello.

A veiled lady comes along the road. "Let us watch her," says the Don, drawing Leporello aside. She sings with bitter sadness of the man who first seduced, then deserted her ("Ah! chi mi dice mai"). The Don's first thought is that he can possibly make another conquest here, especially as she seems to be very sad and in need of consolation. "I must comfort her," he decides. "As he has comforted eighteen hundred others," says Leporello, aside. In offering that consolation, the Don discovers to his dismay that the lady is none other than Donna Elvira, whom he had betrayed years before in Burgos, and that at the moment she is in search of him to take her revenge. She recognizes the Don and upbraids him for deserting her after having declared her his wife forever. He tells her he had good reason. Since she doubts him, he tells her that "this honest fellow" (pushing Leporello forward) will give her a complete explanation. Giovanni escapes while Leporello diverts her attention.

When Elvira discovers that Giovanni has slipped away again, she sadly seats herself. Leporello, unable to escape, tells her not to bother—that Giovanni is not worth the trouble. "But he has betrayed me!" she exclaims. "Console yourself," says Leporello maliciously. "You are neither the first nor the last. Look here." Leporello then goes into the famous comic aria, "Madamina! il catalogo." Taking a book from his pocket, he unfolds, like a map, page after page as he lists the Don's conquests of women: 640 in Italy, 231 in Germany, 100 in France, only 91 in Turkey, but 1,003 in Spain; there are country maids, city girls, countesses, duchesses, old ones, young ones, fat ones, thin ones, rich ones, poor ones. If it is a woman, he makes it his duty to win her, "as *you* well know." By the time he finishes, pages from Leporello's book are stretched across a large part of the stage. Then he runs off.

The insult in the last line of Leporello's aria infuriates Elvira anew. Now that she knows better than ever the nature of the Don, she is determined upon revenge.[1]

[*Scene Three*] A village green near a tavern. It is later the same morning. Joyous festivities, singing, and dancing are in progress. Zerlina, a bright and gay little peasant girl, and Masetto, a thick-skulled but amiable bumpkin, are going

---

[1] Sometimes this scene closes with the recitative, "In quali eccessi," and the aria, "Mi tradì quell' alma." In this powerful and dramatic recitative and aria Elvira predicts the doom of Giovanni. Remembering the past, she cannot forget the misery he has caused her, and yet she still loves him. This aria, not originally in the opera, was added by Mozart in 1788, and practice differs widely in placing it. It is more commonly inserted at the opening of the first scene of Act Two; sometimes at the end of Scene Two, Act Two.

to be married, and they merrily sing and dance with their companions ("Giovinette, che fate all' amore").

The audacious Don Giovanni arrives with Leporello. His eye quickly perceives the attractive Zerlina. Leporello also anticipates a wide field for himself among the other girls. Giovanni approaches and makes a great show of friendship toward Zerlina and Masetto. Feigning generosity, he orders Leporello to take the company to his palace nearby and entertain them, and to pay special attention to Masetto. He stays behind with Zerlina. Masetto is reluctant to leave Zerlina, despite Leporello's assurances that Giovanni will "take good care of her." Zerlina, too, says she will be safe, but Masetto continues to protest until the Don touches his sword and tells him to run along. Masetto goes, making servile obeisance to the Don and growling jealously at Zerlina ("Ho capito, Signor, sì"). Leporello pushes him along.

Giovanni loses no time in making love to Zerlina, even going so far as to propose marriage. Shyly she avoids him at first, but he finally gains her hesitant acquiescence in the charming duet ("Là ci darem la mano"). Meanwhile, Donna Elvira has appeared and is watching everything from the background. As Giovanni is about to lead Zerlina off, Elvira intercepts them, calling Giovanni a scoundrel and declaring that she is just in time to save this poor innocent girl. In spite of his aside to Zerlina that this is just a poor woman infatuated with him, whom he humors out of pity, Elvira succeeds in exposing his true nature ("Ah! fuggi il traditore"), and leads Zerlina away.

Donna Anna and Don Ottavio arrive as Don Giovanni curses his luck. For a moment Giovanni thinks he is trapped, but when Ottavio greets him by name he knows he is still safe. They have no idea that he is the man who killed Anna's father; in fact, Anna appeals to him to help her find the villain. Relieved to know he is not recognized, he places himself at her service.

Elvira returns at this moment. In the quartet that follows ("Non ti fidar, o misera") she warns Anna and Ottavio against placing any trust in Giovanni's word, but Giovanni maneuvers her aside and whispers to the others that she is demented. Elvira hears him and insists that they must not believe him. Anna and Ottavio do not know what to think, but their suspicions are aroused. Finally Giovanni succeeds in leading Elvira away, telling Anna and Ottavio that he must go now to take care of the poor raving creature but to call on him when they need him.

As he leaves, Anna, in an impressive recitative ("Don Ottavio! son morta!"), tells Ottavio that she recognizes Giovanni's voice as that of the murderer. Ottavio is horrified that Giovanni, a nobleman and his friend, should be the one. Anna tells him the whole story: how Giovanni entered her chamber, his features hidden, and tried to ravish her; how she fought him off and shrieked for help; how she clung to him to prevent his escape; how her father came and was killed. Leading into the aria, "Or sai, chi l'onore," she calls on Don Ottavio to renew his vow of vengeance for her father's death.

As she leaves, Ottavio still finds it difficult to believe a noble-born friend would be such a villain. He determines to get at the truth. The scene closes as Ottavio steps to the front of the stage for his lovely, quiet aria, "Dalla sua pace," in which he declares that his peace of mind depends on his loved one, Donna Anna.

[*Scene Four*] The garden of Don Giovanni's palace. It is late afternoon of the same day. Leporello enters, still complaining, followed by Giovanni. Leporello tells the Don how he carried out his orders about entertaining the peasants and of the trouble the jealous Masetto gave him. He relates also how Elvira came in with Zerlina and denounced Giovanni at length, while he said nothing till she was finished and could say no more, then led her out and locked the door. In the exuberant *Champagne Aria* ("Finch' han dal vino") Giovanni orders Leporello to summon the peasants for a great party. These country maids are to his taste, he says, and while the others are reveling in wine and dancing he will be adding several more names to his list. Leporello goes off to do as he is told, and Giovanni enters his palace.

Zerlina and Masetto now come upon the scene, Masetto scorning and scolding his peasant love for her attentions to the Don. Zerlina replies to her jealous lover with the coquettish aria, "Batti, batti, o bel Masetto," as she amusingly teases him to good humor, patting his face and kissing him.

Don Giovanni's voice is heard inside as he gives the final orders for the party. Zerlina is flustered and wants to hide. Masetto is immediately suspicious. "You are afraid I shall learn what there is between you," he accuses her. "I shall hide here and see what goes on," he says. Giovanni comes out accompanied by servants. Zerlina draws back into an arbor. The guests arrive. Giovanni is looking everywhere for Zerlina; finally he sees her as she tries to hide. He signals Leporello to take the others inside, while he attempts to lead Zerlina into the arbor. Suddenly confronted by Masetto, he is confused but quickly recovers himself. "Masetto," he says, "you have deserted your bride. Come, join the dancing." They go inside.

At this time three figures come upon the scene in domino costumes, wearing masks over their eyes. They are Elvira, Anna, and Ottavio. They consult together on their plan for vengeance. A minuet drifts out. Leporello comes to open a window and sees them. Mistaking them for revelers, he informs Giovanni, who orders them to be invited in. They accept gladly. Before entering, all three unmask and sing softly the touching, beautiful *Mask Trio* ("Protegga, il giusto cielo"), a prayer to heaven for vengeance. They resume their masks and enter the palace.

[*Scene Five*] The ballroom in Don Giovanni's palace. It is now evening. There are three orchestras. Drinks are flowing freely; Giovanni is paying pretty compliments to the girls, and Leporello is doing much the same. The Don again turns his attention to Zerlina. Masetto is burning with jealousy, while Zerlina flirts with Giovanni. Anna, Elvira, and Ottavio enter, masked, and are made welcome.

One orchestra starts to play. It is the celebrated *Don Giovanni Minuet*, one of the most charming ever composed. Ottavio dances the minuet with Anna. Giovanni draws Zerlina away, ordering Leporello to distract Masetto's attention. A second orchestra breaks into a country dance; a third one starts a waltz. Giovanni swings Zerlina into the country dance. Leporello, feigning solicitude for Masetto, seizes his arms and forces him to waltz with him. As Giovanni and Zerlina pass a door he leads her into the next room. Masetto breaks loose from Leporello, and Leporello goes to warn his master, while Anna, Elvira, and Ottavio closely watch what is going on.

Zerlina's cries for help come from the next room. There is sudden confusion, and all turn toward the door as Zerlina rushes into the ballroom and seeks the protection of the masked trio. Don Giovanni knows he is in a tight spot and plays a comedy. He bursts in, sword in hand, turns to his poor servant, Leporello, and tries to throw the blame on him with threats of punishment. The guests, this time, are not convinced. Ottavio, Anna, and Elvira unmask and confront Giovanni, telling him his lies will help him no longer. The men approach Giovanni threateningly as he leans on his sword. This tumultuous scene ends with the impressive septet, "Trema, trema, scellerato!" as all denounce Giovanni for his crimes, while thunder (sounding his doom) is heard offstage. Still courageous and unrepentant, he only laughs at his fate. Seizing Leporello, he fights off Don Ottavio and escapes.

Act Two

[*Scene One*] A street in Seville in front of Donna Elvira's house. It is night. Donna Elvira is alone. Her recitative ("In quali eccessi") and aria ("Mi tradì quell' alma"),[2] in which she predicts the doom of Giovanni but still proclaims her love for him in spite of the way he has misused her, open this act. Elvira, hearing voices, then enters her house and Gio-

[2] This is now the customary place for this recitative and aria. As noted previously, it sometimes is placed at the close of Scene Two, Act One; sometimes at the end of Scene Two, Act Two. In those cases, this act opens with Leporello and Giovanni entering the scene.

vanni and Leporello come on the scene. Leporello, as usual, is complaining. Giovanni tries to laugh him out of his mood, but Leporello is more persistent this time. The Don has tried to kill him, and that is no joke. Giovanni finally appeases him somewhat with a purse of money. "Well, all right this time," says Leporello, "but you must give up women." "Give up women!" exclaims Giovanni. "Why, I need them more than I need food." "Must you deceive the whole sex, then?" asks Leporello. "It is not deceiving," says the Don. "It is love. But I love all women, and I can't neglect any of them. In their small way of thinking, they call this deceiving."

Well, what now? Leporello wants to know. The Don's roving eye has been attracted to Elvira's pretty serving maid. In order to try his fortune with her, he says, he wants to appear as a servant himself, and so he makes Leporello change cloak and hat with him. Elvira meanwhile has appeared at an upper window and sings the opening of an exquisite trio, "Ah, taci, ingiusto core," as she gazes with melancholy at the moon and tries to quell her heart's rebellious longing for the seducer. Giovanni, ever alert, takes advantage of the situation. Standing behind Leporello, who now wears the Don's hat and cloak, and making appropriate gestures with Leporello's arms, he sings to her of his love. Leporello can hardly refrain from laughing as she falls into the trap and agrees to come down. All this, of course, is to get the mistress out of the house and out of the way, so that Don Giovanni can make love to the maidservant.

While Elvira is on her way down to join him Don Giovanni tells Leporello to take her off somewhere and make love to her. Elvira appears, and Leporello begins to enjoy his assignment. Don Giovanni, acting the part of a street ruffian, pretends to attack them and thus frightens them away. His scheme having worked, the Don picks up his mandolin and begins the *Serenata* to Elvira's maid ("Deh vieni alla finestra").

Just as the girl appears at the window his singing is interrupted by the entrance of Masetto and a crowd of armed peasants seeking Giovanni. Being protected by his disguise as Leporello, he is not alarmed. In fact, he feigns willingness

Don Giovanni

to help in the hunt and rids himself of Masetto's followers by sending them off on fools' errands in all directions ("Metà di voi quà vadano"). He tells Masetto to stay with him, leads him around, off the scene and on again. He asks Masetto if he is resolved upon killing the Don—or wouldn't a beating be sufficient? "I'll kill him and cut him up into pieces," says Masetto. "Show me your weapons," says Giovanni, whereupon the simple peasant hands over his musket and pistol. Thereupon Giovanni unmercifully beats him with the flat of his sword and goes off, leaving the bewildered Masetto groaning on the ground.

Zerlina now appears with a lantern. She hears Masetto's groans. He tells her he was beaten by Leporello or some fiend who looked like him. "I told you your silly jealousy would bring you trouble," says Zerlina. "Where has he hurt you?" Masetto lists the various places in which he is hurt. She sympathizes with him and tends his injuries, and in a lovely aria, "Vedrai carino," consoles him with the pretty thought that love (and particularly hers) can heal all wounds. On this sweet note the curtain falls.

[Scene Two] A courtyard adjoining Donna Anna's house. Leporello, tired of the part he is playing, is trying to escape from Elvira, who still thinks he is Giovanni. "Do not leave me," she cries. Then, trembling with apprehension, she sings the opening lines of a sextet ("Sola, sola, in bujo loco"), while Leporello is groping his way about the courtyard, looking for a way out. He finds an exit, but just as he is about to leave, Don Ottavio and Donna Anna enter through it. She is grieving over her father's death, and Ottavio is attempting to console her. Elvira starts looking for Leporello, who is still searching for a way out. He finds another exit, but again, just as he is about to go out, Masetto and Zerlina enter and confront him. Masetto, Ottavio, Zerlina, and Anna close in on him, thinking he is the Don. They approach him menacingly. Elvira pleads for him, claiming him as her husband. It looks for a moment as though Leporello's life is in great danger, but he whips off the cloak and reveals his identity.

"So it was you who almost killed my Masetto!" cries Zerlina. "Ah, and you have deceived me!" adds Elvira. "You must be wearing those clothes for some mischievous purpose," says Ottavio. As they quarrel about who will punish him, Leporello pleads that the misdeeds are Giovanni's and that anything he has done wrong he has been forced to do by the Don ("Ah, pietà! Signori miei!"). Then, watching his chance, he escapes.

Ottavio is now convinced beyond any doubt of Giovanni's guilt. As the scene ends Don Ottavio sings the great tenor aria, "Il mio tesoro." This is a calm, smooth melody, and in it he swears to avenge his Donna Anna, for he wishes, above all, to bring her comfort.[3]

[*Scene Three*] A cemetery. It is about two in the morning. In the rear is a life-size statue of the murdered Commendatore on horseback. Don Giovanni leaps lightheartedly over the wall. "Ah," he cries, "this is a good place to hide. I wonder how Leporello made out with Donna Elvira?"

Just then Leporello scrambles over the wall. He is still frightened from his narrow escape, and angry, but Giovanni is in a frolicsome mood. "I have had some gay adventures since we parted, but I'll tell you only one of them," he laughs. "About a woman, no doubt," says Leporello.

"That's right," answers the Don. He tells how he met one of Leporello's own conquests, who, mistaking him for Leporello because of the clothes, was quite agreeable to his advances. However, she soon became aware of her error and screamed, and he had to run off. Leporello is not amused. "Suppose," he says, "it had been my wife—would you laugh then?" "All the louder," answers the Don.

[3] In some presentations the scene ends with the sextet. Leporello makes off as soon as he discloses himself, and his aria is omitted. In that case, Ottavio's aria is moved to a later scene.

Following this scene as it is given here is one which Mozart wrote in at a later date, but it is seldom used now. In it, Zerlina, razor in hand, drags in Leporello. She ties him to a chair, and they sing a comic duet ("Per questa tue manine"). While Zerlina goes off to get the others Leporello drags himself off, chair and all.

It is sometimes at this point that Elvira stays after the others have gone in pursuit and sings the recitative, "In quali eccessi," and the aria, "Mi tradì quell' alma," in which she predicts the doom of Giovanni, then proclaims her love for him in spite of the way he has misused her.

The moon, meanwhile, has broken through the clouds and shines with a ghostly light on the statue. A solemn voice speaks near them; it is the statue: "Your mirth shall have an end before the morning dawns." "Who spoke there?" asks the Don. Leporello, frightened out of his wits, claims it is a ghost, but Giovanni, grasping his sword, again asks, "Who spoke there?" Again the head of the statue leans forward and says: "Audacious villain, be quiet. Let the dead sleep in peace."

"Someone must be outside," says the Don. Then, with indifference and contempt, he looks up and says: "Isn't this the statue of the Commendatore? Go over and read the inscription." "Oh, excuse me," says the frightened Leporello, "I never learned to read in light so pale." "Read it, I say!" cries the Don threateningly.

Leporello, shaking with fear, reads: " 'Here I await vengeance from heaven on him who slew me.' " The reckless Don is not taken aback, though Leporello trembles. He says: "O venerable fool of fools! Tell him to come and have supper with me this evening." Leporello, shaking from head to foot, hangs back, but under the threat of his master's sword he blurts out the invitation in the duet, "O statua gentilissima." "Most noble statue," he begins, but he cannot get it all out. Under the Don's goading he tries again and again and finally succeeds, but almost dies when the statue nods. At this point the brazen Don addresses the statue himself. "Speak if you are able," and he mockingly adds: "Will you come to supper?" The statue answers, "Yes." Still undaunted, the Don drags Leporello off to prepare the meal.

[*Scene Four*] A small room in Donna Anna's palace. There is a picture of the murdered Commendatore hanging on the wall, with large candles burning at each side. Here once more Don Ottavio is trying to comfort the inconsolable Donna Anna. He urges her to marry him and tells her that the villain, Don Giovanni, will soon be brought to justice. Donna Anna declares she loves him, but until her father's murderer is punished she cannot think of happiness. This is the sentiment of the great aria which closes this scene ("Non mi dir, bel idol mio").[4]

[*Scene Five*] Don Giovanni's banquet hall. The Don is seated at a table with two beautiful ladies as his guests. He sings of the pleasures he enjoys. Leporello is serving from a side table filled with good things to eat, occasionally helping himself. Giovanni eats and drinks and teases Leporello. All the while his private orchestra entertains him with music.[5]

Into this gay scene Donna Elvira comes rushing, bringing an entirely different note. She throws herself on her knees and begs Don Giovanni to mend his ways before it is too late— to show just one virtue if he has one. The Don and Leporello just mock her and invite her to stay for supper. She leaves in despair, but just outside the door she screams. The Don orders Leporello to go and see what it is all about. The servant goes to the door, but returns almost speechless with fright. It is the statue he has seen approaching! "Oh, my lord, it is the man of stone. The man in white. Can't you hear his heavy footsteps?"

Loud knocking resounds. The Don orders Leporello to open the door, but the terrified servant's knees tremble so that he cannot obey his master. The Don goes himself, but before he can open it, the wind howls, thunder crashes, the door blows open, and, to the accompaniment of the dramatic chords heard in the overture, the statue in white stone armor enters and stands in the pale light in the doorway. The Don's guests leave hurriedly, and Leporello hides under the table.

"You invited me, Don Giovanni," says the statue, "and here I am." The Don, though amazed, repeats his offer of hospitality and orders Leporello to set another place. The statue, how-

[4] Sometimes Ottavio's great aria, "Il mio tesoro," is sung here instead of at the conclusion of Scene Two of Act Two, as noted at that place.

[5] Although Don Giovanni was supposed to have lived at some indefinite period in the past, Mozart inserted tunes that were popular at the time this opera was first produced: a melody from Martin's *Una Cosa Rara;* another from Sarti's *I Due Litiganti;* a third from his own *Nozze di Figaro.* This was Mozart's little joke on his contemporaries and on himself. The melodies are parodied, and as the last one begins—it was one of the most popular tunes of the day—Leporello remarks, "I've heard too much of that!"

ever, refuses, because the spirits of heaven no longer can dine on mortal food. In turn he asks the Don to be *his* guest, and with wicked fortitude Giovanni accepts despite Leporello's pleas from under the table that he should decline on the grounds of a previous engagement. "Give me your hand on it then," says the stone figure, and the doomed man places his hand in that of the statue, which closes upon it like a vise. A cry of horror bursts from Giovanni's lips, and a chill shakes his frame. At last he is impressed—and frightened. Still not so frightened, however, that he will repent when the statue urges him to. "No, no," he cries. "I scorn repentance. Away, you old driveler!" And with this refusal the statue drops Don Giovanni's hand, pronounces him doomed, and sinks into the ground as flames shoot up.

The Don in desperation tries to escape, but every exit to which he rushes is blocked by fire and smoke. Finally the entire scene is enveloped in flames, and Don Giovanni disappears as demons from below proclaim the tortures that await him.

[*Epilogue*] A road near the cemetery. Anna, Elvira, Zerlina, Ottavio, Masetto, and Leporello all appear. Leporello excitedly relates the events that took place at the Don's palace. In the closing sextet they all rejoice in the justice meted out to the Don, and their closing words may be summarized as: "Thus do the wicked find their end!"[6]

---

[6] In many presentations this Epilogue is omitted. Originally it was written as part of the last scene: the five enemies of Don Giovanni entering with the police immediately after the death of Giovanni, and Leporello, crawling out from under the table, telling the story of what has happened.

Faust

by CHARLES GOUNOD
[1818–1893]

Libretto by
JULES BARBIER *and* MICHEL CARRÉ

Based on Goethe's tragedy
FAUST, Part One

CHARACTERS

Faust	*Tenor*
Méphistophélès	*Bass*
Wagner, a young student	*Baritone*
Valentin, a soldier, brother of Marguerite	*Baritone*
Siebel, a youth in love with Marguerite	*Soprano*
Marguerite	*Soprano*
Martha Schwerlein, neighbor and companion of Marguerite	*Contralto or mezzo-soprano*

Soldiers, students, villagers, dancers, demons

Place: A village in Germany
Time: Sixteenth century
First performance: Théâtre Lyrique, Paris, March 19, 1859
Original language: French

THE LEGEND of *Faust*, or *Dr. Faustus*, had its beginning in antiquity. It remained for the German poet Goethe to immortalize this drama of the human and the divine in his *Faust*, one of the most stupendous achievements in all literature. The episode of Faust and Marguerite, however, on which Gounod's opera is based, appears only in Goethe's poem and was not part of the legend.

The brief prelude opens with a meditative phrase followed by a short fugue. This leads into the refrain of Valentin's aria in Act Two, after which the prelude comes to a quiet, simple close.

Act One

Faust's study—a gloomy, medieval room. Faust, a venerable and bearded scholar, is seated at a table littered with papers and books. After a somber, reflective phrase in the orchestra, he raises his eyes from the book before him and voices his weariness and despair ("En vain j'interroge"). For years he has queried and searched, but the answer to the riddle of life has eluded him. Faust cries for death and, in sudden resolve, seizes a flask of poison and pours some of it into a goblet. Holding it aloft, he sings that if death will not come to him, he will go forth to seek it. He is about to drink when he hears the carefree singing of villagers outside. Taunted by their gaiety, Faust utters a terrible curse on life and all human aspirations ("Maudites soyez-vous") and calls upon Satan to come to his aid.

There is a vivid flash of light. Méphistophélès stands before him, suavely announcing himself, "Me voici." After a brief colloquy he assures Faust that he can grant him anything he asks—money, fame, power. But Faust scorns all his offers and says he desires only the greatest treasure of them all—his youth.

"Well and good!" the devil replies. When Faust asks the price, Méphistophélès replies that it is but a trifle. Here on earth, he explains, he will do Faust's bidding. Later, in the underworld, Faust will wait upon *him*. When the philosopher hesitates in the face of this grim bargain, Méphistophélès conjures up a vision of Marguerite at her spinning wheel. Faust exclaims in wonder ("O merveille!"), while in the orchestra throbs the passionate theme symbolizing Marguerite.

Impetuously he signs the paper Méphistophélès puts before him. The devil hands him the goblet, saying that it no longer contains poison, but the elixir of life itself. Faust drinks and is instantly transformed into a handsome young man. Méphistophélès tells him that he may see Marguerite that very day. The two then sing a duet hailing the joys of love and beauty now in prospect. ("A moi les plaisirs"). They rush out of the study as the curtain falls.

Act Two

The square of a German village.[1] A kermis, or fair, is in progress, with villagers, students, and soldiers milling about. A group of students strike up a rollicking tune in praise of drinking ("Vin ou bière"). This leads into a rousing chorus in which all eventually join.

As all except the students and soldiers leave the square, Valentin and Siebel enter. In recitative, Valentin muses about the medallion given him by his sister Marguerite to charm away danger ("O sainte médaille"). When he expresses concern about Marguerite, who will be left alone when he goes to war, Siebel promises to act as her guardian. Valentin extends his hand to Siebel in thanks and then begins the famous aria, "Avant de quitter ces lieux" (familiarly translated as "Even bravest heart may swell"). Commending his sister to the care of God, he reflects on the sadness of farewell to home and friends, then sings of the glory of victory in battle. After the aria, Wagner, a student, calls for wine and proposes a song. Jumping upon a table, he begins the *Song of the Rat* ("Un rat plus poltron que brave"). He has sung only a few bars when he is interrupted by Méphistophélès, who suddenly appears and politely asks if he may join the group. If Wagner will end his song, the devil says, he will oblige the company with a much better one. Wagner tells him to begin at once. Thereupon Méphistophélès sings the *Song of the Golden Calf* ("Le veau d'or est toujours debout"). With biting scorn he describes how all men worship gold.

The listeners, although somewhat awed, lustily echo the

[1] *Faust* is generally performed in four acts instead of five, as written. This then becomes Scene Two of Act One.

closing phrases of the song and express their approval. Valentin, however, is suspicious of the stranger. When Wagner hands Méphistophélès a drink, the devil glances at the student's hand and remarks that his life line foretells death in battle. At that, Siebel asks to have his fortune told. Méphistophélès tells the youth that every flower he touches will shrivel and die—particularly the bouquets destined for Marguerite. The mention of her name brings an angry protest from Valentin. The devil coolly tells him to be careful, for his fate too is waiting for him.

Now Méphistophélès exclaims in disgust at the taste of the wine. He strides up to the wine cask used as the tavern sign and strikes it with his sword. As a stream of wine spurts forth, he bids the amazed onlookers to join in a toast to Marguerite. Valentin, infuriated, whips out his sword, whereupon Méphistophélès swiftly draws a circle around himself on the ground with his own weapon. Valentin lunges at Méphistophélès, then draws back gasping that his sword has been shattered.

Siebel, Valentin, Wagner, and their companions confront Méphistophélès and, holding up the hilts of their swords to form the sign of the cross, they sing the dramatic *Chorus of the Swords* ("De l'enfer qui vient émousser"). The men regard him warily as they move off.

At that point Faust appears and demands to be taken to the maid he saw in the vision—if, indeed, she is more than a vision. Méphistophélès reassures him, but warns that it will not be easy to win the girl, for Heaven itself protects her. A lofty theme symbolizing divine guidance underscores this thought. But Faust insists that the devil keep his promise.

Méphistophélès declares that Marguerite will soon appear. A smoothly flowing waltz rhythm is heard as he advises Faust to try his luck during the dance. The villagers meanwhile throng into the square, singing as they dance the well-known chorus, "Ainsi que la brise légère." An interlude of musical dialogue follows. Méphistophélès calls Faust's attention to the ardent glances of the maidens, but Faust impatiently bids him be silent—he wishes to be left alone with his thoughts. Siebel enters, voicing his longing for Marguerite. Several girls approach and ask him to dance, but he shyly declines. Faust now espies Marguerite and cries out ecstatically. Siebel rushes forward, calling her name, but Méphistophélès deliberately bars his way. Meanwhile Faust hesitantly approaches Marguerite and asks if he may escort her home. Coolly replying that she is not in need of an escort, Marguerite goes on her way. Faust, though rebuffed, rapturously sings that he loves her ("O belle enfant! Je t'aime!"). Siebel sighs in disappointment. Méphistophélès, who has been observing the scene with obvious relish, sarcastically remarks that Faust apparently needs some lessons in love-making. The waltz music, rising to a glowing climax, brings the act to a close.

Act Three

Marguerite's garden.[2] At one side is her cottage. At the rear is a wall with a gate. After a short prelude, Siebel enters. Pausing near a bed of flowers, he sings his melodious serenade imploring the flowers to carry the message of his love to Marguerite ("Faites-lui mes aveux"). But when Siebel picks a bloom it shrivels in his hand. Recalling the stranger's menacing prophecy, he steps swiftly to a small shrine in the garden and dips his fingers in holy water. He picks another flower, exclaiming joyfully as it remains unharmed in his hand. Resuming his serenade, Siebel gathers a bouquet and goes toward another part of the garden.

Faust and Méphistophélès enter through the garden gate. Catching sight of Siebel, the devil warns Faust that his rival is approaching. The youth places the bouquet at Marguerite's door and steals away. Méphistophélès also leaves, while Faust slowly approaches the cottage. Musing on the strange emotion that stirs in his heart, he begins the beautiful aria, "Salut! demeure chaste et pure." Here, he sings, dwells a being of divine innocence, whose humble cottage is blessed with riches beyond measure.

At the conclusion of the aria Faust stands as if spellbound. His reverie is interrupted by Méphistophélès, who appears

[2] This is Act Two when the opera is played in four acts.

carrying a casket of jewels. He shows the gems to Faust and then places the casket next to Siebel's flowers. Quickly he leads Faust through the garden gate.

Marguerite now comes from the cottage, reflecting on the comely stranger who spoke to her so gallantly. Deep in thought, she sits at her spinning wheel and sings the ballad of the *King of Thule* ("Il était un Roi de Thulé"). It is the ancient legend about the old and gentle king who treasured a golden cup made in memory of his beloved queen. Throughout the song Marguerite interrupts herself to recall the stranger's gentle voice and manly bearing.

At length she rouses herself from her reverie and thinks of Valentin. After a moment she notices Siebel's bouquet and is touched by this token of his devotion. Then she spies the casket and the key beside it. She unlocks the casket and cries out in surprise and delight at its dazzling array. In childlike excitement, she wonders if she may dare try on the earrings. "Who would not be a coquette?" she murmurs as she finds a mirror in the casket.

Marguerite gives voice to her happiness in the brilliant aria known as the *Jewel Song* ("Je ris de me voir"). With naïve delight she puts on the earrings, holds up the mirror, and asks her reflection if it is really herself whom she sees. Perhaps some magic has transformed her into a princess. If only the handsome lord were here, she sighs, he would find her beautiful beyond compare. She tries on a bracelet, exclaiming that it is like a gentle hand laid on her arm. Joyously she repeats the first theme of her song, bringing it to a thrilling climax as she bedecks herself with jewels. At the end of the aria she remains kneeling before the casket, admiring herself. Martha enters and gapes in astonishment at Marguerite's glittering adornment.

While the two women examine the jewels, Méphistophélès and Faust enter. The devil addresses Martha by name and informs her in lugubrious tones that he is the bearer of bad news: her beloved husband is dead, but sends his parting benediction. Hearing Martha's startled exclamation, Marguerite fears that something is amiss and hurriedly begins taking off the jewels. The four voices then blend in an ensemble in which contrasting sentiments and musical figures are ingeniously interwoven. Marguerite and Faust ponder over the wonder of their awakening passion, while Méphistophélès makes love to Martha, combining his amorous compliments with insulting asides about her age and appearance. Faust impetuously takes Marguerite in his arms. She frees herself and runs away, but he eagerly pursues her. Méphistophélès manages to escape from Martha, who hurries off in search of her new-found cavalier.

Presently Méphistophélès stalks back into the deserted garden. Gloatingly he predicts that the hour of destiny is at hand for the lovers and intones a baleful invocation to night ("O nuit, étends sur eux ton ombre!"). Let blind passion enslave the souls of the lovers, he sings, and may these flowers, now cursed by his hand, work their evil sorcery in Marguerite's heart. With a gesture of malevolent triumph, he vanishes into the gloom.

Faust and Marguerite reappear and pour out their love in an exquisite duet. It begins with Faust's impassioned phrase, "Laisse-moi contempler ton visage" (popularly translated as "Let me gaze on the vision before me"). Marguerite repeats the refrain to sing rapturously of the mysterious enchantment of this night of love. Clasped in each other's arms, the lovers exclaim with passionate intensity, "Eternally!"

Suddenly Marguerite, troubled by a premonition of disaster, begs Faust to leave her lest he break her heart. He finally goes after she promises to see him on the morrow. On his way out of the garden he encounters Méphistophélès, who bids him wait only long enough to hear what Marguerite will say to the stars. At that moment Marguerite flings open her window. Softly she murmurs, "Il m'aime," then, in unrestrained joy, she sings a refrain of such impassioned ecstasy that Faust rushes to her arms. Méphistophélès, watching the lovers, breaks into fiendish, taunting laughter as the curtain falls.

Act Four

[*Scene One*] After a short and mournful prelude the curtain rises on Marguerite's room.[3] She is seated at her spinning wheel. From outside come the voices of a group of girls, cruelly taunting Marguerite about the lover who ran away. Marguerite sings the dolorous *Spinning Wheel Song*, voicing her love and longing for Faust, even though he has dishonored her.

As she finishes the aria in grief-stricken tones, Siebel rushes in and comments anxiously over her tears.[4] He gently takes her hand and sings the simple and touching aria, "Si le bonheur à sourire t'invite," recalling how he has shared Marguerite's joys and sorrows. Deeply moved by Siebel's devotion, Marguerite thanks him, then says that she will go to church to pray for her errant lover and the child she will bear him.

[*Scene Two*] The interior of the cathedral. Organ music vibrates softly as Marguerite enters, kneels, and begins to pray. Suddenly the voice of Méphistophélès calls harshly that she must not pray ("Non! tu ne prieras pas!"). As Marguerite cowers in terror, a tomb opens and Méphistophélès stands before her, thundering that the devils in hell are clamoring for her soul. Marguerite cries out in horror and bewilderment. The choir behind the scenes chants of the awful Day of Judgment ("Quand du Seigneur le jour luira"). As Marguerite prays, Méphistophélès again proclaims her doom, then vanishes. She faints with a piercing cry as the curtain falls.

[*Scene Three*] A square not far from the cathedral.[5] In

---

[3] When the opera is played in four acts, this becomes Scene One of Act Three.

[4] The score indicates that the *Spinning Wheel Song* can be eliminated, in which case the scene opens with Siebel's entrance. In some performances Scene One is omitted entirely, the act opening with the scene in the cathedral.

[5] As originally written, this scene preceded the church scene. It has become customary to play these two scenes in reverse order for the sake of the climactic effect of the *Soldiers' Chorus* and Valentin's death.

the brief but stirring prelude we hear the familiar strains of the *Soldiers' Chorus*. Noisily welcomed by the townspeople, the soldiers, led by Valentin, enter the square. Valentin greets Siebel and asks about Marguerite. Siebel evasively tells him that perhaps she is in the church. Now follows the rousing *Soldiers' Chorus* ("Gloire immortelle de nos aïeux," usually translated as "Glory and love to the men of old"). The men hail the glorious traditions of bravery in combat and describe the joy of returning home. After the chorus, soldiers and townspeople gradually drift away from the square.

Valentin, remaining behind with Siebel, becomes suspicious when the youth tries to dissuade him from entering Marguerite's house. When Siebel finally blurts out, "You must forgive her," Valentin rushes across the square and enters Marguerite's dwelling. Siebel, breathing a prayer for Marguerite, goes toward the church. Faust now appears, followed by Méphistophélès, who is carrying a guitar. They approach Marguerite's house. Flinging back his cloak, the devil strums his guitar and begins his famous serenade ("Vous qui faites l'endormie"). This remarkable song, with its flippant orchestral accompaniment, is a masterpiece of innuendo and insult. Méphistophélès mockingly parodies a lover's song to his "Catherine," advising the lady not to admit her swain until the ring is safely on the proper finger. Though the panting lover begs for kisses, the devil sings, never open the door without the ring. Méphistophélès climaxes his song with a burst of diabolical laughter.

The devil's guffaws bring Valentin rushing from the house, angrily asking the two strangers what they wish ("Que voulez-vous, messieurs?"). His words introduce a fiery trio. Méphistophélès informs him contemptuously that the serenade was not for his ears. Valentin retorts that his sister heard it only too well, then with a blow of his sword knocks the guitar out of the devil's hands. Faust exclaims in surprise as Valentin mentions his sister.

When Valentin asks whom he must fight to avenge his sister's honor, Faust draws his sword. The duel begins.

Adroitly aided by Méphistophélès, Faust finally plunges his sword into Valentin's body. As the stricken soldier falls, the devil looks down at him and snarls that the vaunted "hero" is now stretched on the ground ("Voici notre héros étendu sur le sable"). Swiftly he drags Faust from the scene.

Martha and a crowd of villagers, attracted by the noise of the fight, throng into the square. Horrified, they approach the dying Valentin. Marguerite rushes from the house and kneels at her brother's side, but he roughly repulses her. Siebel tries to comfort her. Raising himself, Valentin wildly accuses his sister of surrendering decency and honor to satisfy her reckless desires. He utters a curse upon her, then falls back dead. Slowly the villagers bare their heads and kneel, murmuring a prayer for his soul. Marguerite falls sobbing upon his body. The curtain descends.

ACT FIVE

[*Scene One*] Walpurgis Night on the Brocken in the Harz Mountains.[6] A chorus of women sings about the souls of the dead who have been released to roam at will on this night of fearful revelry. Méphistophélès leads Faust in and bids him gaze upon the spectacle. At the devil's command, the celebrated beauties of history—Cleopatra, Laïs, Helen of Troy, Phryne, and the Trojan Women—emerge from the mists in a wild, voluptuous dance. Faust drains cup after cup of magic wine, then laughs in drunken disdain at the voice of his conscience. Suddenly he is brought to his senses by a horrible vision of Marguerite with a fiery ribbon encircling her neck like a wound from a sharp blade. In a frenzy he commands Méphistophélès to take him to her.

[*Scene Two*] A prison cell.[7] The music of the prelude is somber and foreboding. As the curtain rises, Marguerite is

---

[6] This scene depicts, in a spectacular ballet, the lurid revelry held—according to the *Faust* legend—on the first night of May. Gounod composed the ballet for the Grand Opéra version of *Faust* presented in 1869. It is usually omitted in present-day performances.

[7] This is usually played as the final act of the opera.

seen asleep on a pallet of straw. In her madness and despair she has killed her child and has been condemned to death. It is just before dawn on the morning of her execution. Méphistophélès and Faust enter. The demon urges Faust to help Marguerite escape while there is still time—before the break of dawn. Tormented by remorse, Faust ignores him and calls to Marguerite.

Dreamily she murmurs that she hears her lover's voice despite the tormenting laughter of the demons who surround her. Then in ecstasy she sings that she is no longer afraid of death now that he is near. Wildly Faust implores Marguerite to come with him, but cries out in despair when he realizes that she does not hear. Now Méphistophélès strides out of the shadows with the warning, "Away, or you are lost." His words introduce the intensely dramatic trio which concludes the opera ("Alerte! Alerte!").

Marguerite finally sees Méphistophélès as the devil he really is and implores Faust to drive him away. With death upon her, she sings the exultant refrain in which she pleads to be carried to heaven ("Anges purs, anges radieux"). Faust distractedly entreats her to come away with him before it is too late, while Méphistophélès grimly intones that the fatal hour has come. The three voices, repeating the theme in successively higher keys, bring this great trio to an overwhelming climax.

At its conclusion Marguerite turns to Faust and in piercing tones asks him why his hands are stained with blood, then bids him go. "You fill me with horror," she gasps, and dies. Faust utters a terrible cry as Méphistophélès drags him away to his doom, thundering that he is condemned ("Jugée!"). Marguerite's lifeless form is bathed in a golden light, while a majestic chorus of angels is heard proclaiming her redemption ("Sauvée! Christ est ressuscité!"). The curtain falls.

La Forza del Destino

by GIUSEPPE VERDI

[1813–1901]

Libretto by

FRANCESCO MARIA PIAVE

Based on the Duke de Rivas's play
Don Alvaro o la Fuerza del Sino

CHARACTERS

The Marquis of Calatrava	Bass
Leonora, his daughter	Soprano
Curra, her maid	Mezzo-soprano
Don Alvaro, a young nobleman of Inca origin	Tenor
The Alcalde of Hornachuelos	Bass
Don Carlo di Vargas, brother of Leonora	Baritone
Mastra Trabuco, a muleteer	Tenor
Preziosilla, a gypsy fortuneteller	Mezzo-soprano
Brother Melitone, a friar	Bass
Father Guardiano, Superior of the convent	Bass
A military surgeon	Baritone

Soldiers, peasants, beggars, pilgrims, monks, dancers, an innkeeper and his wife

Place: Spain and Italy
Time: Eighteenth century
First performance: St. Petersburg, November 10, 1862
Original language: Italian

This opera, along with *Un Ballo in Maschera,* marks the high point in what has been called the "second period" in Verdi's career. At this stage his music developed a greater dramatic significance as well as richer and more versatile harmonic patterns.

There is a long and dramatic introduction entitled the *Sinfonia*. It begins with a series of powerful trumpet blasts symbolizing Fate. Then follows a theme in a haunting, uneasy mood that is associated with Leonora. Other dominating themes are those of Leonora's prayer in Act Two and Don Alvaro's entreaty to Don Carlo before the fatal duel in Act Four.

Act One

A paneled hall in the palace of the Marquis of Calatrava in Seville. At the rear are two windows, one of which is open, affording a glimpse of the moonlight outside. Between the windows is a wardrobe. Doors at right and left lead into various rooms. One, toward the back, opens on a terrace. The Marquis has brought his daughter Leonora to the privacy of his palace in Seville to keep her from seeing Don Alvaro, with whom she is in love. Her father bitterly opposes the romance because Don Alvaro is a foreigner with Inca blood in his veins. The Marquis, a proud and haughty Spaniard, refuses to consider him a worthy suitor. Leonora, however, has resolved to elope with Don Alvaro this very night.

The Marquis is bidding Leonora good night. Curra, her maid, waits in the background. Noting that Leonora seems restless and unhappy, the Marquis tries to calm her. He tells her that here she is safe from the attentions of her unwelcome suitor and urges her to leave the cares of the future in his hands. Embracing her affectionately, the Marquis retires to his room. As Leonora, weeping softly, sinks into a chair, Curra begins taking clothing from the wardrobe and packing it in a traveling bag. Leonora sobs that her father's kindness has almost broken her resolve to leave and has brought her to the verge of confessing her plan to elope. Curra reminds her

La Forza del Destino

that to have mentioned Don Alvaro's name to her father would have meant her lover's doom.

In a moving soliloquy Leonora grieves over the harsh destiny that forces her to disobey her father for the sake of a tormenting love ("Me pellegrina ed orfana"). Curra warns that it will soon be time to leave. Just then the sound of galloping horses is heard, and in another moment Alvaro, booted and spurred, enters the hall and rushes into Leonora's arms.

A long and dramatic duet begins with Alvaro's passionate greeting ("Ah, per sempre o mio bell'angiol"). He sings that his love for Leonora has made him defy a thousand deaths to rush to her side. The horses are ready, he goes on, and a priest is waiting at the altar. Soon they can be married, and then their glorious life together will begin. But Leonora, losing all her courage, cries that she must see her father once more and begs Don Alvaro to wait until tomorrow. Angry and incredulous, Don Alvaro exclaims that it is clear that she no longer loves him and that now their marriage would be a mockery. At that Leonora avows that she is his forever and will follow him to the end of the world. The duet rises to a feverish climax as the lovers sing that nothing will part them.

As they are about to rush out, the Marquis, sword in hand, storms in, followed by his servants. Don Alvaro draws his pistol, while Leonora rushes to her father and falls on her knees before him. He roughly thrusts her aside. Don Alvaro, declaring that he alone is to blame, puts up his pistol, bares his chest, and tells the Marquis to strike him down. The Marquis, snarling an insult about Don Alvaro's race, orders the servants to seize him. Thereupon Don Alvaro again draws his pistol and warns that no one but the Marquis may touch him. When the Marquis shouts that he will hang for betraying his daughter Don Alvaro swears that Leonora's honor is unsullied. On that assertion, he says, he will stake his life and will face his accuser unarmed. With those words he throws down his pistol. The weapon discharges on striking the floor and fatally wounds the Marquis.

As he falls Leonora rushes to his side, but with his dying breath he utters a terrible curse upon her. Leonora and Don

Alvaro cry out in horror and despair. As the servants carry the Marquis to his room Don Alvaro leads the distracted Leonora toward the terrace. The curtain falls.

Act Two

[*Scene One*] The kitchen of an inn in the village of Hornachuelos. At one side is a door leading to the street. At the rear is a fireplace. A stairway leads to a room on a balcony. The innkeeper and his wife are preparing supper. The Alcalde (mayor of the town) is seated beside the fireplace, and at a nearby table a student is sitting alone. The student actually is Don Carlo di Vargas, son of the slain Marquis of Calatrava. He has come to Hornachuelos on the strength of reports that Leonora and Don Alvaro have been seen in the neighborhood, having fled from Seville. Don Carlo has sworn to kill them both in revenge for his father's death and the presumed betrayal of his sister.

At the back of the room several men and women are dancing the *Seguidilla*. A group of peasants and muleteers lounge about, watching them. Soon they break into a brief but lively chorus saluting the muleteers ("Hola! Ben giungi, o mulattieri"). The Alcalde brings the singing and dancing to a halt by announcing that supper is ready. The men and women gather around the tables, and a schoolteacher is prevailed on to say grace.

Don Carlo, remaining apart from the others, stares moodily into space, muttering about the futility of his quest. At that moment Leonora, dressed in men's clothes, comes out on the balcony and catches sight of him. Recognizing him instantly, she quickly returns to her room. Noticing that one of the muleteers, Trabuco, has not joined the others at the table, Don Carlo goes over to him and asks why he is not eating. Trabuco replies that it is Friday and he is fasting. Don Carlo then begins questioning Trabuco about the young man he brought to the inn, but he is interrupted by the entrance of Preziosilla, a gypsy fortuneteller, who comes dancing in. The

La Forza del Destino

crowd gives her a hearty greeting and the men invite her to sit with them and tell their fortunes. Don Carlo joins the group.

Preziosilla urges the men to enlist in the Italian army and fight the Germans. Shouting defiance of the enemy, the men enthusiastically promise to join up. The fortuneteller strikes up a martial refrain describing the glories of battle ("Al suon del tamburo"). A stirring ensemble is built up as all respond in chorus. Going from one man to another, Preziosilla reads their palms. In a solo interlude she foretells that this one is destined to be a corporal, that one a captain, another a general. But when she comes to Don Carlo there is a sudden silence. Looking closely at his palm, the fortuneteller says that she sees bad luck. There is more to the prophecy, she goes on softly, for his hand reveals that he is not a student. Dismissing the matter with a mocking phrase, she resumes the gay martial refrain, in which all join.

The people suddenly fall silent as chanting is heard outside and a group of pilgrims is seen passing the inn door. The Alcalde explains that they are making a festival pilgrimage and then asks all in the room to kneel and pray. Their voices blend with those of the pilgrims in an impressive prayer ("Padre Eterno, Signor"). Leonora, who has come out on the balcony at the sound of the chanting, prays that she may be saved from her brother's vengeance.

When the pilgrims have passed, Leonora returns to her room, while the guests go back to the tables. Don Carlo again begins questioning Trabuco about the young traveler, remarking banteringly that he seems to be a shy young man who has not even grown a beard. Trabuco, for reasons of his own, parries Don Carlo's questions and pointedly indicates that he is not interested in other people's personal affairs. Annoyed by Don Carlo's persistent queries, Trabuco finally declares that he is going out to the stable and sleep with his mules. They, he observes, are neither clever nor burdened with learning and will no doubt leave him in peace. The crowd laughs.

When he has gone Don Carlo suggests to some of the

others that, as the young traveler does not have a beard, it would be amusing to paint mustachios on him. His hearers are delighted with the idea, but the Alcalde sternly forbids playing that kind of trick on a guest of the inn. Turning to Don Carlo, he remarks that it would be more entertaining if he would tell his own story—who he is and where he is going. Don Carlo obliges in a graceful and rhythmic refrain ("Son Pereda, son ricco d'onore").

His name is Pereda, he begins, and he is an honor student at Salamanca, where he is soon to receive his doctor's degree. At Salamanca, he relates, he made friends with another student, one Don Vargas, who invited him to his home in Seville. When the two arrived there they found that a stranger had abducted Vargas's sister and murdered his father. The two students went from city to city in search of the betrayer but found no trace of him or the girl. Then they heard a report that the girl had perished with her father and that the slayer had fled to America. Don Vargas sailed in pursuit of him. And so, sings Don Carlo, concluding his narrative, he parted from his friend and became a student once more.

His listeners, naïvely thrilled with this exciting tale, repeat his closing phrases in chorus. Preziosilla, apparently suspecting that there is more to Don Carlo's story than he cares to tell, queries him about his "friendship" with Don Vargas. With a knowing laugh she repeats the mocking phrase she sang when she read his palm.

The Alcalde rises and announces that it is time to go to bed. The people begin to leave. Some, however, pause to take up the dance again. Don Carlo, starting for his room, repeats a phrase of his narrative, singing that he is the student Pereda. Preziosilla, watching him, answers with her characteristically flippant phrase. As all sing good night in chorus the curtain falls.

[*Scene Two*] In the mountains near Hornachuelos. At one side is the entrance to the church of the Madonna degli Angeli, the door of which is closed. A light shines through the window above the door. At the other side is the entrance

La Forza del Destino

to the convent. Not far from the door stands a rough stone cross. It is a bright moonlight night.

Leonora, still in male attire, comes in weary and travel-worn. She exclaims in relief at finding the goal of her journey—the convent, where she hopes to take refuge. She thinks of her brother telling his story to the people at the inn and then remembers that he told them that Don Alvaro had fled to America. Now, she cries, her lover has left her alone with her misery. Falling to her knees, she sings a deeply moving prayer in which she implores forgiveness and asks that peace may come to her soul ("Madre, pietosa Vergine"). Her voice soars over the chanting of the friars within the church. Rising, Leonora hesitantly approaches the door of the convent, meanwhile praying for courage and strength.

As Leonora pulls the bell rope a window in the door is opened, and Brother Melitone's scowling face is revealed as he holds up a lantern and peers out. When Leonora asks to be taken to the Superior, Melitone snaps that the convent does not open until five o'clock. Saying that she has come from Father Cleto in the village, she begs Melitone to have pity on her. The friar growls that it is much too early for pity but finally consents to announce her. At length the door is opened and Father Guardiano appears, followed by Melitone. Guardiano dismisses the friar, who retires, grumbling.

The Superior gently asks Leonora why she has come. She makes it known that she is a woman and then begs him to save her, for she is under a curse and fears eternal damnation. When Guardiano protests that such a task is beyond a poor friar Leonora asks if he received a letter from Father Cleto concerning her. In shocked surprise Guardiano exclaims that she must be Leonora di Vargas. He solemnly exhorts her to kneel before the cross.

Devoutly kissing the cross, Leonora sings that already the burden of her father's curse seems to have been lifted from her soul ("Più tranquilla l'alma"). Her refrain leads into a dramatic duet. She tells Guardiano that she desires to enter the convent and devote her life to God. The Superior warns that the life of the penitent is harsh and expresses doubt that

Leonora, in her tender youth, could meet its stern demands. But Leonora exults that since she has come to this place she no longer can hear the voice of her father cursing her. In answer to Guardiano's further questions she relates how her lover accidentally caused her father's death and how her brother is determined to kill her in revenge.

When Guardiano suggests that she could perhaps find greater comfort in a cloister Leonora turns to the cross and embraces it, crying that she will never leave its shelter. Guardiano, singing that the will of God must prevail, finally relents. He tells Leonora that she may go to a cave hidden in the rocks, where no human being will ever see her again. With that he calls Melitone and orders him to assemble the friars. In a continuation of the duet Guardiano tells Leonora that she shall enter her penitential cave at dawn. As Leonora expresses her gratitude in soaring phrases, the two voices blend in an impressive climax. Leonora and the Superior enter the convent.

The doors of the church now swing open, revealing the brightly lighted altar and two processions of friars carrying candles. Majestic organ chords peal forth as Father Guardiano leads Leonora, now dressed in a monk's robe, out of the church, with Melitone and the other friars following. They group themselves around the Superior, and Leonora kneels as he raises his hands in blessing, marking the beginning of the great ensemble which concludes the act ("Il santo nome di Dio"). Guardiano proclaims that a penitent has come to the convent to expiate her sins and that she will live in the secret grotto. It will be her refuge forever. Whoever dares invade the grotto, violating the holy solitude of this penitent, will be forever cursed. The friars repeat the curse, "Maledizione, maledizione!"

Bidding Leonora rise, Guardiano tells her to go her way in peace. He and the friars commit her to the protection of the Holy Virgin ("La Vergine degli angeli"). Leonora kisses the Superior's hand and then slowly moves toward the grotto. As Guardiano extends his hands in blessing and the chorus swells to a close, the curtain falls.

La Forza del Destino

ACT THREE

[*Scene One*] A battlefield near Velletri, Italy. It is night. Don Alvaro, in the uniform of a Spanish grenadier, walks in wearily. He is plunged in gloomy thought. Unseen soldiers, apparently playing cards around a campfire, are heard in a brief chorus as they call out their bids ("Attenti al gioco").

After a mournful orchestral interlude Don Alvaro muses bitterly over his ill-starred existence. He thinks of Seville and of Leonora, whom he believes to be dead. Crying out against the cruel destiny that has haunted him since birth, he reveals something of his past. His father had fought to free his country from foreign domination and had married the last of the Inca princesses in an effort to establish a royal throne and a royal line. But he was overthrown, and he and his wife were put into prison. There Don Alvaro was born, while both parents later perished on the scaffold. Overwhelmed by these tragic memories, Don Alvaro sings the poignant aria, "Oh, tu che in seno agli angeli." He prays to Leonora, imploring her to look down from heaven and take pity on his misery.

At the conclusion of his aria there are sounds of fighting from the direction of the camp, and a moment later several officers are seen running across the background. Alvaro rushes out and returns shortly with Don Carlo. The latter explains that a quarrel broke out during the card game and then thanks Don Alvaro for saving his life. Saying he had just arrived from headquarters, he introduces himself as Don Felice de Borros, adjutant to the commander. Don Alvaro identifies himself as Don Federico Herreros, captain of the grenadiers. Clasping hands, they swear to be friends in life and death ("Amici in vita e in morte"). A bugle call is heard in the distance as a signal for battle. Don Alvaro and Don Carlo rush off as the soldiers are heard in chorus hailing the coming fray.

[*Scene Two*] A room in the headquarters of the Spanish army in Italy. The noise of battle is heard outside. A surgeon and several orderlies hurry in and rush to the windows to watch the fighting. Peering through a telescope, the surgeon cries that Herreros was leading the charge and has been wounded. The adjutant, he goes on, is now rallying the retreating men. Again they go forward, he exclaims, and now it is the Germans who are in flight. The watchers jubilantly hail the victory, and then the surgeon announces that the wounded Herreros is being brought to headquarters.

Don Alvaro, unconscious, is carried in on a stretcher. At his side is Don Carlo, his uniform torn and covered with dust. The surgeon, examining Don Alvaro, reports that a bullet has lodged in his chest. Don Alvaro revives and gasps weakly that death is near. Don Carlo, assuring him that the surgeon will save his life, tells him that he will be rewarded with the Order of Calatrava. At the sound of the name Don Alvaro utters an exclamation of surprise. In feverish excitement he tells Don Carlo that he must speak to him privately. At a sign from Don Carlo the surgeon and the orderlies withdraw.

Painfully raising himself, Don Alvaro begins the famous duet, "Solenne in quest'ora." In somber tones he asks Don Carlo if, in this fateful hour, he will carry out one last request. When the other swears he will do so Don Alvaro gives him a key to his valise and tells him to take from it a certain packet of papers and burn them without reading their contents. Deeply moved, Don Carlo promises to do what he asks. In relief and gratitude Don Alvaro sings that now he can die in peace. The duet rises to a powerful climax as Don Carlo, embracing Don Alvaro, tries to give him courage and comfort. After poignant farewells, Don Alvaro is carried into another room, where the surgeon is to operate in an attempt to save his life.

Left alone, Don Carlo recalls Don Alvaro's surprise at hearing the name of Calatrava. Suddenly he is stunned by the thought that perhaps Alvaro is the very man he is seeking. Hastily he unlocks the valise and takes out the packet of papers. For a moment he struggles against the impulse to open them, then remembers his promise to the man who saved his life. Throwing down the packet, he launches into an intensely dramatic monologue in which he voices horror over the evil impulse that is goading him to open the fateful packet and thus dishonor his oath ("Urna fatale del mio destino").

In a frenzy of excitement he again searches through the valise in an effort to find another clue. He comes upon a small box and after a moment's hesitation opens it. There before him is Leonora's picture. As he is gloating over this final proof of Don Alvaro's identity the surgeon opens the door and tells him that Don Alvaro will live. Don Carlo bursts forth into the great aria in which he savagely exults that his archenemy will survive to be the victim of the revenge so long delayed ("Egli è salvo! oh gioia immensa!"). Not only Don Alvaro, but Leonora—wherever she is hiding—will die by his hand. After the fiery climax of the aria Don Carlo rushes away. The curtain falls.

[*Scene Three*] The camp at Velletri. Among the tents is a peddler's booth and another where refreshments are sold. It is nearly morning. A patrol marches in, making the rounds of the camp. In a hushed chorus the men describe their guard duties ("Compagni, sostiamo"). Their voices die away as they continue on their rounds.

As the dawn grows brighter Don Alvaro appears. Though recovered from his wound, he lives in dread of the evil fate that seems to be hounding him. While he is reflecting Don Carlo appears, and Don Alvaro greets him warmly. Don Carlo inquires if his wounds have healed, and when Don Alvaro assures him that they have, he asks if he is well enough to fight a duel. As Don Alvaro stares at him in consternation Don Carlo reveals that he knows his real name. A stormy duet follows as Don Alvaro furiously accuses Don Carlo of having broken his oath ("Sleale! Il segreto fu dunque violato").

Don Carlo retorts that he did not open the packet but that Leonora's picture revealed the secret. Now, he goes on, they will fight it out. Alvaro refuses to fight, saying he will not break the bond of friendship they pledged each other. He protests that the spirits of Don Carlo's father and Leonora will bear witness that he did not kill the Marquis in cold blood. Don Carlo calls him a liar, saying that he has learned that Leonora is not dead. She has fled to relatives in a distant part of the country.

Don Alvaro almost forgets the quarrel in his happiness over the news that Leonora is alive. While Don Carlo threatens that he intends to kill her also, Don Alvaro sings that he will marry his beloved and confer on her his own royal name. But when Don Carlo persists in his threats and insults, Don Alvaro, losing all control, turns on him, crying that *he* shall be the first to die. After the wild climax of the duet the two men begin dueling fiercely. Members of the patrol rush in, separate the combatants, and drag Don Carlo away. Don Alvaro, crying that his every good intention is met with violence, throws away his sword. In a despairing phrase he declares his resolve to seek oblivion in a cloister ("Al chiostro, all'eremo"). Bowed in misery, he walks away.

It is now sunrise and the camp stirs into activity. The scene that follows is an ingenious musical panorama of camp life. The soldiers come out of their tents and busy themselves cleaning their equipment. Vivandières appear and begin selling refreshments to the soldiers. Preziosilla is seen at a booth, telling fortunes. There is a roll of drums and then a spirited chorus in a catchy, martial rhythm ("Lorchè pifferi e tamburi"). In a solo passage Preziosilla invites all to have their fortunes told.

Trabuco appears with a box of trinkets, calling to the soldiers to buy or barter ("A buon mercato"). They crowd around him and in a lively chorus haggle over his prices. A number of beggars wander in and stretch out their hands for bread. Some of the younger recruits begin complaining that they were forced to leave their mothers and go to war ("Povere madri deserte"). This introduces an amusing ensemble. The vivandières approach the whimpering recruits and try to cheer them, saying they will gladly act as mothers and sweethearts. Preziosilla, disgusted at this show of weakness on the part of the recruits, pulls them away from the girls and berates them for acting like schoolboys. But everyone takes it in good humor, and soon the vivandières and the recruits begin dancing a tarantella. They sing a merry chorus as they dance ("Nella guerra è la follia").

When the fun is at its height Melitone comes in and looks on disapprovingly. Finally making himself heard, he begins preaching to the people, denouncing them for their sinful and heathenish behavior ("Toh, toh! Poffare il mondo!"). After listening for a while the soldiers shout him down and threaten to beat him. Bellowing dire warnings of doom, Melitone runs away, the soldiers at his heels. Preziosilla saves the friar from a thrashing by snatching up a drum and beating a lively tattoo. As soldiers, recruits, and vivandières gather round her she leads them in the rousing *Rataplan* chorus.

Act Four

[*Scene One*] The courtyard of the convent of Madonna degli Angeli near Hornachuelos. At one side a door opens onto the road. On the other side is the door to the cloister. Father Guardiano, reading his breviary, passes through the courtyard. A motley throng of beggars comes in from the road. Holding out plates and bowls, they clamor for food.

There is a great uproar as Melitone and another friar carry in a large kettle of soup, which they set down in the middle of the courtyard. The beggars, pushing and shoving, hold up their bowls, each trying to get a larger portion than his neighbor. Brandishing a soup ladle, Melitone roars at them to be quiet. Father Guardiano appears and reminds him that he must be patient with these poor unfortunates, but Melitone fumes that they are a lot of whining, ungrateful gluttons.

When the beggars sneeringly refer to the soup as "scrapings," Melitone loses his temper completely and threatens them with his ladle. They wail that Father Raphael treated them much better. Melitone bellows that the good Father Raphael evidently had his fill of dispensing charity, for now the long-suffering Brother Melitone has been left to deal with this rabble. A humorous ensemble develops. The beggars monotonously repeat that Father Raphael was an angel ("Padre

Raffaele era un angelo"). The louder they chant his praises, the angrier Melitone becomes, until finally he kicks over the soup kettle and chases the beggars from the courtyard.

Mopping his brow, he approaches Father Guardiano, who gently rebukes him for flying into a rage because the beggars seemed to prefer the ministrations of Father Raphael. Thereupon Melitone remarks that Raphael has been acting strangely of late, staring wildly and talking to himself. Melitone relates that yesterday he made a joking reference to the dark color of Raphael's skin and remarked that he was acting like a wild Indian. At that, Father Raphael ran screaming from his cell.

Melitone asks Father Guardiano the reason for Raphael's strange behavior. Over somber chords in the orchestra Guardiano sings that the burden of the man's misfortunes and the strain of repentance and fasting have unhinged his mind ("Del mondo i disinganni"). The refrain marks the beginning of a striking duet, Melitone repeating Guardiano's words. As the duet ends a bell rings sharply. Guardiano leaves as Melitone goes to open the door. Don Carlo, muffled in a cloak, strides in and inquires about a certain Father Raphael. There are two here, Melitone replies; one is fat and the other dark and lean. He asks which one is wanted. The demon, answers Don Carlo. Melitone bustles off to fetch the lean Father Raphael, muttering that he undoubtedly is the devil in disguise.

While waiting for Father Raphael, who, of course, is Don Alvaro, Don Carlo exults that now nothing stands between him and his revenge. Don Alvaro, in a friar's robe, appears and gasps in dismay as he recognizes the other. Don Carlo snarls that now he has found the man whom he has sought for five long years. A long and dramatic duet follows ("Col sangue sol cancellasi").

Don Carlo cries that Don Alvaro's blood must flow to wipe out the dishonor done to the name of Vargas. As Alvaro is a friar and unarmed, he goes on, he has brought two swords. Don Alvaro refuses to take a sword, whereupon Don Carlo calls him a coward. Controlling himself with a great effort,

La Forza del Destino

Don Alvaro kneels before his adversary and implores him to forgive. He swears that Leonora was never betrayed. Don Carlo pours forth insults which he climaxes with a contemptuous reference to Don Alvaro's race.

At that Don Alvaro snatches a sword from Don Carlo. He is about to lunge when he throws the sword away, crying that he will not yield to his baser instincts. Snarling that Don Alvaro is a weakling, Don Carlo slaps his face. Raging that now Don Carlo has sealed his fate, Don Alvaro picks up the sword. The duet comes to a furious climax with the two shouting for death. They rush away to fight their duel in a spot behind the convent.

[*Scene Two*] A wild rocky place in the mountains not far from the convent. At the rear is a grotto with a door. It is near sunset. Leonora, her pale face bearing the marks of years of suffering and penance, emerges from the grotto. Standing at the door, she voices her desperate longing for peace and forgiveness in the magnificent aria, "Pace, pace mio Dio!" She thinks of Don Alvaro and laments over the cruel fate that parted them. As she goes to the rock where Father Guardiano has left her a few morsels of food she hears the sound of angry voices. She hurries back to the grotto. Her aria ends in a ringing phrase as she calls down a curse on whoever is venturing to disturb her solitude.

Sounds of clashing swords come from beyond the grotto. Suddenly Don Carlo's voice is heard crying out that he is dying and imploring for absolution. Don Alvaro rushes in, sword in hand, shouting that he has again spilled the blood of a Vargas. Wildly he rings the bell at the door of the grotto.

After warning him away from within, Leonora opens the door. She and Don Alvaro stand transfixed as they recognize each other. Then Don Alvaro staggers back, warning Leonora not to approach because his hands are stained with blood. Pointing to the background, he tells her that a man is dying there—it is her brother, whom he was forced to kill. Leonora runs to the spot, while Don Alvaro raves that fate has mocked him again—he has found Leonora, only to meet her when his hands are stained with her brother's blood.

Leonora's voice is heard in a cry of pain, and after a moment she staggers in, aided by Father Guardiano. She gasps that Don Carlo, determined to expiate her sin, stabbed her as she held him in her arms. Don Alvaro curses his destiny. Guardiano exhorts him not to rail against heaven but rather to ask forgiveness ("Non imprecare, umiliati").

This introduces the stirring trio which concludes the opera. The dying Leonora implores Alvaro to seek salvation in prayer. He at first spurns all comfort but at last cries out that heaven has pardoned him. Leonora sings that she will go before him to heaven, where there is no hatred and love alone rules. As Alvaro distractedly begs her not to leave him alone with his guilt Leonora gasps his name and dies. Crushed by despair, Don Alvaro groans, "Mortal!" Father Guardiano, lifting his hands in blessing, murmurs that Leonora is with God, "Salita a Dio!" The curtain falls.

Gianni Schicchi

by GIACOMO PUCCINI

[1858–1924]

Libretto by

GIOACHINO FORZANO

Based on the story of Gianni Schicchi, a citizen of medieval Florence

CHARACTERS

Zita (also called La Vecchia—the Old Woman),
  cousin of Buoso Donati, the deceased .... *Mezzo-soprano*
Marco, son of Simone .... *Baritone*
La Ciesca, wife of Marco .... *Soprano*
Rinuccio, nephew of Zita .... *Tenor*
Simone, cousin of Buoso .... *Bass*
Gherardo, nephew of Buoso .... *Tenor*
Nella, his wife .... *Soprano*
Gherardino, their son .... *Mezzo-soprano*
Betto di Signa, brother-in-law of Buoso .... *Baritone*
Gianni Schicchi .... *Baritone*
Lauretta, his daughter, in love with Rinuccio .... *Soprano*
Spinelloccio, a doctor .... *Bass*
Amantio di Nicolao, a lawyer .... *Bass*
Pinellino, a shoemaker .... *Bass*
Guccio, a dyer .... *Bass*

Place: Florence
Time: 1299
First performance: Metropolitan Opera House, New York, December 14, 1918
Original language: Italian

GIANNI SCHICCHI is part of a trilogy of one-act operas which includes *Il Tabarro* and *Suor Angelica*. The hero of the opera is modeled on an actual historical character who lived in Florence at the end of the thirteenth century and whose escapades made him famous.

The bedroom in the home of Buoso Donati, a wealthy Florentine, who has just died. At the four corners of the canopied bed on which the body lies are four lighted candles. In front of it is a candelabrum with three candles unlighted. At one side of the room a staircase leads up to a small balcony. Buoso's relatives, kneeling in prayer, are grouped around the bed. Their occasional outbursts of grief—"Povero Buoso! Povero cugino! Povero zio!"—are obviously forced. Gherardino, a boy of about seven, is seated on the floor, somewhat apart from the others, amusing himself by playing with marbles. Finally he grows restless and is sent out of the room.

Betto, whose threadbare clothing and timid manner mark him as the lowliest of the relations, hesitantly mentions a rumor he has heard about Buoso. It is to the effect that the old man has left most of his possessions—even his mill—to a monastery. In excitement and dismay the relatives appeal to Simone, who, as one-time sheriff of the town, presumably has a constructive opinion about the matter.

Simone ponders a moment and then, with an air of weighty deliberation, declares that if Buoso has filed his will with the town clerk, then all is lost. If, however, the will is still here among his personal effects, the situation may yet be turned to the advantage of the relatives. Instantly there is a mad scramble to find the will, with everyone ransacking cupboards and drawers. Rinuccio, in an ardent strain ("Lauretta, amore mio"), expresses the hope that the document will be found for the sake of his romance. While the others are searching the room he ascends to the balcony and looks through the contents of a chest.

Betto, ignored by everybody, surreptitiously pockets a silver seal and a pair of scissors and finally manages to conceal a silver tray under his coat. There is a momentary uproar as Simone comes upon a document, which, however, proves to be the wrong one. Suddenly Rinuccio, holding up a parchment he has found in the chest, cries out, "Salvati! Il testamento di Buoso Donati!" As he descends the stairs the others rush toward him with hands outstretched, but he holds the document out of their reach. In a brief refrain he reminds them that it was he who found the will ("Zia, l'ho trovato"). He asks Zita, as head of the family, if she will consent to his marriage with Lauretta, in the event that Buoso's legacy provides the clan with wealth. When Zita and the others impatiently assure him that he may marry anyone he likes, he calls Gherardino and sends him off to bring Schicchi and his daughter.

Taking the parchment from Rinuccio, Zita unrolls it and reads the greeting, which is addressed to her and Simone. The latter, murmuring the premature thanks to Buoso for his generosity, lights the three candles at the end of the bed. Breathlessly crowding around Zita, the relatives silently read the will as an appropriately dignified theme is given out by the orchestra. But as they read their faces take on expressions of stunned surprise and dismay. Simone slowly walks over to the bed and extinguishes not only the three candles he has just lighted but the other four as well. Turning back to the relatives, he bursts out that the rumor really was the truth. ("Dunque era vero!"), and these words introduce an agitated ensemble. One outdoes the other in expressions of envious rage over the fact that the monks and nuns will grow fat on Buoso's wealth. In spiteful mockery they deride each other as disappointed heirs, now left as poor as they were before.

Rinuccio eventually succeeds in quieting them and then says that there is one man who can help—Gianni Schicchi. The relatives, however, assuming that he is concerned only with furthering his romance, scornfully reject his suggestion. At that moment Gherardino rushes in to announce that Schicchi and his daughter are approaching. A vigorous argument now ensues during which Rinuccio stoutly defends Schicchi as a man of resourcefulness and sagacity. He is the type of man, cries Rinuccio, who is a credit to the noble city of Florence. In a melodious aria he rhapsodizes over the city, telling how its splendors attract men of genius and talent the world over ("Firenze è come un albero fiorito"). Gianni Schicchi, he concludes, contributes much to the glory of Florence.

At the conclusion of the aria Schicchi enters with Lauretta, who ardently greets Rinuccio. Schicchi, taking in the situation at a glance, indicates his distaste over the rapacity and pretended grief of the relatives. Zita furiously tries to drive him away, fuming that she will never allow her nephew to marry someone beneath his station. Schicchi, stung to anger, denounces her for her selfish interference, while the two lovers pledge their devotion to each other. The four voices blend in a brief quartet.

Schicchi, disgusted with the wrangling, starts to leave, but Rinuccio implores him to give his attention to the problem of the will. Lauretta adds her entreaties in a touching aria ("O mio babbino caro"). With a deliberate show of unwillingness Schicchi finally takes the will and begins reading. He slowly paces back and forth, and the relatives, their eyes fixed on him, follow in a comical procession. Suddenly he stops as though struck by an idea. He glances at Lauretta and then sends her out on the terrace. When she is out of earshot he asks the relatives if the news of Buoso's death has been given out. Not even the servants know of it, they answer. At Schicchi's bidding they take Buoso's body, along with the candelabrum, into another room.

Just as they are rearranging the bed there is a knock on the door and Spinelloccio, the doctor, announces himself. While the relatives, speaking through the partially opened door, assure the doctor that Buoso is much improved, Schicchi conceals himself behind the bed. Spinelloccio insists on seeing the patient. Schicchi, imitating Buoso's voice, calls out that he is much too tired to see anyone at the moment and tells him to return in the evening. Spinelloccio leaves, first pausing to observe that none of his patients ever dies, thanks to his superior medical knowledge.

Emerging from his hiding place, Schicchi asks if his imitation was convincing. On being assured that it was, he explains his plan in an amusing aria ("Si corre dal notaio"). The relatives are to call the notary at once, telling him that

Gianni Schicchi

Buoso is at the point of death and wants to make his will. By the time the notary arrives Gianni Schicchi will be in the bed to play the role of Buoso and will dictate the will to the satisfaction of all concerned. The relatives hail Schicchi for his brilliant inspiration.

Then, one by one, they declare their claims to various pieces of Buoso's property—neighboring farmlands—and a loud argument develops over the disposition of the mule, the palace, and the sawmill at Signa. The dispute is interrupted by the tolling of a bell announcing a death. Panic-stricken, the relatives wonder how the news of Buoso's death was made known. Schicchi sighs that now his plans have gone awry. Gherardo hurries out to investigate but returns a moment later with the cheering news that the knell is being sounded for the mayor's Moorish assistant who died of a stroke.

With expressions of happy relief the relatives help Schicchi prepare for his masquerade. Each one, watching his chance, tries to bribe Schicchi into bequeathing him the coveted mule, palace, and mill, and Schicchi solemnly makes them all the same promise. When he is finally arrayed in Buoso's nightgown and cap, Zita, La Ciesca, and Nella push him toward the bed, singing an amusing trio, in which they pretend to coax a little child to go to bed ("Fa' presto, bambino").

Before he gets into bed Schicchi turns to the relatives with a word of advice ("Prima un avvertimento!"). He warns them of the severe penalty which, according to the Florentine law, will be inflicted on all of them if their participation in the fraud is discovered: the right hand cut off—and exile. Gesturing toward the window through which the city is visible, he sings a mock-serious farewell to Florence. It is echoed by all in chorus.

There is a knock at the door. Schicchi jumps into bed and pulls up the covers, while the relatives darken the room. The notary enters, followed by Pinellino and Guccio, who are to witness the will. After appropriate formalities Schicchi begins dictating. The relatives nod approvingly when he assigns a modest sum for his funeral and an equally nominal one for the monastery. There are further expressions of satisfaction as the farmlands are duly disposed of.

When the supposed Buoso comes to the mule, the palace, and the mill, there is a feverish stir of expectancy. These, as well as the house in Florence, he declares, are to be left to his cherished friend, Gianni Schicchi. This brings anguished protests from the relatives, but Schicchi quiets them by repeating the refrain of his adieu to Florence, with its significant reference to waving farewell with a handless arm. He adds to their distress by ordering Zita to reward the notary and the witnesses with a handsome fee out of her own purse. When the will is duly signed and sealed the three leave with effusive expressions of gratitude.

No sooner have they gone than the relatives fling themselves on Schicchi with furious denunciations. Standing up in the bed, he snatches Buoso's stick, which is hanging from a bedpost, and wields it with telling effect. Roaring that the house is now his, he orders them out. As he pursues them around the room they snatch up everything they can lay their hands on and finally rush out, their arms laden with booty. Schicchi dashes after them.

While the music gradually quiets down to rich, sustained chords, Rinuccio and Lauretta go to the rear of the room, where the youth opens a large window, revealing a view of Florence glowing in the sunshine. The lovers sing a beautiful duet ("Lauretta mia") and then stand in a fervent embrace. Schicchi returns with part of the loot, which he drops on the floor. He sees the lovers, oblivious to everything in their rapture. Turning to the audience, he points to the lovers and, in spoken words, asks if Buoso's wealth could serve any better purpose. The relatives, he says, have consigned him to hell for this bit of skulduggery. With all due respect to Dante, he hopes that the audience will acquiesce in the verdict of "Not guilty." Schicchi starts the applause and bows. The curtain falls.

Hänsel und Gretel

by ENGELBERT HUMPERDINCK
[1854–1921]

Libretto by
ADELHEID WETTE

Based on a fairy tale of the same name by Grimm

CHARACTERS

Hänsel	*Mezzo-soprano*
Gretel	*Soprano*
Peter, their father, a broommaker	*Baritone*
Gertrude, their mother	*Mezzo-soprano*
The Sandman	*Soprano*
The Dewman	*Soprano*
The Witch	*Mezzo-soprano*

The fourteen angels, woodland voices, children

Place: A forest in ancient Germany
Time: The distant past
First performance: Weimar, Germany, December 23, 1893
Original language: German

HUMPERDINCK'S DELIGHTFUL fairy-tale opera was one of the most important works for the lyric stage to come out of Germany after the era of Wagner. Based on authentic German folklore, it is truly Germanic in spirit, and in its musical structure it represents a high level of German technique.

The composer met Wagner while the latter was at work on *Parsifal,* and the two became close friends. Humperdinck not only aided in copying the *Parsifal* score but also assisted in preparing the opera for production. His intense admiration for Wagner's work and his close association with him account for the strong Wagnerian influence that is evident, particularly in the score of *Hänsel und Gretel*.

The overture begins with a stately chorale in the horns—the melody of the *Children's Prayer* which dominates the entire opera. This is followed by a lively rhythmic strain which has to do with the spell cast upon the children by the witch. It gives way to a more deliberate melody that will be heard again at the beginning of Act Three, when the children are awakened by the Dewman. These identifying melodies are interwoven with the prayer theme.

Act One

[*Scene One*] A small and sparsely furnished room in the forest cottage of Peter the broommaker. Hänsel sits near the door, busily making a broom. Gretel is seated at the fireplace, knitting. She sings an ancient German folk tune about "Susie," telling of the poor geese who have no shoes. Hänsel, taking up the melody, sings that there is not even a farthing at hand to buy sugar and bread. Impetuously he flings the unfinished broom into a corner and jumps to his feet. If Mother would only come home, he frets. Gretel whimpers that she is terribly hungry. When Hänsel continues grumbling, his sister bids him remember what Father says when Mother complains. To the theme of the prayer the girl repeats the old proverb, "When need is direst, God stretches forth His hand" ("Wenn die Not auf's Höchste steigt"). Gretel then takes up a broom and pretends that she is sweeping out their tribulations, singing a merry little tune as she does so ("Griesgram hinaus"). Hänsel joins his voice in a pleasing duet. But Gretel remembers there is work to be done and warns Hänsel to get busy. He scoffs at the idea, saying he would much rather dance and have fun. Gretel exclaims that she loves to dance—and now they will do so to the little song that Auntie once taught them. Clapping her hands to keep time, Gretel tries to teach Hänsel the steps as she sings ("Brüderchen, komm tanz' mit mir").

She performs for his benefit—first the feet—tap-tap-tap—then the hands—clap-clap-clap. Forgetting their troubles—as well as their work—they dance and sing with carefree abandon, continuing with such vigor that they finally trip over each other and fall to the floor.

As they lie their laughing and out of breath, they hear their mother calling outside. Both spring to their feet in guilty fear. Gertrude storms in, angrily demanding the reason for the uproar. Hänsel explains that it was Gretel's doing, while she in turn blames her brother. Declaring she will thrash the children for not doing their work, Gertrude goes to fetch her stick. In her excitement she knocks over a pitcher of milk on the table.

There goes the pitcher, the Mother wails, and now there is nothing left for supper! Angrily she sends Hänsel and Gretel off to the woods to gather strawberries. She warns that if they dare come back without a full basket they will get the worst beating of their lives. When the children are gone Gertrude sinks sobbing into a chair and bemoans her misfortunes. Pillowing her head in her arms, she sobs herself to sleep.

Then from the distance comes the voice of Peter the broommaker, singing a lusty refrain—"Ra-la-la-la, ra-la-la-la!" As he draws nearer we hear the burden of his song: Hunger is the greatest chef! Carrying a huge basket on his back, Peter bursts in, still roaring his song. Of what use is a great chef, he goes on, when the kettle is empty! As for himself, brandy is the staff of life, he remarks, setting a half-empty bottle on the table. With that he reels over to his sleeping wife and gives her an enthusiastic kiss.

Gertrude wakes up, rubs her eyes in bewilderment, and asks who is making all the din. Peter tries to kiss her again, but she angrily pushes him away and berates him for wasting his time drinking at the tavern. He jovially tells his wife to forget her troubles and begins to unpack his basket. Gertrude exclaims in surprise and delight as he brings forth a tempting array of foodstuffs. Arm in arm the broommaker and his wife dance about the room. As Gertrude prepares supper Peter explains how it all happened. There was a great celebration in the village, he relates, and people were in the mood to buy. He made the most of his opportunity and sold his wares at the highest prices.

Suddenly he asks where Hänsel and Gretel are. In answer Gertrude relates the events of the afternoon—how the milk pitcher came to be broken and how, in anger, she sent the children into the woods. For all I care, she adds spitefully, they can be at Ilsenstein. Horrified, Peter asks his wife if she has not heard of that gruesome spot deep in the forest where the fiend has her lair. In a somber dramatic aria Peter tells about the "Crust Witch" ("Die Knusperhexe"). At midnight she and her evil brood, astride their brooms, ride on their fiendish errands. During the day, Peter goes on, she lures little children into her Crust Cottage, bakes them into gingerbread children *(Lebkuchenkinder)*, then gobbles them up. With a despairing cry for help Gertrude rushes from the house. Peter pauses to pick up the bottle of brandy from the table, then dashes out after his wife. The curtain falls.

[Scene Two] Without pause the orchestra begins the prelude, *The Witches' Ride*.[1] The curtain rises on a quiet forest glade, with the gloomy Ilsenstein rising in the background. We find Gretel sitting on a mossy tree trunk making a garland of wild roses, while Hänsel is looking for strawberries among a clump of bushes at the left. The scene gradually darkens.

Gretel sings a song (again a German folk tune) about a little man, wearing a fine purple cloak and a black hat, who stands on one leg all alone in the forest ("Ein Männlein steht im Walde"). Hänsel interrupts, shouting that his basket is full of strawberries. The children turn again to their games, meanwhile eating up all the strawberries. They hear a cuckoo in the distance and amuse themselves by imitating its call. Suddenly they become aware of the gathering darkness, and Hänsel confesses that he does not know the way home. Gretel sobs in terror, thinking she sees a ghost among the trees. Hänsel challenges it with a call which is re-echoed behind

[1] Originally written as Act Two.

the scenes by a chorus of women's voices. The children clasp each other in fright.

At the height of their terror a little gray man with a sack on his back steps through the rising mist, singing that he is the Sandman ("Der kleine Sandmann bin ich—sh!"). He loves little children, he says, and delights in dropping upon their eyes the magic grains that bring deep and restful slumber. The children gradually become calmer as he strews sand over their eyes. They kneel and sing the famous *Children's Prayer*, about the fourteen angels who gather in pairs around their bed to guard them while they sleep ("Abends, will ich schlafen gehn"). At the end of the duet the children sink back upon the ground and fall asleep in each other's arms.

As the orchestra softly echoes the prayer theme total darkness envelops the scene. Suddenly a bright light breaks through the mist, bringing into view a long staircase at the rear. Fourteen angels in flowing garments descend the staircase in pairs, group themselves about the children, then join hands and move about in a slow, dreamlike dance as the curtain falls.

Act Two

The prelude begins with a brief phrase which is part of an ancient song-game familiar the world over. It will be heard again later in the act when the Witch sings that someone has been nibbling at her house. Following this comes the dawn motive. After it has been stated the curtain rises. The scene is the same, except that the angels have disappeared.[2]

The Dewman appears and sprinkles drops from a bluebell over the sleeping children to the accompaniment of a little song ("Der kleine Taumann heiss' ich"). He proclaims that he travels with the sun and pries open sleepy eyelids with golden shafts of light. As he wanders off, Gretel sits up and rubs her eyes. Hänsel turns over on his other side and goes back to sleep. In wonder and surprise, Gretel muses at find-

[2] Originally written as Act Three.

ing herself in the forest. She awakens Hänsel, meanwhile imitating a birdcall. He springs to his feet and gives his own imitation of a rooster's crow. The two voices join briefly in a sparkling duet ("Ti-re-li-re-le, 's ist nichtmehr früh"). The children then tell each other of their wonderful dreams about the guardian angels.

Suddenly they cry out in astonishment. At the back the mists have now cleared, revealing the Witch's house at Ilsenstein. In transports of delight Hänsel and Gretel sing a duet describing the wonders of the gingerbread house ("Von Kuchen und Torten ein Häuslein gemacht"). Hand in hand they tiptoe toward the house. Hänsel, ignoring Gretel's warning, creeps up to the cottage and breaks off a piece from the corner.

With that a voice, singing the phrase of the song-game music heard in the prelude, calls out from within, asking who is nibbling at the house ("Knusper, knusper, Knäuschen, wer knuspert mir am Häuschen?"). Hänsel, startled out of his wits, drops the piece of cake. He asks Gretel if she heard the voice. They decide that it was only the wind, then break off more pieces from the house. At that moment the upper part of the door opens and the Witch peers out, unobserved by the children. While they are merrily feasting the Witch steps quickly out of the house and throws a rope around Hänsel's neck. He cries out in terror and tries desperately to get away, but the Witch merely cackles in fiendish glee. Then she invites the children into the house, promising them all the sweets they can eat. But Hänsel flatly refuses to enter. He cautions Gretel not to mind the Witch, then whispers that they will try to run away.

By that time Hänsel manages to free himself. He and Gretel start to run. Thereupon the Witch draws a stick from her belt, raises it like a wand, and utters her incantation—"Hokus, pokus, Hexenschuss!" Instantly the children are stopped. The scene darkens. As she intones the spell the end of the stick begins to glow eerily. She leads Hänsel into a nearby cage and locks the barred door. Shaking a warning finger at Gretel, who is motionless in the grip of the spell, the

Witch disappears into the house. Hänsel tells his sister that she must watch carefully everything the Witch does and pretend to obey her. In a moment the Witch returns, bringing a basket of sweetmeats with which to fatten Hänsel. He pretends to be asleep. Then she frees Gretel from the spell and orders her to work about the house.

Hurrying over to the oven, the Witch throws a handful of wood on the fire, slams the door, and rubs her hands in evil delight. Gloatingly she muses on how Gretel is to be "coaxed" into the oven. She will ask her to bend down and look inside. Then, one big push, bang goes the door, and—presto! Gingerbread! In her mad joy over the plan the Witch bestrides a broom and races wildly around the house, chanting a nonsensical refrain about her broomstick horse ("Hopp, Galopp, mein Besengaul!"). Suddenly she stops and dismounts, awakens Hänsel, and tells him to show her his tongue. She examines it closely, smacking her lips. Now then, show me your finger, she orders. Hänsel instead holds forth a small stick, whereupon the Witch complains that he is still much too bony.

Calling to Gretel, she orders her to bring more raisins and almonds for Hänsel. While the Witch is feeding him Gretel cautiously picks up the magic wand and softly repeats the incantation. When the Witch turns to look at the oven, Hänsel, freed from the spell, escapes from the cage. The Witch calls to Gretel and tells her to look into the oven to find out if the gingerbread is ready. Gretel, pretending to be very stupid, asks the Witch to show her how one looks into an oven. Hänsel sneaks closer. As the Witch bends over in front of the open oven the children push her in and slam the door. They shout in mocking imitation of her own words: "Und bist du dann drin—schwaps! Geht die Thür—klaps [One big push, bang goes the door, and—presto]!"

Hänsel and Gretel prance around singing the *Knusperwalzer* (*Crust Waltz*), in which they exult over the death of the Witch. They dance together toward the Witch's house. Hänsel breaks away and rushes inside. In another moment he appears at one of the upper windows and begins throwing down apples, pears, oranges, gilded nuts, and an assortment of sweetmeats. Gretel catches them all in her apron.

All at once the oven begins crackling furiously, then explodes and collapses into smoking debris. Hänsel and Gretel drop their booty in fright and stare in astonishment. They become even more bewildered as a crowd of children, their gingerbread crusts fallen away, throng about them. The strangers, their eyes closed, sing in a soft chorus that now they are forever free ("Erlöst, befreit, für alle Zeit") and urge Hänsel and Gretel to touch them so that they may awaken. Gretel timidly touches the nearest child, who opens its eyes and smiles at her. Eagerly she touches the others, who likewise respond. Hänsel meanwhile waves the Witch's wand and repeats a phrase of the incantation. Instantly the spell is broken. The children rush up to Hänsel and Gretel, join hands, and dance around them, singing a joyful chorus ("Die Hexerei ist nun vorbei").

The ensemble is interrupted by the sound of the broom-maker's jolly "Ra-la-la-la" from the distance. As Peter and Gertrude appear their children rush up to them with glad cries of greeting. Two boys then drag from the ruins of the oven the figure of the Witch, now an enormous gingerbread cake. Peter bids the children observe how the Witch was destroyed by her own evil magic ("Kinder, schaut das Wunder an!")—thus heaven punishes evil.

In a variation of the prayer theme he intones the words of the *Children's Prayer*—"When need is direst, God stretches forth His hand." The children respond in a great chorus. Then, as they join hands and joyously dance around in a circle, the curtain falls.

Lohengrin

by RICHARD WAGNER
[1813–1883]

Libretto by the Composer

Based on a medieval legend

CHARACTERS

King Henry I of Germany	*Bass*
Count Frederick Telramund of Brabant	*Baritone*
A herald	*Bass*
Ortrud, wife of Count Frederick	*Mezzo-soprano*
Elsa of Brabant	*Soprano*
Lohengrin, a knight of the Holy Grail	*Tenor*
Gottfried, brother of Elsa	

Nobles of Saxony and Brabant, pages, ladies and gentlemen of the court, attendants

Place: Antwerp
Time: Early part of the tenth century
First performance: Weimar Theater, Germany, August 28, 1850
Original language: German

WAGNER began work on *Lohengrin* in 1845, having gathered material for the libretto from several Teutonic legends dealing with the mythical knight of the Holy Grail. The legend of *Parsifal*, in particular, supplied the background not only for *Lohengrin* but also for the later music-drama, *Parsifal*. In Act Three of *Lohengrin* the knight reveals that he is the son of Parsifal and a knight of the Holy Grail. The Grail knights were the holy warriors whose duty it was to guard the sacred cup in which the blood of the crucified Christ had been poured.

The composer wrote the opera in reverse order, beginning with the third act, and completed it early in 1848. Forced into exile for political reasons, Wagner at length sent the score to Franz Liszt at Weimar and prevailed on him to produce the opera. Wagner himself did not see a performance of it until 1861.

The prelude opens with the ethereal motive symbolizing the Holy Grail. This leads into the refrain of Elsa's prayer in Act One. The music rises to a tremendous climax, then concludes with an exquisite reiteration of the Grail theme.

Act One

An open field on the banks of the Scheldt River, beyond the walls of Antwerp. King Henry is seated on his throne under the Oak of Judgment, surrounded by his Saxon nobles. Facing them some distance away sits Frederick Telramund, with Ortrud at his side. He is attended by noblemen of Brabant.

The King's herald comes forward and signals four trumpeters to sound a fanfare. He announces that King Henry is summoning the men of Brabant to the defense of the German kingdom. Vigorously the Brabantians pledge their loyal efforts in behalf of their country. The King now rises and greets his vassals ("Gott grüss euch"). In solemn tones he tells them that the Hungarian hordes are threatening Germany on the eastern borders. A nine years' truce has expired, and now the Hungarians are clamoring for battle. King Henry says he has come to urge the Brabantians to march with him at once to Mainz and engage the enemy. Turning to Telramund, he asks why Brabant, on which he counted for support in this crucial hour, is torn by civil strife and unrest.

Telramund thanks the King for coming to act as arbiter ("Dank, König, dir, dass du zu richten kamst!"), then gives his explanation. He relates that the Duke of Brabant, on his deathbed, placed in his hands the care of the Duke's two children, Elsa and Gottfried. One day Elsa left the palace with her brother and later returned alone. Gottfried was never found. Convinced by her guilty manner and evasiveness that Elsa was responsible for her brother's disappearance, Telramund continues, he renounced the right to make her his bride—a right granted him by the Duke—and married Ortrud instead. Telramund then charges Elsa with the murder of her brother and claims the throne of Brabant. There is a murmur of surprise and dismay from the people of the court over this alarming state of affairs.

When Telramund hotly continues that Elsa further plotted to rule Brabant with a secret lover at her side, King Henry silences him. The Saxons and Brabantians draw their swords and sing that their weapons will remain unsheathed until the King's judgment on the accused has been proclaimed. The herald summons Elsa.

To the accompaniment of a tender and exalted theme Elsa approaches to take her place before the King. The men softly comment that he who has dared to accuse so pure a being must indeed be certain of her guilt. King Henry asks if she is Elsa von Brabant ("Bist du es, Elsa von Brabant?"). She bows without speaking. When he inquires if she knows the nature of the accusations against her she nods calmly. The King asks if she confesses her guilt ("So bekennst du dein Schuld?").

As if in a trance, Elsa murmurs about her brother. Then she begins the dramatic soliloquy known as *Elsa's Dream* ("Einsam in trüben Tagen"). Lost and alone, Elsa sings, she prayed for help and a cry of anguish burst from her lips. As its echoes died away she sank to the ground in sleep. Then in a vision there appeared before her a knight in shining armor. It is he who will be her champion in this hour of deep distress.

Deeply moved by her strangely exalted manner, King Henry beseeches Telramund to think carefully before he presses his charges any further. In answer Telramund furiously challenges to combat anyone who questions the truth of his assertions. Turning to Elsa, the King asks whom she will choose as her champion. In an ecstatic refrain ("Des Ritters will ich wahren") she repeats that the warrior of her vision shall fight in her behalf. Her hand shall be his reward.

Excitedly the men sing that a royal prize indeed awaits the warrior who will take up this challenge. After a fanfare the herald commands the champion to step forward. There is a long pause. When there is no answer Telramund cries out that his accusations are justified and that he is in the right. Elsa implores the King to sound the call again. Once more it is met with silence. Falling to her knees, Elsa sings the eloquent and moving prayer, "Du trugest zu ihm meine Klage," in which she pleads that her knight may appear. The ladies of her retinue join their entreaties in chorus.

Suddenly the men near the bank of the river cry out that a boat drawn by a swan is approaching. Others join their voices to exclaim that a warrior in resplendent armor is standing in the boat, guiding the swan with reins of gold. The chorus rises to a tremendous crescendo as Lohengrin's boat nears the riverbank. Elsa, standing as if spellbound, does not turn to look. King Henry watches the scene in amazement. Telramund looks on in mingled fear and anger, while Ortrud stares in terror at the swan.

Lohengrin, clad in magnificent armor, stands leaning on his sword as the boat touches the shore. A great shout of welcome bursts from the throng ("Gegrüsst, du gottgesandter Held!"). There is an expectant hush as Lohengrin steps from the boat, then turns and addresses the swan ("Nun sei bedankt, mein lieber Schwan"). He thanks the swan and bids it return to the magic land whence they have come and sorrowfully sings farewell as it departs. The chorus comments in tones of awe.

Lohengrin pays his respects to the King and, as the Grail theme sounds softly in the orchestra, tells him that he has come to protect the maiden who has been grievously accused. Turning to Elsa, he requests the privilege of being her champion knight. Elsa rapturously greets her hero and savior ("Mein Held, mein Retter"). A dramatic colloquy ensues, in which she pledges herself to Lohengrin if he wins in combat. In return he exacts from her the promise that she will never ask his name or seek to know whence he came ("Nie sollst du mich befragen"). When Elsa fervently declares that she will keep faith with him Lohengrin takes her in his arms, crying out that he loves her ("Elsa! Ich liebe dich!").

While the chorus sings softly of the strange enchantment of this scene, Lohengrin escorts Elsa to King Henry, committing her to his care. Swiftly confronting Telramund, he declares that Elsa is guiltless and that the charges are false. When Telramund is warned by his own henchmen not to fight this heaven-sent adversary he answers that he would rather die than prove a coward ("Viel lieber tot, als feig!").

Thereupon the nobles mark off the area of combat. After the herald announces the rules of the contest and the two principles invoke divine aid, King Henry offers a dignified and solemn prayer that right may triumph ("Mein Herr und Gott, nun ruf' ich dich")—known as *König's Gebet*. All intone the prayer in a majestic chorus. As trumpets sound, the King strikes his shield three times with his sword as a signal for the combat.

The two knights lunge at each other, and there is a brief but furious clash of weapons. With a mighty blow Lohengrin strikes Telramund down, then stands over his vanquished foe with the sword point at his throat. In a dramatic phrase the knight sings that he will spare Telramund's life. As the chorus hails the victor with a great shout, Elsa pledges herself to Lohengrin in impassioned phrases ("O fand ich Jubelweisen"). A magnificent chorus of praise and rejoicing follows. It is sung by all except Telramund and Ortrud, who lament their defeat and shame. Overcome by anger and humiliation, Telramund collapses at Ortrud's feet, while Elsa and Lohengrin are borne away in triumph at the brilliant climax of the chorus. The curtain falls.

Act Two

The fortress of Antwerp. At the rear is the Pallas, the abode of the knights. Toward the foreground is the Kemenate, or women's chambers. It is night. Lights glow in the windows, and sounds of gaiety come from within. On the shadowy steps of the cathedral opposite the royal dwellings, Telramund and Ortrud are seated. They have been deprived of their royal prerogatives and are clad in beggars' clothing. Telramund is sunk in thought, while Ortrud glares malevolently at the glowing windows. Suddenly Telramund turns upon his wife in bitter wrath, saying that it was her evil sorcery that led him to forfeit his honor in combat.

Ortrud answers him with sneering contempt, remarking that his anger is too late—had he directed it against his foe, they would have been spared this disgrace. Yet one hope is left them, Ortrud says, for she knows the secret of the spell which enabled Lohengrin to conquer. Once the knight reveals his name and race, his magic power will be broken. Elsa alone can draw that secret from him, and she must be persuaded—or forced—to question the knight. Deliberately she goads Telramund to wilder fury by telling him that if he had drawn but one drop of blood from Lohengrin that, too, would have rendered him helpless. In a dramatic and powerful refrain sung in unison Ortrud and Telramund swear that they will exact a terrible revenge ("Der Rache Werk").

As their voices die away to a menacing whisper Elsa appears on the balcony of the Kemenate and stands for a moment in happy reflection. The ardent phrases of her song mark the beginning of what is known as the *Balcony Scene* ("Euch Lüften, die mein Klagen so traurig oft erfüllt"). Ortrud sends Telramund away and in dolorous tones calls to Elsa. Maliciously pretending remorse and repentance, she wails that she meant no harm and that Telramund acted in thoughtless and unreasoning anger. Elsa, moved by her apparent distress, tries to comfort her. She bids Ortrud to wait and hurriedly re-enters the chamber. Alone, Ortrud calls in savage exultation on Odin and Freia, the pagan gods, to aid her in accomplishing her revenge. When Elsa reappears with two ladies in waiting Ortrud kneels before her in servile entreaty. Elsa, in transports of joy over her approaching bridal, assures Ortrud of forgiveness and says she will also seek a word of pardon from her champion.

Lohengrin

Craftily Ortrud warns Elsa not to love too rashly and expresses the hope that she may never be deceived in her affections. Though momentarily frightened by the ominous sound of Ortrud's words, Elsa fervently urges her to believe that faith alone can bring happiness in love ("Lass mich dich lehren"). Aside, Ortrud sardonically observes that Elsa's very triumph shall prove her undoing. ("Dieser Stolz, er soll mich lehren"). The voices of the two women blend in a brief but impressive duet which brings their colloquy to a close. Ortrud permits Elsa to lead her into the Kemenate. As the women enter the dwelling Telramund appears. Gazing after them, he muses gloatingly that Ortrud's evil sorcery will destroy those who have robbed him of his honor.

Trumpet blasts from various towers of the citadel now herald the dawn. Telramund quickly conceals himself behind an abutment of the cathedral to avoid being seen by the servants who go about their morning duties. Soon the space before the Pallas is filled with courtiers and men from the fortress. In a stirring chorus ("In Früh'n versammelt uns der Ruf") they sing of the glorious events that will mark this day. All then turn to face the herald, who comes out of the Pallas. He proclaims the King's edict branding Telramund a traitor and placing anyone who aids him under the pain of death. The men curse him vehemently. The herald further announces that Elsa's champion has declined the title of Duke and has asked to be named Protector of Brabant. The chorus lustily hails the hero.

After a trumpet call silences the throng the herald informs them that today Elsa's champion invites all to join him in his wedding festivities. Tomorrow, however, they must turn to the stern duties of war. The men pledge their loyalty in an exultant chorus ("Zum Streite säumet nicht"). While the people and the warriors are milling about in great excitement, four Brabantian noblemen, former henchmen of Telramund, draw aside and sullenly protest among themselves at marching against an enemy who has never challenged them. At that moment Telramund stealthily approaches. He declares that he is resolved to unmask their would-be leader as a pretender and a renegade. Astounded at Telramund's boldness, they warn him against betraying himself and try to shield him from the eyes of the throng.

Four pages now announce Elsa and her bridal retinue. To the accompaniment of a stately refrain the procession emerges from the Kemenate, while the nobles and the populace range themselves on either side of the great court. There is a tremendous chorus of acclaim ("Heil dir, Elsa von Brabant") as Elsa and the ladies move toward the cathedral. In the procession is Ortrud, now clad in royal garments.

Just as Elsa is about to ascend the cathedral steps Ortrud advances and stands before her. In suppressed fury she declares that she will no longer follow like a lowly handmaiden but will force Elsa to relinquish her place. When Elsa angrily rebukes her Ortrud fiercely defies her to speak the name of the knight whose bride she is to be. Perhaps there is good reason, she cries, why he forbids questions about his origin. In a dramatic, sweeping phrase ("Du Lästerin! Ruchlose Frau!") Elsa denounces Ortrud's slanderous accusations. She calls upon the assemblage to bear witness that her knight is a stainless champion who spared the life of his treacherous enemy. Furiously Ortrud retorts that this unknown warrior is an evil impostor.

At this point trumpets signal the approach of King Henry, Lohengrin, and their followers, who advance in majestic array from the Pallas. Alarmed by the disturbance, the King and Lohengrin hurry forward. Elsa rushes distractedly into the knight's arms, imploring him to protect her. Imperiously Lohengrin commands Ortrud to leave, then tenderly bids Elsa accompany him to the cathedral.

The procession moves onward. Suddenly Telramund breaks through the throng, confronts the King, and wildly demands to be heard. The warriors cry out against him, while the King orders him to be seized. As the crowd shrinks back in awe at his frenzy Telramund launches into a bitter tirade ("Den dort im Glanz ich vor mir sehe"). He brands Lohengrin a sorcerer

Lohengrin

and demands that he reveal his name and race. Violently he declares that he who came among them under such mysterious circumstances has much to explain. The people begin murmuring suspiciously.

Lohengrin vehemently replies that no false accusations can impugn his honor. Not even the King, he says, can force him to speak. To one only is he answerable—Elsa. As he utters her name in a ringing phrase he turns to her, only to recoil at her terrified expression. The great closing chorus of the act now begins as the onlookers voice their bewilderment and confusion ("Welch ein Geheimnis muss der Held bewahren?"). Ortrud and Telramund exult that the poison of suspicion is doing its deadly work in Elsa's heart. Elsa herself frantically voices her doubts and fears, while Lohengrin vows that his accusers shall be brought to account.

Led by the King, the nobles crowd around Lohengrin and assure him of their support. Telramund swiftly approaches Elsa and treacherously begs her to betray Lohengrin into his hands. One drop of blood, he tells her, will rob the knight of his protecting magic and also render him powerless to leave her. Elsa distractedly tries to drive Telramund away. Seeing the two in conversation, Lohengrin rushes between them and in a terrible voice commands Telramund to go.

Elsa, stricken with shame at her doubting, sinks to the ground at Lohengrin's feet. Gently he raises her, asking if she wishes to put to him the fateful question. In a moving refrain she answers that love has conquered every doubt ("Mein Retter, der mir Heil gebracht"). Lohengrin thereupon escorts her to the King. As the assemblage hails the bridal pair in the brilliant climax of the chorus, the King leads them to the top of the cathedral steps. Elsa and Lohengrin embrace. In that moment Elsa sees Ortrud standing below with her arm upraised in a gesture of venomous triumph. Controlling herself with a supreme effort, Elsa quickly turns and enters the church with Lohengrin and the King. The curtain falls.

Act Three

A richly appointed bridal chamber. At one side is an open casement window. The brilliant prelude, familiar as a concert number, sets the mood for the wedding festivities which open the act. At the conclusion of the prelude doors at the rear open and the bridal procession enters, led by pages carrying lighted tapers. The women escort Elsa, while the men accompany King Henry and Lohengrin. The entire assemblage sings the world-famous *Wedding Chorus* ("Treulich geführt").

Elsa and Lohengrin embrace. Pages remove their robes of state, and then the King approaches and gives the pair his blessing. The men and women, with the King, now retire to the strains of the *Wedding Chorus*. Their voices fade away in the distance as the pages close the doors.

Lohengrin leads Elsa to the couch and tenderly begins the magnificent love duet, "Das süsse Lied verhallt." In passionate phrases soaring over a sensuous orchestral accompaniment the lovers give voice to their rapture. But when Lohengrin ecstatically sings Elsa's name and she responds there is a subtle change of mood. Elsa murmurs that her name sounds sweet on his lips ("Wie süss mein Name deinem Mund entgleitet"), but the harmonies darken when she entreats Lohengrin to allow her to speak his name.

Lohengrin evades her request with fervent protestations of love, singing that all he asks in return for his measureless devotion is her abiding faith in him. But Elsa's mood grows more feverish as she insists that he reveal his secret. When he tells her that he came from realms of light to save her and win her love, she cries despairingly that by those very words she knows her love is doomed. Now, she laments, each day will bring the tormenting fear that he will leave her to return to the enchanted country from which he came. In alarm she imagines she sees the swan returning on its fateful errand. Lohengrin distractedly begs her to cease her questioning, as once again we hear the warning theme associated with the words "Nie sollst du mich befragen." Mad with doubt and fear, Elsa demands to know his name, his destiny, and his race ("Den Name sag' mir an! Woher die Fahrt? Wie deine Art?").

At that moment Telramund and his four henchmen burst into the room with drawn swords. Screaming in terror, Elsa seizes Lohengrin's sheathed sword, which he had placed beside the couch. As she holds the scabbard, Lohengrin draws the sword, whirls about, and kills the onrushing Telramund with one terrible blow. Thereupon the four nobles drop their weapons and kneel at Lohengrin's feet. Elsa faints in his arms.

There is a long, tense pause. Then Lohengrin sadly murmurs that all happiness has ended ("Weh! Nun ist all' unser Glück dahin!"). He lifts Elsa to the couch. She revives momentarily and gasps a prayer. Lohengrin then commands the noblemen to bear Telramund's body before the King. Summoning two ladies in waiting, he bids them array Elsa in her bridal finery and escort her to the throne. He slowly leaves the chamber as the stricken Elsa is cared for by her attendants. The dawn grows brighter, and pages extinguish the tapers.

Here the curtain is lowered for a moment. Trumpet calls are heard in the distance. The scene changes to disclose the meadow on the banks of the Scheldt, as in the opening of the opera. In magnificent pageantry King Henry and the nobles arrive with their retinues. They arrange themselves in formal array as the King again takes his place on the throne under the great oak. In a heroic refrain ("Wie fühl' ich stolz mein Herz entbrannt") he bids his followers prepare to march against the foe, then inquires about the hero who is to lead them.

At that point the four nobles enter, carrying Telramund's body on a bier, which is placed before the throne. The King and assemblage exclaim in horror and surprise. Elsa, bowed in sorrow, now appears with her retinue, followed shortly by Lohengrin. Clad in battle armor, he comes forward with solemn dignity as King Henry and the warriors hail him as the hero of Brabant.

Then as the men listen incredulously the knight declares

that he cannot lead them into battle. He comes not as warrior but as accuser, he says, and with those words throws back the covering from Telramund's body. Explaining the circumstances of the attack, Lohengrin demands judgment on the slaying of Telramund. In a vigorous chorus the King and the warriors proclaim the justice of his deed.

But there is yet another charge, Lohengrin continues. Dramatically he tells the tense throng that Elsa, through vile treachery, has been betrayed into breaking her promise by asking his name and race. Now, he announces, the destined moment has come to reveal his secret. He does so in the famous aria, "Im fernem Land."

As the exalted Grail theme sweeps through the orchestra he sings of the shining temple on the mountain of Monsalvat, where reposes a sacred cup—the Holy Grail. Its divine power is renewed each year by the visitation of a dove from heaven. The Grail is in the keeping of a company of consecrated knights. It is the duty of these sinless warriors to go forth in the defense of those who are beset by earthly evil. But once the name of the knight is known, he must depart forever from those whom he has redeemed. It was as a knight of the Grail that he himself was sent here, Lohengrin continues. In the ringing climax of his song he proclaims that he is the son of Parsifal, chief among the knights of the Grail, and Lohengrin is his name.

The people murmur in amazement and wonder over his enthralling story. Elsa gives a cry of remorse and approaches Lohengrin with faltering steps. He takes her in his arms as he sings a poignant phrase of sorrow and reproach ("O Elsa! Was hast du mir angethan?"). He mourns the tragic destiny that has destroyed their happiness, then bids her farewell.

Elsa implores him not to leave her. The people add their voices in a dramatic accompaniment to the soaring phrases of her entreaty. But Lohengrin replies that his absence already has provoked the wrath of the Grail and that only in parting can the sin of Elsa's betrayal be expiated. In answer to the plea of the warriors that he remain to lead them against their

Lohengrin

enemy, Lohengrin turns to King Henry and assures him of a glorious victory.

Tremendous excitement stirs the throng as the swan suddenly appears in the distance. As it reaches the shore Lohengrin greets it in sorrowing tones ("Mein lieber Schwan"). Had but the one year of its bondage elapsed, he sings, the power of the Grail would have restored the swan to human shape. In agony and despair he turns to Elsa. If she had kept faith with him for this one year of trial, he says, so that he could have remained with her, the Grail's might would have sent her brother back to his rightful place at her side.

He then hands Elsa his sword, along with his horn and his ring, bidding her give them to her brother when he at length returns. The sword will protect him, the horn will sound a call for help in time of danger, and the ring will remind him of the champion who came to the defense of his sister. Lohengrin passionately kisses Elsa in farewell, while she stands as if transfixed. In somber tones the people lament his going.

Suddenly Ortrud rushes forward. Tauntingly, she bids Lohengrin to return to his home. ("Fahr' heim, du stolzer Held"). Now she can tell his unhappy bride the truth. The swan that draws the boat is none other than the transformed heir of Brabant. The chain around its neck is the instrument of sorcery with which she robbed the boy of his human shape.

In fierce exultation she turns on Elsa, saying that but for her betrayal in revealing his name Lohengrin would have freed her brother from the spell at the end of a year. Now the evil enchantment is still in force. The boy must remain a swan—and this very swan will take Elsa's champion away forever. At these words the people cry out violently against Ortrud.

Lohengrin kneels in prayer. Then, as the Grail theme rises triumphantly in the orchestra, the dove of the Grail circles over the boat. The knight swiftly unfastens the chain from the swan's neck, whereupon the swan sinks beneath the surface of the water. At the spot where it disappeared there rises a handsome boy in glittering princely raiment. Leading him forward, Lohengrin asks all to look upon the Duke of Brabant ("Seht da den Herzog von Brabant").

Ortrud screams in terror and falls to the ground. Lohengrin leaps into the boat, and the dove, taking the golden chain in its beak, draws the craft away from the shore. Gottfried slowly approaches Elsa, while the assemblage makes obeisance. As she takes him in her arms she turns her gaze toward the river, calling to her husband ("Mein Gatte! Mein Gatte!"). A bend in the stream momentarily hides Lohengrin. As he reappears, standing in the boat and bowed over his shield, a great cry of sorrow bursts from the throng. The curtain falls.

Lucia di Lammermoor
by GAETANO DONIZETTI
[1797–1848]

Libretto by
SALVATORE CAMMARANO

Based on Sir Walter Scott's novel
THE BRIDE OF LAMMERMOOR

CHARACTERS

Lord Enrico Ashton of Lammermoor, a Scotch nobleman....*Baritone*
Lucia Ashton, his sister ....*Soprano*
Sir Edgardo of Ravenswood, last of his family ....*Tenor*
Raimondo Bidebent, Lucia's tutor ....*Bass*
Alisa, Lucia's companion ....*Mezzo-soprano*
Lord Arturo Bucklaw, an influential nobleman ....*Tenor*
Normanno, Lord Enrico's captain of the guard ....*Tenor*
   Friends, relatives, pages, soldiers, and servants of Lord Enrico

Place: Scotland
Time: About 1702
First performance: Teatro San Carlo, Naples, September 26, 1835
Original language: Italian

THE NOBLE FAMILIES of Lammermoor and Ravenswood, deadly enemies for many years, have sworn to exterminate each other. Only one member of the Ravenswood clan is left: young and fearless Sir Edgardo. His father was slain by Lord Enrico, who has also taken his lands.

ACT ONE

The park of Ravenswood Castle. The scene is a rocky wooded section, with a lake in the background. A group of guards, headed by their leader, Normanno, are excitedly searching the grounds and talking about a stranger who has been seen prowling about the place.

Lord Enrico enters with Raimondo. He laments to Normanno and Raimondo that he has lost his fortune and is still menaced by his old dispossessed enemy—Edgardo of Ravenswood. He adds, however, that his sister Lucia can save him from ruin if she will marry the man he has chosen to be her husband, but that she dares to refuse. Kindhearted, elderly Raimondo urges him to remember that she is mourning the death of her mother and cannot think of love. "Cannot think of love," sneers Normanno. "Her heart is burning with love." He then relates how Lucia was rescued by a hunter from the attack of a mad bull; that every morning she secretly meets her protector at that very place, near her mother's grave. Enrico asks if he knows the man and Normanno answers that he thinks the mysterious lover is Sir Edgardo.

Enrico is infuriated ("Cruda funesta smania"). Just then some of the guards return to tell that they have seen a man on horseback dash away from the ruined tower. Their suspicions are confirmed: it is Edgardo ("Come vinti"). Enrico's fury rises. He swears vengeance on Lucia and Edgardo ("La pietade in suo favore"), and the guards pledge their support as they all leave. Raimondo has pleaded for Lucia in vain, and he departs despondent.

While the scene darkens somewhat, a lovely harp interlude is heard. Soon Lucia and Alisa, her companion, enter the park to meet Edgardo. Alisa fears Enrico's wrath if they should be discovered. Lucia feels that she must warn Edgardo of his danger. She then tells Alisa how on this very spot, according to legend, a Ravenswood once murdered a maiden who loved him and threw her body into the fountain nearby. Her unhappy spirit still haunts the park. In a beautiful and dramatic aria ("Regnava nel silenzio") she relates how she once encountered this unhappy spirit and was warned by it of a wretched ending to her secret love affair. Alisa begs her to give up Edgardo before some tragedy occurs, but Lucia, her spirits rising, can sing only of the ecstasy of her love for Edgardo ("Quando rapita in estasi"). With misgivings, Alisa sees Edgardo approaching and leaves to keep watch while the lovers are together.

Edgardo begs Lucia's forgiveness for asking her to meet him at such a time, but explains he must leave Scotland that night on a political errand to France. Before he goes, however, he wants to seek peace with her brother and to seal the friendship by asking for her hand. But Lucia knows that Lord Enrico will never consent to their marriage and asks Edgardo to keep their love secret.

Edgardo is resentful. "Is it not enough," he asks, "that he killed my father and stole my heritage? Will only my death satisfy him?" He recites how he had sworn revenge at his father's tomb, but Lucia's love had since cooled his ire ("Sulla tomba che rinserra"). In mounting anger, he states that he can still fulfill his vow.

Lucia, in a state of commingled love and sorrow, persuades him to let love prevail. With sudden determination he asks her to swear to be his forever. He places a ring on her finger as a token of his plighted faith, and Lucia gives him one of her rings as she pledges undying devotion. The act closes with a brilliant love duet as they bid each other a tender farewell ("Verranno a te sull'aure").

Act Two
(The Marriage Contract)

A hall in Lammermoor Castle. When the curtain rises, several months have elapsed since Edgardo left for France. In the meantime Lord Enrico has been going ahead with a nefarious scheme to separate the lovers. It is not only hatred of the Ravenswood clan that prompts him to plot against Edgardo, but the fact that he is in desperate financial straits. By arranging a marriage between Lucia and Lord Arturo Bucklaw, he can improve his fortune.

At the beginning of the act we find Enrico talking to Normanno. He tells him he has invited all his friends and kinsmen to celebrate the coming wedding, but he fears Lucia may still refuse to marry Arturo. Normanno calms his fears by reminding him that they have intercepted all the letters between the lovers and have spread a rumor that Edgardo loves another. As they see Lucia approaching, Enrico asks Normanno for the letter which together they have forged in order to make Lucia believe that Edgardo has chosen to marry another. Normanno hands him the letter and then leaves to escort Lord Arturo to the castle.

Presently Lucia enters. She comes forward listlessly, looking fixedly at her brother. He comments on her sad and anguished expression, saying he had hoped to see some signs of happiness. She replies that he knows the cause of her sorrow and implores him to give up his resolve ("Il pallor funesto, orrendo"), but Enrico only bids her forget her lover and pleads with her to accept a noble husband. Lucia will not hear his suggestions and replies that she has already pledged her faith to another. Then the cruel brother produces the forged letter, which he commands her to read, saying that it will prove she has been betrayed. With trembling hands Lucia takes the note and reads. Overcome with horror and dismay, she is about to faint. He rushes to her aid. In a flowing duet she bemoans her misery and wishes for death, while he entreats her to forget her traitorous lover ("Soffriva nel pianto").

Suddenly sounds of festive music are heard. Enrico tells Lucia that the crowds are greeting Lord Arturo Bucklaw, whom he has selected to be her husband. At her insistence that she will not marry but now waits only for death, Enrico in despair confesses to her that unless she consents, his own death and the ruin of the family will result, for he has committed treasonable acts against the king and only Arturo is powerful enough to save him from punishment. His death will be upon her head and his spirit will haunt her ("Se tradirmi tu potrai"). Lucia still insists that death alone is her future.

As Enrico leaves, Raimondo enters. He, too, is now convinced Edgardo is faithless and tells Lucia it is her duty, in her mother's memory, to come to her brother's aid ("Ah! cedi, cedi"). Lucia is brokenhearted at the prospect of life without Edgardo. Believing he is lost to her forever, and also thinking it is her duty to save her brother, she finally consents ("Guidami tu, tu reggimi"). Weeping, she goes to prepare for the wedding.

Hardly has she left the room when the guests arrive. Arturo, Enrico, Normanno, knights and ladies, pages, squires, guards, and inhabitants of Lammermoor enter, joyfully hailing the coming marriage that will cement the friendship of the Ashtons and the Bucklaws ("Per te d'immenso giubilo"). Arturo proclaims his friendship and his love for Lucia. ("Per poco fra le tenebre"). Enrico introduces him to the assembled guests.

Arturo asks for Lucia. Enrico tells him she will be in presently but bids him not to be astonished if she seems grief-stricken, for she is still mourning her mother's death. Lucia enters, supported on the arm of Raimondo and accompanied by Alisa and her other maids-in-waiting. Enrico presents Arturo to the despondent girl. She shrinks from him, but Enrico whispers to her to be cautious and not ruin his plans. He goes to the table where the marriage contract lies. Arturo signs it. Then Raimondo and Alisa lead the trembling Lucia to the table, and, scarcely aware of what she is doing, she signs the deed.

Suddenly the door opens. A stranger appears, his features concealed. He announces himself—"Edgardo!" There is immediate consternation. As Alisa and the ladies lead the swooning Lucia to a seat, there begins one of the most beautiful and powerfully dramatic ensembles ever written—the famous *Sextet*. It opens with Edgardo's questioning phrase, "What restrains me in such a moment?" ("Chi mi frena in tal momento?") It is, of course, only his love for Lucia that keeps him from drawing his sword and wreaking vengeance on his enemies. Even though she has betrayed his faith, he still loves her. Lucia, meanwhile, is consumed by despair; new fears fill Enrico's heart, and he feels compassion for his sister's plight; Arturo, Raimondo, Alisa, and the assembled guests pray that the impending trouble will pass.

Enrico and Arturo order Edgardo away, rushing at him with drawn swords. Edgardo draws too, saying he may die but others will die with him. Raimondo intervenes and bids them put up their swords. Enrico demands to know why Edgardo has come. Edgardo replies that he has come for Lucia, who has sworn faith to him. That vow is canceled, Enrico tells him, and shows him the marriage contract. Edgardo asks Lucia if it is her signature and she answers that it is.

Edgardo's fury knows no bounds. Stifling with rage, he gives Lucia back her ring and demands his own. Lucia, completely bewildered and hardly conscious of what is going on, takes the ring from her finger. Edgardo snatches it from her, throws it down, and tramples it underfoot.

Lucia swoons. Edgardo is ordered to leave, with a warning that their revenge will seek him out ("Esci, fuggi"). Instead of attempting to defend himself, Edgardo throws away his sword, offers his breast for them to strike, and declares he would gladly perish. Lucia prays for his life. Raimondo, Alisa, and the ladies induce him to flee for the sake of Lucia. After another brilliant concerted number the curtain falls as Edgardo rushes from the hall.

Act Three

[*Scene One*] The great hall of Lammermoor Castle. The first part of the third act is the famous *Mad Scene*. Musically it consists of some of the most beautiful as well as difficult coloratura passages ever composed, while dramatically it portrays a Lucia who cannot help but arouse our pity and sympathy, for in her insanity she believes herself to be with her lover, and so is happy in her madness.

When the curtain rises the hall is well peopled with guests. From adjoining rooms dance music is heard, and also sounds of jubilation ("D'immenso giubilo").

Suddenly Raimondo enters, pale and tense with excitement. He calls to the people to stop their merriment, and, gathering them about him, he tells this tale of horror ("Dalle stanze, ove Lucia"): Hearing a groan of terror from the bridal suite, he swiftly entered to find Arturo dead and Lucia standing triumphantly over his body, still waving the sword with which she had killed him. With glaring eyes fixed on Raimondo, she whispered, "Where is my husband?" and a smile of pleasure flashed over her pale countenance, plainly showing she was bereft of all reason.

He has just finished telling his story to the horror-stricken group when Lucia enters, her disheveled hair coming down over her white gown. She is deathly pale, and evidently unconscious of her surroundings. She thinks she is with her true lover, Edgardo. She imagines she hears his voice. Once again, she thinks, they are in the park, near the fountain. Suddenly she believes the unhappy spirit has risen to separate them. In her bewildered mind they fly to a beautiful altar strewn with roses. She hears celestial harmony. "The tapers are lighted" ("Ardon gl'incensi"), she sings. "There is the priest in his splendid robes. Give me thy right hand, Edgardo," she says in her delirium, "for I am thy bride forever. This blissful moment repays all my suffering." The startled assemblage implores Heaven to have pity on the poor maiden.

Enrico enters angrily and starts to upbraid Lucia for her perfidious crime; but Raimondo draws attention to her pathetic state of mind. He is instantly remorseful. Lucia, believing it is Edgardo who is angry with her, admits she signed the contract, but only because her cruel brother forced her to do so. "I love only you, Edgardo," she says. "Do not leave me."

Now apparently normal once more and realizing that she is dying, she asks them to cast a flower upon her grave but not to weep for her, because she goes to await her true love in heaven ("Spargi d'amaro pianto"). With this aria Lucia falls into the arms of Alisa. Enrico, repenting too late, is overcome with grief. The scene ends with Raimondo assailing Normanno as the cause of all the trouble.

[Scene Two] A section near Edgardo's ruined castle of Wolfscrag. The scene is a weird and eerie place. Lammermoor Castle, brightly illuminated, is seen in the distance, while in the foreground are the tombs of the Ravenswoods. It is night. Here we find Edgardo brooding. He does not know that Lucia has killed her husband and is herself dying. In his great aria ("Fra poco a me ricovero") he sings that he now waits only for an unmourned grave. He is bitter about Lucia's marriage and the happiness he thinks is hers, but anger has gone.

A group of inhabitants of Lammermoor, having left the scene of the tragedy at the castle, enter lamenting. Edgardo asks the cause of their grief, and they recount the whole unhappy story ("Giusto cielo! rispondete"). When he hears that Lucia in her madness is calling only for him, he resolves to see her, but Raimondo, who has come in, restrains him. A tolling bell is heard at that moment. Raimondo tells Edgardo that the bell announces Lucia's death. Edgardo sobs aloud in his grief.

At last realizing the steadfastness of Lucia's love for him, he apostrophizes her pure spirit, declaring that he and she will not be long parted. ("Tu che a Dio spiegasti"). Before the others can stop him, Edgardo stabs himself. While his life ebbs away, the saddened onlookers offer a solemn prayer that Heaven may pardon such human errors.

Madama Butterfly

by GIACOMO PUCCINI
[1858–1924]

Libretto by

LUIGI ILLICA *and* GIUSEPPE GIACOSA

Based on John Luther Long's story and David Belasco's play
MADAME BUTTERFLY

CHARACTERS

Goro, a *nakodo*, or marriage broker	*Tenor*
B. F. Pinkerton, lieutenant, United States Navy	*Tenor*
Suzuki, maid to Cio-cio-san	*Mezzo-soprano*
Sharpless, American Consul at Nagasaki	*Baritone*
Madama Butterfly (Cio-cio-san)	*Soprano*
The Cousin	*Soprano*
Mother of Cio-cio-san	*Mezzo-soprano*
Yakusidé, uncle of Cio-cio-san	*Baritone*
Commissioner	*Bass*
Registrar	*Baritone*
The Bonzo, a Buddhist priest, also an uncle of Cio-cio-san	*Bass*
Prince Yamadori, a suitor of Cio-cio-san	*Baritone*
Kate Pinkerton, wife of Lieutenant Pinkerton	*Mezzo-soprano*
Trouble, Cio-cio-san's child	

Relatives and companions of Cio-cio-san, servants

Place: Nagasaki, Japan
Time: Nineteenth century
First performance: La Scala, Milan, February 17, 1904
Original language: Italian

PUCCINI saw a production of Belasco's *Madame Butterfly* in London and decided immediately to use the play as the basis for an opera. He went to particular pains to give the work authentic local color, both dramatically and musically, basing some of his themes on genuine Japanese music.

The first production, however, was a complete failure. For reasons that no one seems to have been able to analyze, it was greeted with expressions of violent dislike. Revised and presented again four months later, the opera was a brilliant success.

Act One

The terrace and garden of the Japanese house which Lieutenant Pinkerton has leased in Nagasaki. It is on a hill overlooking the harbor and the town. Pinkerton expresses surprise and pleasure over the house as Goro scurries about showing him the ingenious arrangement of sliding panels which form the walls. Suzuki and two other servants enter and are introduced to the lieutenant by Goro. Suzuki addresses Pinkerton in flowery phrases, but Goro cuts her short when he observes that the lieutenant is getting bored by her chatter. He sends her and the two others away, then tells Pinkerton about the people who will be present for the signing of his marriage contract. They will include, he says, some two dozen relatives, the American Consul, Japanese officials, and, of course, Butterfly, the bride-to-be.

Sharpless arrives, panting and complaining about the steepness of the climb to the house. Pinkerton orders Goro to set out drinks, and then the two men sit down to talk. The lieutenant explains casually that he has leased the house for nine hundred and ninety-nine years and has bound himself to marriage with a Japanese for the same length of time—with the convenient provision that both the lease and the marriage can be canceled on a month's notice.

In a vigorous air introduced by a phrase from "The Star-Spangled Banner" ("Dovunque al mondo"), Pinkerton describes how the American seafaring man roams the whole world over in devil-may-care fashion, daunted by nothing, making conquests on his own terms. He cites his marriage ad-

Madama Butterfly

venture as an example. Sharpless observes that Pinkerton's philosophy is very convenient but one that eventually will exact its own price. The two men join in a rousing toast to America.

Goro bustles in, overhears Sharpless ask Pinkerton about his bride, and at once offers to provide one for the consul, who laughingly declines the offer. Pinkerton sends Goro off to bring Cio-cio-san. Sharpless remonstrates with him for taking his marriage so lightly, but Pinkerton, in an ardent refrain ("Amore o grillo"), answers that the geisha so enchanted him with her fragile beauty that he resolved to have her. When the consul warns that he may bring sorrow to an innocent and trusting heart, Pinkerton merely proposes another toast —this time to the American girl who will someday be his real wife.

Now the voices of Butterfly and her girl companions are heard in a jubilant chorus, in which we hear the love theme for the first time. Butterfly appears, charmingly introduces Pinkerton to her companions, and then answers questions about her family. They were once wealthy, she says, but now times have changed. At the mention of her father there is a moment of awkward silence, but Butterfly hastens on to explain about her illustrious uncle, the Bonzo. Apologetically she adds that she has another uncle who, unfortunately, is addicted to the bottle. She coyly asks Pinkerton and Sharpless to guess her age, laughing slyly at their astonishment when she reveals that she is only fifteen.

Pinkerton orders Goro to bring forth the refreshments. At that point the relatives arrive, along with the Imperial Registrar and the High Commissioner. Goro officiously takes charge. In a lively, chattering chorus the relatives comment on the Americans and then ceremoniously pay their compliments as they are introduced by Butterfly. Taking Pinkerton to one side, Butterfly shyly asks if she may be permitted to keep certain of her treasures. From the sleeves of her kimono she brings forth a variety of feminine knickknacks, then finally a long, slender sheath. A brief, somber phrase sounds dramatically in the orchestra. When Pinkerton asks her about the sheath, Butterfly turns away in confusion. Goro steps forward and whispers that it was sent to her father by the Mikado. In further explanation, Goro makes a gesture indicating hara-kiri.

Butterfly then shows Pinkerton a number of figurines, explaining that they are symbolic of the souls of her ancestors. In an impressive refrain ("Ieri son salita") she tells him that for the sake of his love she has repudiated her ancestors and her family. With that she throws the figurines away.

The marriage contract is signed with much ceremony. Sharpless, after a final word of caution to Pinkerton, leaves with the Commissioner and the Registrar. Pinkerton invites the relatives to help themselves to food and drink. In a festive chorus they express their satisfaction, and the sight of Uncle Yakusidé helping himself to the whisky provides considerable amusement.

The celebration is interrupted by the arrival of the Bonzo, who confronts Butterfly and furiously curses her for having renounced the religion of her ancestors. At Pinkerton's threatening command, the Bonzo and the relatives slowly withdraw, shouting denunciations at Butterfly, who buries her face in her hands and sobs bitterly.

As the angry cries die away in the distance, Pinkerton gently takes Butterfly's hands from her face and speaks words of comfort. Twilight approaches. From inside the house comes the sound of Suzuki's voice murmuring evening prayers. Pinkerton gives orders to arrange the house for the night, then seats himself in a chair and lights a cigarette. Suzuki helps Butterfly exchange her wedding dress for a long flowing gown of white.

Butterfly and Pinkerton are left alone, and now the music builds up into the rapturous love duet that concludes the act ("Viene la sera"). Clasped in each other's arms, they gaze up at the starry sky and pour out their ecstasy in the passionate climax of the duet, "Oh, quanti occhi fisi." As they slowly go into the house the curtain falls.

Madama Butterfly

ACT TWO

Butterfly's house. It is three years later. Pinkerton has long since left Nagasaki, and Butterfly has borne him a child. Suzuki is praying before a statue of Buddha, pausing occasionally to ring a prayer bell. Butterfly stands motionless near a screen. Suzuki implores the gods for aid, then shows Butterfly the few coins that are left to buy food. When the maid frets over their plight, Butterfly calmly assures her that Pinkerton will return. He promised, she sings, that he would come back when the robins nest in the spring. In the beautiful aria "Un bel dì" she describes the joy that will be hers on the day Pinkerton's ship sails into the harbor.

Butterfly's happy reverie is interrupted by the arrival of Goro and Sharpless. She welcomes the consul graciously and engages in a polite conversation about the state of his health and the weather. Sharpless, ill at ease, waits his chance to speak of the fateful letter he has received from Pinkerton saying that he has an American wife and that his marriage to Butterfly is a thing of the past. The consul stares in surprise when Butterfly asks him when the robins nest in America. Pinkerton assured her, she continues, that he would return with the robins, but they have already nested three times. Sharpless replies with considerable embarrassment that he is not an expert on ornithology, a word which Butterfly naïvely tries to pronounce.

The scene is interrupted by the arrival of the stupid, bumbling Prince Yamadori. Goro, having learned that Butterfly has been deserted, has lost no time in trying to arrange another marriage, and is offering Yamadori to Butterfly as a likely suitor. But she greets the prince's offers with amused contempt. When she reminds him that she is already wed, Goro says that desertion constitutes grounds for divorce. That may be the law in Japan, Butterfly retorts, but not in America. To Sharpless's dismay, she turns to him for confirmation.

After much lugubrious pleading, Yamadori leaves with Goro. Sharpless finally manages to read Pinkerton's letter, and as gently as possible he makes its tragic meaning clear. Butterfly recoils as if struck. After a moment she recovers, hurries from the room, and returns with her baby. In a dramatic and moving air ("Chi vide mai a bimbo"), she proudly tells Sharpless that here is Pinkerton's son. He must be told, she says, and when he knows that his wonderful child is waiting for him, he will allow nothing to stand in the way of his return. Clasping the child in feverish ecstasy, Butterfly sings that perhaps one day the Emperor will pass by and see this boy, with his heavenly blue eyes. He will be so taken by his beauty that he will make him a prince of the kingdom. Sharpless asks the boy's name. His name now is Trouble, Butterfly replies, but when Pinkerton returns it will be Joy. Deeply moved and distressed, Sharpless leaves, promising to tell Pinkerton of his son.

Suzuki bursts in, dragging the whimpering Goro. She tells Butterfly that he has been saying that her baby's father is unknown, and that in America such a child would be held in disgrace. Infuriated, Butterfly threatens to kill Goro with her dagger. Suzuki intervenes and pushes him out of the room.

A cannon booms in the harbor, announcing the arrival of a ship. With the aid of a telescope Butterfly identifies it as the *Abraham Lincoln*, Pinkerton's ship. In wildest excitement, she orders Suzuki to bring all the flowers from the garden to decorate the house. As they arrange the flowers they sing the lovely duet "Scuoti quella fronda di ciliegio," in which they joyously declare that they will rob the cherry tree of all its petals and the garden of all its blooms and scatter them in handfuls over the house in honor of this great occasion. After the duet Butterfly puts on her wedding gown, while Suzuki dresses the baby, then closes the *shosi*, a sliding wall with paper panes, facing the harbor. Butterfly makes three small holes in the *shosi*, one for herself, one for Suzuki, and a third for the baby. In the gathering darkness the women take up their vigil. From behind the scenes comes a melancholy, hummed chorus sung in slow, sweeping phrases over a plaintive melody in the orchestra. Suzuki and the baby gradually fall asleep. The faithful Butterfly remains standing motionless as the humming finally dies away and the curtain falls on this quiet but highly emotional scene.

Act Three

The same scene as at the end of Act Two.[1] There is a melodious prelude which echoes the theme of the first-act love duet. From the harbor come the shouts of sailors and the clanking of anchor chains. The early morning sun streams into the house. Butterfly, at length ending her vigil, rouses Suzuki and takes up the baby. At Suzuki's urging she retires to her room to rest.

Pinkerton, his wife Kate, and Sharpless approach. The two men go to the door, while Kate waits in the garden. Suzuki answers at their knock and tells them that Butterfly waited all night for Pinkerton after she had seen his ship in the harbor. Sharpless tells her that they have come to ask her aid in making arrangements for the future care of Pinkerton's child. When Suzuki learns that the strange woman in the garden is Pinkerton's wife, she sinks to the ground, sobbing in despair. A brief, dramatic trio follows ("Lo so che alle sue"). Sharpless implores Suzuki to break the news to Butterfly, assuring her that Mrs. Pinkerton will give the child her loving care. Suzuki begs to be spared this task, while Pinkerton gives way to his remorse.

At length Sharpless persuades Suzuki to go into the garden to meet Kate. He turns on Pinkerton in angry reproach for having caused all this sorrow, and then somewhat contemptuously suggests that he leave without seeing Butterfly in her agony. The lieutenant pauses long enough to sing a heartbroken farewell ("Addio fiorito asil").

Suzuki re-enters with Kate Pinkerton, and at that moment Butterfly appears at the doorway of her room. Suzuki vainly tries to keep her from coming in. Eagerly Butterfly looks for

---

[1] The opera was originally written in two acts. When Puccini revised it he divided Act Two into two parts, which are usually played as Act Two and Act Three.

Pinkerton. As she gazes from one to the other, the terrible truth dawns upon her, and she stares at Kate as if hypnotized. Kate tries to approach, but she motions her away. When Kate begs her forgiveness, Butterfly quietly bids her to tell Pinkerton that she will somehow find peace. He may have the child, she says in answer to Kate's request, if he will return for him in half an hour. Kate and Sharpless sadly leave.

The orchestra intones a dolorous theme as Butterfly orders Suzuki to close the doors and draw the curtains and then tells the sobbing maid to join the child in the garden. After a long time Butterfly takes a white veil from the shrine and throws it over the screen. She takes the dagger from its sheath, kisses it, and slowly reads the inscription: "Death with honor is better than life without honor."

She poises the dagger at her throat. At that moment Suzuki pushes the child into the room. In wild anguish Butterfly clasps him to her and sings a poignant farewell to her "little idol" ("Piccolo Iddio"). Brooding chords throb in the orchestra as she seats the child on a small stool, puts an American flag and a doll in his hands, and then blindfolds him. Dagger in hand, she steps behind the screen. In the next moment the knife thuds to the floor and the white veil slides slowly from the screen.

Butterfly, with the veil around her neck, creeps over to the child and collapses at his feet. She dies as Pinkerton, shouting her name, bursts into the room, followed by Sharpless. Powerful chords sound out the theme of the refrain which Butterfly sang when she mused that the Emperor might admire her beautiful child. The curtain falls.

Die Meistersinger von Nürnberg

by RICHARD WAGNER
[1813–1883]

Libretto by the Composer

Based on actual events in the history of the mastersingers
of sixteenth-century Germany

CHARACTERS

Eva, daughter of Veit Pogner	Soprano
Walther von Stolzing, a young knight of Franconia	Tenor
Magdalene, Eva's nurse	Mezzo-soprano
David, apprentice to Hans Sachs	Tenor
Hans Sachs, cobbler	Bass
Veit Pogner, goldsmith	Bass
Sixtus Beckmesser, town clerk	Bass
Kunz Vogelgesang, furrier	Tenor
Fritz Kothner, baker	Bass
Hermann Ortel, soap boiler — mastersingers	Bass
Balthazar Zorn, pewterer	Tenor
Conrad Nachtigall, buckle maker	Bass
Augustin Moser, tailor	Tenor
Ulrich Eisslinger, grocer	Tenor
Hans Foltz, coppersmith	Bass
Hans Schwarz, stocking weaver	Bass
Night watchman	Bass

Journeymen and apprentices of the guilds, burghers,
townspeople, musicians, children

Place: Nürnberg, Germany
Time: Mid-sixteenth century
First performance: Munich, June 21, 1868
Original language: German

The story of *Die Meistersinger* centers around the traditional song competitions held in Germany by the medieval guilds. Artistically inclined craftsmen in the principal cities formed singers' guilds and admitted to membership only those who successfully met the requirements of a song test governed by strict rules relating to rhyme, tune, and subject matter.

One of the most distinguished of the mastersingers was Hans Sachs, who lived in Nürnberg during the early part of the sixteenth century. A shoemaker by trade, he was also a poet of considerable renown. The names of the other mastersingers in the opera were likewise taken directly from history.

The magnificent overture, familiar as a symphonic number, states the dominating themes of the opera—the dignity and authority of the mastersingers as exemplified by Hans Sachs, and the love of Eva and Walther.

Act One

In the church of St. Katherine in Nürnberg. At one side, behind an openwork partition, may be seen a section of pews, in which members of the congregation are standing as they sing the final chorale of the service—the *Kirchenchor* ("Da zu Dir der Heiland kam"). The foreground represents the open space in front of the choir. Among the worshipers are Eva and Magdalene. Standing beside a pillar a short distance away is Walther von Stolzing. He intently watches Eva, who glances at him occasionally as she sings. Magdalene, noticing this, looks at her in stern reproof.

As Eva and her nurse leave at the conclusion of the service Walther approaches and earnestly requests Eva to give him an answer to his suit. While Magdalene flutters about anxiously, Eva explains that she is destined to be the bride of the man who wins the mastersingers' contest, which is to be held the next day. During their conversation David enters and draws a curtain across the partition at the back, screening off the rest of the church. When Walther, deeply perturbed at Eva's answer, turns away for a moment, Eva begs Magdalene to help her win her lover, whom she compares to the biblical David of Albrecht Dürer's portrait.

Magdalene repeats the famous biblical name with a sigh of emotion, whereupon David, the apprentice, comes forward and asks who is calling him. He is carrying a ruler and swinging a piece of chalk at the end of a string. In the throes of youthful love for Magdalene, he looks at her ardently as he answers her questions about the preparations he is making. He tells her that he is arranging accommodations for the masters, who are going to hold a preliminary song trial for a number of apprentices trying for membership in the guild. Magdalene advises Walther to make the most of this opportunity and present himself to the masters as a possible candidate for the final competition, where he can perhaps win the beloved Eva as his bride. The lovers manage to arrange for a rendezvous in the evening before the nurse hurries Eva away.

A number of apprentices enter, and David puts them to work. They arrange the benches, set up a special chair for the contestant, and begin building a platform. David meanwhile explains to Walther the details of the song competition, and the knight, deep in thought, seats himself in the contestant's chair. He listens attentively as David tells how he is being taught both versifying and singing by Hans Sachs. To be a master, David says, one must be not only a singer but a poet as well. Walther decides to enter the contest. David now turns his attention to the apprentices, finds that they have built the platform too large, and makes them rebuild it to smaller dimensions. On it they place a chair, a small desk, and a blackboard, then enclose the entire platform with a black curtain. When they have finished they join hands and dance around it, singing a chorus in which they derisively wish Walther good luck in his venture.

They withdraw to a bench at the rear as the mastersingers enter. Walther seats himself on a bench in the foreground. Pogner appears first, accompanied by Beckmesser, who harasses him with entreaties to plead his case with Eva. Walther interrupts to greet Pogner, and Beckmesser looks him over suspiciously, muttering about the prospects of a rival at this crucial moment. Pogner introduces Walther to the others and gives him leave to sing at the preliminary trial.

The roll is called, after which the masters seat themselves. But before they take up the business of the day Pogner speaks to them in a long monologue which is known as *Pogner's Address* ("Das schöne Fest"). He has traveled about Germany and is particularly distressed over the fact that the burghers apparently are held in low esteem by the public. The impression is, he says, that they are interested solely in material things and money-making, to the exclusion of culture and art. To prove to the people that the burghers are not crass materialists, Pogner declares, he is making a special contribution to the annual song competition—he is offering his daughter Eva as bride to the man who wins the contest.

The majority of the burghers voice their approval, but Hans Sachs protests that, in all fairness, the bride should be given some choice in the matter of a husband. The people, too, he adds, are entitled to voice their opinion, particularly as to the qualifications of the singer. When some of the masters express their doubts as to the judgment of the public in matters of art, Pogner suggests, as a compromise, that Eva be permitted to reject the winner of the contest, with the stipulation that only a mastersinger be considered eligible as a future bridegroom. After considerable argument Pogner's plan is adopted.

Pogner now formally introduces Walther as a contestant. The masters ask him where he learned the art of singing, and he replies in the melodious aria, "Am stillen Herd." He studied the art, he says, from the book of the ancient minstrel, Walther von der Vogelweide, and from nature. Sachs expresses his approval, but the others are rather dubious about this unconventional type of training. They ask the knight what subject he will take for his song, and he announces that love will be his theme. He seats himself in the singer's chair. Beckmesser takes his place on the marker's platform, pausing to warn Walther spitefully that he will be allowed only seven mistakes.

Walther's ardent love song ("Fanget an! So rief der Lenz in den Wald"), being a spontaneous expression of his emotions, breaks practically every one of the traditional rules, and violent indications of disapproval are heard from the marker's platform. Despite the furious scratching of chalk on slate, Walther continues undaunted until Beckmesser pulls aside the curtains and holds up the slate, which is covered with chalk marks.

Beckmesser sarcastically enumerates the flaws in the song, and several of the masters add their criticisms. Kothner points out one inexcusable infraction of the rules—Walther rose from his seat as he sang. Hans Sachs protests against the arbitrary judgment of the masters, but he is shouted down by Beckmesser, who gathers his colleagues around him and elaborates on the singer's errors. With the exception of Sachs and Pogner, they are unanimous in their disapproval. Walther, angry and impatient over their haggling, expresses his contempt for their hidebound rules, proclaiming that henceforth he will sing according to the dictates of his heart. With that he strides angrily out of the church.

Sachs, who has listened intently to Walther's song, voices his approval of the knight's talent and courage. Beckmesser calls for an official decision, and the masters signify that the contestant is rejected. Loudly discussing the matter, they leave as the apprentices take down the platform and put away the benches. The voices of the men and boys blend in a lively chorus ("Glück auf zum Meistersingen"). Hans Sachs stands to one side, and as the apprentices remove the contestant's chair he makes a gesture of resignation.

Act Two

A street in Nürnberg, intersected at the center by a narrow alley that winds toward the rear, with houses on both sides. On one side of the intersection, toward the foreground, is

Pogner's home. Directly opposite is Hans Sachs's shop and living quarters. It is a summer evening. The apprentices are putting up the shutters of the houses, singing as they work. David is attending to the windows of Sachs's shop.

Magdalene comes out of Pogner's house, calls David to her, and asks about the song trial. He tells her that Walther was rejected. The nurse hurries back into the house, while the apprentices dance around David and tease him about talking to Magdalene. He is about to retaliate when Sachs appears and sends him back into the shop. The street becomes quiet again as the apprentices go to their homes.

Pogner and Eva approach arm in arm down the alley, talking about the song competition. They seat themselves on a stone bench under a tree in front of their home, and shortly Magdalene calls them in to supper. As Pogner enters the nurse manages to detain Eva and whisper the news about Walther. Much distressed, Eva decides to appeal to Hans Sachs for advice.

The shoemaker meanwhile has seated himself at his workbench, which David has placed near the door. He closes the lower half of the door, sends David off to bed, and prepares to work. In a long soliloquy ("Wie duftet doch der Flieder") he muses over Walther's song. Eva interrupts his reflections, and an interesting musical dialogue ensues ("Gut'n Abend, Meister"). Sachs reveals his warm affection for Eva, who indicates that she would be well content if the cobbler himself were to win the contest and claim her for his bride. She scornfully dismisses Beckmesser as a suitor. Sachs, touched by her devotion, tells her gently that he himself is much too old for her.

When the talk turns to Walther the cobbler deliberately speaks disparagingly of him. In her annoyance over his remarks Eva is at last betrayed into revealing her true feelings. As she leaves in response to Magdalene's call, Sachs decides with satisfaction that his conjectures about the romance were correct. He withdraws into his shop, leaving the upper half of the door slightly ajar.

Magdalene tells Eva that Beckmesser plans to serenade her

Die Meistersinger von Nürnberg

this evening with the song he has written for the contest. Just at that moment Walther appears, and Eva rushes to him with an ardent greeting. Walther tells her mournfully that the decision of the mastersingers has put an end to all his hopes. He bursts out in anger and impatience over their blindness and obstinacy, then implores Eva to elope with him. Suddenly the watchman's horn sounds, and Eva tells her lover to hide until he has passed. She runs into the house. In his quaint, medieval chant, the watchman announces that it is ten o'clock, swinging his lantern as he goes on his way. Sachs, having overheard the conversation between the lovers, peers cautiously out, remarking that the two must be prevented from taking so indiscreet a step.

Eva, dressed in Magdalene's clothes, steals out of the house and rushes into Walther's arms. As they start toward the alley Sachs flings open his door, catching them in the light of his lamp. Quickly they dodge into the shadows, Eva warning that they must not be seen by the shoemaker. Walther listens in dismay as Eva tells him that the shoemaker is Sachs and that, far from being his friend, he has taken sides with the other masters against the newcomer. Walther is about to rush over to the shop and demand explanations when Beckmesser comes down the alley.

Pausing in front of Pogner's house, he begins tuning his lute, then looks up at Eva's window, where Magdalene, in Eva's clothes, has seated herself. Thereupon Sachs brings his workbench just outside his door and fits a shoe on the last. Beckmesser is about to begin his serenade when Sachs starts hammering away and bellowing out a lusty refrain, "Jerum! Jerum! Halla-hallo-he!" Beckmesser, trying to control his temper, begs Sachs to be quiet, but the shoemaker replies that he must finish his work. In desperation Beckmesser suggests that Sachs act as marker for his song and pound only when he hears a mistake. He has sung only a few quavering bars of his clumsy ballad ("Den Tag seh' ich erscheinen") when the pounding begins again, and the louder he sings, the faster Sachs pounds. At length Sachs takes the shoe from the last and holds it up in triumph. He sings in praise of the "marker's shoe" ("Mit den Schuhen ward ich fertig schier"), calling it that because he fashioned it while the blows of his hammer recorded the mistakes of a would-be mastersinger. A shoe, like a song, he observes, must be well made. Meanwhile, Beckmesser bellows his serenade at the top of his lungs.

Soon heads pop out of windows, and in an angry chorus the neighbors call for quiet. David looks out of his window and, seeing Beckmesser serenading at the house of his ladylove, rushes out with a club and begins whacking away at his rival. This sets off a tremendous row, in which all the people of the neighborhood—burghers, journeymen, apprentices, women, and children—eventually join.

At the height of the uproar Walther and Eva emerge from their hiding place. Drawing his sword, the knight tries to force a path through the crowd. Sachs rushes from his shop, seizes Walther, and pushes Eva up the steps of her house. Still holding fast to Walther, the shoemaker turns around, manages to catch hold of David, drags both his captives into his shop, and slams the door. Beckmesser, out of David's clutches at last, limps hastily away.

The watchman's horn sounds above the tumult, and the crowd melts away as if by magic. By the time he appears to call out the hour of eleven ("Hört ihr Leut', und lasst euch sagen"), the street once again is deserted and quiet. A full moon rises over the housetops. The themes of the fight and Beckmesser's serenade run softly through the orchestra as the curtain falls.

Act Three

The interior of Hans Sachs's shop. The prelude, also a concert favorite, is dominated by the themes associated with Hans Sachs. It is morning, and sun floods the room. Sachs is sitting in a huge armchair, deep in a book. David enters carrying a basket. Seeing that Sachs is unaware of his presence, he takes a piece of pastry and a sausage from the basket and begins to eat.

Startled by the sound of a turning page, he puts aside the food and respectfully takes his place before Sachs. He tells him that he has delivered the shoes to Beckmesser and then tries to make amends for his behavior of the night before ("Ach, Meister, woll't Ihr mir verzeih'n!"). It was all for the sake of Magdalene, he explains, because she has always been so kind to him. Sachs suddenly snaps his book shut and David sinks to his knees in fright. But the cobbler's thoughts are elsewhere. Casually he forgives David, then tells him to repeat his verses for the day. The boy replies with a naïve song about St. John, on whose festival day the song competition is being held ("Am Jordan Sankt Johannes stand"). With his mind still on his encounter with Beckmesser, David sings the first line to the tune of the ill-fated serenade. At Sachs's startled look he corrects himself in confusion. Sachs hears him through and then sends him about his duties.

Left alone, Sachs sings the magnificent aria ("Wahn! Wahn! Überall Wahn!") in which he ponders over the hate and discord that are rife in the world—even here in peaceful Nürnberg. At the slightest pretext, he muses, his good neighbors will strike out at each other in blind anger, as though they were under some mischievous spell. He resolves to turn the folly of the good burghers to some useful purpose.

As he finishes, Walther enters from the other room. Sachs greets him affectionately, and a melodious dialogue follows ("Grüss Gott, mein Junker"). Walther tells Sachs that he had a dream so wonderful that he scarcely dares speak of it for fear that its magic may vanish. Sachs urges him to tell it, saying that man's finest inspirations are born of dreams. In the phrases of the *Prize Song*—sung in its entirety later at the competition—Walther describes his dream, while Sachs, listening with growing excitement, writes it down as he sings. Walther breaks off occasionally to discuss the meaning of the song with Sachs. The shoemaker, realizing that this is the song destined to win the prize, makes certain suggestions as to rhyme and musical form so as to ensure the approval of the masters. He calls for a second stanza and Walther answers with the beautiful refrain in which he describes how the vision of his beloved came to him at close of day ("Abendlich glühend"). It was then that he heard the magic song which now inspires him. Sachs advises Walther to try for the prize, then both leave to prepare for the festival.

Beckmesser now enters. He is resplendent in his festival costume but limps about, groaning in pain from the beating of last night. Muttering in anger and discomfort, he looks stealthily around and finally catches sight of the paper on which Sachs has written Walther's song. Now that scoundrelly Sachs's intentions are clear, he fumes as he examines it, for this proves that he is planning to enter the contest. Hearing the door behind him open, Beckmesser stuffs the paper in his pocket just as Sachs enters.

The shoemaker greets him genially, but Beckmesser angrily accuses him of trying to eliminate him from the competition by deliberately involving him in a street brawl ("O Schuster, voll von Ränken"). He charges Sachs with plotting to clear the field of all rivals so that he can win the hand of Eva. Drawing forth the paper from his pocket, he shakes it under Sachs's nose, sputtering that *here* is proof of the shoemaker's skulduggery. His jaw drops in surprise when Sachs offers him the song as a present. When he finally convinces himself that Sachs is not playing a trick on him, he limps from the shop in triumph, loudly assuring Sachs that he will reward him someday for this noble deed.

As Sachs looks after him, sadly shaking his head, Eva enters. Their conversation ensues in a fine duet ("Sieh, Evchen!"). In charming confusion she tells him that one of her new shoes is too tight. Well aware of her real reason for coming, Sachs kneels down to examine the shoe, and as he does so Walther opens the door and stands in the entrance. He is wearing the splendid costume of a knight, and Eva gasps in delighted surprise. Sachs takes the shoe to his bench, turns his back on the scene, and begins working.

Walther, gazing at Eva in rapture, breaks into the refrain of his dream song, to which Eva listens as if enchanted. Sachs, returning with the shoe, bids Eva to mark the song well, for it is a masterpiece. Overcome by emotion, Eva bursts into tears

Die Meistersinger von Nürnberg

and throws herself into Sachs's arms. Deeply moved, he gently frees himself and gives her over to Walther.

In a glowing refrain that has in it certain echoes of the *Tristan und Isolde* music ("O Sachs, mein Freund!") Eva pours out her love for Sachs, saying that if fate had not decreed otherwise she would be his bride. Sachs answers rather ruefully that the circumstances remind him of the sad story of Tristan, and that he would prefer to spare himself the role of King Marke. A theme from *Tristan* sweeps through the orchestra to underscore his words.

The entrance of Magdalene and David breaks the mood of the scene. Welcoming them, Sachs proclaims, in an ensuing refrain ("Aha! da streicht schon die Lene"), that a new song has been born and needs christening. He and Eva are to be its godparents, while Magdalene and David are to be witnesses. To make the boy eligible as a witness, Sachs promotes him to journeyman then and there by ordering him to kneel and giving him a box on the ear—the traditional symbol of the bestowal of this new rank.

Eva bursts into a joyous refrain ("Selig, wie die Sonne"), introducing the magnificent quintet which closes the scene. Eva sings that Walther's magic song has banished all her sorrow, while Walther exclaims that it was her love that inspired it. Though rejoicing with Eva, Sachs confesses a pang of regret that her love now belongs to another. Magdalene and David express their happiness over the fact that now they may wed, David having attained the rank of a freeman. At its conclusion Sachs bids all to hurry to the festival. The curtain descends as the music continues on a stirring festive theme mingled with the fanfare of trumpets. At its climax the curtain rises on the colorful scene of the song competition.

An open meadow outside Nürnberg, with the river Pegnitz visible in the background. At one side is a raised flag-draped platform for dignitaries and judges of the contest. Gaily bedecked tents and booths line the other side of the open space. Townspeople crowd in upon the scene and are noisily welcomed by the apprentices, who dance about with the girls.

The various guilds now parade in, waving their identifying

banners and singing lusty choruses. Then the masters enter in a stately procession and take their places on the platform. When all have gathered, the apprentices silence the throng and Hans Sachs steps forward. He is greeted with a majestic hymn of acclaim, "Wach' auf, es nahet gen den Tag."

In moving tones Sachs acknowledges the greeting ("Euch wird es leicht"), speaks a friendly word to Pogner, and then formally opens the contest. First he calls on Beckmesser, who has been desperately scanning Walther's song in a last-minute effort to memorize the words. The apprentices conduct him to the singer's place, a mound of turf. He stumbles in his excitement, complains that the mound is shaky, and orders the boys to settle it more firmly. Laughing among themselves, they pound it vigorously.

With an exaggerated bow to Eva, Beckmesser launches into his song. He tries to fit the words of Walther's poem to the tune of his serenade, with ludicrous results. Distracted by the snickers of the crowd, he forgets the words and sings on in an aimless panic. As he finishes in a final, desperate effort, the throng bursts into a roar of derisive laughter. Rushing over to the platform, he flings the paper in Sachs's face, shouting that the cobbler tricked him into singing his miserable ditty. Shaking with fury, he storms through the crowd and disappears.

Sachs quietly announces that he merely wrote down the words of the song, which is the inspiration of a distinguished visitor who can sing it as it should be sung. At his command Walther steps forward and sings the great *Preislied (Prize Song)*, the high point of the opera ("Morgenlich leuchtend im rosigen Schein"). It is a poetic description of the miracle which inspired his song. He sings of wandering into a magic garden, where, under an enchanted tree, he saw a beautiful maiden. As he stood beside her he knew that this lovely maiden and his Muse were one and the same. His Muse, he sings exultantly, is Eva, and the music she inspired will transport them both to the heights of Parnassus and to Paradise. The masters and the people, in a choral accompaniment to the final phrases of the song, comment in surprise and wonder at its beauty. Walther is accorded the prize by unanimous acclaim.

Eva places the victor's wreath on his head, then both kneel before Pogner to receive his blessing. When Pogner, however, proffers the knight the gold chain of the Masters' Guild, he spurns it with some show of bitterness. At that Sachs steps forward and in an eloquent refrain ("Verachtet mir die Meister nicht") exhorts him not to scorn the masters' prize. Though their rules may seem stern and unyielding, he continues, it is they who keep sacred the standards of German art. Those who revere that art must safeguard it in time to come, when the land will be threatened by evil from without.

The people echo his words in a triumphant chorus. Eva takes the wreath from Walther's head and bestows it upon Sachs. He, in turn, takes the gold chain from Pogner and presents it to Walther. Pogner kneels before Sachs, while the masters make a gesture of homage. In a dazzling chorus the people hail the beloved shoemaker of Nürnberg ("Heil Sachs! Hans Sachs!").

Mignon

by CHARLES LOUIS AMBROISE THOMAS
[1811–1896]

Libretto by
MICHEL CARRÉ *and* JULES BARBIER

Based on Goethe's novel
WILHELM MEISTER'S LEHRJAHRE

CHARACTERS

Lothario, an Italian nobleman (first seen as a wandering minstrel)	*Bass*
Philine, an actress	*Soprano*
Laërtes, an actor	*Tenor*
Giarno, leader of a gypsy band	*Bass*
Mignon, a young girl kidnaped by gypsies, in reality the daughter of Lothario	*Mezzo-soprano*
Wilhelm Meister, a young student on a tour	*Tenor*
Frédéric, also a student, in love with Philine	*Contralto*
Antonio, a servant	*Bass*

Townspeople, gypsies, peasants, actors, actresses, comedians, ladies and gentlemen, servants

Place: Germany and Italy
Time: Eighteenth century
First performance: Opéra-Comique, Paris, November 17, 1866
Original language: French

THE COMPOSER of *Mignon* was a brilliant musician and one of the acknowledged masters of *opéra comique*. He wrote a great number of operettas, operas, and ballets, as well as choral works and instrumental pieces. Although he had little faith in *Mignon*, it was enormously successful.

Mignon

The overture, familiar as a concert piece, is dominated by the theme of Mignon's aria, "Connais-tu le pays?" and the principal motive of Philine's air, "Je suis Titania."

Act One

The courtyard of a hostelry in Germany, with the entrance at one side. On the second floor a door opens on a balcony, from which a staircase leads down to the courtyard. Townspeople and peasants are seated at tables, singing a lively chorus about the joys of drinking and companionship. Lothario, carrying his harp, wanders in and is invited to one of the tables. The people become quiet and listen as he sings a melancholy air in which he describes his weary, endless search for his lost child ("Fugitif et tremblant"). Some of his listeners comment that this tragedy of the past has driven him partly mad. They try to console him and bid him drink to forget his sorrow.

A number of gypsies enter and begin to dance for the entertainment of the crowd. Philine and Laërtes, coming out on the balcony to watch them, join the others in a gay choral accompaniment to the dancing. At its conclusion Giarno steps forward and announces that Mignon will now perform her famous dance on eggs. He orders Zafari, the fiddler, to play his best tune, while other gypsies spread a carpet on the ground and place eggs upon it. Giarno rouses Mignon, who is lying asleep under a blanket in a gypsy cart, and tells her to get ready to dance. Philine, watching this, asks Giarno if the child is a boy or a girl. "Neither," replies Giarno with a laugh as he throws back the blanket. "It is Mignon."

Climbing out of the cart, Mignon looks sullenly over the crowd and then says that she will not dance. Giarno threatens to beat her, while the gypsies comment in an agitated chorus. As Giarno brandishes his stick, Lothario strides up and puts his arms protectingly around Mignon. Giarno angrily orders him away, and at that moment Wilhelm, attracted by the commotion, rushes to the rescue with drawn pistol. Mignon, in a charming gesture of gratitude, divides her bouquet between Lothario and Wilhelm. Philine and Laërtes, as well as the other onlookers, wonder who this unknown young man may be. Lothario, stirred by the incident to memories of the past, sings about a mysterious knight clad in heavy armor. Mignon offers a prayer of thanks for her deliverance, while Wilhelm muses over this strange adventure.

The crowd gradually scatters, and soon the courtyard is deserted except for Wilhelm and Laërtes. The latter comes down from the balcony, introduces himself, and explains that he and Philine have recently arrived with a theatrical troupe which is now out of employment. Wilhelm, in turn, reveals that he is a student from Vienna. He has become bored with university life, he says, and has decided to see the world. He expresses his carefree philosophy in a florid aria, declaring that he intends to wander through the world as he pleases, tasting all its pleasures ("Oui, je veux par le monde").

The talk soon turns to Philine, and Laërtes warns that she is a heartless flirt who is interested solely in adulation and gaiety. Philine, appearing on the balcony at that moment, overhears Laërtes and with ironical good humor thanks him for singing her praises. The conversation, on the general topic of love, continues in the form of a charming trio, which begins with Wilhelm's comment on Philine's beauty ("Que de grâce et de charmes!").

Philine, making it obvious to Wilhelm that she wishes to see him again, leaves with Laërtes. Mignon approaches and shyly thanks Wilhelm for coming to her aid. In ensuing recitative she tells him as much of her past as she can remember. She has no other name than Mignon, she says. Her mother is dead, and so is the "great devil" who was her first master. All she knows of her past, she continues, is that one summer evening she was seized by a band of men and carried from her home. She recalls her homeland in the famous aria "Connais-tu le pays?" When she sings of a land of warm sunshine and blue skies, where a palace awaits her, Wilhelm concludes that it is Italy.

Mignon

The scene is interrupted by the appearance of Giarno. Wilhelm decides then and there to buy Mignon's freedom and leaves with the gypsy to arrange the terms. Mignon is beside herself with joy. Lothario enters, and when he tells Mignon that he has come to say good-by she expresses a desire to accompany him on his wanderings. Taking his harp, she sings a song about the free and untroubled flight of the swallows, "Légères hirondelles," which concludes in duet form as Lothario joins his voice with hers. Hearing Philine's laughter behind the scenes, Mignon quickly leads Lothario away.

Philine enters with Frédéric, who is dusting off his riding habit, complaining that he wore out his horse in his hurry to see her. She taunts him coquettishly. They meet Wilhelm and Giarno and learn that Wilhelm has bought Mignon's freedom, an act of kindness which brings warm words of praise from Philine. Satisfied with his bargain, Giarno leaves. Wilhelm is introduced to Frédéric, and while they are talking Laërtes enters with a letter for Philine. It turns out to be an invitation to Philine, Laërtes, and their actor companions to visit the castle of Baron de Rosemberg, Frédéric's uncle. Philine promptly invites Wilhelm to join them, saying that he can assume the role of a poet. She gives Frédéric to understand that he will be decidedly unwelcome, whereupon he rushes away in a jealous fury.

As Philine and Laërtes go into the inn, Mignon rushes up to Wilhelm exclaiming that now she is free she is ready to follow him wherever he goes. Wilhelm tries to dissuade her. Hurt by his rebuff, Mignon declares that she will go with Lothario, who approaches at this moment. The minstrel welcomes her as his companion in a melodious aria ("Viens! la libre vie est douce"). The prospect of committing her to the dubious protection of the old man, however, prompts Wilhelm to change his mind. The three join in a brief trio in which Wilhelm consents to take Mignon, who fervently thanks him ("Envers qui me délivre"). Lothario, again bemused by his dreams, prays that he may be allowed to go on hoping and singing.

Philine and Laërtes, accompanied by the other members of the troupe, emerge from the inn, ready to leave for the castle. The gypsies also prepare to go on their way. The townspeople assemble to bid them good-by, and all join in a stirring chorus. In a solo interlude Philine sings that whoever loves her will follow her, a pointed hint to Wilhelm ("Qui m'aime, me suive"). When he responds by accepting her invitation, she impudently snatches Mignon's bouquet out of his hands. Mignon flares up momentarily in jealous anger. Turning to the gypsies, she bids them farewell, assuring Giarno that she forgives him. The chorus continues to an impressive climax.

Act Two

[*Scene One*] The entr'acte is the familiar gavotte. At the rise of the curtain we see Philine seated at a dressing table in a sumptuously appointed boudoir. With great delight she examines the notes and flowers from various admirers.[1] Laërtes's voice is heard in a merry refrain. He appears shortly and, looking around the room, exclaims over its luxurious appointments. Philine tells him that the baroness has given her the use of her boudoir, whereupon Laërtes banteringly remarks that the baron no doubt has the key. With exaggerated gallantry he strikes up a madrigal, in which he describes the fatal effect of Philine's bewitching glances on the heart of a lover ("Belle, ayez pitié de nous"). Philine teasingly observes that his passionate love-making reminds her of Frédéric.

Wilhelm enters. Laërtes informs him that the troupe will perform *A Midsummer Night's Dream*, by one William Shakespeare, a rather talented playwright. Philine is to play Titania. As he leaves to arrange for the performance he meets Mignon outside the door. She is dressed as a page. In answer to the questioning looks of Philine and Laërtes, Wilhelm ex-

[1] In the original score an aria, written for the London production, is indicated here. In it Philine voices her pleasure over her romantic conquests ("À merveille! j'en ris d'avance").

plains that, as the girl insisted on remaining with him, he has decided to take her along as his servant. Philine, with deliberate condescension, invites Mignon in, saying that she will have an opportunity to perform her egg dance.

At Wilhelm's urging, Mignon seats herself at the fireside. Philine comments with malicious delight on the spectacle of the master serving the servant, while Mignon smarts under her mocking laughter. As the actress busies herself at making up for her performance, Wilhelm, completely enchanted by her loveliness, stands in attendance. Philine sings a brilliant air describing how her admirers sigh for the privilege of waiting on her ("Je crois entendre"). Wilhelm's voice blends with hers as he sings passionately of her beauty.

Mignon, curled up at the fireside, feigns sleep but watches every move. Wilhelm, lost in adoration, entreats Philine for one word of encouragement. Her reply is a gay, mocking refrain. Mignon, aside, heartbrokenly sings that she longs for sleep so that she may be spared this tormenting scene. The three voices blend briefly, and then Philine and Wilhelm leave.

Resigning herself to the situation for the sake of being near Wilhelm, Mignon soon forgets her troubles in admiration of her luxurious surroundings. Her attention is caught by the cosmetics on Philine's dressing table. She rouges her cheeks, examines the effect in a mirror, and then expresses her delight in a brilliant refrain called the *Styrienne*—"Je connais un pauvre enfant." Then, determined to make the most of this escapade, she goes into an adjoining dressing room to put on one of Philine's costumes.

While she is out of the room Frédéric enters through a window. He expresses his satisfaction at being in the boudoir of his ladylove in the tuneful gavotte "Me voici dans son boudoir." Wilhelm suddenly returns. He stares at Frédéric in mingled surprise and amusement. There is an exchange of words over Philine, the argument coming to a climax when Frédéric draws his sword and challenges Wilhelm as a rival. Just as the two cross swords Mignon, dressed in one of Philine's costumes, rushes in and intervenes.

Frédéric, relishing Wilhelm's discomfiture, puts up his sword and swaggers from the room. Seeing Mignon for the first time in appropriate feminine attire, Wilhelm suddenly realizes that she is a beautiful young woman. As diplomatically as possible he points out that he can no longer retain her as his page and tells her that they must part. In a tender aria he bids her farewell ("Adieu, Mignon, courage!"). Mignon sadly sings that she will go back to her old life, wandering about and begging for food. Deeply moved by her despair, Wilhelm realizes that he cannot bear to be parted from her.

Philine returns with Frédéric and comments with mocking disdain on Mignon's appearance. Stung to fury, Mignon rips the lace from the dress and then runs into the dressing room. Frédéric complacently remarks that she is probably jealous of him. Laërtes, costumed for his role as Theseus, enters and announces that the play is about to begin. All leave. Mignon, once more in her gypsy dress, reappears. In a burst of jealous fury, she cries out, "Cette Philine! je la hais [That Philine! I hate her]!" The curtain falls.

[*Scene Two*] The park outside Baron de Rosemberg's castle. At one side is the shore of a small lake. At the rear can be seen the brilliantly lighted windows of the conservatory, where the play is being performed. Mignon appears, gazes at the castle, and laments that Wilhelm is there with her hated rival. Tormented by jealousy and despair, she is about to throw herself into the lake when she hears the strains of a harp.

Lothario enters. On seeing Mignon he first thinks she is his lost daughter, Sperata. Recognizing Mignon and noticing her grief, however, he takes her in his arms and tries to comfort her. In a tender refrain he sings that, like her, he has wandered alone, scorned by the world, to lead a life of suffering ("Pauvre enfant! pauvre créature!"). Their voices join in a duet as they sing of their loneliness and sorrow. Suddenly there is a burst of applause from the conservatory. Tortured by the thought that the acclaim is for Philine, Mignon prays that lightning may set the castle on fire. Distractedly she rushes away. Lothario repeats the word "fire" and slowly walks toward the castle.

The play having ended, members of the audience and the actors—the latter still in their costumes—emerge from the conservatory. In a brief chorus all acclaim Philine for her performance. She comes forward and sings the brilliant *Polonaise*, "Je suis Titania." (A ballet sometimes follows.)

Wilhelm enters, and Philine chides him for not having joined in the chorus of praise. He answers that he is looking for Mignon. As Philine takes him aside, Lothario and Mignon appear. The old man tells her that to avenge her he has set the castle on fire. Wilhelm sees Mignon and eagerly hurries toward her, whereupon Philine approaches and asks Mignon to go into the castle and bring back Wilhelm's bouquet, which she has left behind.

No sooner has Mignon gone inside than Laërtes appears, crying that the castle is on fire. Wilhelm dashes into the burning building. Just as the walls fall into blazing ruins he reappears with Mignon unconscious in his arms. Clutched in her hand is the withered bouquet. The onlookers hail the rescuer in a dramatic chorus as the curtain falls.

ACT THREE

The hall of the Cipriani castle in Italy. At the back is a large door, and on either side are smaller doors through which a lake may be seen in the distance. It is to this castle that Wilhelm has brought Mignon to aid her recovery from the illness which was caused by the harrowing experience of the fire. The hall is deserted as the curtain rises. A harp is heard, and from the distance come the voices of a chorus singing a barcarolle about the soft wind sweeping over the lake ("Au souffle léger du vent"). Lothario appears at the door of the room where Mignon is lying ill and sings the *Berceuse*, in which he muses that Mignon's tormenting fever has subsided and that now angels guard her peaceful slumber ("De son coeur j'ai calmé").

The servant Antonio, carrying a lamp, enters with Wilhelm. He explains that the owner of the castle disappeared many years ago and that the property is now for sale. Wilhelm tells him that he will make a decision on the purchase tomorrow. Antonio leaves. Wilhelm approaches Lothario, who tells him that Mignon is greatly improved. Thereupon Wilhelm declares that he has decided to buy the castle of Cipriani for Mignon. At the mention of Cipriani, Lothario becomes strangely excited. Striding up to a large door at the back, he tries to open it, saying that no one has entered the room for fifteen years. He tries another door, finds it open, and goes through it.

Musing over the old man's mysterious behavior, Wilhelm goes to the door of Mignon's room, and as he softly opens it he hears her speak his name in her sleep. In the well-known aria "Elle ne croyais pas" he voices the hope that when she recovers she will reveal the secret that is troubling her. As he stands in the doorway gazing at her Antonio brings him a letter from Laërtes informing him that Philine has followed him to Italy. He is about to enter Mignon's room when she herself, now awake, steps from her chamber. She looks about in wonder, murmuring that it is as if she had seen this place in a dream. In sudden excitement she calls Wilhelm's name. He hurries to her, and a passionate duet follows ("Je suis heureuse! L'air m'envivre!"). Mignon revels in the thought that the fresh, pure air of this land has renewed her vigor, while Wilhelm begs her to forget the past.

In spite of her rapture, however, Mignon is haunted by the thought of Philine, and as though to justify her fears, Philine's voice is heard in the distance, singing her aria, "Je suis Titania." Wilhelm vainly tries to calm Mignon, assuring her that he loves her alone and that he has forgotten Philine. Mignon bitterly laments that her rival will yet destroy her happiness. Their voices blend in a dramatic climax, after which Mignon, overwhelmed by excitement and fear, faints in Wilhelm's arms.

Mignon

When she revives, Wilhelm tells her that her fears were imaginary, but Mignon is inconsolable. She calls to Lothario, who enters at that moment. His greeting, "Mignon! Wilhelm! Salut à vous!" introduces the dramatic concluding trio of the opera. The lovers are dumfounded when they see him in the attire of a nobleman. His manner has changed to one of dignity and assurance, his mind having been restored by contact with familiar surroundings. When he announces that he is the owner of the Cipriani castle, Wilhelm, not realizing what has happened, exclaims it is another delusion.

Lothario hands Mignon a small casket and tells her to open it. As she wonderingly examines its contents, Lothario softly calls "Sperata," but it stirs only a vague memory in Mignon's mind. Suddenly she finds a prayer book, and at Lothario's bidding she begins reading a prayer, "O Vierge Marie." After the opening phrase Mignon raises her eyes from the book and repeats the prayer from memory. Excited and shaken by the onrush of memories, she asks what country she is in. Lothario tells her it is Italy. Thereupon she dashes into an adjoining room and after a moment reappears, crying out that she has seen the portrait of her mother. In transports of happiness Lothario greets his long-lost daughter, Sperata, while Wilhelm voices his joy over the reunion. Mignon swoons from sheer ecstasy, but quickly revives. The trio, dominated by the theme of "Connais-tu le pays?" rises to a moving climax as the curtain falls.

Norma

by VINCENZO BELLINI
[1802–1835]

Libretto by
FELICE ROMANI
Based on a play by Alexandre Soumet

CHARACTERS

Oroveso, the Arch-Druid, father of Norma	*Bass*
Pollione, the Roman proconsul	*Tenor*
Flavio, his centurion	*Tenor*
Norma, high priestess of the Druids	*Soprano*
Adalgisa, a temple virgin	*Contralto*
Clotilda, Norma's companion	*Mezzo-soprano*

Druids and Druidesses, temple virgins, attendants,
Gallic soldiers, the two children of Norma

Place: Gaul
Time: During the Roman occupation, about 50 B.C.
First performance: Teatro La Scala, Milan, December 26, 1831
Original language: Italian

THE DRUIDS, about whom the story of *Norma* revolves, were members of a religious order which wielded great influence among the ancient tribes of Gaul, Britain, and Ireland. They were regarded as having the gift of prophecy, and all civil and military affairs required their sanction. Their authority was above that of kings and military leaders. Serving in the temples, the Druids were under severe self-imposed discipline. The high priestesses, in particular, committed themselves to rigorous devotion and took the vows of chastity. The high priestess Norma betrayed her vows, loved the Roman proconsul, Pollione, and bore him two children. At the time the story begins Pollione has grown tired of Norma and has become infatuated with Adalgisa, a temple virgin.

The stirring overture opens with a warlike fanfare and then takes up the theme of the opening chorus of Druids and Gallic warriors.

Act One

A clearing in the center of a sacred grove of the Druids. It is dominated by a huge oak tree, with its great branches thickly entwined with mistletoe. Beneath the tree is a large stone altar. To the accompaniment of a grave, martial air, Druid priests and Gallic warriors come into the grove in solemn procession. The last to appear is the Arch-Druid Oroveso. As the men arrange themselves in formal order Oroveso issues his command to the priests, "Ite sul colle, O Druidi." They are to ascend to the mountaintop to watch for the rising of the new moon. When it is sighted, the great bronze shield of the war-god Irminsul is to be struck three times, a signal for the cutting of the mistletoe, the sacred ceremony which Norma is to perform.

The men respond in one of the great choruses for which the opera is famous, "Dell' aura tua profetica." They implore the aid of Irminsul in destroying the Roman legions and driving them from their land. Rome's days are numbered, they cry. As they sing, the men make their way up the paths leading to the mountaintop. Their voices die away in the distance.

When the grove is deserted Pollione and Flavio appear. Flavio reminds the proconsul that Norma has warned them that they risk death in coming to this sacred spot. At the mention of her name Pollione recoils. Flavio, surprised, asks him why he is troubled at hearing the name of the woman he loves. Pollione then confesses that he no longer loves Norma but has become enamored of Adalgisa, a beautiful young virgin of the temple. Norma's vengeance, he admits, would be terrible to contemplate, were she to learn she has a rival. In a dramatic refrain he tells Flavio of a vision ("Meco all'altar di Venere"). He was kneeling with Adalgisa before the altar of Venus in Rome. Her hand was clasped in his, and they were rapturously happy. Suddenly an awful mist enveloped the altar, blotting out the daylight. When he turned to look at Adalgisa, Pollione continues, she had vanished, and only a moan answered his anguished cry for her. Then a terrible voice reverberated through the temple, intoning that thus Norma avenges herself on her false lover ("Norma così facempio, d'amante traditor").

Pollione's narrative is interrupted by a fanfare of Druid trumpets and the booming of the war shield. The voices of the returning Druids are heard in the distance ("Sorta e la luna, o Druidi"). Flavio warns the proconsul to flee, but Pollione cries that he will defy these barbarians. In an ensuing aria he declares that the flame of his new love will not only protect him but will destroy the infidels and their altars ("Me protegge, me difende"). Yielding to Flavio's pleas, he rushes away with him just before the Druids reappear.

Accompanied by virgins and priestesses, the Druids and warriors assemble in the grove and sing a mighty chorus acclaiming Norma and invoking the protection of Irminsul ("Norma viene"). Attended by her retinue of maidens, Norma ascends the steps of the main altar. She is dressed in a flowing robe and on her head is a wreath of sacred flowers. In her hand she carries a golden sickle with which to cut the mistletoe.

She rebukes the Druids for demanding war on Rome without the sanction of divine authority. The fate of Rome, she declares, will be pronounced not by mortals, but by gods. When Oroveso, in angry impatience, asks when Rome's tyranny will cease, Norma replies that the city will be destroyed from within by its own evil. Until that day, she says, there must be peace. With that she cuts a few branches of mistletoe, symbolic of a peace offering, and drops them into a cloth held by priestesses.

Norma then sings the great aria, "Casta Diva." The first

part is an entreaty to the pure Queen of Heaven to cleanse the hearts of her people from lawless and warlike emotions, so that peace may prevail. In the second part ("Ah! bello a me ritorna") she voices her distress over the fact that the hatred of the Druids is directed against the man she loves—the proconsul. She expresses her longing for one word from him indicating that his love for her has reawakened. The sentiments of the Druids, dominated by thoughts of vengeance, find expression in a choral accompaniment to her aria. After its climax Norma leaves the grove, the Druids following in procession.

Adalgisa now appears and hesitantly approaches the altar. She laments that, although Pollione's love has caused her to betray her religion, she cannot drive away her thoughts of him. Confused and frightened, she throws herself on the steps of the altar and implores the gods to save her from this fatal love ("Deh! proteggimi, o Dio!"). As she prays Pollione rushes in. He tries to embrace her, but she repels his advances and entreats him to leave. A long and dramatic colloquy follows. Pollione at first reproaches her for spurning him when he willingly would sacrifice himself on the altar of her gods for the sake of her love ("Va, crudele").

Repeating the refrain, Adalgisa sings that the burden of sin weighs heavily on the soul of a maiden whose innocence has been betrayed. Pollione begs her to flee with him to Rome, where they can be forever happy ("Vieni in Roma"). Yielding at length to his fervent entreaties, Adalgisa rushes into his arms, crying that she will follow him no matter what her fate may be. He asks her to meet him at this same spot tomorrow at the same hour, after which they will escape. Their voices blend exultantly as the curtain falls.

The scene changes to Norma's home, a huge rocky cave.[1] Animal skins are hung about the walls. The furniture consists of rough benches and a couch covered with skins. Through the doorway at the back the Druid temple is visible, and beyond it the wild countryside. It is a rude and barbaric scene.

---

[1] *Norma* was originally written in two acts but is sometimes played in four. In that case, this becomes Act Two.

Norma comes in leading her two children. With her is Clotilda, her companion. Norma, greatly agitated, confides that Pollione has been recalled to Rome but as yet has given her no sign that she is to go with him. She cries that the thought of his deserting her would drive her to madness. Hearing someone approach, she tells Clotilda to take the children away.

As they are led from the room Adalgisa timidly enters. Noting the girl's troubled demeanor, Norma quietly tells her to approach and unburden herself. Adalgisa then confesses that she has yielded to love and has resolved to flee from the temple. When Norma asks how it happened, Adalgisa describes how she and her lover first met and tells of the ecstasy of her awakening love. Overwhelmed by recollections of her own experience, Norma scarcely seems to hear. She murmurs that she once tasted the same bliss.

Fearing punishment, Adalgisa implores Norma to give her strength to resist the lure of her passion. In answer, Norma embraces the girl and absolves her from her sacred vows. In a tender refrain she describes the joys of love that will be hers ("Ah! si, fa core e abbraccia"). The voices of the two women blend melodiously as Adalgisa asks Norma to repeat the words she has longed to hear. Norma then asks who her lover is. A Roman, the girl replies, and at that moment Pollione appears in the doorway. Norma is transfixed with horror, while Pollione, gazing at Adalgisa, waits tensely for the storm to break. Adalgisa, bewildered and uncomprehending, looks from one to the other. Confronting the proconsul, Norma breaks into a wild denunciation of his treachery. Cowering in fear, Adalgisa brokenly implores Pollione to explain what has happened.

A fiery trio now ensues. Seizing Adalgisa's arm, Norma forces her to look at Pollione, crying out that this man, in duping an innocent girl, has committed a double crime of deceit and betrayal. Adalgisa, now realizing the enormity of Pollione's offense against the high priestess, sings that the thought of Norma's anguish numbs her own. Pollione implores Norma to let her wrath fall on him alone, declaring that his passion for Adalgisa makes him defy hell itself. He tries to force Adalgisa to go with him, but she cowers terror-stricken in Norma's arms and refuses to leave.

In wild fury Norma then orders Pollione out of her sight ("Vanne, sì, mi lascia indegno"). The proconsul defies her rage, while Adalgisa gives way to despair. As the trio rises to a powerful climax the voices of the Druids are heard in the temple, warning Norma that the god Irminsul is summoning her. Above the surge of voices comes the booming of the shield, the signal for the temple rites. Norma, her arms protectingly around Adalgisa, moves toward the door. With a gesture of baffled fury Pollione rushes away.

Act Two

Norma's home.[2] The two children are seen asleep on the couch. During a somber orchestral prelude Norma enters carrying a lamp. In one hand she holds a dagger. Setting the lamp on the table, she gazes wildly at the children, resolving to kill them. Their helpless innocence makes her pause, however, and she voices her love for them in a brief but moving air ("Teneri figli"). Then, remembering that they are also the children of the treacherous Pollione, her hatred returns. But no sooner has she raised her dagger to strike than she falls to her knees beside the bed, sobbing that she cannot kill her own children. Calling Clotilda, she tells her to summon Adalgisa.

When Adalgisa appears, Norma, now determined to end her life, tells the girl to take the children to Pollione in the Roman camp. In a moving refrain she commits the children to Adalgisa's care ("Deh! con te li prendi"). Adalgisa, trying to dissuade Norma from taking her life, cries that she has resolved never to leave the temple. Instead, she will go to Pollione and entreat him to come back to the woman who loves him and who bore his children. When Norma distractedly asks her to leave Adalgisa leads the two children before their mother, bids them kneel, and lifts up their hands in a gesture

[2] Act Three when played in four acts.

of entreaty. Then begins the beautiful duet, "Mira o Norma." Adalgisa exhorts the high priestess to let her heart be swayed by a mother's love.

At first abandoning herself to despair, Norma is gradually won over by the fervor of the girl's entreaties. Adalgisa finally convinces her that she has forever rejected Pollione's love and that she will go to him only to plead for Norma. Deeply moved, Norma embraces Adalgisa. Calling Clotilda, she signals her to take the children away. In the lyrical concluding phrases of the duet Norma and Adalgisa pledge their eternal friendship and devotion.

The scene changes to a wild rocky clearing in the sacred forest.[3] The Gallic warriors meet with the Druids to report on the movements of the Romans, and the conference is carried on in a dramatic chorus ("Non partì? Finora è al campo"). The warriors sing that the hated proconsul has not yet withdrawn his forces, and the Druids join them in declaring that they must bide their time until they can strike at the foe with full strength.

Oroveso now appears and informs them that Pollione is to be succeeded by an even more tyrannical commander. The men angrily ask if Norma still counsels peace. Oroveso answers that the high priestess keeps silent. When the men ask what course they are to take Oroveso replies in a dramatic aria ("Ah! del Tebro al giogo indegno"). Though the Romans hold them in bondage, he declares, they must appear to submit meekly while gathering their forces. Then, when the foe is lulled into a false sense of security, they will rise and drive him from the land. Druids and warriors echo Oroveso's sentiments in an accompanying chorus.

There is a change of scene to an open court at the entrance of the temple of Irminsul.[4] In the center of the court is a stone altar. Near it hangs the shield of Irminsul and the club that is

[3] Scene One of Act Four when played in four acts.
[4] Scene Two of Act Four when played in four acts.

used to strike it. Norma, standing near the altar, waits for the return of Adalgisa with the repentant Pollione.

Her hopes are dashed, however, when Clotilda rushes in with the news that Adalgisa's entreaties were useless. Far from yielding, Pollione tried to force her to go with him. Adalgisa managed to escape and flee to the temple, and the proconsul has even tried to pursue her into the sacred precincts.

In a frenzy of rage Norma rushes to the shield and strikes it three times. At this signal for war Oroveso appears, followed by Druids, Druidesses, and warriors, who throng in from all sides. Standing with upraised arms on the altar steps, Norma shouts that the gods have decreed war. The people answer in a fiery chorus ("Guerra! le Galliche selve"), in which they swear to wipe the Romans from the face of the earth.

When the chorus is stilled Oroveso steps forward to say that no sacrifice has been prepared for the altar of the wargod. Norma grimly assures him that the rite will take place. At that moment there is a commotion outside, and Clotilda hastens in, crying that a Roman has desecrated the temple by entering it. As she speaks Pollione is brought in by warriors and led before the altar, where he stands with folded arms, gazing arrogantly at the crowd. Oroveso takes his sacrificial knife from his belt and advances toward the proconsul. Norma snatches the knife from her father's hand and is about to plunge it into Pollione's breast when she pauses. The people murmur in surprise. Announcing that she wishes to question the prisoner to ascertain if some traitor perhaps aided him in gaining access to the temple, Norma asks Oroveso and the others to withdraw. They slowly leave the court.

Dagger in hand, she approaches Pollione. A dramatic duet follows ("In mia man alfin tu sei"). Reminding the proconsul that he is in her power, she tells him that she will spare his life if he will give up Adalgisa. He fiercely refuses. Norma then threatens to kill his children, whereupon he begs her to let him be the victim if she must have revenge. Furious over his refusal to relinquish Adalgisa, Norma declares that the girl must die because the gods demand a sacrifice. At that Pollione kneels before her and entreats her to take his life. Norma scornfully answers that she will torture him to the utmost by sacrificing the woman he loves.

After the stormy climax of the duet Norma turns toward the altar. Desperately the proconsul tries to snatch the dagger away from her. She flings him off, mounts the steps of the altar, and calls to Oroveso and the Druids. Pollione stands transfixed as the people gather to hear Norma's judgment. In ringing tones she cries that she offers a new victim for the sacrifice—a virgin who has not only broken her vows of chastity but has betrayed her country. As the crowd angrily demands her name, Pollione, certain that she will doom Adalgisa, implores Norma not to speak.

Then, answering the roar of the crowd, Norma proclaims that the guilty one is herself ("Son io"). With that she slowly takes the wreath from her head and lets it fall to the ground. Quietly she orders the sacrificial pyre to be prepared. Pollione distractedly protests Norma's self-accusation.

Turning to Pollione, Norma sings that, despite his treachery, her love will bind them together beyond the grave ("Qual cor tradisti"). He replies that he has learned too late the depth of her devotion and begs to be allowed to share her fate. Oroveso and the Druids exhort Norma to repudiate her judgment, saying that it must have been uttered in a moment of madness. But Norma approaches her father and declares that she is guilty beyond hope of pardon. She asks only that he take her innocent children into his care so that they will not be left to the mercy of the Romans. Oroveso refuses.

Kneeling before him, Norma makes a final desperate plea in behalf of her children ("Deh! non volerli vittime"), while several priests come forward holding the black veil of death which is placed over the heads of sacrificial victims. Norma's refrain leads into the powerfully dramatic ensemble which concludes the opera. Oroveso, now yielding to his daughter, promises to protect her children and then asks her to embrace him in farewell. Pollione sings that his only wish is to mount the sacrificial pyre with Norma. The Druids and Druidesses grimly intone that this sacrifice will cleanse their altar and temple of defilement.

Throwing the black veil over Norma's head, the priests command her to go to her doom ("Vanne al rogo"). She embraces Oroveso and then sinks into Pollione's arms. Surrounded by the priests, Norma and Pollione walk slowly toward the pyre. As the chorus rises to a climax the curtain falls.

Le Nozze di Figaro
(The Marriage of Figaro)

by WOLFGANG AMADEUS MOZART
[1756–1791]

Libretto by
LORENZO DA PONTE

Based on Beaumarchais's comedy
LE MARIAGE DE FIGARO

CHARACTERS

Figaro, valet to Count Almaviva	*Baritone*
Susanna, fiancée of Figaro and maid to Countess Almaviva	*Soprano*
Dr. Bartolo	*Bass*
Marcellina, Dr. Bartolo's housemaid	*Soprano*
Cherubino, page to Count Almaviva	*Soprano*
Count Almaviva	*Baritone*
Don Basilio, a music teacher	*Tenor*
Countess Almaviva	*Soprano*
Antonio, a gardener, uncle of Susanna	*Bass*
Don Curzio, a lawyer	*Tenor*
Barbarina, daughter of Antonio	*Soprano*

Peasants, townspeople, servants

Place: The palace of Count Almaviva, near Seville
Time: Seventeenth century
First performance: Burgtheater, Vienna, May 1, 1786
Original language: Italian

ALTHOUGH *Le Nozze di Figaro* is a sequel to *Il Barbiere di Siviglia*, it was the first play of the Figaro trilogy to be produced as an opera. Rossini's *Il Barbiere* did not come along until some thirty years later. The principal characters, of course, appear in both operas. Rosina, who was wooed by Count Almaviva in *Il Barbiere*, appears in *Figaro* as the count's wife. Figaro, who has become the count's valet, is planning to marry Susanna, maid to Countess Almaviva. Don Basilio appears again as a music teacher, while Dr. Bartolo, still sulking over his failure to win Rosina and her fortune, continues his plotting against Figaro.

The brilliant overture is familiar to all concertgoers.

ACT ONE

Figaro's apartment, not yet completely furnished. Susanna is trying on a hat, critically observing the effect in a mirror. Figaro is measuring the room. In a brief duet Susanna asks Figaro his opinion of the hat, while he tries to divide his attention between measuring and giving Susanna the proper answer ("Cinque, dieci, venti, trenta").

In recitative he explains that he is trying to find out if the room will accommodate the bed which the count has given them as a wedding gift.[1] Susanna promptly objects to using this room as their bedroom. The two argue the matter in an ensuing duet in which Figaro points out how convenient the arrangement would be, with the count's apartment on one side and the countess's on the other ("Se a caso madama la notte ti chiama"). Should they call at night, it would be but two steps to their respective doors. Suppose, Susanna retorts, the count should send Figaro on a journey for a few days. It would be very convenient for his lordship to have Susanna's room but two steps from his own.

To Figaro's complete astonishment, Susanna reveals that the count is infatuated with her and is determined to take advantage of his feudal rights as master of the house (the right

[1] In present-day performances most of the recitatives are given in spoken dialogue.

to woo a maid in his service before she is wed to another servant). Susanna leaves to answer the countess's ring.

Now it is clear, muses Figaro, why he and Susanna have been asked to accompany the count to London, where he is to serve as minister. He expresses his thoughts on the matter in the well-known aria "Se vuol ballare, Signor Contino." If that is the way Sir Count wishes to dance, sings Figaro, he shall be glad to play the tune. Meanwhile he has a few tricks of his own up his sleeve. At the conclusion of his aria he leaves.

Bartolo and Marcellina enter, discussing the contract signed by Figaro stipulating that he will either pay back the money he borrowed from Marcellina or marry her. The two then plot to turn the count against Susanna, in the hope that he will support Marcellina in her attempts to marry Figaro. In a spirited aria Bartolo describes how he will launch a campaign of vengeance that will bring this scoundrel Figaro to his knees ("La vendetta!"). After he stalks pompously from the room Marcellina encounters Susanna returning from the countess's room with one of her mistress's dresses and a ribbon. The two women address each other with studied courtesy and then, in a sparkling duet, proceed to exchange feminine insults ("Via resti servita"). Finding herself no match for Susanna, Marcellina rushes furiously from the room.

While Susanna is still calling choice sarcasms after her, Cherubino enters. The page, in great distress, explains that the count, having caught him with his arms around Barbarina, is about to send him away. He cannot bear to leave, he sighs, because of his current passion for the countess. Susanna is to be envied, he goes on ardently, for she is always near his beloved. Cherubino manages to snatch the countess's hair ribbon out of Susanna's hands, offering in exchange a love song he has just written. It is a song for all the beautiful women in the world, he exclaims, and then sings the charming and amorous serenade "Non so più cosa son."

Susanna warns him that the count is approaching, and Cherubino quickly hides behind an armchair. Almaviva seats

Le Nozze di Figaro

himself in the armchair, much to Susanna's alarm, and adds to her confusion by making love to her. As he tries to persuade her to meet him in the garden that night, Basilio's voice is heard outside. The count starts to go behind the chair, whereupon Cherubino, screened by Susanna, deserts his hiding place and slips into the chair. Susanna flings the countess's dress over him just as Basilio enters.

Looking around suspiciously, Basilio asks Susanna if she has seen the count, adding that Figaro is looking for him. He continues with insinuating references to the count's attentions to Susanna and hints at her flirtation with Cherubino. He advises her to warn the page to restrain his affection for the countess, because it is becoming obvious to everyone in the palace. At that the count emerges angrily, and an excited trio follows ("Cosa sento!").

When the count orders Basilio to bring the page to him at once, Basilio smugly protests that the boy meant no harm. Susanna almost faints, but manages to prevent the two men from leading her to the armchair. Basilio deliberately keeps harping on the subject of Cherubino. The count tells how he caught the page in Barbarina's room only yesterday. Demonstrating how he found the culprit, he walks over to the chair and pulls away the dress, only to find Cherubino in virtually the same predicament.

Angry and chagrined, Almaviva determines to call in Figaro and tell him that Susanna has been deceiving him with Cherubino. He changes his mind, however, when he realizes that the page overheard him making love to Susanna herself only a few moments ago. To hide his confusion he turns angrily on Cherubino, but is interrupted by the entrance of a group of peasants carrying flowers and singing the praises of the count. With them is Figaro, holding a bridal veil.

He explains that the demonstration is honoring the count for having revoked the laws of feudal privilege, adding that he and Susanna wish to be the first to take advantage of his enlightened action by being married this very day. He requests the count to place the bridal veil on Susanna's head in token of his blessing. Almaviva, well aware of Figaro's ruse, asks that the wedding celebration be postponed until evening. Then, he murmurs in an aside, he will thwart Figaro's plans by bringing Marcellina on the scene. The peasants withdraw as they repeat their chorus. Cherubino begs the count not to be too harsh with him, and Susanna and Figaro add their entreaties. Determined to send the page away from the castle, Almaviva decides to give him the post of ensign in his regiment, with the stipulation that he join immediately. The count and Basilio leave.

Figaro offers Cherubino some parting advice in an amusing aria, "Non più andrai," a delightful parody on military heroics. He tells the page that he must now give up his amorous exploits for the sterner duties of war and describes the glories of coming back as a hero—assuming, of course, that he will be lucky enough to come back alive. Joined by Susanna, they march off in mock-military style. The curtain falls.

Act Two

The countess's apartment. At one side is the entrance door of the apartment and near it the door of an adjoining room. On the other side is the door of the dressing room. At the rear is a window. In the moving aria "Porgi amor" the countess laments that the count no longer loves her. Susanna enters, and the two discuss Almaviva's wayward affections. They are interrupted by Figaro, who informs them that the count, nettled because Susanna has thwarted his romantic schemes, has gone over to the enemy—that is, Marcellina. But, says Figaro, he means to trap the count in his own intrigues. Basilio has been sent to the count with an anonymous letter warning him that the countess has arranged to meet an admirer in the garden tonight during the ball. Meanwhile Susanna is to ask the count to meet her in the garden at the same time, but Cherubino, dressed as a girl, will go in her place. The countess will then surprise her husband and thus have him at her mercy. While he is preoccupied with his difficulties, Susanna and Figaro will be quietly married. The three plotters decide to act at once, because the count is away hunting. Figaro goes to fetch Cherubino, and as he leaves he repeats a phrase of his aria, "Se vuol ballare, Signor Contino."

When the page arrives to try on Susanna's clothes, he is persuaded to sing another one of his compositions. With Susanna accompanying him on the guitar, he sings the famous aria "Voi, che sapete," in which he describes how he is tormented by the pangs of young love. While the countess compliments him on his singing, Susanna locks the door of the apartment and then goes into the dressing room. Cherubino shows the countess his commission, and she remarks in surprise that it still lacks the official seal.

An amusing scene now follows, in which Susanna, having brought out a dress, gives Cherubino a lesson in feminine mannerisms. She explains how he is to act in the delightful aria "Venite inginocchiatevi." The page proves so adept at imitation that Susanna is quite overwhelmed by his charm. The countess discovers that he has bound her ribbon around his arm to bandage a cut. She asks to have it back, but is touched by his ardor when he implores to be allowed to keep it. Susanna goes into an adjoining room to bring a new ribbon. In her absence Cherubino declares his love to the countess.

His avowals are interrupted by a knock at the door, and the count's voice is heard outside. Cherubino rushes into the dressing room and locks the door, while the countess, trying to control her agitation, opens the apartment door. Almaviva enters with Figaro's letter in his hand. He first demands to know why the door was locked, then asks her to explain the letter. As he watches her suspiciously, there is a noise in the dressing room. The countess explains that Susanna is trying on her wedding gown.

A lively trio follows. The count orders Susanna to come out, while the countess warns her to stay inside. Susanna, who has meanwhile slipped unnoticed out of the adjoining room and is hiding in an alcove, calmly appraises the situation. When the countess refuses to open the dressing-room door, Almaviva furiously declares that he will bring tools to force the door, then orders his wife to come with him. As they leave, the count locks the apartment door from the outside.

Cherubino bursts out of the dressing room. When Susanna tells him that he is locked in the apartment, he rushes panic-stricken to the window and jumps out. There is a tremendous crash below. Susanna looks down, sees that he has made his escape, then runs into the dressing room and locks the door just as the count and the countess re-enter. Unaware that Cherubino has fled, the countess confesses that it was the page who locked himself in her dressing room. In a fury Almaviva forces his wife to give him the key, unlocks the door, and, drawing his sword, commands Cherubino to come out.

Susanna appears, demurely greeting the count, who stares at her in bewilderment, while the countess nearly faints in surprise and confusion. When the count rushes in to search the room, Susanna assures the countess that Cherubino has safely escaped. Making the most of the situation, the countess roundly upbraids her husband for his suspicions. Abjectly he begs her forgiveness. As to the anonymous letter, the countess and Susanna decide to make an end to their plotting and confess that Figaro wrote it.

They have almost succeeded in placating the count when in walks Figaro. Questioned by Almaviva, he denies writing the letter. The countess and Susanna, having failed to warn him in time, try to pass the letter off as a joke. They implore the count to put no further obstacles in the way of the marriage. Almaviva fumes because Marcellina has not arrived.

To make matters worse, Antonio the gardener now enters. He is quite drunk and is carrying a broken flowerpot. He loudly complains that for some time a variety of rubbish has been flung out of the castle windows into his flower beds. Now the limit has been reached: someone threw down a man. Susanna and the countess, in a desperate aside, implore Figaro to save the situation. He makes an attempt by declaring that he himself jumped out of the window. When Antonio remarks that the man he saw seemed much smaller and younger, the count angrily exclaims, "Cherubino!" Figaro quickly says that the page evidently returned on horseback,

Le Nozze di Figaro

because he left for Seville this morning. Antonio says that he saw no horse fall from the window.

Figaro, in growing panic, repeats that it was he who jumped. He tells the count that he was waiting for Susanna when he heard the count outside. Fearing his master's wrath because of the letter, he made his escape via the window. He limps about, saying he hurt his ankle.

At this crucial point Antonio shows Figaro a paper which he found in the flower bed. The count snatches it away, and the others are horrified to discover that it is Cherubino's commission. Figaro stammers that the page left it with him because it had not yet been stamped with the official seal. Completely out of patience, Almaviva tears up the document.

Matters are now brought to a climax with the appearance of Marcellina, Dr. Bartolo, and Don Basilio, who present Figaro's contract to the count and demand that the barber be made to fulfill his obligations. The count, seeing his opportunity to revenge himself on Susanna and Figaro, promises to give the matter proper consideration. A brilliant ensemble ends the act.

Act Three

A hall in the palace, decorated for the wedding festivities. The count, pacing about, is musing on the complicated state of affairs of his household. When his back is turned the countess and Susanna enter, the countess urging her maid to arrange a rendezvous with her husband in the garden. She herself will then meet him there. When Susanna mentions Figaro, the countess suggests leaving him out of things for the moment.

The countess steals away, and Susanna approaches Almaviva, overhearing him say to himself that he will force Figaro to marry Marcellina. At that Susanna makes herself known and calmly tells him that she will buy off Marcellina with the dowry the count himself has promised her. She lures him into again declaring his love for her. They arrange the meeting in the garden as they sing the charming duet that begins with the count's fervent expression of his love, "Crudel! perchè finora."

Almaviva now leaves as he hears Figaro approaching. Unfortunately, he overhears Susanna exclaim to Figaro that now they have won their campaign. In fury over Susanna's perfidy, the count resolves to thwart her plans. Even though they have bought off Marcellina, he fumes, he will persuade Antonio not to allow his niece to marry Figaro. He will arouse the gardener's exaggerated sense of family pride by telling him that Figaro is of dubious parentage. Then, in the imposingly dramatic aria "Vedrò mentr'io sospiro," he swears he will have revenge.

He is about to go when he encounters Marcellina, the stammering lawyer Don Curzio, Bartolo, and Figaro. Then and there Marcellina's suit is to be settled, Don Curzio having decided that Figaro's contract is valid—he must either pay his debt or marry Marcellina. Figaro protests that he is of noble birth and cannot marry without the consent of his parents. Unfortunately, he continues, he was stolen from them in babyhood, but he has proof of his identity in a certain birthmark. Marcellina asks him if it is under his right elbow. Figaro answers that it is, whereupon Marcellina joyfully exclaims that she is his mother and Bartolo his father—to Bartolo's acute discomfiture.

Another ensemble number follows. Figaro and his parents fondly greet each other, while Don Curzio and Almaviva express surprise and disappointment. Susanna runs in with money to pay Figaro's fine, only to find him embracing Marcellina. Storming that Figaro is deserting her for her rival at the crucial moment, she boxes his ears. During the ensuing sextet, however, things are explained to her satisfaction. After the number Curzio and the count leave, muttering darkly that the happiness of the others will be short-lived. Marcellina and Bartolo decide on a double wedding and give Figaro back his contract, along with a purse, as a dowry. Susanna hands him the money which was to pay the fine. They all leave happily together.

Le Nozze di Figaro

Barbarina enters with Cherubino, who has returned secretly from Seville. In order to conceal his presence from the count, he decides to dress himself as a girl and join the flower maidens in presenting bouquets to the countess. The two go on their way. Then the countess enters, expressing deep concern about the probable results of Susanna's rendezvous with the count. In the beautiful, stately aria "Dove sono" she recalls the happiness of the past with her husband and voices the fervent hope that she may win back his love. After the aria she leaves to look for Susanna.

The count appears briefly with Antonio, who, showing him Cherubino's cap, insists that the page has returned. The countess, re-entering with Susanna, tells her she must write a note to the count, definitely fixing the time and place for the rendezvous. The engaging *Letter Duet* follows ("Che soave zeffiretto"). Susanna, writing at the countess's dictation, repeats the words after her in answering phrases. Instead of sealing the letter, they use a pin, writing on the paper that the pin is to be returned with the bearer.

Susanna hides the note in her dress as the peasant girls approach for the flower ceremony. Singing a brief chorus, they present bouquets to the countess, who, catching sight of Cherubino in girl's costume, remarks on "her" resemblance to the page. Antonio, entering with the count, makes his way through the crowd to Cherubino, snatches off his girl's hat, and puts the soldier's cap on his head. There is great consternation, and the count threatens Cherubino with dire punishment. Thereupon Barbarina naïvely reminds the count that he promised her, in return for kisses and embraces, to grant anything she asked. She then requests his permission to marry Cherubino. Confused and embarrassed, Almaviva makes an evasive answer, and to himself he fumes that every move he makes works to his own disadvantage.

Figaro enters, gaily bidding all to prepare for the wedding dance. The count and Antonio, trying to trap him, present Cherubino, saying that the page has admitted jumping from the window. But Figaro imperturbably remarks that one man can leap from a window as well as another.

As the music of the bridal march begins, the count and countess seat themselves on a dais to welcome the wedding guests, who sing a chorus of praise as they march by. They then dance a fandango, during which Susanna secretly gives the count her letter. In opening it he pricks his finger with the pin, which he lets fall. Figaro, dancing near by, takes due note of this and observes to Susanna that the count evidently has received a letter from another admirer. The count invites the people to the wedding celebration which is to be held in the evening. They sing joyfully of the festivities in prospect.

Act Four

The garden of the palace, with arbors to the right and left. Barbarina enters carrying a lantern, and in a plaintive aria ("L'ho perduta") she laments over something she has lost. Figaro and Marcellina appear. Barbarina tells them that she has lost the pin which the count gave her to take back to Susanna with the message that it was to remind her of the "pine tree." Figaro, assuming, of course, that his fiancée is deceiving him with the count, rushes furiously away, swearing to revenge himself on the whole race of womankind. Marcellina, remarking that women must act together in their own interests, declares that she will warn Susanna.[2] Marcellina leaves, and Figaro reappears to sing his stormy aria, "Aprite un po' quegl' occhi" ("Open your eyes a little"), in which he voices his disillusionment and gives vent to his rage over woman's conniving and deceit. After the number he conceals himself in the background.

The countess and Susanna, dressed in each other's clothing, now enter, followed by Marcellina, who whispers that Figaro is near by. Deliberately raising their voices, the countess and Susanna talk about the rendezvous, and then the maid asks

[2] Following this, in the original score, is an aria for Marcellina, after which there is a short scene involving Figaro, Bartolo, and Basilio, then an aria for Basilio. Because of their relative unimportance—musically and dramatically—these scenes are generally omitted.

to be left alone. She sings the beautiful aria "Deh vieni, non tardar," an ardent expression of her love, not for the count but for Figaro, who she knows is listening.

As he looks on from his hiding place, raging over Susanna's treachery, Cherubino comes upon the scene. Obeying his natural impulse to woo every pretty woman he meets, he promptly begins making violent love to Susanna, not knowing, of course, that it is the countess in disguise. An exciting ensemble follows. While the countess is trying to fend off the page, the count rushes in with an ardent greeting to the supposed Susanna. Just as Cherubino tries to kiss her, the count interposes himself, and the page kisses him instead. He turns to slap Cherubino but hits Figaro, who has rushed into the melee at this point. The page makes his escape.

Figaro and Susanna now withdraw to different parts of the garden, while the count makes ardent love to his own wife, thinking she is Susanna. He gives her a ring as a pledge of his devotion. Figaro returns in time to see the count lead the disguised countess toward the arbor at the right. Lurking about in the darkness, Figaro encounters Susanna and, believing her to be the countess, tells her that now they both may trap the faithless pair. Susanna tries to disguise her voice, but in an unguarded moment she forgets, and Figaro realizes who she is. He deliberately continues the masquerade and, addressing her as the countess, passionately declares his love. Susanna, provoked to fury, boxes his ears. Figaro happily accepts the blows, convinced by this show of temper that Susanna really loves him.

The count now enters looking for the supposed Susanna, who has meanwhile eluded him. Figaro, catching sight of him, kneels before his "countess" in an exaggerated gesture of adoration, then both he and Susanna rush for the arbor to the left of the stage. Almaviva captures Figaro and shouts furiously for his servants. As Basilio, Bartolo, and Curzio rush in, he denounces his valet and declares that he will now unmask his partner in infidelity.

Storming into the arbor, the count drags forth, in comical procession, Cherubino, Barbarina, Marcellina, and Susanna.

The others, seeing Susanna still dressed as the countess, are dumfounded. As Susanna begs the count to forgive her, the countess herself emerges from the right-hand arbor. The situation now becomes clear to Almaviva. Thoroughly chastened and repenting his jealous suspicions, he implores his wife's forgiveness and is duly pardoned. All voice their joy over the happy denouément.

Otello

by GIUSEPPE VERDI
[1813–1901]

Libretto by
ARRIGO BOÏTO

Based on Shakespeare's tragedy
OTHELLO, THE MOOR OF VENICE

CHARACTERS

Montano, Otello's predecessor as governor of Cyprus	*Bass*
Cassio, Otello's lieutenant	*Tenor*
Iago, Otello's ensign	*Baritone*
Roderigo, a Venetian gentleman	*Tenor*
Otello, a noble Moor in the service of Venice	*Tenor*
Desdemona, Otello's wife	*Soprano*
Emilia, Iago's wife and Desdemona's companion	*Mezzo-soprano*
Lodovico, Ambassador of Venice	*Bass*
A herald	*Bass*

People of Cyprus, Venetian soldiers and sailors, innkeeper, servants, Venetian ladies and gentlemen

Place: A seaport in Cyprus
Time: Late fifteenth century
First performance: La Scala, Milan, February 5, 1887
Original language: Italian

THE OUTLINE of the opera's story follows closely Shakespeare's tragic play, *Othello*. Turkey is threatening the supremacy of the Venetian state in the Mediterranean and has launched an attack against the Venetian-held island of Cyprus. The Duke of Venice has sent out a fleet under Otello, an exceptionally brilliant general, who is also governor of Cyprus.

There is no overture. The curtain rises quickly after a few introductory bars.

Act One

An open square outside Otello's castle overlooking the sea. In the foreground is a tavern and in the background a quay. It is night and a storm is in full blow with much thunder and lightning. A ship has been sighted and identified as Otello's. A large crowd of people, including many soldiers, has gathered, all looking anxiously out to sea. Among the crowd are Iago, Roderigo, Cassio, and Montano.

The opening chorus describes the storm and voices the fear that the ship will be wrecked on the rocks. Iago, in an aside to Roderigo, says he would just as soon see the ship go down. But the danger passes and Otello comes safely ashore, followed by soldiers and sailors. In a brief solo beginning with the exclamation "Esultate!" he announces his overwhelming defeat of the Turks. The crowd cheers and sings of victory as Otello enters his castle, followed by Cassio, Montano, and the soldiers. The storm now subsides and the people start to build a bonfire.

Iago talks with Roderigo, a young gentleman who is much in love with Desdemona, Otello's wife. Roderigo is in despair over the hopelessness of his love, but Iago tells him to have courage and patience, for Desdemona will soon tire of Otello. Iago professes his friendship for Roderigo, adding that he hates Otello, though serving him and posing as his friend. Cassio re-enters and Iago points to him while pouring forth his scorn and envy. Cassio had been made Otello's lieutenant, a post Iago coveted for himself. Iago instead was named Otello's ensign, a lower post. It is this slight that has made Iago, in his burning ambition, hate Otello. He takes Roderigo aside to tell him more.

Otello

The bonfire has been lighted and the festive crowd sings of the brightly burning flame ("Fuoco di gioia"). As the firelight dies, servants set out colorful Venetian lanterns in the arbor adjoining the tavern. The soldiers gather about the tables and Iago, Roderigo, and Cassio join them in drinking. After several rounds, Iago urges Cassio to have another beaker of wine, but Cassio at first refuses, saying he has had enough. Iago then toasts the fair Desdemona and Cassio joins in the praise of her beauty. This fits in well with Iago's scheming. Now he works on Roderigo's passion and jealousy, telling him that Cassio, too, seeks Desdemona's love, and he cleverly points out how Cassio has just exalted her. "We must make him drink," Iago tells Roderigo. "If he drinks he is ruined."

Pressing more wine on Cassio, Iago surges into the rollicking yet sinister *Brindisi*, or drinking song ("Inaffia l'ugola!"). The chorus takes up the song. Cassio sings and drinks, gradually becoming so befuddled with wine he can sing no more. Iago had kept the song going for just this purpose. Having already slyly built up an active resentment to Cassio in the mind of Roderigo, he now urges him to provoke the drunken Cassio to combat so that an uproar will result and thus arouse Otello.

At this point Montano arrives to tell Cassio it is time for him to stand guard. He is concerned when he sees Cassio's condition, and Iago plays upon his apprehension, telling him that Cassio is always that way before going to sleep. Meanwhile Cassio has grown boisterous and quarrelsome. Roderigo provokes a fight by laughing at him. Montano attempts to intervene, telling Cassio he is drunk, whereupon Cassio draws his sword and attacks Montano.

Iago sends Roderigo off to sound the alarm, then turns to the furiously fighting pair and hypocritically orders them to stop. Montano is wounded. Finally the alarm sounds and Otello appears, followed by men with torches. The fighting ceases.

Otello demands an explanation. Iago innocently claims that he cannot understand it. They were as the closest of friends, then suddenly, as if mad, they drew their weapons. Cassio, ashamed, has nothing to say.

Awakened by the tumult, Desdemona enters. Otello, in great anger, dismisses Cassio from his service for provoking the disturbance. This, of course, is just what Iago had hoped to accomplish. Otello dispatches Iago to quiet the city and Montano is assisted into the castle. The crowd disperses.

Otello and Desdemona are left alone. The act closes with a tender love duet ("Gia nella notta densa") in which the Moor and Desdemona recall the hours they spent together when he beguiled her with his stories of danger and hardship in battle, and she thus came to love him. Their joy overwhelms them. Three times Otello kisses Desdemona ("Un bacio . . . un bacio . . . ancora un bacio") to the accompaniment of the kiss motive, the words and music of which are repeated at the very end of the opera with such telling effect. The storm clouds have now passed and the scene is bathed in moonlight. With their arms about each other Desdemona and Otello return to the castle as the curtain falls.

Act Two

A room on the ground floor of Otello's castle. At the rear an arched doorway leads out to a garden. When the curtain rises Iago is conversing with Cassio, telling him that Desdemona is usually to be found in the garden at noontime and that his best chance of mending his fortune lies in persuading her to plead his cause before Otello. "She is our general's general and of a kind nature. She will obtain your pardon."

Cassio agrees that Iago's plan is a good one and walks into the garden to await Desdemona. Iago gazes after him with a look of contempt and then, as Cassio disappears among the trees, gives voice to his cynical and altogether contemptible philosophy of life, singing the famous *Credo* ("Credo in un Dio crudel che m'ha creato"). This is an extremely effective aria that reveals the full treachery and villainy of his character. He believes in a cruel God who has fashioned him in His own image. He believes that life is made but to feed death and that good, honest men are only wretched actors whose so-called virtues—pity, love, unselfishness, and honor—are but falsehoods. (The text of the *Credo*, incidentally, is Boïto's own invention and doesn't occur in Shakespeare's play.)

Iago pauses as Desdemona comes into the garden, then calls out softly to Cassio, "Go to her. This is the moment." Cassio approaches her. While Iago expresses his satisfaction in the progress of his plot, Cassio and Desdemona walk back and forth at the end of the garden in earnest conversation.

Iago's luck continues. He sees Otello approaching but pretends not to. Leaning against a column and staring toward the garden, he talks as though to himself: "I don't like that." His words arouse Otello's curiosity. The Moor glances out into the garden just as Cassio and Desdemona are disappearing from view. He quickly turns to Iago, asking if that was not Cassio with his wife. Iago answers evasively and craftily arouses the Moor's suspicions by means of hints and continued questions. He asks, for instance, if Cassio knew of Otello's passion for Desdemona in the days when he wooed her. Otello answers: "Yes, why do you ask?" "Just for the satisfaction of my thought," replies Iago. "I did not think he knew her then." "Oh yes," says Otello, "he was often my messenger to carry tender words to her." Iago murmurs: "Indeed," as if to imply that Otello had been too trusting.

Otello sees that Iago has something on his mind and begs him to come out with it; but Iago again replies in riddles, telling him to beware of jealousy, "the green-eyed monster which doth mock the meat it feeds on." Furiously Otello says he will cast aside suspicion and jealousy and will require proof before he doubts. Playing up to his mood, Iago agrees that proof is needed. "Watch closely," he advises, "so that your faith may be restored or your suspicions confirmed."

At this point Desdemona returns to the garden, surrounded by women, children, and sailors who bring her flowers and gifts. They sing Desdemona's praises, accompanying themselves on mandolins and small harps ("Dove guardi splendono"). This scene emphasizes the noble gentleness of Desdemona's nature and the utter contrast between her character and that of the unprincipled, scheming Iago. Otello's attitude toward her softens.

At the conclusion of this little scene Desdemona comes through the archway from the garden into the house, followed by her serving woman, Emilia, who is Iago's wife. Desdemona, of course, knows nothing of the suspicion which Iago has planted in Otello's mind, and in a generous-hearted way begs her husband to reinstate Cassio. He tries to avoid the subject, but she insists. This only seems to arouse Otello's suspicions still further. He begins to think Iago is right and that Desdemona might actually be in love with Cassio. She notices the troubled look on her husband's face and, being a loving wife, asks if he is ill. "Are you not well?" "I have a pain upon my forehead here," he answers. She tries to soothe him by binding her handkerchief around his head, but Otello rudely snatches the handkerchief and throws it to the floor. Desdemona is astonished and dismayed, especially as the handkerchief she offered him was his own first gift to her—a handkerchief with little strawberry designs on it. Emilia recovers the handkerchief.

A dramatic quartet follows in which Desdemona declares her love for Otello and begs forgiveness if she has ever offended him ("Se inconscia, contro te, sposo, ho peccato"). The Moor tells himself that his heart is broken and his golden dream of love scattered in the dust. Iago, who has seen Emilia pick up the handkerchief, demands that she give it to him. Suspicious that he is up to some wicked scheme, she refuses, but he grasps her arm and snatches it from her. He gloats that now he has them in his meshes, while Emilia prays to God to save them from disaster.

Otello orders them all to leave him. Iago admonishes Emilia to say nothing of the incident. Desdemona and Emilia leave, but Iago moves only to the door at the rear as Otello throws himself into a chair and cries out the grief that is in him. Behind him, Iago carefully examines the handkerchief, then puts it away, saying: "Trifles are as good proof as holy writ to the jealous. I will lose this napkin in Cassio's house and let him find it." He watches Otello with grim satisfaction. "The Moor already changes with my poison." Then, approaching Otello cordially: "General, no more of that."

Otello accuses Iago of causing his grief by arousing his suspicion. " 'Tis better to be much abused than but to know it a little," he states. In a touching melody he says farewell to peace of mind, to his thoughts of fame, to his whole military career ("Ora e per sempre addio sante memorie").

Iago pretends to soothe Otello's feelings. This merely infuriates Otello, who throws himself on Iago. Grasping him by the throat and throwing him down, he demands that he prove his accusations. Iago, rising, feigns wounded vanity that his honest efforts should thus be treated, and he is reluctant to speak. He allows Otello to press him for proof. Finally he tells of spending the night with Cassio recently and hearing Cassio murmur of his love for Desdemona in his sleep ("Era la notte, Cassio dormia, gli stavo accanto"). He goes still further: "Have you not sometimes seen a handkerchief spotted with strawberries in your wife's hand?" "It was my first gift to her," answers Otello. "I have seen it in Cassio's hand lately," Iago states. Otello is now beside himself with jealousy. He kneels, lifts his arms heavenward, and cries out a great oath of vengeance ("Sì, pel ciel marmoreo giuro!"). Iago's duplicity at this point is almost unbelievable. As Otello is about to rise, he holds him down and, kneeling beside him, he too swears to avenge himself upon those who have wronged Otello. Their voices blend in ringing phrases, and upon this duet the curtain falls.

Act Three

The great hall of the castle. At one side is a large portico. At the rear is a terrace. The room is vast and richly appointed. At one side is a raised throne.

After a brief orchestral introduction the curtain rises on Otello and Iago in the hall. From the portico a herald announces that a galley bringing ambassadors to Cyprus has been sighted. Otello dismisses the herald and, turning to Iago, urges him to go on with the tale he has been telling. Iago explains to Otello that he has agreed to meet Cassio very shortly in the great hall of the castle, and that if Otello wants proof of Desdemona's guilt he should hide and listen. As Desdemona approaches, Iago leaves, but he makes one last reference to the handkerchief with the strawberry design.

Desdemona comes into the hall, and in one of the most dramatic scenes in the opera, Otello tries to trap her into confessing her love for Cassio. Desdemona's innocence and the Moor's unreasoning suspicion are displayed in a duet ("Dio ti giocondi"). Desdemona attempts to speak again in behalf of Cassio, but Otello, claiming a cold, asks to borrow her handkerchief. She offers one, but of course it is not the handkerchief with the strawberry pattern. He asks for the one that was his gift to her, but she tells him she does not have it with her. Warning her of great woe if she loses it, Otello says his mother received it from an Egyptian charmer who put a spell on it. He insists that she fetch it, but Desdemona replies that it is a trick to prevent her from speaking for Cassio. She, of course, is moved simply by pity for a fine, brave officer who in a weak and thoughtless moment had endangered his career; but to Otello it seems as if her mind were always on Cassio. He grows even more wild-eyed and insistent. In spite of her earnest assurances of fidelity, he calls her false. Poor Desdemona does not understand this fury. She falls on her knees to assure him of the purity of her love for him ("Esterrefatta fisso lo sguardo tuo tremendo"), but Otello is in no mood to listen or believe.

Sending her rudely away, he utters his sorrowful soliloquy ("Dio! mi potevi scagliar tutti i mali della miseria"). Singing hardly above a whisper, he reveals how completely heartbroken he is now that his illusions have been shattered.

Iago returns and hurriedly whispers to Otello to watch and listen from behind a column, for Cassio is coming. Otello retires out of sight, and as Cassio walks in, Iago begins his craftily planned conversation, which is designed to torture Otello's mind still further. He cunningly induces Cassio to talk of his affairs with Bianca, a woman of the town, but speaks her name so softly that Otello cannot hear it. As they indulge in their half-whispered conversation punctuated by laughter, Iago keeps Cassio at a distance where Otello can hear only snatches of what is said, knowing that Otello will think Cassio is talking of Desdemona. Cassio mentions in an undertone that he has found a lady's handkerchief in his room and wonders how it came there. Iago asks to see it, and he holds it behind him so that Otello can view it from his hiding place. In the trio that follows ("Quest' è una ragna"), Iago pretends to sense a true romantic symbol in the handkerchief. Cassio takes it back from Iago and admires it too while Otello swallows the "proof," doubting not the slightest now that Desdemona has betrayed him.

There is a flourish of trumpets and a cannon shot, the signal of the arrival of the ships from Venice. Iago hurries Cassio off to avoid having him meet Otello in the great hall. In a murderous rage Otello strides from his hiding place and asks Iago to tell him how he can slay Cassio. Iago fans his anger by recalling Cassio's laughter and the reference to the handkerchief. Otello orders Iago to procure poison to kill Desdemona that very night, but Iago advises him instead to strangle his wife as she sleeps. Otello signifies his approval of this method of vengeance, while Iago remarks that he himself will "take care" of Cassio. Impetuously the Moor raises Iago to the rank of lieutenant on the spot, and Iago sardonically thanks him. He announces that the ambassador from Venice is approaching and suggests that Desdemona be present in order to avoid any suspicion. Otello agrees and directs Iago to call her.

During this dialogue, shouts of greeting from those aboard the ships are heard outside. Now the company enters the great hall and in an imposing chorus hails Otello as the "Lion of San Marco." In the forefront of the throng are Iago, the Venetian ambassador Lodovico, Roderigo, Desdemona, and Emilia. Lodovico sings a formal greeting to Otello and hands him a parchment. Otello acknowledges the message, kisses the seal of the scroll, opens it, and begins to read.

Meanwhile, Lodovico pays his respects to Desdemona and she responds. In an aside to Emilia she comments on Otello's angry demeanor. Iago joins the group with a bland greeting to Lodovico, who asks for news of Cassio. Iago replies that Cassio has incurred Otello's displeasure, whereupon Desdemona predicts that the lieutenant will soon be restored to favor. Otello, overhearing this remark, is instantly suspicious. He mutters threateningly to Desdemona while pretending to read the parchment. Desdemona is bewildered, but Lodovico says casually that Otello has misunderstood. Iago deliberately repeats Desdemona's remark about Cassio, and with innocent sincerity Desdemona says she would do her utmost for Cassio out of her affection for him.

Still pretending to read the document to Desdemona, Otello warns her in a fierce undertone to hold her tongue. Distressed, Desdemona asks his forgiveness. In uncontrollable fury Otello bursts out, "Silence, demon!" and raises his hand as if to strike his wife. Lodovico holds him back while the crowd exclaims in horror. Otello orders Cassio to be brought in, then softly tells Iago to watch Desdemona when the lieutenant enters. In shocked amazement at Otello's conduct toward Desdemona, Lodovico seeks an explanation from Iago. He unctuously shrugs his shoulders and asks to be spared from expressing his opinion.

Cassio enters, and Otello again warns Iago to watch closely. The Moor announces loudly that the Doge has recalled him to Venice. In an aside he snarls an insult to Desdemona. Roderigo, frustrated in his love for Desdemona, cries out in despair. Otello goes on to proclaim that Cassio will succeed him as governor of Cyprus. At those words Iago curses in angry surprise, realizing that Otello's departure will spoil his plans. The Moor and Cassio signify their obedience to the senatorial decree. In a whisper Otello calls Iago's attention to Cassio's discomfiture. He again addresses the company—pausing for another sarcastic aside to Desdemona—declaring that the city's defenses will be left in Cassio's hands. Lodovico, pointing to the stricken Desdemona, implores Otello to speak

Otello

some word of comfort. Otello's only answer is that they will sail tomorrow.

Suddenly, in wild fury, he seizes Desdemona, orders her to kneel, then hurls her to the ground. In the confusion Otello drops the parchment. Iago snatches it up and slyly reads it. Desdemona, helped to her feet by Emilia and Lodovico, then begins the tragic aria in which she laments the loss of Otello's love ("A terra!—si, nel livido"). She cries out that she lies helpless in the dust and already feels the icy hand of death. She mourns Otello's tender greeting, his smile, his kiss. Nothing now can dry her tears. The aria is continued over the accompaniment of a dramatic chorus in which all join. Those in the throng comment on Otello's mad behavior, then attempt to console Desdemona. Iago approaches and urges Otello to take his revenge on Desdemona before his wrath cools, while he himself swears to kill Cassio. Then turning to jeer at Roderigo, he reminds him that if Otello leaves for Venice, Desdemona will be out of his reach forever. He conspires with Roderigo to murder Cassio in order to prevent Otello's departure from Cyprus and warns him to do as he is told, sneering at him for being a weakling and a coward.

As the chorus rises to a tremendous climax Otello violently orders everyone to leave. The throng falls back in terror. When Desdemona rushes toward Otello imploringly, he turns on her with a terrible curse. The people flee, and Desdemona is led away by Emilia and Lodovico.

Otello and Iago remain alone. Mad with anger, Otello cries for blood and rants about the handkerchief. Convulsed by his rage, he falls fainting to the ground. Iago looks down at him and remarks that the poison is beginning to work. From outside the castle come the shouts of the throng, hailing Otello. In a powerful, unaccompanied musical phrase, Iago exults that at this moment no one could prevent him from grinding his heel into Otello's face. The crowd again hails the "Lion of Venice." Iago points to the prostrate Otello and in arrogant, venomous triumph sings: "Ecco il Leone!" ("Behold the Lion!"). The curtain falls.

Act Four

There is a short orchestral interlude, based on the plaintive theme of the *Willow Song*, which Desdemona sings later in the act. The curtain rises on Desdemona's bedroom. Near the bed is a prie-dieu, and above it the image of the Madonna. A candle burns on the table. Emilia, helping Desdemona as she prepares to retire, inquires about Otello. Desdemona says that he has ordered her to await him. She directs Emilia to make up the bed with her wedding sheets. If she should die, the maid is to use one of the sheets for Desdemona's shroud.

Desdemona seats herself before her mirror and quietly begins a recitative in which she tells the sad story of her mother's maid, Barbara, whose lover went mad. She sang a song of "Willow" to console herself. This evening, Desdemona muses, the song keeps running through her mind. Then she begins the mournful melody of the *Willow Song* ("O Salce! Salce!"). Desdemona gives her ring to Emilia and asks her to guard it. She takes up the song again, then suddenly stops to listen, imagining she hears a sigh or a knock at the door. It is only the wind, Emilia says.

Desdemona ends her song in a simple, unaccompanied phrase of infinite sadness. She bids Emilia good night. Her eyes are aching, she says, and wonders if that foretells weeping. There is a long quiet note in the orchestra, and Desdemona again whispers, "Good night." As Emilia is about to go, Desdemona, shaken by a premonition of doom, pours out an impassioned phrase of farewell. She embraces Emilia, who then leaves her. Desdemona kneels at the prie-dieu and sings a profoundly moving prayer to the Madonna, the quiet, beautiful *Ave Maria*. For several moments she remains in a prayerful attitude, then goes to bed and lies down.

As the orchestra begins a sinister, foreboding theme, Otello steps through a secret door. He lays his scimitar on the table, pauses before the candle, looks at Desdemona. He blows out the candle and stalks toward the bed. Parting the curtains, he gazes for a long time on his sleeping wife, then kisses her three times as the kiss motive sounds in the orchestra. Desdemona awakes and calls his name. With sinister deliberation Otello asks if she has prayed this night—if there is any unforgiven crime on her conscience—for he does not wish to kill her soul. Terror-stricken, she pleads for mercy.

Otello warns Desdemona to think upon her sins, but she sobs that her only sin is the love she bears Otello. Must she die because of that love? she asks in desperation. Furiously Otello accuses her of loving Cassio. Desdemona denies it. Otello says he saw her handkerchief in Cassio's hands. Ignoring Desdemona's frantic protests, Otello scornfully tells her not to perjure herself on her deathbed by denying her guilt.

Desdemona implores Otello to call Cassio and thus establish her innocence. Otello retorts coldly that Cassio is dead. As Desdemona voices her despair, Otello rages like a madman at her tears, which he imagines are for Cassio. Desdemona begs the Moor to banish, not to kill, her. As Otello curses her in maniacal fury, Desdemona entreats for one moment more to pray. With a terrible cry Otello strangles her.

There is a knock at the door. The clamor of the orchestra dies down to somber, brooding chords as Otello, looking down at his wife, intones, "Calma, come la tomba" ("Calm as the grave"). More knocking is heard at the door. Emilia rushes in with the news that Cassio has killed Roderigo and that Cassio himself still lives. Desdemona stirs in her death agony and cries out that she is dying guiltless. Horror-stricken, Emilia asks who has done this deed. Desdemona gasps that she herself has done it but that she is innocent. Then she dies.

Otello cries out that Desdemona lies and that he himself has killed her. He tells Emilia that Iago proved to him that Desdemona was unfaithful with Cassio. When Emilia brands Otello a fool for believing Iago, the Moor threatens her. Emilia rushes to the door and loudly calls for help. Lodovico, Cassio, and Iago come in. Emilia denounces Iago's perfidy to his face. Montano enters at that moment and adds the news that Roderigo, before he died, confessed his part in the plot against Otello and exposed Iago's treachery. When Otello calls on Iago to answer the charge, Iago dashes for the nearest door and escapes.

Otello strides to the table, picks up his scimitar, and in an agony of remorse calls down lightning from heaven. Lodovico tries to take his sword, but Otello fends him off. Softly, as if to himself, he sings that although he has still another weapon this moment alone seals his doom. He drops the sword, goes to the bed, and looks upon Desdemona. In a final, tragic monologue he mourns her evil fate. Swiftly he draws a dagger from his doublet and stabs himself. Cassio, Lodovico, and Montano exclaim in horror.

Then Otello sings the Italian equivalent of Shakespeare's immortal lines: "I kissed thee ere I killed thee; no way but this, killing myself. . . ." He sinks upon the bed and, as the kiss motive throbs in the orchestra, he sings the impassioned phrases: "Un bacio, un bacio ancora, un altro bacio!" ("A kiss, again a kiss, and yet another kiss!"). Otello falls dead across Desdemona's body and the curtain slowly descends.

Pagliacci

by RUGGIERO LEONCAVALLO
[1858–1919]

Libretto by the Composer

CHARACTERS

Canio, head of a troupe of strolling players ("Pagliaccio,"
  First Clown, in the play) ....*Tenor*
Nedda, his wife ("Columbine" in the play) ....*Soprano*
Tonio, an actor ("Taddeo," Second Clown, in the play)....*Baritone*
Peppe, or Beppe, an actor ("Harlequin" in the play) ....*Tenor*
Silvio, a villager, lover of Nedda ....*Baritone*
Peasants and villagers

Place: Montalto, province of Calabria, Italy
Time: Between 1865 and 1870
First performance: Teatro dal Verme, Milan, May 21, 1892
Original language: Italian

In the minds of opera lovers *Pagliacci* is inevitably linked with *Cavalleria Rusticana*, for these two operas have provided a favorite double bill for years. The careers of Leoncavallo and Mascagni, in fact, bear a remarkable similarity. Each achieved lasting fame with a single opera, while their other works sank into comparative obscurity. It is said that the success of *Cavalleria Rusticana* inspired Leoncavallo to write his opera.

"Pagliacci" was the name given to the mimes and comedians who were the trade-mark of the strolling players of sixteenth-century Italy. The plot is in the familiar play-within-a-play pattern, in which the actors suddenly assume real-life roles. In this instance, the on-stage play is the pantomime of old Italian comedy, with its well-known characters of Columbine, Harlequin, and Clown. Leoncavallo once wrote that in Montalto, the town of his boyhood and the locale of the opera, an actor killed his wife after a performance. The composer's father was judge at the trial. The episode made so deep an impression that Leoncavallo later immortalized it in *Pagliacci*.

The prelude begins with a vivacious theme descriptive of the festive spirit which accompanies the visit of the strolling players to the village on the day of the Feast of the Assumption. Next we hear a brief strain of the aria, "Ridi, Pagliaccio," sung by Canio at the end of Act One. This is followed by several bars of the love music sung by Nedda and Silvio. Then the music reverts to the staccato of the opening phrases.

Prologue

Tonio, the hunchbacked clown, steps before the curtain to sing the *Prologue* ("Si può? Signore! Signori!"). Announcing himself ("Io son il Prologo"), he explains that, in this old play, the author is presenting something true to life. Inspired by poignant memories ("Un nido di memorie"), the playwright wrote down his thoughts to the cadence of his sobs and tears. The result will be a pageant of powerful human emotions. In a ringing phrase Tonio cries, "Andiam! Incominciate [Come then! Let the play begin]!"

Act One

A sunlit village street. At one side a small traveling theater has been set up. From the distance come the sound of a trumpet and the thumping of a drum. Villagers enter, shouting that Pagliaccio has returned. They pause to stare at Tonio, who sullenly lies near the steps leading up to the small stage. The townspeople sing a chorus of welcome ("Viva Pagliaccio") as Canio, Nedda, and Peppe, dressed in their familiar pantomime costumes, enter in a donkey cart. Canio pounds his big drum for silence and then invites the crowd to attend the play about the great Pagliaccio, which is to be given in the evening. As Canio climbs down from the cart Tonio limps up to help Nedda alight, but Canio roughly pushes him aside and boxes his ears. The crowd laughs derisively and some urchins begin to tease Tonio. He strikes out angrily at them, then retreats into the theater, muttering threats against Canio. Peppe drags away the cart.

Several villagers invite Canio to drink with them. Peppe promptly invites himself. Throwing down his whip at the steps of the theater, he rushes inside to take off his costume. Canio asks Tonio if he is coming along. The hunchback replies that he must first take care of the donkey. One of the villagers hints that Tonio only wants to remain behind so that he can make love to Nedda. Canio, suppressing his anger, sings that if he, as Pagliaccio, found his ladylove with a rival, he would either trounce them both, or make the best of it and perhaps get a beating into the bargain. But were he to find Nedda in such a situation, he says, the end of the play would be much different.

Nedda, aside, exclaims in alarm. Canio, recovering himself, says he adores his wife, and as proof gives Nedda a kiss. The men leave. Soon the villagers appear on their way to vespers, and now follows the well-known *Chorus of the Bells* ("Din, don, suona vespero"). It fades gradually as the people wander off.

Nedda, left alone, recalls Canio's strange outburst and wonders if he suspects her. Dismissing the thought, she muses about the birds, wheeling in the sunshine ("O che bel sole"). This introduces the famous *Ballatella*, one of the best-known soprano arias in operatic repertoire. Nedda sings of the free and joyous flight of the birds ("Stridono lassù").

At the end of her aria Tonio appears, telling her that he was so enthralled by her singing that he could not leave to join the other men. When he ardently declares his love Nedda tells him to save his love-making for the stage. Stung to fury by her insolence and contempt, he advances threateningly, whereupon Nedda snatches up Peppe's whip and slashes him across the face. Shouting that he will have his revenge, Tonio limps away.

In another moment Silvio appears at the wall behind the theater. The love theme vibrates in the orchestra. When Nedda tells him about Tonio, Silvio implores her to end this wretched existence and go away with him. The two voices blend in a long and moving duet[1] ("Silvio! a quest'ora"). While they are singing Tonio steals in, listens for a moment, then slinks away. At last Nedda yields, promising to meet Silvio that night when the play is over.

Tonio and Canio appear just in time to hear Nedda call after the fleeing Silvio that she will be his tonight and forevermore ("A stanotte—e per sempre tua sarò!"). Canio springs forward with a cry of rage. Nedda tries to bar his way as he leaps over the wall in pursuit of Silvio, while Tonio laughs gloatingly. Canio returns. Dagger in hand, he confronts Nedda, demanding the name of her lover. When she coolly refuses to answer he lunges toward her. Peppe, who has been busy behind the theater, rushes forward on hearing the commotion. Just in time he leaps between the two, wrenches the knife out of Canio's hand, and hurls it away. He begs Canio to control himself, for the people are already leaving the church and are coming to see the play.

Tonio, also trying to calm Canio, advises him to bide his time, for the lover may come to the play and there betray his identity. Peppe tells Canio to put on his costume and bids Tonio to beat the drum to announce the performance. He and Tonio retire behind the theater.

Canio, standing alone, sings the great aria, "Vesti la giubba," voicing the tragic fate of the clown. On with costume and make-up! The public pays and must be amused. If Harlequin steals your Columbine, laugh—and win the ap-

[1] Because of the length of this number an optional cut is indicated in the score.

plause! Change your tears into laughter, Clown—"Ridi, Pagliaccio!" As the orchestra repeats the powerful theme of his lament Canio staggers up the steps of the theater and disappears inside. The curtain falls.

Act Two

After a brief intermezzo the curtain rises on the same scene as Act One. It is evening of the same day. While Peppe blows a trumpet and Tonio beats the drum, the people seat themselves on benches arranged in front of the theater. In a lively chorus the villagers express their excitement over the play. Silvio enters and cautiously approaches Nedda, who is passing around a plate for admission money. She whispers that she will be at the rendezvous, then continues on her rounds. A bell rings backstage, and the play begins.

We see a small crude stage, where Nedda, dressed as Columbine, is seated at a table. The orchestra plays a minuet which continues as accompaniment to the scene. Columbine sings that her husband Pagliaccio will come home late this evening, then frets because the servant Taddeo has not returned from the market. From behind the scenes comes the voice of Peppe, as Harlequin, singing his serenade, "O Columbina, il tenero fide Arlecchin [O, Columbine, here waits your faithful Harlequin]."

After the serenade, Tonio, costumed as Taddeo, enters carrying a market basket. Columbine asks him if he has brought the chicken, whereupon Taddeo kneels down before her and bids her look in the basket. Then he makes ardent love to her. Ignoring him, Columbine goes to the window and signals outside. With deliberate emphasis Tonio sings that Columbine is the soul of innocence—as pure as the driven snow ("È casta al par di neve!"). Harlequin, carrying a bottle of wine, climbs through the window, sneaks up behind Taddeo, gives him a kick, and tells him to be off. The goodhearted Taddeo offers to stand guard for the lovers and then exits.

Columbine and Harlequin sit down at the table and feast gaily on the chicken and wine. Harlequin gives Columbine a sleeping potion for Pagliaccio. Taddeo bursts in and warns the lovers that Pagliaccio is approaching. Harlequin leaps out of the window. Just as Canio—now Pagliaccio—enters, Nedda repeats, as part of the play, her parting words to Silvio —"A stanotte—e sempre tua sarò."

Canio's anger gives a harsh edge to the familiar accusations of infidelity which are part of the play. Tonio, taking up his cues as Taddeo, calls from outside with sardonic emphasis that Columbine could not possibly utter a falsehood. Canio commands Nedda to tell him her lover's name. When she reproachfully exclaims, "Pagliaccio," Canio cries out, "Pagliaccio non son [Pagliaccio no longer]!" In a dramatic aria he sings that his honor as a man must be revenged and bitterly reproaches himself for having loved a woman who is not worth all the anguish she has caused him.

Nedda taunts that if he considers her so worthless he may send her away, whereupon Canio declares that she will remain here until she names her lover. Trying desperately to continue the play, Nedda, singing to the accompaniment of a gavotte, assures Canio that nothing tragic has happened. But Canio cries out that Nedda either will name her lover or die. The villagers voice their bewilderment at the strange scene. Peppe tries to rush toward the furious couple but is restrained by Tonio.

Suddenly Canio, shouting "Il nome," stabs Nedda. Silvio draws his dagger and rushes to the stage. As Nedda, with her last breath, gasps out his name, Canio whirls and buries his knife in Silvio's heart. He drops his knife, then gasps the closing lines of the tragedy: "La commedia è finita [The comedy is ended]!" The curtain falls.

Parsifal
by RICHARD WAGNER
[1813–1883]

Libretto by the Composer

Based on Wolfram von Eschenbach's poem
PARSIFAL
a fourteenth-century manuscript known as the
MABINOGION
and Chrétien de Troyes's
PERCIVAL LE GALOIS, OU CONTES DE GRAIL

CHARACTERS

Gurnemanz, an elderly knight of the Grail	*Bass*
Four esquires	*Sopranos / Tenors*
First knight	*Tenor*
Second knight	*Baritone*
Kundry, part sorceress, part mortal woman	*Soprano*
Amfortas, King of the knights of the Holy Grail	*Baritone*
Parsifal	*Tenor*
Titurel, father of Amfortas, former King of Monsalvat	*Bass*
Klingsor, a sorcerer	*Bass*

Knights of the Grail, boys and youths, Flower Maidens of Klingsor's garden

Place: In and about the castle of Monsalvat in the Spanish Pyrenees
Time: Middle Ages
First performance: Festspielhaus, Bayreuth, July 26, 1882
Original language: German

Wagner regarded *Parsifal* as something beyond mere theatrical entertainment. Because of its profound theme—the spiritual redemption of man through the sacrifice of a Saviour—he designated it as a consecrational festival play and expressly prohibited its performance at any other theater than the Festspielhaus at Bayreuth. Its first presentation outside Bayreuth was in New York in 1903, and it was not introduced to European opera houses until 1914.

The magnificent prelude, familiar as a symphonic piece, states the motives which underlie the central idea of the Holy Grail. First we hear the theme of the Eucharist, after which there emerges the Grail theme—with its *Dresden Amen*—symbolizing the sacred cup of communion. These are followed by the motive of faith and the motive of the lance.

Act One

A shadowy forest grove near the castle of Monsalvat. At one side is a road leading to the castle. At the rear is a lake. It is dawn. Gurnemanz and two esquires are seen asleep under a tree. At the sound of a stately fanfare from the castle Gurnemanz awakens and rouses the esquires, who kneel with him in morning prayer as the horns sound forth the faith and Grail themes. Gurnemanz orders the esquires to prepare to assist Amfortas when he is brought to the lake to bathe the spear wound in his side. Two knights enter, and Gurnemanz inquires as to the King's condition, expressing the hope that the balm which the knight Gawain has found will help heal him. The knights answer that Amfortas lay in sleepless agony all through the night. Gurnemanz sadly muses that only one remedy and one man can heal the wound. The knights ask him to explain, but at that moment a galloping rhythm sounds forth in the orchestra and the esquires exclaim that the sorceress is approaching.

Kundry rushes in. She is an eerie figure in a rough, black gown, with her hair flying and eyes staring in wildest excitement. She hands Gurnemanz a small vial of balsam, crying that if this does not heal Amfortas, then all the potions of Arabia will be of no avail. With that she falls exhausted to the ground.

Amfortas is borne in on a litter carried by knights. Racked by pain, he voices the hope that the lake's pure waters will relieve his agony. A knight tells him that Gawain did not find the herb for which he sought and has ridden forth again to look farther. Deeply troubled, Amfortas sings in the music of the promise motive that he must wait for the one who is destined to save him—the Innocent Fool. Gurnemanz hands him Kundry's flask, bidding him try the potion. When Amfortas tries to thank Kundry she sullenly answers that she wants no words of gratitude. At the King's signal the knights continue on their way to the lake.

The esquires, going about their duties, look contemptuously down on Kundry, who is still cowering on the ground, and jeer that her potion will do more harm than good. Gurnemanz rebukes them, pointing out that Kundry faithfully performs her duties as messenger to Grail knights on far-off battlefields. Since she has found refuge in Monsalvat, he goes on, she seeks to expiate her past sins through devoted service.

In answer to the questions of the esquires concerning Amfortas and Kundry, Gurnemanz launches into a long monologue ("O wunden-wundervoller heiliger Speer!") recalling the legend of the Grail. He relates how Titurel, while fighting pagan hordes, was visited by a host of angels, who gave into his keeping the sacred chalice from which Christ drank at the Last Supper, and the spear which pierced His side as He hung on the cross. Titurel then built Monsalvat as a sanctuary for these treasures and recruited a band of sinless knights to guard them. These guardians are the knights of the Holy Grail, whose duty it is to ride forth into the world and fight on the side of justice and mercy.

Klingsor sought admission to the Grail company but was refused because he could not conquer his evil instincts. Enraged and determined on revenge, Klingsor gave himself over to heathen magic and learned the arts of sorcery. He transformed a deserted spot near Monsalvat into a luxurious garden and peopled it with surpassingly beautiful and voluptuous women, the loveliest of whom was Kundry. These creatures enticed a number of Grail knights into the garden, where Klingsor kept them as slave-warriors. Amfortas, who was made ruler of Monsalvat by the aging Titurel, took up the sacred lance and invaded Klingsor's domain in an attempt to destroy the sorcerer and free the knights. Kundry, however, tempted him and betrayed him into Klingsor's hands, whereupon the sorcerer seized the monarch's spear, plunged it into his side, then fled with the weapon. Amfortas made his way back to Monsalvat, where he has since been lying tortured by the wound which will not heal.

Klingsor now has the sacred lance and is plotting to gain control of the Grail itself. Only he who retrieves the spear can release Monsalvat from the evil which has brooded over it since the day of Amfortas's tragic encounter with Klingsor. One day, Gurnemanz goes on in the conclusion of his narrative, when the wounded Amfortas was praying for help, a celestial voice spoke to him, saying that his redeemer will be an Innocent Fool, made wise through compassion.

Suddenly cries of alarm are heard in the direction of the lake. Knights and esquires rush forward, their eyes on a swan fluttering overhead. The bird plunges to the ground. As a knight steps forward and pulls an arrow from its body Parsifal is dragged in. The knights and esquires, pointing to the bow he is carrying, cry out that it was he who killed the swan. Gurnemanz asks him if he is guilty. As the Parsifal motive peals out, the youth unhesitatingly admits shooting the bird. In majestic anger Gurnemanz denounces him for this wanton killing. Overcome with shame and remorse, Parsifal snaps his bow in two and hurls away his arrows.

Gurnemanz questions Parsifal further but receives only vague answers. The youth says that he does not know who his parents are, nor anything about his origin. He does not even know his own name. Gurnemanz, though irked by his apparent stupidity, is determined to learn more about him.

He curtly orders the knights to return to the King, who is still at his bath. They leave, while the esquires carry the swan away.

In response to Gurnemanz's queries Parsifal finally says that he remembers that his mother's name was Herzeleide (Heart's Sorrow) and that his home always has been in the forest. He made his own bow, he explains, to protect him from wild animals. Gurnemanz remarks on his noble bearing and wonders why his mother did not provide him with better weapons. Kundry, who has been crouching at one side, suddenly interrupts. The lad was reared fatherless, she says harshly. His father was Gamuret, who was slain in battle. The boy's mother, seeking to shield him from a warrior's fate, kept him hidden from the world and did not teach him the use of arms.

Listening to her in growing excitement, Parsifal exclaims that he recalls a troop of knights in shining armor passing through the forest. He followed after them for many days. Kundry breaks in to say that the youth encountered men and beasts in his wanderings and that men learned to fear him in the fury of combat. In naïve wonder Parsifal asks who it is that fears him. The evil ones, Kundry replies. Puzzled at this, Parsifal desires to know who, then, is good. The mother whom he has deserted, Gurnemanz says gently. The boy's mother is dead, Kundry declares. She herself was asked by the dying woman to bear her last greeting to this fool. Furious at her contemptuous tone, Parsifal flings himself at Kundry. Gurnemanz rushes to her aid and rebukes the youth. Shaken by his outburst, Parsifal sinks to the ground in a faint. Kundry aids Gurnemanz in reviving him, then makes her way to a thicket in the background and disappears.

The knights are seen in the distance carrying Amfortas back to the castle. Gurnemanz helps Parsifal to his feet and starts off with him in the direction of the castle, musing to himself that this innocent youth may well be the Grail's destined redeemer.

Now follows what is generally referred to as the *Trans-*

formation Scene.[1] As Parsifal and Gurnemanz begin walking the scene gradually changes to the accompaniment of an orchestral interlude in which the themes of the cry of the Saviour, the bells of Monsalvat, and the Eucharist predominate. The two men climb through a rocky pass and disappear. As the Grail theme soars up through the sound of the bells of Monsalvat, the huge hall of the castle, with its vaulted dome, becomes visible. Parsifal and Gurnemanz enter. In the center are two long tables, extending from the front of the scene to the rear. Knights of the Grail enter and seat themselves at the tables in preparation for the Communion Feast, hailing the ritual in a majestic chorus ("Zum letzten Liebesmahle").

Amfortas is brought in and carried to a couch at the center of the hall toward the rear. Before it is a stone altar on which stands the shrine of the Grail, draped with a cloth. The litany of the Holy Grail is intoned in an intensely moving chorus ("Den sündigen Welten"), which is sung by a choir of youths at the middle height of the dome and a boys' choir at the top.

At the conclusion of the chorus the voice of Titurel is heard as though issuing from a tomb. He exhorts Amfortas to perform the office of Holy Communion, and in so doing expiate his guilt. As the esquires move forward to uncover the Grail, Amfortas stops them with the cry, "Lasst ihn unenthüllt [Leave it undisclosed]!" He launches into a long monologue of bitter self-reproach, protesting that his guilt has rendered him unworthy of this sacred task. He prays for divine forgiveness, so that he may die in peace.

Spent by his confession, he falls back in a faint. The voices of the invisible choir exhort him to put his faith in the Innocent Fool who will come to redeem him, while the knights urge him to perform the holy office. The esquires uncover the golden shrine, take out a crystal cup, and set it before Amfortas, who slowly revives. He remains with bowed head before the chalice, while the theme of the Eucharist sings

[1] Wagner's original stage directions called for moving scenery to give the illusion of the journey from the grove to the castle. In present-day productions the curtain is generally lowered for a scene change.

softly in the orchestra. The scene gradually grows darker until it is enveloped in complete blackness.

Suddenly the cup begins to glow in a wine-colored light which spreads through the darkness. Amfortas lifts it up and moves it from side to side in a gesture of consecration. Titurel's voice is heard in an exultant phrase. Then Amfortas sets the cup on the table, while its glow fades and the scene again brightens. The esquires replace the cup in the shrine, then pass the Bread and Wine for the Communion Feast.

Gurnemanz, who has seated himself at the table with the knights, motions to Parsifal to sit beside him and partake of the Bread and Wine. The youth, who has been watching the scene as though spellbound, neither moves nor speaks. The knights join with the invisible choir in singing of the Last Supper ("Blut und Leib der heil'gen Gabe"). At the conclusion of the chorus the knights advance to the center, embrace each other, and then prepare to leave. Amfortas, with his wound torn open as the result of his feverish ecstasy, is borne groaning from the hall, followed by the company. Parsifal, transfixed by the scene, puts his hand to his side in a convulsive movement as he hears Amfortas's cry of pain. Gurnemanz approaches and asks him if he has understood what he has just seen. As though his senses were dulled by pain, Parsifal shakes his head and does not answer. In angry impatience Gurnemanz drives him out of the hall through a side door and then follows after the knights. From far above in the dome a voice repeats the theme of the Innocent Fool. It is answered in a soft phrase by the invisible choir. The curtain falls.

Act Two

The open top of the tower of Klingsor's castle. Steps at one side lead up to the battlements. Objects used in the performance of magic arts are scattered about. In the brief but dramatic prelude we hear the motives of Klingsor, the magic, and Kundry. As the curtain rises Klingsor is seated before a magic mirror into which he gazes to see events of the future. He murmurs with evil satisfaction that the Innocent Fool is making his way to the castle. With mysterious motions and incantations he summons Kundry, who seems to rise up from the black depths beyond the tower at the back. She moves as though in sleep. Gradually awakening, she utters a cry of terror at the sight of Klingsor. He jeers at her for humbling herself in the service of the knights and then reminds her that she is still in his power. Now that he wields the sacred spear, he adds, he will enslave the holy knights as well.

But now he must be on his guard, he continues, for one who is more dangerous than any of the knights is on his way to the castle. He is the Innocent Fool, and Kundry must tempt him to his ruin as she did the knights. When Kundry recoils in horror Klingsor warns that he is master and must be obeyed. Ignoring her protests and lamentations, he goes to the battlement to observe Parsifal's approach. He takes up a horn, blows a signal, then commands the enslaved knights below to give battle to the intruder. With savage delight he describes how the confused and stupefied warriors are routed by the youth, exclaiming over the lad's fearlessness and his prowess with the sword. Kundry, now helpless in the grip of Klingsor's spell, vanishes, shrieking, to prepare herself to lure Parsifal to his doom. Gazing down from the battlement, Klingsor gloats that Parsifal will soon be his slave.

At a gesture from the sorcerer the tower disappears and in its place is a lush, tropical garden. Parsifal, standing on the ramparts at the rear, gazes on the scene in awe and wonder. The Flower Maidens, beautiful young girls dressed in light flowing garments, enter in great excitement. In an agitated chorus they lament that their knightly lovers have been wounded by a cruel intruder. Seeing Parsifal, they curse him for bringing this sorrow upon them.

Parsifal, completely enchanted by their beauty, advances slowly. The maidens shrink back in fear, but when they see that he does not intend to harm them they draw close to him. Their hostile manner changes to gaiety and delight over his handsome features and friendly demeanor. Soon they move about him in a sensuous dance, and in an alluring chorus they invite him to share the delights of love with them. At first Parsifal gently fends them off. Finally, annoyed by their voluptuous entreaties, he impatiently orders them away and turns to leave the garden.

At that moment Kundry's voice, tenderly singing Parsifal's name, comes from the depths of the garden. The youth pauses in astonishment, murmuring that his mother once called to him thus in a dream. At the sound of Kundry's voice the Flower Maidens withdraw to the castle, regretfully bidding Parsifal farewell. Kundry gradually becomes visible in the background. Now in the disguise of a ravishingly beautiful woman, she is lying on a bed of flowers, her arms temptingly outstretched.

Wonderingly the youth asks why she called him by the strange name of Parsifal. Kundry answers that it is a name she coined from the one his father gave him—"Falparsi"—signifying innocence in folly and folly in innocence, and to tell him this at long last, she has come to the garden. In an ensuing monologue ("Ich sah das Kind an seiner Mutter Brust") Kundry tells Parsifal of his mother, Herzeleide, and the events of his youth. The narrative is dominated by the Herzeleide theme. Kundry deliberately stirs his emotions by telling him that his mother died of a broken heart when he left her to roam about in the world.

As Parsifal gives way to his remorse, Kundry, pretending to console him, draws him to her side with tender caresses. Parsifal laments that in his folly he has forgotten his mother's love, then is suddenly haunted by a torturing thought. As the theme of Amfortas's agony flashes through the orchestra he presses his hand to his side.

Kundry, gathering him in her embrace, sings that by confession to her he will absolve himself of the sin against his mother. Obedient to her wish, Kundry goes on, she has come to teach him love. With that she presses her mouth to his in a long, passionate kiss, while the magic motive sweeps through the orchestra.

Suddenly Parsifal, clutching his hand to his heart, leaps to his feet with a terrible cry of pain ("Amfortas! Die Wunde!"). As though in a delirium, he raves that the spear wound is burning in his side, then in feverish ecstasy he recalls the scene of the Communion. In rising frenzy he cries out that he hears the agonized voice of the Saviour calling on him to redeem the Grail from the thralldom of sin.

Using all her powers of seduction, Kundry tries to turn his thoughts to her. In a sudden flash of understanding Parsifal exclaims that it was with these very caresses that Kundry tempted Amfortas and lured him to his doom. Furiously he struggles out of her embrace. Kundry turns on him in bitter reproach, asking why—if he is indeed the appointed redeemer—he does not save her. In the intensely dramatic aria ("Seit Ewigkeiten harre ich deiner") she tells of the curse that is upon her. At the Crucifixion she looked on the Saviour and laughed at His agony. Since that day she has been condemned to wander about the earth, seeking one who will redeem her from the curse. But always when she is in reach of salvation the fatal, mocking laughter seizes her and dooms her again to torment and frustration. Distractedly she implores Parsifal to take her in his arms for but one hour so that she may find atonement.

Parsifal answers that were he to yield to her they both would be damned forever. He can redeem her only if she will cleanse her heart of its carnal desires. Now at last, he sings, he knows the torment of humanity's struggle between good and evil. At these words Kundry exults that her kiss has bestowed manhood's wisdom on Parsifal. Her love, she tells him, can make him a god and at the same time deliver her from the curse of her laughter. Parsifal consents to help her if she will lead him to Amfortas. Furiously Kundry refuses, declaring that she will leave the fallen monarch to his ruin. Moreover, she warns that she will use the spear that wounded him against Parsifal himself if he dares to spurn her love. In a final desperate effort she tries to embrace Parsifal, but he pushes her violently away.

Leaping to the battlement, she shouts for Klingsor. Turning

back to Parsifal, she cries upon him the curse that will doom him to wander, like herself, over the earth in an endless quest for salvation. Klingsor springs upon the battlement with the sacred lance upraised. He hurls it, but it remains motionless in the air above Parsifal's head. There is a remarkable orchestral effect here as a harp glissando vividly portrays the spear's flight toward its target. Parsifal grasps the weapon and makes the sign of the cross with it, proclaiming in ringing tones that the sorcerer's spell is broken forever.

Instantly Klingsor vanishes and the castle collapses into ruins, while the garden is transformed into a desert. Kundry falls to the ground with a despairing cry. Parsifal, leaving the scene of desolation, pauses and turns to her, saying that she will know where to find him. The curtain falls.

Act Three

A meadow at the edge of a forest near Monsalvat. At one side is a rude hut. It is an early morning in spring. The introduction reflects the mood of despair that hangs over Monsalvat and then states the theme descriptive of Parsifal's wanderings. As the curtain rises, Gurnemanz, greatly aged and clad as a hermit, comes out of the hut. Hearing groans issuing from a thicket at the edge of the woods, he goes to investigate. He finds Kundry lying unconscious on the ground, carries her into the clearing, and tries to revive her. Finally she opens her eyes and utters a cry of alarm. She is dressed in the rough robe of a penitent, and there is a marked change in her demeanor. Her feverish, excited manner has given way to a calm humility. She looks at Gurnemanz for a long time in silence. When he expresses surprise at her seeming lack of gratitude toward him for saving her life she only mutters, "Dienen—dienen [Service—service]."

Gurnemanz sadly tells her that now the knights have no need for her services. They go no more to distant battlefields and are fending for themselves in the forest like wild animals. Without a word Kundry busies herself about the hut, then goes to bring water from a nearby spring. While there, she sees a stranger approaching and points him out to Gurnemanz. After a moment Parsifal enters. He is clad in black armor, with the visor of his helmet closed, and carries a spear. Slowly, as if deep in thought, he seats himself on a grassy slope. He remains silent when Gurnemanz questions him. The old man tells him that he has come to a holy place where it is forbidden to carry weapons, especially on this day of all days—Good Friday.

Thereupon Parsifal thrusts his spear into the earth, places his sword, shield, and helmet beside it, and kneels before his weapons in prayer. Gurnemanz is astonished to find that he is the youth who killed the swan. Kundry also indicates that she knows the knight—and his spear as well. Parsifal rises at length and approaches Gurnemanz. Recognizing him, he holds out his hand in greeting. In answer to the old man's questions he tells his story ("Der Irrnis und der Leiden Pfade").

Hounded by a curse, he relates, he wandered over the earth seeking the Holy Grail, which he has sworn to restore to its rightful power. He fought many a battle but never once profaned his spear by using it in combat. Now at last he has reached his goal with the sacred lance unstained. Gurnemanz exults over the miracle that has brought the knight to Monsalvat to perform his destined task. He then tells Parsifal of the sad plight of the knights—how Amfortas, tortured by physical and spiritual agony, refuses to perform the rite of Holy Communion and is obsessed with the desire for death. The knights, deprived of the sacred food, have lost their strength and can no longer go forth into combat. Gurnemanz says that he himself has retired to a hermit's hut to wait for death, while Titurel, having been denied the Grail's sustaining power, has died like any mortal.

Parsifal cries out that he is to blame for the misery and suffering inflicted on the company of the Grail. Shaken by anguish and remorse, he sinks unconscious to the ground. Gurnemanz and Kundry bear him gently to the spring and remove his armor. Reviving, Parsifal asks if he may now see Amfortas. Gurnemanz tells him that they both will go to the castle today to attend the funeral rites for Titurel, during which Amfortas is to serve Holy Communion. As he speaks, the somber burial theme sounds in the orchestra.

To the accompaniment of the baptism theme Kundry and Gurnemanz perform a ceremony symbolic of purification. They anoint Parsifal's head and feet with the contents of a small golden vial which Kundry takes from her gown. Gurnemanz then baptizes Parsifal with water from the spring, after which the knight baptizes Kundry. Shaken by sobs, she remains on her knees before him. Gazing about him, Parsifal exclaims over the fresh beauty of the spring morning, and now the great music of the *Good Friday Spell* surges up from the orchestra. Over the music Gurnemanz sings to Parsifal of the meaning of Good Friday—the day when all mankind looks up in gratitude and joy at the cross, where humanity was redeemed by love's sacrifice. Kundry raises her eyes to Parsifal with an expression of humble entreaty. In compassion and tenderness he kisses her on the forehead.

Bells sound in the distance, while in the orchestra the theme of Titurel's burial begins. Gurnemanz brings his Grail mantle from his hut and, with Kundry's help, places it around Parsifal's shoulders. The knight takes up his spear, and then he and Kundry follow Gurnemanz to the castle. The scene changes gradually as in the first act, while the burial theme throbs powerfully in the orchestra. As the bells toll louder the hall of the Grail comes into view.

From one side a procession of knights enters carrying Titurel's coffin. From the other side comes a second procession of knights bringing in Amfortas. The two groups sing antiphonally. Amfortas is borne to the couch behind the altar, while the coffin is placed in front of it. The knights entreat Amfortas to perform the office of Communion, but his only answer is an expression of anguish. Titurel's coffin is opened, whereupon a cry of lamentation rises from the assemblage. Painfully raising himself, Amfortas entreats the spirit of his father to intercede for him in heaven, so that he may be granted the boon of death. The knights crowd toward him, begging him to reveal the Grail.

Frantic with pain and remorse, Amfortas leaps from the couch, tears aside his robe, and bares his wound. Wildly he begs the knights to slay him, the vilest of sinners, and thus bring about the Grail's redemption. As the knights draw back in terror and dismay Parsifal strides forward and places his spear point on Amfortas's wound, declaring that the weapon that caused the wound now heals it ("Nur eine Waffe taugt"). The King, his anguish suddenly turned to joy, reels back and is supported by Gurnemanz. Parsifal sings that his sins have been forgiven and that through the King's suffering the Innocent Fool has received the gift of wisdom.

As the Parsifal motive thunders out, the knight proclaims that he has brought back the sacred lance, which now has been purified by the very blood it once drew. He orders the shrine to be uncovered and the Grail chalice brought forth. Parsifal kneels before the altar. Again the hall darkens, while the cup glows with its mysterious roseate light. The voices of the knights blend with the invisible choir in an exultant hymn of praise to the Redeemer. As a piercingly brilliant ray from above illumines the chalice a white dove flutters down from the dome and hovers over the head of Parsifal. Kundry, her eyes fixed on the knight, sinks to the ground and dies. Parsifal raises the chalice in the gesture of consecration. The motives of faith and the Grail soar upward as the curtain slowly falls.

Rigoletto

by GIUSEPPE VERDI
[1813–1901]

Libretto by
FRANCESCO MARIA PIAVE

Based on Victor Hugo's drama
LE ROI S'AMUSE

CHARACTERS

The Duke of Mantua	Tenor
Borsa, a courtier	Tenor
The Countess Ceprano	Mezzo-soprano
Rigoletto, the Duke's jester, a hunchback	Baritone
Count Ceprano, a nobleman	Bass
Marullo, a courtier	Baritone
Count Monterone, a nobleman	Baritone
Sparafucile, a professional assassin	Bass
Gilda, daughter of Rigoletto	Soprano
Giovanna, Gilda's nurse	Mezzo-soprano
A page	Soprano
A herald	Baritone
Maddalena, sister of Sparafucile	Contralto

Courtiers, ladies and gentlemen of the court, servants

Place: Mantua, Italy
Time: Sixteenth century
First performance: Teatro La Fenice, Venice, March 11, 1851
Original language: Italian

VICTOR HUGO'S DRAMA of intrigue, treachery, and revenge at the court of François I of France greatly impressed Verdi as material for an operatic plot. Asked to write an opera for the

Teatro La Fenice, he insisted that Piave prepare a libretto based on the play. Although the rather insinuating title, *Le Roi s'amuse*, was changed to *La Maledizione (The Curse)*, the libretto provoked difficulties with the censor. Because of current political unrest, the authorities deemed it unwise to present a story of royal decadence and philandering. Consequently the locale of the opera was changed to the palace of the Duke of Mantua, a petty Italian nobleman, and the opera was retitled *Rigoletto*. Both Verdi and the authorities were satisfied. He wrote the opera in about six weeks, and the production was a spectacular success.

The first theme we hear in the brief prelude is that of the curse laid upon Rigoletto by Count Monterone. This somber, brooding music gives way to a brilliant, rhythmic strain as the curtain rises.

Act One

[*Scene One*] The glittering ballroom in the palace of the Duke of Mantua. It is thronged with cavaliers and their ladies. Some are dancing. The Duke, in conversation with Borsa, enters. He tells the courtier about a beautiful girl whom he has been observing at Mass for the past three months. He has learned that she lives in a remote part of town and that each night a mysterious stranger is admitted to the girl's home. The Duke then turns his attention to the ladies in the room, exclaiming that Count Ceprano's wife is the most beautiful of all. Borsa warns that Ceprano may overhear him and inform a "certain lady" of his roving eye. "That would be most unfortunate," is the Duke's rejoinder. He sums up his cynical philosophy about women in the graceful and carefree aria, "Questa o quella." One woman is as welcome to him as another, he sings. Fidelity has no appeal for the true lover, who cherishes his freedom to rove. He scorns the husband's jealous fury and mocks the lover's rage.

The guests now begin a minuet, and the Duke gallantly leads the Countess Ceprano forward to be his partner. Much to her discomfiture, he proceeds to make violent love, then escorts her out of the room before Ceprano's very eyes. Rigoletto, who has entered just in time to mark the Duke's exit, sneers at Ceprano's anger and embarrassment. The Count strides out of the room to follow the Duke. Rigoletto joins the courtiers, who exclaim in malicious glee over his sallies about the Duke's latest amorous exploit. The jester then limps away, while the courtiers laugh uproariously. There is a brief interlude during which the guests join in the *perigourdine*, a stately court dance. The courtiers remain at one side, looking on.

Suddenly the music changes to the spirited refrain heard at the beginning of the scene. Marullo enters, hurries up to the courtiers, and tells them that Rigoletto has decided to play the lover—he has a young sweetheart. "An elegant Cupid," the courtiers observe sarcastically. At that moment the Duke reappears, followed by Rigoletto. The Duke asks his jester how to dispose of Ceprano, because the Countess has completely ensnared his heart. The jester suggests that the Duke carry off the Countess. As for Ceprano, he says viciously, let him be arrested or beheaded.

Ceprano, who has re-entered, overhears the conversation and exclaims in fury. Rigoletto continues to torment Ceprano until he threatens to draw his sword. The jester's cruel raillery brings an angry warning from not only the Duke but the courtiers as well, but Rigoletto boasts that no harm can touch him.

These various sentiments introduce a dramatic chorus as the courtiers join their voices to sing "Vendetta del pazzo!" They all turn on Rigoletto, declaring that they will no longer tolerate his evil jests. He arrogantly repeats that he is safe from their vengeance. The mood of the music changes as the dancers crowd in from the other rooms. The entire ensemble sings about the festivity and merriment that rule the evening.

As the chorus ends, the voice of Count Monterone is heard outside, demanding admittance. With an angry exclamation he bursts into the room and accuses the Duke of dishonoring his daughter. Goaded to fury by Rigoletto's taunts, the Count challenges the Duke to condemn him to death, saying that his curses will haunt the betrayer and that he will demand vengeance from God himself.

Angrily the Duke orders the Count's arrest. Monterone, whirling on Rigoletto, thunders, in ringing tones, "You who laugh at a father's anguish, be accursed!" Rigoletto recoils with a gasp of horror. The entire assemblage denounces Monterone for interrupting the festivities, and they order him to leave. Monterone reiterates his curse, while Rigoletto voices a foreboding of disaster. The Count is led away by guards and the people follow him out of the room. The curtain falls.

[*Scene Two*[1]] A deserted street near Rigoletto's house. At the side of the house is a walled courtyard with a door leading into it from the street. In the courtyard is a tree. The balcony of the house rises above the wall, with a stairway leading from it to the courtyard. Across the street is another high wall, over the top of which the gable of Count Ceprano's house is visible.

Rigoletto, muffled in his long cloak, comes slowly down the street. Ominous chords reverberate in the orchestra as he recalls Monterone's curse—"Quel vecchio maledivami." Sparafucile approaches and introduces himself as a man who can properly dispose of an enemy or a rival. There are such, he adds significantly. "Inside there," says Sparafucile, nodding his head toward Rigoletto's house, "you have a woman...." Rigoletto, fearing that the man may know about Gilda, quickly asks him his price for killing a nobleman. The price is as may be, Sparafucile answers casually. At any rate, half must be paid in advance.

The assassin goes on to explain that, with the aid of his beautiful sister, he lures his victims to his tavern on the outskirts of the town and there quietly dispatches them. Telling Rigoletto he may be found at this spot nightly, Sparafucile slinks away, murmuring his name.

Rigoletto, staring after him, sings a bitter soliloquy ("Pari siamo"). "We are equal—the murderer and I," he reflects. "He

[1] Originally written in three acts, *Rigoletto* now is generally played in four, and this then becomes Act Two.

strikes with a knife by night, I with a malicious tongue by day." In despair the jester cries out that nature, in her cruel caprice, has created him as a monstrous caricature of a man ("O uomini! o natura!"). Then he pours out his hatred and contempt for the courtiers. Finally shaking off these tormenting thoughts, he enters the courtyard.

The music becomes livelier as Gilda rushes out of the house and embraces her father. After they affectionately greet each other ("Figlia!" "Mio padre!") their voices blend in a long and melodious colloquy. Gilda entreats him to tell her of the secret grief that seems to overshadow their lives. Evading her question, he asks her if she has left the house today. When Gilda replies that she has gone only to Mass, he is reassured.

Earnestly Gilda begs Rigoletto to tell her about her mother. Yielding at length to her pleas, he tells her, in a touching refrain, that her mother died long ago ("Deh non parlare al misero"). Now, he says, they are left alone, surrounded by enemies and threatened by a strange curse. Their voices blend in a moving climax as they express their sorrow over the past and pledge their devotion to each other.

Gilda then wishes to know why she is not allowed to go into the city. Greatly agitated, Rigoletto asks if she has ever ventured beyond the neighborhood. In an aside, Gilda, thinking of the handsome stranger she has seen at church, betrays a twinge of conscience. Her father warns her never to leave home. Calling Giovanna, the nurse, he orders her to keep close watch over Gilda, who assures her father that all will be well.

Stepping out through the courtyard door, Rigoletto looks carefully up and down the street. As he does so, the Duke, disguised as a student, steals up behind the jester and enters the yard through the door without being noticed either by Rigoletto or Gilda. Before Rigoletto re-enters, the Duke tosses a purse to Giovanna with a gesture to be quiet and then conceals himself behind the tree. He is astounded when the jester comes back and addresses Gilda as his daughter. In poignant phrases the two bid each other good-by. After Rigoletto has left, Gilda muses about her unknown admirer. As she sings the Duke comes forward, signaling Giovanna to leave. Kneeling before Gilda, he declares his love in a phrase which completes her sentence and begins on the note Gilda has just sung ("T'amo, ripetilo!").

This introduces an impassioned duet in which they both confess their love. Eagerly Gilda asks the Duke his name. Walter Maldè, a humble student, the Duke replies. At that moment Count Ceprano and Borsa are seen cautiously approaching the house. They satisfy themselves that it is the home of Rigoletto, then withdraw. Giovanna rushes in, saying she heard footsteps. Gilda tells the nurse to lead the Duke out through the house. The lovers tenderly bid each other farewell.

Gilda, gazing after him, ecstatically repeats the name he gave—"Walter Maldè." Then she begins the famous aria, "Caro nome che il mio cor," a brilliant and rhapsodic expression of her newly awakened love. At the end of the aria Gilda goes into the house and reappears shortly after on the balcony, carrying a lantern to light her lover on his way. Softly she repeats several phrases of her aria, her voice trailing off into silence as she re-enters the house.

Meanwhile, Ceprano, Marullo, Borsa, and other courtiers have stealthily gathered in the street below. There they encounter Rigoletto returning home. In the dark street he does not recognize them. Marullo identifies only himself and says they have come to abduct Ceprano's wife. Rigoletto, who has been nervous at finding the courtiers so near his own home, is relieved and agrees to join them. He consents to mask himself, as the others are disguised. Marullo places a mask over his eyes and at the same time slips a handkerchief over the mask. Rigoletto, thinking he wears only the mask, remarks that it has grown very dark. Taking advantage of his confusion, the conspirators lead him to his own house and tell him that he is going toward Ceprano's. They explain that he is to hold the ladder up to the wall.

As the courtiers force their way into the house they sing a striking chorus ("Zitti, zitti, moviamo a vendetta"), in which they exult over their trick on Rigoletto. At the end of the ensemble some of the courtiers emerge carrying Gilda, gagged and bound. Now from the distance comes the muffled voice of Gilda calling for help, then a shout of triumph from the conspirators.

Rigoletto, still at the foot of the ladder, puts his hands to his face and discovers that his eyes are bandaged. He tears off the handkerchief and mask. In the light of a lantern left by the courtiers he catches sight of Gilda's scarf. Like a madman, he rushes into the house and reappears, dragging the bewildered Giovanna. For a moment Rigoletto's frenzy leaves him choking and speechless. Finally he bursts out in tones of anguish "Ah! la maledizione [The curse]!" He collapses, fainting, as the curtain falls.

Act Two

A room adjoining the Duke's chambers in the palace.[2] The Duke enters and in an excited soliloquy discloses that he returned to Gilda's house only to find the door locked and the premises deserted. In a brief but melodious aria the Duke voices his sincere longing for Gilda ("Parmi veder le lagrime"). His tender musings are interrupted by the entrance of the courtiers, who, in a spirited chorus ("Scorrendo uniti remota via"), inform him that they succeeded in abducting Rigoletto's maiden. When they reveal that they have brought the girl to the palace the Duke ardently sings of his joy over the prospect of seeing his beloved again. At the end of the number he hurries from the room, leaving the courtiers gaping in astonishment over his unusual demeanor.

From behind the scenes comes the voice of Rigoletto in a phrase of careless gaiety. As he enters the courtiers mockingly bid him good morning. Rigoletto looks furtively around for possible signs of his daughter's presence, hiding his anxiety by singing to himself as he limps about. He spies a handker-

[2] Act Three when given in four acts.

chief lying on the floor at the back of the room. Surreptitiously picking it up, he glances at it, then mutters that it is not Gilda's.

When Rigoletto asks about the Duke the courtiers answer that he is still sleeping. They likewise evasively answer the Duchess of Mantua's page, who has just entered. All this subterfuge finally rouses Rigoletto's worst suspicions. Confronting the courtiers, he cries that the girl must be in the chamber with the Duke and demands that they give him back his daughter. "His daughter!" the courtiers exclaim in astonishment. As the jester lunges toward the door of the chamber the courtiers bar his way. At this point Rigoletto sings the intensely dramatic aria ("Cortigiani, vil razza dannata"), denouncing the treachery of the courtiers. Again he tries to force his way into the chamber, crying, "Open the door, murderers!" Rigoletto then wildly implores the courtiers to give him back his child. The great aria ends with a cry for mercy—"Pietà, signori!"

As the courtiers look contemptuously down at the jester the door of the chamber suddenly opens and Gilda rushes out. She throws herself into her father's arms. Joyously he greets her, then becomes alarmed at her tears. "I am disgraced, Father!" she gasps. As Rigoletto recoils in horror she pathetically begs him to hide her shame. He turns on the courtiers and commands them to leave. A single note repeated insistently in the orchestra lends striking emphasis to his words.

Flinging himself into a chair, Rigoletto orders Gilda to speak. In the brief aria which introduces the dramatic closing scene of the act ("Tutte le feste al tempio") she confesses meeting her youthful admirer, then tells how she was torn from her home and brought to the palace.

Rigoletto is shaken with horror. In a duet reminiscent of the one in the first act, father and daughter attempt to console each other. Rigoletto declares that they must leave the palace at once. Just at that moment Monterone, surrounded by guards, crosses the room on his way to prison. Dramatically he pauses before a portrait of the Duke, saying that his curse has been in vain, for the Duke still triumphs in his sins.

Rigoletto

As the guards lead Monterone away Rigoletto calls after him that vengeance is not far off. Glaring at the Duke's portrait, Rigoletto swears revenge, while Gilda prays that she may be able to protect the man she loves. Their voices blend in a duet of thrilling power. As they both rush from the room the curtain falls.

Act Three

Sparafucile's inn, partly in ruins, on the outskirts of Mantua.[3] The stage setting shows both the interior, with a broken staircase leading to a loft, and the road in front of the inn. The Mincio River is visible in the background. Sparafucile is seated at a table inside the tavern, cleaning a leather belt. Rigoletto and Gilda, standing in the roadway, are talking excitedly.

The jester asks his daughter if she still loves the Duke. "Always," she replies, whereupon Rigoletto bids her peer into the tavern through a chink in the wall. At that moment the Duke, dressed as a soldier, comes in calling loudly for a room and some wine. While he is being served he sings the brilliant aria, "La donna è mobile [Woman is fickle]," which vividly characterizes him as a gay philanderer. He sings that woman's affections are as wayward as the breeze, and he who tries to capture her heart does so to his sorrow.

Sparafucile enters, places a jug of wine and glasses on the table, then knocks on the ceiling with the hilt of his sword. At that signal Maddalena comes down from the upper room. The Duke promptly tries to embrace her, but she evades him. Sparafucile steps outside and asks Rigoletto if he is to kill the victim immediately or later. Rigoletto tells him to await instructions. Sparafucile walks away toward the river.

Then begins the great Rigoletto quartet, "Un di, se ben rammento mi." The Duke, inside the tavern, woos Maddalena,

[3] Act Four when given in four acts.

who coyly responds. Outside, Gilda and Rigoletto express their humiliation and anger. The conflicting sentiments are skillfully blended to bring the quartet to a magnificent climax.

Rigoletto tells Gilda to don boy's clothing and ride to Verona, where he will meet her. When she leaves, Sparafucile reappears. Rigoletto pays the assassin half his fee, then says he will return at midnight to carry the body to the river. Thunder rumbles in the distance as he goes, while behind the scenes a humming chorus gives the effect of the rising wind of the storm.

As Sparafucile re-enters the Duke informs him that he has decided to stay at the inn overnight. Sparafucile offers the Duke his own room, then leads him upstairs. When Sparafucile returns, Maddalena, now completely under the spell of the Duke, desperately tries to persuade her brother not to kill him. While they are arguing, Gilda, wearing a man's costume, with boots and spurs, appears outside. She sings that her love for the Duke has drawn her here despite her father's orders to leave, then peers into the tavern.

Maddalena sings to Sparafucile that she adores the Duke and cannot let him die. In answer Sparafucile tosses her a large sack and harshly orders her to mend it so that it will hold the victim when he is borne off to the river. Maddalena suggests that Sparafucile murder Rigoletto instead of the Duke when the hunchback returns to pay the rest of his fee. Gilda is beside herself with horror.

Sparafucile finally compromises by agreeing to substitute for the Duke the first person who arrives at the inn before midnight. A brief but dramatic trio follows. Gilda prays desperately for help; Maddalena exults that the stormy night will aid her plan; Sparafucile reiterates the terms of his compromise. The storm increases in violence. A clock strikes. Determined to sacrifice herself for her lover, Gilda knocks at the inn door. As Sparafucile answers she tells him that she is a stranger and has lost her way. She enters, and Sparafucile flings himself upon her with drawn dagger.

There is a musical interlude which depicts the storm rising

to a furious climax, then slowly subsiding. As the sounds of the storm die away Rigoletto approaches, grimly musing that the hour of revenge has come at last. The clock strikes midnight as he knocks at the door of the inn. Sparafucile answers, then drags forth the sack in which he has placed Gilda's body. Rigoletto pays him the rest of the fee, takes up his burden, and starts for the river. Suddenly he hears the Duke's voice singing the refrain of "La donna è mobile." He listens as if hypnotized, and as the Duke's voice dies away in the distance he tremblingly tears open the sack, only to find his dying child.

Gilda suddenly stirs in her death agony and calls to her father. Quietly she tells him that she has sacrificed herself for the man she loved. Her voice blends with Rigoletto's in a final duet of farewell, and then she dies in her father's arms. Brokenly the jester sobs, "My Gilda! Dead!" In a paroxysm of despair he bursts out, "Ah! la maledizione!" He collapses over the body of his child as the theme of the curse reverberates in a mighty fortissimo. The curtain falls.

Der Ring des Nibelungen

by RICHARD WAGNER

[1813–1883]

Libretto by the Composer

Based on Germanic, Scandinavian, and Icelandic sagas,
particularly the *Nibelungenlied* (*Nibelungen saga*)

Das Rheingold

CHARACTERS

Woglinde ⎫	Soprano
Wellgunde ⎬ Rhinemaidens	Soprano
Flosshilde ⎭	Mezzo-soprano
Alberich, king of the Nibelungs	Bass
Fricka, wife of Wotan	Mezzo-soprano
Wotan, ruler of the gods	Bass-baritone
Freia, sister of Fricka, Goddess of Youth and Beauty	Soprano
Fasolt ⎫ giants	Bass
Fafner ⎭	Bass
Froh ⎫ brothers of Freia	Tenor
Donner, the thunder god ⎭	Baritone
Loge, the fire god	Tenor
Mime, brother of Alberich	Tenor
Erda, the earth-goddess	Mezzo-soprano

Place: Legendary Germany
Time: Antiquity
First performance: Munich, September 22, 1869
Original language: German

Das Rheingold

WAGNER began work on the prose poem of *Der Ring des Nibelungen* in 1848, with the writing of *Siegfrieds Tod (Siegfried's Death)*, which embodied the core of the drama. But after completing it he realized that it required prefatory explanation and therefore wrote *Der Junge Siegfried (The Young Siegfried)*. Finding it necessary to preface this poem (which became the present *Siegfried*) with still more explanatory material, he wrote *Die Walküre* and then *Das Rheingold*. The original *Siegfrieds Tod* became *Die Götterdämmerung*. Wagner completed the *Ring* poem in 1852, and in 1853 began composition of *Das Rheingold*, which he designated as the prologue to the drama. The entire score of the *Ring* was completed in 1872. The first complete performance of the *Ring* cycle took place at the Festspielhaus, Bayreuth, in August 1876.

The prelude to *Das Rheingold* is remarkable for the fact that it continues for 135 measures without a change of key. It is presumably symbolic of the calm, undisturbed depths of the Rhine and the elemental state of creation at the time the drama opens. This striking passage embodies what may be considered the first *leitmotiv*, or leading motive, of the *Ring* drama. Although it does not occur again in its original form, a number of other leading motives are constructed out of its harmonic element—that is, the perfect major chord. Among those which will be recognized are the motives of *Rhinemaidens*, *Gold*, *Norns*, *Destruction of the Gods*, *Rainbow*, *Sword*, *Ride of the Valkyries*, and *Brünnhilde's Sleep*. The first leading motive of *Das Rheingold* becomes strongly apparent at the end of *Die Götterdämmerung*, when the ring is finally engulfed by the Rhine. The simple, strong chord that dominates the music symbolizes the return to the primordial state of creation.

Because of the vast and complicated plot of the *Ring*, there are numberless other leading motives that symbolize characters and dramatic situations. As developed by Wagner, the leading motive was not merely a musical imitation of characteristic sounds, such as the galloping of horses, the sound of laughter, or the roaring of the wind—Wagner's leading motives—he was not the first nor the only one to use them—express in music the psychological factors of a dramatic situation as well as the identifying characteristics of an individual. A given motive will be heard not only when a character appears on the scene but also when that character is linked with a certain dramatic situation. Thus, in Act Two of *Die Walküre*, when Fricka rebukes Wotan for allowing Siegmund to steal Hunding's wife, we hear leading motives of persons or things as they are referred to in the conversation—*Hunding, Sword, Ring, Love, Spring,* and *Treaty.*

[*Scene One*] The rocky bed of the Rhine.[1] In the greenish-blue depths of the river the Rhinemaidens are swimming about at play. As they glide to and fro, Alberich, an evil-looking misshapen dwarf, emerges from the shadows at the base of the rocks and begins to climb upward, gazing in fascination at the mermaids. His passion stirred by their beauty, he tries awkwardly to lure them into his grasp, but they only laugh at his efforts. The dwarf curses in fury as they elude him.

Suddenly a yellowish light begins to glow at the peak of one of the largest rocks, and the Rhinemaidens, swimming around it, hail the gold of the Rhine. They sing that their father, who imposed on them the duty of guarding the treasure, told them that a ring forged from it would make its owner lord of all the world. But only he who is willing to renounce love forever can forge this ring.

Alberich, staring up at the gold, listens as if hypnotized, then climbs slowly toward the top of the rock. Reaching it at last, he shouts his renunciation of love, then tears the gold loose from the rock. Clutching the treasure, he scrambles down the rock and disappears, while the Rhinemaidens pursue him with angry cries. The waters recede as darkness envelops the scene and a thick mist begins to rise. When it clears and the stage gradually brightens again, a mountaintop becomes

[1] The opera is in one act and four scenes and is generally given without lowering the curtain. Scene changes are indicated by cloud and mist effects as the stage is darkened. Sometimes the opera is divided into two acts at the end of Scene Two.

visible. At one side of an area of flat rocks Wotan and Fricka are lying asleep.

[Scene Two] The morning light discloses, in the background, the shining castle of Walhalla, the newly built home of the gods, above the valley of the Rhine. Wotan and Fricka awake as the stately Walhalla motive sounds in the orchestra. Wotan, gazing proudly at the castle, declares that a dwelling worthy of the gods, built by the giants Fasolt and Fafner, at last is completed. Fricka reminds him that he has offered her sister Freia to the giants as payment for building the castle and bitterly reproaches him for his evil bargain. She adds that this castle, instead of satisfying Wotan's lust for power and glory, seems to have sharpened his desire for wandering about the world bent on conquest. When she accuses him of being heartless and cruel toward her, he retorts that there is proof enough of his devotion in the fact that he sacrificed one of his eyes to win her as his bride.

At that point Freia appears, imploring protection from the giants, who are now coming to claim their fee. Wotan, very much disturbed, fumes that Loge, his clever and crafty adviser in affairs of state, should be present, because he has devised a plan to ransom Freia. Confronted by the giants, the god spars for time, suggesting that they ask for some other reward. In angry surprise, they remind Wotan that the contract was written on his sacred spear and that as chief of the gods he must keep his word. Just as they start toward Freia her brothers, Donner and Froh, rush in. With his hammer upraised, Donner threatens the giants, but Wotan steps between the quarreling gods.

To the accompaniment of the Magic Fire music, Loge appears. Wotan, attempting to shift from himself the blame for the rash agreement with the giants, tells Loge that he would never have heeded his advice on the matter if the fire god had not promised him to find some way out of the contract. Loge, somewhat taken aback, points out that Fasolt and Fafner have satisfactorily performed their task and now may justly claim their fee. Furthermore, he says, he has wandered over the earth seeking some treasure that could be given them in place of Freia. But nowhere, he says, did he find a treasure for which men would be willing to sacrifice the love of womankind.

One man alone, the evil Alberich, has renounced love for gold, continues Loge, and he then tells the gods how the Nibelung king stole the hoard and forged the magic ring. Loge adds that he promised the Rhinemaidens he would present to Wotan their plea to restore their treasure. But Wotan, his thoughts on the ring and its terrible power, listens carefully as Fricka, Donner, and Froh—prompted by the wily Loge—counsel him to steal the treasure from Alberich. The Rhinemaidens, Fricka says scornfully, deserve their fate.

Fasolt and Fafner now offer to abrogate the contract and relinquish Freia if Wotan will agree to give them Alberich's treasure instead. Wotan contemptuously refuses, whereupon the giants seize Freia and carry her off. Transfixed with horror, the gods stare helplessly after her.

Loge, watching the others, cries out that they are growing pale and old before his eyes. Then he realizes what has happened. He tells Wotan that, because the Goddess of Youth and Beauty has been taken away, the gods are doomed to mortal old age. He warns that they will now be deprived of the golden apples from the tree which she guarded and with which they sustained their immortality. Spurred to action by the plight of the gods, Wotan decides to descend to Alberich's lair in search of the treasure that can ransom Freia.

Bidding the gods wait until he returns, Wotan follows Loge through an opening in the rocks and disappears. Clouds of smoke darken the scene. The Magic Fire music surges up and then gives way to a rhythmic figure as the beating of hammers on anvils is heard. A red glow flickers through the murk. Finally the smoke lifts and a gloomy cavern becomes visible. This is Nibelheim, the home of the Nibelungs, deep in the earth.

[*Scene Three*] Alberich enters, dragging the yelping Mime by his ear and abusing him for not having finished his forg-

Das Rheingold

ing. As Mime is being cuffed about he drops a piece of metalwork that somewhat resembles loosely woven chain mail. It is the tarnhelm, which makes its wearer invisible. The strange Tarnhelm motive sounds in the orchestra. Mime tells Alberich that he must keep it a while longer because it is not quite completed. Examining it closely, Alberich says he can find no flaws, then angrily accuses Mime of plotting to keep the tarnhelm for himself. To test its power, he puts it on his head and instantly vanishes, a puff of smoke appearing in his place. Mime looks distractedly about as he hears Alberich's voice, then wildly tries to ward off invisible blows. We hear savage, exulting laughter, and then the voice fades as Alberich goes to his slaves deep in another part of the cave.

Wotan and Loge now make their way into the cave, come upon Mime crouching in the shadows, and lift him to his feet. Sobbing in pain and terror, the dwarf tells them how Alberich forged the magic ring and with its aid discovered unlimited treasure in the earth. He has set the Nibelungs to digging up the hoard for him, giving them no rest night or day. Mime also explains about the tarnhelm.

At that point Alberich reappears, driving before him a group of Nibelungs burdened with gold, which they pile up at one side of the cave. The tarnhelm is hanging at his belt. Catching sight of Wotan and Loge, he drives Mime and the other dwarfs back into the cavern, ordering them to dig up more gold. Howling under his blows, they disappear.

Eying the gods suspiciously, Alberich asks why they have come. Wotan replies that they have heard of Alberich's wonderful treasures and would like to see for themselves. Through subtle flattery, Loge finally leads Alberich into boasting how, with the aid of his ring and his gold, he will rule not only the whole world but the gods as well. Craftily Loge asks what good all this gold would do him if someone should steal the ring and thus deprive him of his power. Alberich replies that with his tarnhelm he not only could make himself invisible but could assume any shape he pleases. Thus anyone who tried to steal the ring could never escape him.

Loge deliberately expresses doubt as to the power of the

tarnhelm, whereupon Alberich puts it on and becomes a great snake, which writhes and hisses on the ground before the gods. They pretend to be terrified. When Alberich resumes his human shape, Loge asks if he can change himself into a small creature as well as a large one—say, for example, a toad. Alberich again vanishes, and the gods see a toad crawling on a nearby rock.

Instantly Wotan puts his foot on the creature, while Loge snatches up the tarnhelm. Alberich, changed back to his own shape, curses and struggles under Wotan's foot. Tying him securely, the gods drag him out of the cavern. The scene darkens, fires glow through billowing smoke, and the sound of the hammers again is heard. The characteristic rhythmic beat in the orchestra is superseded by the Walhalla motive as the smoke lifts and the scene grows brighter. Once more we see the mountaintop near Walhalla, but the clinging mists hide the castle in the background.

[Scene Four] Wotan and Loge, dragging Alberich, enter through a pass in the rocks by which they had descended to Nibelheim. The dwarf curses in helpless rage as Loge taunts him unmercifully. Wotan tells him that he may buy his freedom with the hoard. To himself Alberich mutters that as long as he has his ring he can replenish his treasures at will, and thus the price of freedom will not, after all, be too dear. Asking Loge to loosen his right hand, he raises the ring to his lips and utters an incantation that brings his slaves up from the depths with the treasure. No sooner have they been sent back below than the gods declare that they will keep the tarnhelm as part of the ransom. As Loge tosses it on top of the mound of gold, Alberich shouts that they are a brace of greedy scoundrels, saying to himself, however, that he can easily force Mime to make him another.

Loge asks Wotan if the prisoner may now be released. In answer, the god points to the ring and demands it as the final item of ransom. Frantically Alberich protests, accusing Wotan of treachery and cynical lack of respect for the terms of a bargain. He warns that whoever robs him of his ring will be

Das Rheingold

forever accursed. With a sneer at his warning, Wotan ruthlessly pulls the ring from Alberich's finger, slips it on his own, and gazes at it in triumph.

He tells Loge to set Alberich free. Staggering to his feet, the dwarf shouts his terrible imprecation. Let this ring, acquired by a curse, bring anguish and death to all who possess it, he intones. Warning Wotan again that he shall never escape the ring's curse, Alberich disappears. Loge remarks sardonically on his "blessing," while Wotan stares at the ring as if hypnotized.

Suddenly Loge exclaims that Fasolt and Fafner are approaching with Freia. At that moment Fricka, Donner, and Froh enter, and Loge proudly shows them the hoard. The giants, with Freia between them, confront Wotan, who tells them that the ransom is ready. Thrusting their staffs into the ground on each side of Freia as a measure of her height and width, they order the gods to pile up the gold until it hides her from their sight. When all the gold has been placed in front of her, Fafner says he can still see Freia's hair and orders the tarnhelm to be thrown on top of the heap. Sullenly the gods obey. Fasolt, examining the mound, exclaims that he cannot part with Freia as long as he can see her eyes through one small hole that remains unfilled. The ring on Wotan's finger, he says, must serve to hide her completely from his sight. At Wotan's flat refusal to give up the ring, Fasolt drags Freia from between the two staves and starts to take her away.

While the gods plead desperately with Wotan a light begins to glow in a crevasse at the side of the clearing, and Erda, the earth-goddess, rises out of the ground. In ominous tones she sings that she is the all-wise goddess who knows all that has happened and all that is to be ("Weiche, Wotan, weiche!"). Through her three daughters, the Norns, who spin the web of fate, Wotan has gained his wisdom. But she herself has come to warn him that the gods are doomed. He must give up the ring. Slowly Erda disappears into the earth.

Suddenly resolved, Wotan raises his spear, orders the giants to release Freia, then throws the ring on top of the hoard. Freia is joyously embraced by the gods. In the next moment the giants begin quarreling furiously over the division of the spoils. Loge maliciously advises Fasolt to take the ring and give the rest of the treasure to Fafner. Fasolt snatches the ring, whereupon Fafner kills him with a blow of his staff and tears it from his grasp. The gods exclaim in horror, while Wotan muses uneasily that the curse has already begun its work. He resolves to go to Erda for further counsel.

Fricka, noting her husband's troubled look, urges him to go to the castle, where he can find respite from his cares. Wotan orders Donner to dispel the mists which still hide the castle. Donner summons up a thunderstorm, calls Froh to help him, and then both vanish in the swirling clouds. Meanwhile Fafner drags away the body of Fasolt and the sack containing the treasure. The blows of Donner's mighty hammer are heard in the distance; lightning blazes and thunder rolls. As the Rainbow theme soars up from the orchestra, the clouds lift, revealing a shining rainbow bridge that arches from the castle across the valley to the feet of the gods. Over the accompaniment of the Walhalla motive, Wotan proclaims that the shining fortress will be called Walhalla ("Abendlich strahlt"). He takes up a sword which Fafner, in dragging away the treasure, has left behind, points with it toward Walhalla as the Sword theme rings out, and bids the gods follow him to their destined abode. Hand in hand with Fricka, he starts across the bridge. Only Loge remains behind, remarking cynically that the gods will think themselves safe in their new home. He muses that perhaps it would be better to go his own way rather than join the gods in their fool's paradise of self-complacency. He will think it over, he decides, then casually follows after the gods.

From below comes the poignant lamentation of the Rhinemaidens bewailing the loss of their gold. Wotan looks uneasily downward and orders Loge to quiet them. When he calls down to the Rhinemaidens in jeering tones, the gods laugh and continue on their way. The sorrowing voices of the maidens are engulfed in the triumphant Walhalla motive as the curtain falls.

Die Walküre

CHARACTERS

Siegmund } Sieglinde }	Wälsungs, mortal son and daughter of Wotan .	{ Tenor { Soprano

Hunding, husband of Sieglinde ....Bass
Wotan ....Bass-baritone
Brünnhilde, daughter of Wotan and Erda,
  and eldest of the Valkyries ....Soprano
Fricka, wife of Wotan ....Mezzo-soprano

Gerhilde, Ortlinde, Waltraute, Schwertleite, Helmwige, Siegrune, Grimgerde, Rossweise } Valkyries, other daughters of Wotan and Erda .... { *Sopranos, mezzo-sopranos, and contraltos*

Place: Legendary Germany
Time: Antiquity
First performance: Munich, January 26, 1870
Original language: German

Wotan, realizing that Alberich would make every effort to get the magic ring away from Fafner, usurp world power, and then destroy the gods, was forced to take action to forestall his enemy. In order to safeguard Walhalla, he gave to his nine daughters, the Valkyries, the task of bringing from the world's battlefields the bodies of the bravest heroes. Transformed into immortals, they served as protectors for the gods.

Meanwhile Wotan has been ranging over the earth seeking the hero who would recover the ring from Fafner. The giant had dragged the hoard into a cave in the forest, where, in the form of a dragon, he was guarding his loot. Wotan now hopes that his earthly son Siegmund will be the one to wrest the treasure away from Fafner. (Siegmund and Sieglinde were Wotan's children by a mortal woman, with whom he lived for a time in the guise of Wolfe, or Wälse, creating the race of Wälsungs.) At the time *Die Walküre* opens, Siegmund, fleeing from a hostile forest tribe, has found refuge in the home of Hunding.

Act One

A primitive dwelling in the forest, built of rough logs around a huge tree which branches up through the rafters. From the trunk protrudes the hilt of a great sword. At one side of the room is a fireplace, and at the back are large double doors. The fury of the storm raging outside is vividly portrayed in the brief prelude. At its climax the doors swing open and Siegmund enters. Exhausted and out of breath, he staggers over to the hearth, flings himself down on a large bearskin, and lies there motionless.

Sieglinde enters from another room and exclaims in surprise as she sees the stranger. As she bends over him for a closer look, Siegmund revives and calls for water. Sieglinde brings him a beaker made of horn, and while he drinks, the Love motive sounds in the orchestra. Gazing at her intently, he asks who she is. Sieglinde replies that she is the wife of Hunding and that this is his home. Siegmund explains that, in combat with enemy tribesmen, his sword and shield were destroyed and he was forced to flee. As he goes on with his story, Sieglinde gives him mead to drink for further refreshment.

His strength somewhat restored, Siegmund rises and starts to leave. When Sieglinde invites him to rest awhile, he answers sadly that he must go in order to spare this household the misfortune that seems constantly to pursue him. Sieglinde observes that he could not bring trouble to the place where trouble itself dwells. The two pause as though spellbound,

Die Walküre

gazing at each other with growing ardor as the Love motive again sounds forth.

They are interrupted by the entrance of Hunding, who mutters a surly greeting and eyes Siegmund suspiciously. Abiding by the traditional rules of hospitality, however, he invites Siegmund to share his meal, noting with increasing surprise the close resemblance between the stranger's features and those of his wife. In answer to Hunding's questions, Siegmund explains more about himself. He is called Wehwalt (Woeful), he says, and he is of the tribe of Wälsungs (Wolfings). For a time he lived happily in the forest with his father, Wälse (Wolfe), his mother, and his twin sister. One day he and his father came home from the hunt to find their home burned to the ground and the mother murdered. They searched the ruins, but found no trace of the sister. The perpetrators of this deed, Siegmund says, were the Neidings, a hostile tribe that had long been feuding with the Wälsungs. He relates that his father was eventually slain in combat, leaving his son to wander alone through the forest, doomed to misery and defeat.

Siegmund then tells how one day he went to the rescue of a maiden who was being taken by her tribesmen to the house of a man they were forcing her to marry. After a furious combat in which the girl herself perished, Siegmund says, he was forced to flee for his life.

Hunding springs to his feet, angrily exclaiming that those whom Siegmund had attacked were his own kinsmen, and that now his enemy is under his roof. He offers Siegmund sanctuary for the night, but warns him to be ready to defend himself in the morning. With that Hunding orders Sieglinde to prepare his night drink and leave the room. His wife, following him, tries unobtrusively to direct Siegmund's eyes to the sword in the tree. Siegmund, however, fails to read the meaning of her glances.

Alone, Siegmund laments that he is unarmed in the house of his foe and wonders why he does not have the sword which his father promised he would find in his hour of need ("Ein Schwert verhiess mir der Vater"). But his thoughts soon turn to Sieglinde's beauty. He does not notice how the gleam from the dying fire is occasionally reflected in the hilt of the sword in the tree.

As the fire flickers out, leaving the room in darkness, Sieglinde re-enters and steals to Siegmund's side, whispering that she has mixed a sleeping potion with Hunding's drink. She then tells how she was forced to marry Hunding, and how, during the wedding feast, a one-eyed stranger entered the house unbidden. With a single stroke he thrust a great sword into the tree saying that it would belong to the warrior who could draw it forth again. Siegmund leaps to his feet in great excitement. Ardently Sieglinde sings that she longs for someone to unsheathe the sword and avenge her, then rushes into Siegmund's arms.

At that moment the doors at the rear swing open, showing the forest flooded with spring moonlight. Siegmund sings rapturously of love and spring in the beautiful aria "Winterstürme wichen dem Wonnemond," which Sieglinde answers in the equally ecstatic refrain, "Du bist der Lenz." They discover that they are Wälsungs—brother and sister—and are overwhelmed with joy at their reunion. Siegmund now realizes that it was his own father who thrust the sword into the tree and that he himself is destined to draw it forth.

Siegmund repeatedly cries "Wälse" in powerfully swelling and rising tones, then, hailing the sword ("Nothung! So nenn' ich dich Schwert!"—"Needful, I name this sword!"), he wrenches it free. He and Sieglinde passionately embrace, then rush out into the night. The curtain falls.

Act Two

A desolate mountain overlooking a deep ravine. Wotan, clad in full armor and carrying a spear, is standing in the foreground. Before him is Brünnhilde in the armor of a Valkyrie. He orders her to summon the other Valkyries and ride to the aid of Siegmund, who must soon face Hunding in combat. Brünnhilde climbs to a rocky ledge in the background

Die Walküre   303

and there sings her magnificent battle cry, "Hojotoho!" Looking down the valley, she informs Wotan that Fricka is approaching, then leaves as she continues her battle call.

Fricka angrily confronts Wotan, and a dramatic colloquy follows. Bitterly she reproaches him for permitting Siegmund to steal Hunding's wife. As the Goddess of Marriage, whose duty it is to see that nuptial vows are kept inviolate, Fricka demands that Wotan punish the guilty lovers. Wotan protests that the gods are sorely in need of a mortal champion who can perform a service that they themselves cannot accomplish. For that task, says the god, he has destined Siegmund, and that is why he is protecting him. Fricka denounces Wotan for shielding a sinful mortal, then forces him to promise that he will doom Siegmund.

She stalks away just as Brünnhilde rides up the pass. Curtly she tells the Valkyrie that Wotan has made his decision. Brünnhilde quietly approaches her father, who is overwhelmed by humiliation and despair. Trying to console him, she puts aside her shield and weapons and kneels before him. In a long monologue Wotan tells his daughter of his tragic attempts to regain the ring. He reveals how first he went to Erda for counsel, won her love, and sired nine daughters—the Valkyries, who have brought to Walhalla the heroes appointed for its defense. Then he reared Siegmund as a lawless warrior and gave him a magic sword in the hope that he would recover the ring. But now the ring's fearful curse will strike again, because Fricka has forced him to deny Siegmund protection in his coming encounter with Hunding.

Glory and power are gone, Wotan says bitterly, and now there remains only the dismal end. The gods are doomed and Alberich will triumph. That loathsome dwarf, Wotan goes on, has bought a woman with his gold, and she will soon bear him a son who will carry on his evil work. But he, chief of the gods, can find no one who will aid him in redeeming the world. In savage irony the god consigns Walhalla and its power to the Nibelungs with his blessing.

When he tells Brünnhilde that Siegmund must die, she desperately pleads for his life. Her entreaties rouse Wotan to violent anger. Roughly ordering her to obey, he strides from the scene. For a long time Brünnhilde stands motionless, overcome by horror and despair. At last she takes up her weapons and walks slowly to the top of the rocky height. From there she sees Siegmund and Sieglinde in the valley below. She watches them for a while, then sadly descends from the peak and disappears.

The lovers, exhausted by their flight, make their way painfully up through the pass. Sieglinde, beside herself with fear and remorse, begs Siegmund to leave her so that she might die alone in her shame. Delirious with terror, she imagines that Hunding's dogs are about to spring at her with wide-open jaws. With a piercing cry she faints in Siegmund's arms. Cradling her in his embrace, he seats himself and gazes at her in tenderness and concern.

Brünnhilde slowly approaches and stands before him, calling him by name as the Fate motive sounds in the orchestra ("Siegmund, sieh' auf mich!"). To the accompaniment of the Death motive, Siegmund asks who she is. Gravely she tells him that only heroes destined to die in battle may gaze upon her, and that she has come to take him to Walhalla. When Siegmund asks if Sieglinde may go with him, Brünnhilde says that he must part from her forever. Thereupon Siegmund flatly refuses to go, saying that he proposes to defend his beloved and himself with his magic sword. Wotan has disenchanted the sword, Brünnhilde says, and he is fated to be slain by the pursuing Hunding. Impetuously Siegmund raises his sword and cries out that he will kill Sieglinde and then himself rather than part from her. Won over by Siegmund's brave defiance, Brünnhilde promises to aid him in the fight despite Wotan's command. Warning him to prepare for battle, she rushes away.

Hunding's horn is heard in the distance. Siegmund tenderly kisses the sleeping Sieglinde, then strides toward the heights to meet his foe. Lightning blazes and thunder crashes as the two men come face to face. Brünnhilde is seen hovering near Siegmund, trying to protect him with her shield. Suddenly a reddish glow breaks through the clouds, revealing

Wotan with his spear pointed at Siegmund. Brünnhilde falls back in terror. Just as Siegmund aims a deadly blow at Hunding, his sword is shattered against Wotan's interposing spear, and, defenseless, he is killed by Hunding.

During the fight Brünnhilde rushes to Sieglinde, lifts her to her horse, tethered near by, and rides away. Wotan stands for a moment looking down at Siegmund. Then, at a contemptuous gesture of his hand, Hunding falls dead. Furiously vowing punishment for Brünnhilde, the god disappears. The curtain falls.

ACT THREE

The prelude is the thrilling and powerful *Ride of the Valkyries*, during which the curtain rises on a rocky mountain summit bordered by pines. Storm clouds, torn by the wind, swirl across the dark sky. On the highest peak three of the Valkyries await the arrival of the others, who are seen coming through the sky with the bodies of heroes slung across their saddles. The war maidens laugh in savage glee as they exclaim that the horses, carrying heroes who were foemen on the battlefield, rear at each other as though imbued with the hatred of combat.

Suddenly they see Brünnhilde approaching and are dumfounded when they discover that she is carrying not a warrior but a woman, Sieglinde. Brünnhilde tells her sisters about the fight, saying that Wotan, in terrible anger, is pursuing her to punish her for attempting to aid Siegmund. She begs the Valkyries to give her one of their fresh horses, but they refuse, fearing Wotan's wrath.

While the increasing roar of the storm heralds Wotan's approach, Sieglinde begs the Valkyries to save her. They tell her to flee eastward to a cave deep in the forest where Fafner sleeps on his gold. Wotan shuns that spot and will never pursue her there. Brünnhilde bids her have courage, for she is to bear a son who will be the world's most glorious hero—Siegfried. She hands her the fragments of Siegmund's sword.

Sieglinde thanks her ecstatically, then makes her escape.

At the height of the storm Wotan strides in. The Valkyries, retreating farther up the mountain height, surround Brünnhilde and try to conceal her. In majestic anger the god commands Brünnhilde to stand before him. Her sisters beg Wotan to be merciful. He proclaims that henceforth Brünnhilde will no longer be a Valkyrie and furiously orders her sisters to have nothing more to do with her, under the pain of similar punishment. The eight Valkyries flee in terror, while Brünnhilde, crushed by despair, falls at Wotan's feet.

For a long time Brünnhilde and Wotan remain motionless. The storm subsides, the weather clears, and a calm twilight descends. Then follows the magnificent scene of farewell. Brünnhilde eloquently tries to justify her actions, but her father insists she must be punished. She shall be placed in a deep sleep upon this mountaintop until the rightful hero awakens her. Resigned to her fate, Brünnhilde begs him to protect her in her helpless slumber with a wall of fire.

Overcome by his love for her, Wotan clasps her in his arms and sings his heartbreaking song of farewell ("Leb' wohl, du kühnes, herrliches Kind!"). At its conclusion he gently kisses her eyes, singing with infinite sadness, "So küsst er die Gottheit von dir" ("Thus the god takes away your godhood"). Slowly she loses consciousness.

Wotan carries her to a grassy slope under a great tree, closes her helmet, lays her spear at her side, and covers her with her shield. He then calls to Loge, commanding him to encircle the sleeping maiden with fire. He strikes a nearby rock three times with his spear. To the accompaniment of the thrillingly descriptive Magic Fire music, the flickering flames leap forth, ringing Brünnhilde's rock. In the tones of the prophetic Siegfried motive, Wotan, standing in lonely majesty on the lofty eminence, against a background of smoke and fire, holds forth his spear and sings that he who fears this weapon shall never break through the flames. While the Sleep motive wells up through the Fire theme, Wotan turns for a moment to gaze in tenderness and sorrow on Brünnhilde, then vanishes. The curtain falls.

SIEGFRIED

CHARACTERS

Mime	Tenor
Siegfried	Tenor
Wanderer (the god Wotan in disguise)	Bass-baritone
Alberich	Baritone
Fafner (the dragon)	Bass
Forest bird	Soprano
Erda, the earth-goddess	Contralto
Brünnhilde	Soprano

Place: A legendary forest in Germany
Time: Antiquity
First performance: Festspielhaus, Bayreuth, August 16, 1876
Original language: German

SIEGFRIED introduces the central character of the great *Ring* drama. The young Siegfried, son of Siegmund and Sieglinde, has been reared by Mime, the dwarf, in his cavelike home deep in the forest. Sieglinde, fleeing after the death of Siegmund in combat with Hunding (recounted in *Die Walküre*), has been found wandering in the forest by Mime. He took her to his dwelling, where she died giving birth to her son. Now grown to early manhood, Siegfried is about to take up his role of "world hero," destined to triumph because he is oblivious to fear and has learned the meaning of love.

The prelude briefly sounds the dark and mysterious Mime motive and then is dominated by an insistent, pounding rhythm suggestive of hammer strokes. The Slavery motive is heard, while the Sword motive cuts through momentarily. The curtain rises as the music continues without pause.

Act One

Mime's crude cave home in the forest. At one side is a natural stone abutment which serves as a forge, and over it is a bellows. Before the forge is an anvil, at which Mime is working. Swinging his small hammer to the rhythm of the music, he beats futilely away at the blade of a sword. In weariness and disgust he rages over the utter futility of his efforts ("Zwangvolle Plage! Müh' ohne Zweck!"). He fumes that every sword he makes is promptly shattered by the headstrong youth for whom he fashions it. Completely out of patience, he throws down the blade. Staring at it gloomily, he muses that if he could but forge together the broken sword *Nothung (Needful)*, his troubles would be over. Having this mighty weapon, he could persuade that reckless devil of a boy to slay the dragon Fafner for him and recover the Nibelung hoard which the dragon guards with his body. Then, Mime gloats, he would gain possession of the ring and be master of the world.

Complaining about his hard lot, Mime goes back to work. At this point Siegfried comes storming in, leading a bear by a rope. He sets the bear on Mime and roars with laughter at the dwarf's frantic efforts to escape. When he has had enough of this sport he drives the bear out of the cave, remarking that the animal proved pleasanter company than Mime. Taking up the sword on which Mime has been working, Siegfried smashes it to pieces against the anvil, raging at the dwarf for being too stupid to forge a weapon he can use. He sits down on a stone bench and lapses into a sulky silence.

Mime, warily staying out of reach, tries to placate him and finally offers him a dish of food. Siegfried knocks the dish from his hand, whereupon the dwarf launches into a querulous tirade. Has he not lavished fatherly care and devotion on this boy, fed and clothed him, taught him all he knew? And now what is his reward? Nothing but ingratitude and abuse! Siegfried retorts that the only thing he ever learned from Mime was a loathing for Mime himself. He wonders what impels him to return to the cave at all—when the birds and the beasts of the forest are friendlier than Mime could ever be.

Siegfried further annoys the dwarf by his persistent questioning. The animals, he says, live happily together—the male, his mate, and their offspring. The little ones, he has noted, resemble their parents, while he himself knows only a whining, repulsive dwarf as "Father." Fortunately, says Siegfried, he does not in the least resemble him and, what is more, does not believe that Mime is his father. Excitedly he demands to know who his parents are. When Mime tries to evade the question, Siegfried takes him by the throat and cries that he will force the answer from him.

The terrified dwarf thereupon tells Siegfried that long ago he came upon a woman lying helpless and ill in the forest. He took her to his cave, where she gave birth to a child and then died. But before her death, Mime relates, she told him that the child was to be called Siegfried and that she was Sieglinde. Of Siegfried's real father, Mime continues, he learned only that he was killed in combat. When Siegfried asks Mime to produce some proof to substantiate this fantastic story, Mime shows him the sword blade, broken in two. And this, wails Mime, remembering to feel sorry for himself again, was his sole reward for his deed of mercy.

In great agitation Siegfried cries that these fragments shall be forged into his rightful sword. He commands Mime to mend it for him, threatening him with the worst beating of his life if he fails. With that the youth rushes off into the forest, leaving Mime moaning that all his Nibelung's craft and skill will never be able to fashion this hero's sword.

The dwarf, overcome by despair, huddles in front of the anvil. Then, as an impressive passage of chords vibrates in the orchestra, the Wanderer appears at the entrance of the cave. He wears a long dark cloak and a wide-brimmed hat, which droops over the missing eye, and carries a great spear. After solemnly introducing himself to the frightened Mime, he explains that he has been wandering over the world and has learned much of its wisdom. The dwarf ungraciously tells him to be on his way, but the Wanderer, ignoring the remark, strides over to the hearth and sits down.

He observes after a moment that he has discovered in his travels that man is sorely lacking in wisdom. Mime, eying him suspiciously, remarks that he is well content with the wits he possesses. Thereupon the Wanderer proposes a contest of brains, offering his head as forfeit if he fails to answer any three questions Mime asks him. The dwarf agrees, musing that he will certainly trap this interloper in his own folly. First, asks Mime, what race inhabits the depths of the earth? The Nibelungs, replies the Wanderer. Alberich, their ruler, plundered the earth of its gold. With it and the aid of a magic ring, he hoped to enslave all mankind. Mime asks who rules the earth's surface. The giants Fasolt and Fafner ruled there, the Wanderer replies. They gained possession of Alberich's hoard, and in a quarrel over the spoils Fafner slew Fasolt. Fafner, in the form of a dragon, now guards the Hoard. For his third question, Mime asks who rules the skies. The Walhalla motive peals through the orchestra as the Wanderer replies that the gods rule above. Wotan is their monarch. He holds a spear hewn from the world ash, and on it are graven sacred edicts governing man's conduct. With this spear Wotan rules over gods, Nibelungs, and giants alike.

Now, says the Wanderer, settling himself more comfortably, it shall be Mime's turn. First, who are those with whom Wotan is most severe, yet loves above all others? The Wälsungs, answers Mime. Best-beloved were Siegmund and Sieglinde and Siegfried, their son. The Wanderer then asks what sword Siegfried must have to slay Fafner and recover the hoard. "Nothung!" cries Mime, in gleeful self-confidence. The third question—Who will reforge the broken sword Nothung?—throws the unsuspecting dwarf into a panic. Chattering in fear, he admits that he cannot answer.

The Wanderer tells him that only he who knows no fear can mend the sword. Regarding Mime with quiet amusement, the visitor remarks that he will leave his host's head as a prize for the fearless one. With that he leaves.

Mime, staring into the forest, gives way to his panic, con-

Siegfried

juring up horrible dangers. Overcome by terror, he hides in a corner. In another moment Siegfried bursts in, demanding to know if the sword is ready. By way of excuse, Mime says that he has been too concerned with fears for Siegfried's sake to give his attention to the sword. When Siegfried asks the meaning of fear, the dwarf says he will take him to Neidhöhle, the lair of the dragon, where he will learn this important lesson.

Impetuously Siegfried orders Mime to fashion the sword, so that he may be on his way. Mime wails that he is not equal to the task. Fuming at the dwarf, Siegfried picks up the broken weapon and declares that he will forge this sword himself. He builds up the fire and prepares the mold. As he works he sings the jubilant *Forge Song* ("Nothung! Nothung! Neidliches Schwert!"). Mime watches with gloating satisfaction, then begins preparing a magic brew. With this he proposes to poison Siegfried after the lad has slain Fafner and gained possession of the hoard.

Finally the great sword is finished. Siegfried cools it in water, then brandishes it triumphantly aloft. Striding over to the anvil, he splits it from top to bottom with a powerful blow. Laughing joyously, he runs out of the cave. The curtain falls.

Act Two

A dark forest glade. The motives of Fafner, the Ring, the Curse, and Destruction are woven into the gloomy measures of the prelude. Barely visible at the rear is the mouth of a huge cave. Alberich crouches in the shadows, watching by Fafner's cave in the hope that he may recover his lost hoard. Heralded by mysterious flashes of light, the Wanderer appears. Alberich recognizes him as Wotan, his ancient foe, and curses him as a troublemaker. The god himself, he taunts, is being haunted by the fear that the Nibelungs will regain possession of the ring—with obvious consequences.

The Wanderer replies that Mime at this very moment is leading to the cave one who will win the ring—a youth who knows no fear. He suggests that Alberich try to persuade Fafner to give up the ring before the inevitable occurs. Obligingly he awakens Fafner. Alberich calls into the cave that he will be content to let the dragon keep the hoard if he will but surrender the ring. The dragon merely growls back that the treasure is his by right of possession. Wotan laughs at Alberich's disappointment, then disappears with a word of warning. Glaring after him, Alberich savagely vows revenge. He vanishes among the rocks.

The scene grows lighter as the day dawns. Siegfried enters, his sword tied at his waist. Mime shuffles after him, cautiously peering about. Seating himself under a lime tree, Siegfried asks if he is now to have his lesson in fear. Mime points out the cave and tells the youth about the dragon. Its breath is deadly poison, and one drop of its saliva will corrode flesh and bones, says the dwarf in awed tones. It can pulverize a man's bones with a flick of its tail, Mime goes on. This remarkable beast, declares Siegfried, will soon feel the sword Nothung in its heart. He derides Mime for offering him all this nonsense in place of a useful lesson on fear and impatiently tells him to take himself off into the forest. Mime goes, saying he will wait at the nearby spring.

Siegfried lies down under the tree and indulges in pleasant reflection over the beauty of the forest. The orchestra begins the wonderfully descriptive music familiarly known as the *Forest Murmurs (Waldweben)*. Dismissing the unpleasant thoughts of the cringing dwarf, Siegfried muses tenderly about the mother he has never known. A birdcall from the branches above interrupts his thoughts. Intrigued by its song, he fashions a pipe from a reed and tries to blow an answering call. But the notes—amusingly played off-key in the orchestra—bring no response. Siegfried finally gives up and, raising his hunting horn to his lips, sounds his famous *Horn Call*.

At this Fafner awakes and drags his fearsome dragon's body out of his cave. Siegfried whirls and, facing the beast, remarks with an amused chuckle that his efforts have attracted the attention of a handsome stranger indeed. Fafner roars,

Siegfried

shows his teeth, and asks who dares interrupt his slumbers. Siegfried mockingly asks the beast if it can teach him fear. Bellowing with rage, the dragon spews out its poison, while smoke pours from its nostrils. Adroitly avoiding the poisonous spume, Siegfried leaps forward to attack. He lunges at the dragon's tail, then, when the beast rears in pain, turns and drives his sword into its heart.

With its dying breath the dragon asks Siegfried who incited him to this murderous deed. He answers that it was the dragon's own threat that impelled him to use his sword in self-defense. Fafner now realizes that Alberich's ancient curse on the ring has at last struck him down. He warns Siegfried that the one who plotted this deed is planning the youth's death also. Siegfried asks Fafner if *he* knows the riddle of his birth, then reveals his name. The dragon repeats the name and slumps down dead.

Siegfried now pulls his sword from the body and in so doing gets the dragon's blood on his hand. He exclaims that it burns and involuntarily puts his hand to his lips. Through the magic of the blood he finds that he can understand the language of the forest bird, which at that moment begins to sing again. The bird tells him that within the cave is the coveted hoard. Its chief treasures are the tarnhelm, which will help him to accomplish mighty deeds, and the ring, which will bestow world power on its wearer. Thanking the bird for its kind advice, Siegfried enters the cave.

Alberich and Mime now return, and the moment they meet, a violent quarrel ensues over the hoard. Mime is wild with fury when Alberich refuses to share the ring and the tarnhelm and claims the entire treasure for himself. At the height of the argument Siegfried reappears with both the ring and the tarnhelm. He examines them closely, then puts the ring on his finger and hangs the tarnhelm from his belt. The forest bird begins to sing again, telling Siegfried that the taste of the dragon's blood will henceforth enable him to divine the real meaning behind Mime's deceitful words.

A remarkable dialogue follows. The dwarf himself assumes that he is deceiving Siegfried with cunning flattery. However, we hear Mime's words as Siegfried understands them—that he intends to render Siegfried helpless with poison brew, lop off his head with the sword, and then take possession of the ring and the tarnhelm. Mime recoils in angry surprise when the youth's answers show that he understands the true meaning of the words. Nevertheless he extends the drinking horn containing the poison. Siegfried strikes him dead with a single blow of his sword. From the distance comes Alberich's savage, mocking laughter. Siegfried drags the dwarf's body into the cave, then barricades the opening with the carcass of the dragon. The *Curse Motive*, reverberating in the orchestra, reminds us that the ring's curse has claimed another victim.

Wearied by his efforts, Siegfried throws himself down under the lime tree and muses on his loneliness and the mystery of his past. Once more the forest bird sings. It tells Siegfried of Brünnhilde, who lies asleep on a great rock on a mountain height, ringed by flames. Only he who has never known fear can break through the flames and win this glorious maid for his bride. He himself is this hero, Siegfried cries jubilantly, because he had never learned the lesson of fear. Excitedly he implores the bird to lead him to Brünnhilde's rock. The *Fire Music* and the Siegfried motive sound triumphantly as he rushes away to follow the bird's receding voice. The curtain falls.

Act Three

A wild, rocky glen. The brief prelude dramatically states the motives of the Gods' Need and the Treaty, rising to a fiery crescendo with the theme of the Twilight of the Gods. A storm is raging as the curtain rises. Wotan, still in his Wanderer's garb, enters and pauses before a cavernous opening in the rocks. He calls out to Erda, the earth-goddess. An eerie light shimmers in the cavern, and Erda rises slowly from the ground. A long discourse follows. Wotan seeks to learn from the all-wise goddess how the inexorable processes of fate may be halted. Erda pointedly suggests that he ask his own daughter, Brünnhilde, who also was endowed with godlike wisdom. When Wotan reveals how he has punished Brünnhilde—imprisoning her in sleep behind a barricade of flame—Erda berates him for his harshness. She points out that he, with grievous sins on his own conscience, is hardly in a position to punish so severely.

Wotan, however, stubbornly continues. The wisdom that Erda long ago implanted in his heart, he says, has brought him not peace and confidence, but dismay and confusion. Now she must tell him how to conquer the despair that is engulfing his soul. In the face of Erda's evasive reply, Wotan resigns himself to his fate. There is a long pause. Then Wotan somberly declares that he is no longer concerned with the imminent doom of the gods. Siegfried, the hero without fear, has won the ring. With its aid he will also win Brünnhilde, and by that deed of love will redeem the world. As he bids Erda return again to her eternal sleep, she sinks slowly back into the earth.

Wotan, seeing Siegfried approaching in the distance, sits down to await him. The youth rushes in, anxiously following the forest bird, which flutters about for a moment and then disappears. Catching sight of Wotan, Siegfried asks the way to the fire-encircled rock. Instead of answering, Wotan questions the youth, and Siegfried tells him about Mime and killing the dragon with his sword. Asked who forged the sword, Siegfried replies that he himself did it. Wotan wishes to know who first made the fragments out of which he fashioned this sword. Siegfried says that he does not know, adding that the weapon was certainly of no use to him in fragments. That is obvious, remarks Wotan with a good-natured laugh.

Siegfried, rather irked at the stranger's bantering manner, curtly tells him that he has no more time for idle talk. He expresses curiosity, however, about Wotan's appearance, particularly over the fact that he has only one eye. Wotan's devious explanations serve only to make Siegfried more impatient, and he at length orders the god to let him pass on his way to the rock.

In majestic anger, Wotan bars his way. He bids Siegfried

look up at the mountain height, where the glow of a great fire is seen. There the maiden slumbers, he says, but he who dares approach her will be consumed by the flames. Siegfried scornfully attempts to push Wotan aside, whereupon the god holds his spear before him, blocking his path. As Siegfried angrily draws his sword, Wotan warns that this spear once shattered the very sword Siegfried holds in his hands—and will do so again. In a sudden flash of understanding, Siegfried cries out that now at last he faces his father's enemy. Thus his sire will be avenged, he storms, and with a mighty blow splinters the shaft of the spear. There is a blaze of lightning and crash of thunder. Wotan vanishes.

Exultantly Siegfried turns toward the fiery mountain, from which the flaming tide appears to be descending closer. Lifting his horn to his lips, Siegfried blows his horn call, then plunges straight toward the flames. A glowing mist envelops the scene, while the *Fire Music* swells and surges in the orchestra.

When the mist clears we see the sunlit mountain summit where Brünnhilde lies asleep under a huge fir tree. It is the same setting as that of the closing act of *Die Walküre*. The Sleep motive whispers high in the strings. Siegfried appears from behind a rock and gazes on the scene, overcome with amazement. He first notices a fully caparisoned horse near by. Slowly he approaches the sleeping figure in armor and helmet partly hidden by a great shield.

Gently he lifts the shield, gazing in fascination upon the face of the warrior. He carefully cuts through the fastenings of the breastplate with his sword, then lifts off the armor. Completely dumfounded, he discovers that the warrior is a beautiful woman. Siegfried is suddenly gripped by a profound foreboding which he recognizes as fear. Crying wildly for help, he sinks down at Brünnhilde's side.

After a moment he slowly rises, his eyes fixed on Brünnhilde's face. Overwhelmed by her enchanting beauty, he bends down and kisses her passionately on the mouth. Brünnhilde, awakened, hails the sunlit world about her in an ecstatic flood of song. She turns to Siegfried with the soaring phrase,

Siegfried

"Siegfried! seliger Held!" ("Siegfried! Blessed hero!"). Joyously she greets him as the son of the mother whom she befriended in defiance of Wotan.

Siegfried, shaken by the unfamiliar emotion of love, answers her in mingled wonder and rapture. Impetuously he tries to embrace Brünnhilde. She recoils in terror, realizing that in taking away her armor the hero has taken away her godhood. She is no longer a Walküre, but a mortal woman. Desperately she entreats Siegfried to leave her, crying out that she does not want mortal embraces. He sweeps aside her pleas with passionate declarations of his love. Helpless before his ardor, Brünnhilde surrenders, singing that she will follow him to her doom. Jubilantly she bids adieu to Walhalla and the splendor of the gods. Brünnhilde and Siegfried blend their voices in a magnificent duet as they sing of the love that overwhelms them in the dawn of their new world—transfiguring love that laughs at death ("Leuchtende Liebe! lachender Tod!"). They are clasped in each other's arms as the curtain falls.

Die Götterdämmerung

(The Twilight of the Gods)

CHARACTERS

First Norn	Contralto
Second Norn daughters of Erda	Mezzo-soprano
Third Norn	Soprano
Siegfried	Tenor
Brünnhilde	Soprano
Gunther } Gibichungs—children of Gibich and Grimhilde	Bass
Gutrune	Soprano
Hagen, their half brother, son of Grimhilde and Alberich	Bass
Waltraute, a Valkyrie	Mezzo-soprano
Alberich	Bass
Woglinde	Soprano
Wellgunde } Rhinemaidens	Mezzo-soprano
Flosshilde	Contralto

Vassals, warriors, and women

Place: Legendary Germany
Time: Antiquity
First performance: Festspielhaus, Bayreuth, August 17, 1876
Original language: German

PROLOGUE

BRÜNNHILDE'S ROCK (the same as in the closing scenes of *Die Walküre* and *Siegfried*).[1] It is night. From below, in the background, comes the glow of the fire that encircles the rock. In the dim, bluish light of the foreground the three Norns are visible. The First Norn unwinds from about her body the golden cord of Fate, ties one end to a pine tree, and then

---

[1] The opera, written in a prologue and three acts, is sometimes cut because of its great length, the prologue being played as the first scene of Act One.

Die Götterdämmerung

passes it along to the others. As they weave, the destinies of gods and men are decided.

The First Norn sings that one day, as she was weaving beside the spring at the foot of the world ash tree, Wotan appeared and exchanged one of his eyes for a drink of the waters of wisdom. Then he broke a branch from the tree and fashioned a great spear, after which the tree withered and the spring dried up. The Second Norn takes up the story. Winding the cord around a rocky projection, she tells how Wotan engraved on his spear the sacred treaties that gave him world power, and how afterward the spear was shattered by Siegfried. Wotan then returned to Walhalla and commanded the heroes to cut down the ash tree. The Third Norn, catching up the end of the cord, concludes the narrative. The branches of the tree were hewn into pieces and piled up like a rampart around Walhalla. There, the Norn intones, Wotan and his hosts await their doom, which will come when flames obliterate both rampart and castle.

Completing the prophecy, the Norns sing that Wotan will one day plunge his broken spear into the breast of Loge, whom he has bound by magic to Brünnhilde's rock. He will then pull the spear flaming from the fire god's wound, hurl it upon the ramparts of Walhalla, and thus kindle the destroying fire. In frightened tones the Norns exclaim that the sharp edges of the rock are cutting the cord. As they lament that the world's evil and Alberich's curse are severing the strands, the cord suddenly snaps. The Fate motive sounds in the orchestra. The Norns tie themselves together with the torn cord and then disappear, crying that they must now return to their mother Erda.

Dawn slowly brightens over the rocky height. Soon Brünnhilde and Siegfried appear, heralded by their characteristic motives, after which we hear the music played as the introduction to the concert version of *Siegfried's Rhine Journey*. Brünnhilde leads her horse, Grane, by the bridle. Siegfried is clad in armor. In a heroic refrain ("Zu neuen Thaten, theurer Helde") Brünnhilde sings that Siegfried must now go forth to triumph for her. With fateful insight, she reveals she is haunted by the thought that, in sending him forth to conquer, she may lose his love. She has given him divine wisdom at the cost of her godhood. Now she has only mortal love to offer him, and he, as a mortal man, may one day spurn that love. She begs him never to forget their pledges of love. Siegfried promises to accomplish glorious deeds in her behalf, and as a token of faith he gives her the magic ring. In exchange she gives him Grane.

At the end of an ecstatic duet Siegfried, leading Grane through a cleft in the rocks, begins his journey down the Rhine valley. Brünnhilde watches him go, waving to him joyously as his horn call sounds from the distance. The curtain falls during the playing of the familiar *Rhine Journey* music, which continues into the Hagen motive as the curtain rises again.

Act One

The castle of the Gibichungs on the Rhine.[2] Gunther, King of the Gibichungs, is seated on his throne with his sister, Gutrune. They are in conversation with Hagen, who is seated at a table before them. Hagen observes that neither Gunther nor Gutrune is married, and expresses concern about the future of the race of Gibichungs. He would have Gunther marry Brünnhilde, the fairest of women, he says, but her destined bridegroom is the world's greatest hero, Siegfried. Only he was brave enough to penetrate the ring of magic fire that girded the mountain peak on which she lay. Hagen then relates the story of Siegfried's origin and his adventures, adding that a hero of such stature should be the husband of Gutrune. Gunther angrily rebukes him for mocking him with dreams of a bride he cannot win.

At that point Hagen takes Gunther aside and tells him of his evil plan. When Siegfried, journeying down the Rhine, visits the Gibichungs' castle, he can be given a magic potion

[2] Sometimes played as Scene Two of Act One.

Die Götterdämmerung

which will not only put him in Gunther's power but will cause him to forget Brünnhilde and fall in love with Gutrune. Once in the grip of the spell, Siegfried can be persuaded to win Brünnhilde for Gunther in return for taking Gutrune as his own bride.

While they are talking Siegfried's horn call sounds in the distance, and shortly the boat carrying Siegfried and his horse approaches the riverbank. The Curse motive thunders out as he leaps to the shore on his horse. Dismounting, he enters the castle and is greeted by the Gibichungs. Hagen quietly signals Gutrune to retire to her room. Gunther puts his lands, his vassals, and himself at Siegfried's disposal. Siegfried, in return, can offer nothing but his strong muscles and his sword. Moving close to him, Hagen remarks that it has been told that Siegfried has won the Nibelungen hoard. He had forgotten that, Siegfried answers carelessly, because the gold was of no use to him. All he kept of the hoard, he goes on, pointing to the tarnhelm hanging from his belt, was this bit of metal network. He does not know what it is for, he adds. Hagen, saying that it represents the Nibelungs' finest piece of craftsmanship, explains its magic power and then asks Siegfried if he has any other treasure. A ring, Siegfried replies, which is now on the hand of a woman. Gunther betrays great excitement. While he and Siegfried are in conversation, Hagen unobtrusively opens the door of Gutrune's room. She comes out carrying a drinking horn containing the magic potion. Handing it to Siegfried, she courteously invites him to drink.

The draught instantly erases from his mind all memory of Brünnhilde, and he gazes at Gutrune with passionate intensity. Confused and embarrassed by his ardor, she withdraws to her room. Siegfried promises to set out at once to win Brünnhilde for Gunther, saying that, by means of the tarnhelm, he will woo her in Gunther's form. For this service, Gunther assures him, Gutrune shall be his bride. The two men then prick their arms, mix their blood with wine, and drink, swearing an oath of blood brotherhood as their voices blend in a vigorous duet ("Blühenden Lebens labendes Blut"). He who breaks the oath, they proclaim, must pay forfeit with his heart's blood. Hagen declines to drink, saying that his blood is too cold for so fiery a potion.

Taking up their weapons, Siegfried and Gunther leap into the boat and row away on their adventure. Gutrune reappears momentarily, looks after them, and sings Siegfried's name in ecstasy. Hagen, taking up his shield and spear, seats himself in the doorway and watches the two men leave. Sardonically he wishes them godspeed, gloating that their quest for Gunther's bride will bring him the ring ("Hier sitz' ich zur Wacht"). The curtain falls, while the music continues without pause into an interlude dominated by the somber themes of the Nibelungs' Destruction and Triumph. The Gold and Ring motives are heard, and then the Brünnhilde motive. Here the curtain rises again on Brünnhilde's rock—the same scene as the Prologue.[3]

Brünnhilde, gazing in rapture at the magic ring on her finger, is startled by the sound of thunder. As the *Ride of the Valkyries* echoes in the orchestra, Waltraute rides up in wild excitement. Eagerly Brünnhilde asks if she has come with a message of forgiveness from Wotan. Giving Waltraute no opportunity to answer, she sings exultantly that Wotan's stern sentence was a blessing in disguise, for it brought her the boon of love.

The Valkyrie impatiently silences her and tells why she has come. In what is known as *Waltraute's Narrative* ("Seit er von dir geschieden") she describes, virtually in the words of the Norn's prophecy, how Wotan and the gods are awaiting their downfall. Wotan has said that if Brünnhilde will give the ring back to the Rhinemaidens, Alberich's curse will be broken and the peace of Walhalla assured. Waltraute implores Brünnhilde to give up the ring, but Brünnhilde replies that she will never part with this token of her hero's love, even though it means the destruction of the gods. With a cry of warning and despair Waltraute rides away.

The glow of the fire encircling the rock now grows brighter, with the flames leaping into view to the accompaniment of the Magic Fire music. Brünnhilde, looking down into the val-

[3] Sometimes played as Scene Three of Act One.

Die Götterdämmerung 323

ley, ecstatically hails the approach of Siegfried. In a moment he appears, but Brünnhilde recoils in terror and bewilderment as she sees a stranger standing before her. With the tarnhelm on his head, hiding most of his face except his eyes, Siegfried has assumed Gunther's shape. In a disguised voice he tells Brünnhilde that he is Gunther and has come to claim her as his bride. He seizes her and, after a fierce struggle, tears the ring from her finger and then forces her into a cave at the base of the rock. Before he himself enters he unsheathes his sword and—now in his natural voice—cries that the weapon will guard Gunther's bride.

Act Two

Before the entrance hall of the Gibichungs' castle, which is at the right. The sloping bank of the Rhine at the left. To the rear rises a mountain height, on which great stone altars to Wotan, Fricka, and Donner are visible. It is night. Hagen, spear and shield in hand, sits motionless beside one of the pillars of the hall, waiting for the return of Siegfried and Gunther. Alberich is kneeling before him, his hands on Hagen's knees. A strange and somber dialogue follows, throughout which Hagen stares unseeing before him, as though in a trance. Beginning in soft, mysterious tones ("Schläfst du, Hagen, mein Sohn?"), Alberich tells him the story of the ring's curse, then makes him swear that he will regain the ring. The dwarf's voice dies away as he vanishes in the shadows.

Dawn breaks. Hagen is roused by Siegfried, who appears suddenly, explaining that the tarnhelm instantly transported him from Brünnhilde's rock. Gunther and his bride, he says, are following in the boat. Gutrune enters and is joyously greeted by Siegfried. Triumphantly he relates how he won his way to Brünnhilde's side and how his sword helped him keep sacred the oath he swore with Gunther. Telling Hagen to summon the vassals for the wedding festivities, he goes into the hall with Gutrune.

Hagen sounds an oxhorn and calls out to the vassals of the

Gibichungs ("Hoiho! Hoiho! Hoiho!"), and soon the riverbank is thronged with men responding in a vigorous chorus. The hero Siegfried, Hagen proclaims, has won a Valkyrie as a bride for Gunther, and he himself will wed Gutrune. He invites them all to the wedding feast. Meanwhile the boat bearing Brünnhilde and Gunther approaches, and as it touches the shore the vassals cheer.

Gunther proudly leads forth Brünnhilde. She walks beside him with bowed head, her pale features betraying her misery and humiliation. Siegfried and Gutrune, attended by ladies-in-waiting, come from the castle to greet them. Shaken with horror, Brünnhilde sees the ring on Siegfried's finger. She cries out that Gunther forced her to become his bride and tore the ring from her hand, then demands to know why it is now on Siegfried's finger. Gunther, completely confused, protests that he did not give the ring to Siegfried. Wild with anger, Brünnhilde turns on Siegfried and accuses him of betraying her and robbing her of the ring. But Siegfried, still under the influence of the potion, stares at the ring, saying that he wrested it from a dragon, not from the hand of a woman. Thereupon Hagen steps forward, also accuses Siegfried of betrayal, and demands vengeance in Gunther's name. Completely unconscious of his guilt, Siegfried declares that he kept faith with Gunther and that his sword Nothung was the guardian of his trust.

At that Hagen holds forth his spear and demands that Siegfried take an oath upon it. Siegfried places his fingers on the spear point and swears that he was never wed to Brünnhilde ("Helle Wehr!"). Livid with rage, Brünnhilde rushes to the spear and dedicates it to the destruction of Siegfried because of his betrayal and perjury. Unmoved by her fury, Siegfried embraces Gutrune, than gaily invites all to the wedding celebration. He leads Gutrune into the castle, and the people follow.

Brünnhilde, Gunther, and Hagen remain to plan their revenge. When Hagen asks Brünnhilde how he may bring about Siegfried's death, she reveals that with her magic arts she has made the hero invulnerable to attack—all but his back, which he never turns on a foe. That, then, will be the target for his spear, Hagen says malevolently. Gunther, however, thinking of Gutrune, rebels at murdering Siegfried. Hagen whispers that his death will give the Gibichungs possession of the ring. Gutrune need never know how her hero died, he goes on, for tomorrow there will be a great hunting party, during which Siegfried will be killed by a wild boar. As the voices of the plotters blend in a dramatic expression of revenge, the wedding procession emerges from the castle, with the vassals bearing Gutrune and Siegfried on their shields. Hagen compels Brünnhilde to join the procession with Gunther.

Act Three

A forest clearing on the bank of the Rhine. The Rhinemaidens are frolicking about in the water. Siegfried appears on the riverbank, spies the mermaids, and asks them if they have seen the animal he has been trailing. Teasingly they ask if he will give them his ring if they tell him where his quarry is hiding. At his refusal, they taunt him for being miserly. When they find that he is determined to keep the ring, however, their cajolery turns to earnest entreaty, and they warn him that the ring's curse will strike him down that very day. Siegfried's voice blends with theirs in a melodious ensemble as he expresses his contempt for the advice of women.

The Rhinemaidens swim away. Siegfried hears the horns of the hunting party and sounds an answering call. Soon Hagen and Gunther appear, followed by their vassals carrying game. The hunters prepare to feast on their kill. Siegfried tells how he lost track of his quarry and came at length to the bank of the Rhine, where three mermaids told him that he was destined to be killed before nightfall. Gunther, terror-stricken, looks at Hagen, who casually hands Siegfried wine containing a potion that will restore his memory.

As the hunters gather about the campfire, Hagen asks Siegfried to tell of his exploits. When Siegfried, his mind cleared by the potion, relates how he braved the flames and claimed Brünnhilde as his bride ("Mime hiess ein mürrischer Zwerg"), Gunther leaps to his feet in horror. At that moment two ravens circle slowly above and then fly away toward the Rhine. As Siegfried turns to watch them, Hagen plunges his spear into his back. Siegfried falls on his shield, while the murderer vanishes into the darkness. In the final agony of death, Siegfried raises himself and sings a poignant farewell to Brünnhilde.

Now follows the magnificent music of *Siegfried's Funeral March*, which traces in its themes the hero's past and the overwhelming tragedy of his death. The sorrowing vassals lift the shield to their shoulders and slowly move off in a dramatic cortege. Rising mists from the Rhine gradually envelop the scene during this interlude. When they clear away we see the hall of the Gibichung castle, as in Act One.

Gutrune, tortured by a premonition of disaster, starts in fear at the sound of a hunting horn in the distance. The hunting party approaches. Transfixed with horror, Gutrune watches the vassals bring in Siegfried's body and place it in the middle of the hall. When Hagen tells her that Siegfried was killed by a boar, she utters a wild cry of grief and faints over the body. After a moment she revives and accuses Gunther of the murder, but he cries out that Hagen is guilty. In savage defiance, Hagen admits the deed. Siegfried, he declares, swore falsely on his spear, and that very spear has now revenged his betrayal. Shouting that the ring is his by right, he flings himself on Gunther and kills him with a blow of his sword. As he turns to snatch the ring from the hand of the dead Siegfried, the lifeless arm rises slowly, as if in a gesture of warning. The clamoring throng stands frozen with horror.

Brünnhilde now approaches, and with majestic scorn she bids the people cease their childish lamentations because they are unfit for a great hero. Gutrune cries out that Brünnhilde was the cause of all her misfortune, whereupon Brünnhilde tells her contemptuously that she, Gutrune, was never Siegfried's wife, but a mere interloper. Realizing that she too

Die Götterdämmerung

is a victim of Hagen's treachery, Gutrune curses him, and then, crushed by despair, sinks over Gunther's body.

Brünnhilde commands the vassals to build a pyre on the riverbank and to bring to her Siegfried's horse. As the men obey, she looks down upon the hero and pours out her love and sorrow in a heartbreaking strain ("Wie Sonne lauter strahlt mir sein Licht"). Raising her eyes, she bids the gods look upon what they have destroyed, then draws the ring from Siegfried's finger and puts it on her own. She looks toward the Rhine and sings that the Rhinemaidens may soon claim from her ashes their precious ring, cleansed at last of its curse. At her command the two ravens perched near the riverbank start their flight back to Wotan with the message that his doom is upon him. Brünnhilde bids them pause at the fire-encircled rock and tell Loge to join the gods in their final hour. With that she snatches a torch from the hand of a vassal and hurls it upon the pyre, which bursts into flame.

Grane, Siegfried's horse, is led forward. To the music of the great *Immolation Scene*, Brünnhilde hails Siegfried in death, then rides into the flames. The fire billows up fiercely and seems to devour the entire hall, while the terrified onlookers crowd to the foreground. When the flames die down the Rhine surges up in a mighty flood, bearing the Rhinemaidens on its crest. On seeing them, Hagen leaps like a madman into the river to gain the coveted ring, crying, "Zurück vom Ring!" ("Away from the Ring!"). The Rhinemaidens drag him beneath the waves, then reappear, with Flosshilde holding up the ring in a gesture of joyous triumph.

The Rhine subsides. In the distance a glow breaks through a dark band of clouds, revealing Walhalla and Wotan with the gods about him, facing their flaming doom. The music storms to a great climax on the Rhine and Walhalla themes, then dies away as the motive of Redemption by Love soars high in the strings. The curtain falls.

Der Rosenkavalier
(The Rose Bearer)

by RICHARD STRAUSS
[1864–1949]

Libretto by
HUGO von HOFMANNSTHAL

CHARACTERS

Count Octavian Rofrano, a young Viennese nobleman	*Mezzo-soprano*
The Marschallin, Princess von Werdenberg	*Soprano*
Mohamed, her young Negro servant	
Major-domo to the Princess	*Tenor*
Baron Ochs von Lerchenau	*Bass*
Attorney	*Bass*
Milliner	*Soprano*
Vendor of animals	*Tenor*
Widow	
Three orphans	*Soprano* / *Mezzo-soprano* / *Alto*
Singer	*Tenor*
Flautist	
Head cook	
Hairdresser	
Valzacchi, an intriguing Italian	*Tenor*
Annina, his companion	*Alto*
Leopold, Baron Ochs's personal servant	
Four footmen to the Princess	Two tenors / Two basses
Four waiters	One tenor / Three basses

Der Rosenkavalier

Herr von Faninal, a wealthy merchant, recently admitted to the nobility	Baritone
Mistress Marianne Leitmetzer, Sophie's duenna	Soprano
Major-domo to Faninal	Tenor
Sophie, daughter of Faninal	Soprano
Innkeeper	Tenor
Police commissioner	Bass

Guests, musicians, servants, coachmen, stableboys, children, a doctor

Place: Vienna
Time: During the reign of Maria Theresa of Austria in the eighteenth century
First performance: Hofoper, Dresden, January 26, 1911
Original language: German

IN DER ROSENKAVALIER, Strauss turned from the harsh realism of *Salome, Elektra,* and other works in the *verismo* style to romance and lyricism. Subtitled *A Comedy for Music,* the opera contains some of the composer's wittiest and most ingratiating melodies. Its waltz tunes are favorites in concert repertoire.

The brief introduction concerns itself principally with the themes associated with Octavian and the Princess and also states the theme symbolizing their love.

ACT ONE

The boudoir of the Princess von Werdenberg. At one side, in an alcove, is a large curtained four-poster bed. At the other side of the room are large folding doors which lead to an antechamber. At the back, in the center, is a small door, a private entrance. It is late morning and the sun streams in through windows overlooking a garden. The Princess is lying in bed. Only her hand and arm, emerging from the sleeve of her lace nightgown, are visible.[1] Count Octavian, her seventeen-year-old lover, kneels on a footstool beside the bed and addresses her in impassioned phrases ("Wie Du warst! Wie Du bist!"). The Princess answers the Count's exaggerated expressions of devotion with mingled affection and amusement. Octavian frets that the day has dawned. Rushing impetuously to the windows, he draws the curtains, exclaiming that he must hide his beloved from other men's eyes. When a bell tinkles outside he strikes a heroic pose and proclaims that no one shall enter.

At a warning word from the Princess, however, Octavian conceals himself behind a screen near the bed. As he does so the private door at the back opens and Mohamed, the little Negro servant, enters with the Princess's morning chocolate. While he busies himself with putting his tray on a table, the Princess, in an excited whisper, tells Octavian to get his sword, which he has left lying on a chair. Octavian manages to retrieve the sword without being seen by the servant. The latter brings the table forward, places it before a sofa, and then, with a ceremonious bow in the direction of the bed, he trips out.

When all is quiet again the Princess rises, puts on a dressing gown, and sits at the table, where she is joined by Octavian. With mock severity she scolds him for being indiscreet enough to leave his sword lying about in a lady's boudoir. He immediately becomes the tragically misunderstood lover, but the Princess affectionately forgives him. She addresses him as "Quinquin," while he calls her his "Bichette." Over the chocolate they discuss the Field Marshal, who is away on a hunting trip in Croatia. Half-teasingly, the Princess remarks that only last night she dreamed that her husband came home. Octavian fumes with jealousy. When the Princess speaks reassuringly to him, he asks why she has a troubled look. The Field Marshal, answers the Princess, sometimes travels very rapidly.

Even as she is speaking there is a noise outside, and the Princess exclaims in dismay that perhaps the Field Marshal

[1] In some versions the Princess is seated in a chair.

actually is coming home. Octavian, drawing his sword, runs to the doors of the antechamber but is warned back by the Princess, who tells him that out there the footmen are waiting. He runs to the small door, but the Princess calls him back, saying that the private passage also is blocked. At her urgent bidding Octavian hides behind the curtains of the bed. Meanwhile the uproar outside is growing louder. The Princess goes to the door, listens for a moment, and then suddenly laughs with relief as she recognizes the voice of Baron Ochs. Turning toward the bed, she calls to Octavian, telling him that the danger is over. She warns him to remain hidden for the present to avoid being seen by the footmen. Ochs is heard angrily arguing with the major-domo outside.

Puzzling over the reason for the Baron's visit, the Princess recalls that she received a long letter from him several days ago—which she neglected to read. The Baron, she says to Octavian, has undoubtedly come to talk about some matters mentioned in the letter. At that point Octavian, dressed as a maid, emerges from behind the bed. Curtsying, he addresses the Princess in Viennese street dialect. Delighted with his clever disguise, the Princess tells him to leave through the antechamber and walk boldly past the footmen.

The doors are now flung open and the portly Baron stalks in despite the frantic efforts of the footmen to bar his way. He greets the Princess with elaborate gallantry and then looks with a connoisseur's glance at Octavian. He was certain, he says, glaring at the footmen, that the Princess would welcome him despite the early hour. People of quality pay little attention to the time of day when they are in the mood to go calling. There was the Princess Brioche, for example, the Baron goes on, with whom he once chatted while she was in her bath.

The Princess, dismissing the footmen, explains that they were merely obeying orders—she had been suffering from a touch of migraine and did not wish to see any visitors. When she notices the Baron's persistent interest in Octavian the Princess remarks that the "girl" is her new maid, Mariandel. Her country ways, she hopes, will not be too displeasing to the Baron. He exclaims that he is delighted with the young lady. Catching the Princess's knowing look, Ochs hastily changes the subject. He asks if the news of his impending marriage, which he announced in his recent letter, came as a surprise. The Princess adroitly manages to conceal the fact that she never read the letter and, pleading a lapse of memory, asks the name of the bride-to-be. During this conversation, Octavian, despite signals from the Princess to leave the room, deliberately keeps himself within the Baron's range of vision. He looks at the maid with longing glances, at the same time trying to continue his talk with the Princess.

The bride-to-be, says the Baron, is the daughter of one Faninal, who recently has been elevated to the nobility and has been put in charge of provisioning Her Majesty's armies in the Netherlands. Looking over the Baron's shoulder, the Princess again impatiently signals Octavian to go. The Baron, misunderstanding her look, hastens to explain that his affianced is pretty, convent-bred, and an only child, whose father, by the way, is in indifferent health. Moreover, he owns twelve houses and a palace. As the conversation goes on the Baron catches sight of Octavian backing toward the door with the serving tray. Determined to detain the maid, Ochs says that he is hungry, and the Princess orders "Mariandel" to serve him. As he helps himself greedily he looks Octavian over with vulgar approval, muttering amorous proposals in asides.

Ochs tells the Princess that, with her permission, he and his retinue will remain at her palace overnight and then move to the White Horse Inn tomorrow. One of his first duties will be to observe the traditional custom of sending a messenger to his bride-to-be with a silver rose as pledge of his love. He asks the Princess to recommend a proper emissary, and she promises to make some suggestions in the morning. The Baron also asks if he may have a few words with her attorney on the matter of property settlements.

When the Princess endeavors to send Octavian out to summon the attorney, the Baron, grimly determined not to let the maid out of his sight, warns that so young and innocent a child should not be permitted to mingle with the footmen. At that moment the major-domo comes in and announces that the attorney is waiting outside, along with the head cook, the steward, a singer and a flautist recommended by the Duke of Silva, and the usual assortment of morning visitors. While he is speaking to the Princess, Ochs maneuvers Mariandel to the other side of the room and invites her to have supper with him. She coyly demurs.

Dismissing the major-domo, the Princess sees the Baron talking to Mariandel and twits him about taking his fun where he finds it—even on the eve of his marriage. Marriage, answers the Baron, does not mean that he must curb his hunter's instincts. The chase, he says, is the sport of noblemen. In a lilting refrain he goes through the entire category of amorous conquest and expounds at length on the comparative charms of German and Bohemian girls ("Dafür ist man kein Auerhahn und kein Hirsch"). The Princess occasionally interjects a gently sarcastic comment.

Mariandel, pretending to be greatly impressed, listens for a while and then, unable to control herself, bursts out laughing at the Baron's pompous self-esteem. Assuming that the maid is admiring him, Ochs imperturbably brags away. The dialogue continues in trio form as the maid expresses her pretended confusion over the Baron's attentions, while the Princess cautions Ochs to leave her alone. He suddenly asks the Princess if he may take Mariandel to be maid to the Baroness. She would be most acceptable, he says, because he is convinced she has blue blood. The Princess dryly compliments him on his discernment. Ochs observes that it is not unusual for people of position to have servants with a touch of royalty in them. His own servant—a duke's son—has Lerchenau blood as blue as his own. He is outside, the Baron explains, waiting to bring in the silver rose.

As though suddenly struck with an idea, the Princess sends Octavian to bring a medallion from the jewel case in her dressing room. When Octavian returns the Princess shows Ochs the picture it contains and asks if this young nobleman would qualify as the bearer of the silver rose. The Baron enthusiastically approves. The Princess takes pains to point out the strong resemblance between the Count—younger brother of the Marquis Rofrano—and Mariandel. Astonished at the similarity, the Baron hints that it is possibly the result of an amorous adventure on the part of the Marquis. The Princess, implying that she understands, says that the apparent kinship between the Count and the maid prompts her to keep Mariandel in her service. The conversation ends when the Princess finally dismisses the maid. The Baron tries to follow her out, but Mariandel neatly slams the door in his face.

The Princess now turns her attention to her morning interviews. Pandemonium reigns as the folding doors are again flung open, admitting the strange assortment of people who have been waiting. The throng includes the attorney, the head cook, a scullion, the milliner, the scholar, the animal vendor, Valzacchi and Annina, a widow and her three orphans, a tenor, and a flautist. First the three orphans, garbed in black, approach the table where the Princess is seated and appeal melodramatically for help in the name of their noble, departed father. The milliner enthuses over the style and beauty of her selection of hats, while the animal vendor exhibits his apes, dogs and parrots. During the melee the Princess manages to introduce her attorney to the Baron, who is standing at one side of the room. The scholar approaches the Princess with the idea of showing her a book, but Valzacchi brushes him aside and holds forth a copy of a local scandal sheet. After he enumerates the lurid accounts of murders and poisonings it records the Princess impatiently tells him to be off with his trash. The three orphans and the widow, meanwhile having been given a purse, kiss the Princess's hand, whine their thanks, and make their way out.

Now the hairdresser and his assistants bustle in, elbow the others out of the way, and give their attention to the Princess's coiffure. In the meantime the tenor and the flautist come forward. As the flautist plays a cadenza the singer strikes a pose and then launches into a florid Italian serenade, "Di rigori armato." While he is singing three oafish individ-

Der Rosenkavalier

uals enter. They are obviously ill at ease in their liveries and are apparently quarreling among themselves. They turn out to be the Baron's body servant, his almoner, and his chasseur. The servant is carrying a morocco jewel case. All three awkwardly make their way over to the Baron and then stand nearby awaiting instructions.

Ochs is deep in a whispered conversation with the attorney over dowry matters. When the attorney tries to point out to him that the "morning gift" (a gift from husband to wife on the day after the wedding) is customarily given by the groom to the bride, and not vice versa, Ochs loses his temper and begins shouting. The tenor plunges on into the second stanza of his song, but just as he braces himself for the high note of the climax the Baron emits a shout of rage and bangs his fist on the table. Startled out of his wits, the tenor stops short. With a placating gesture the Princess calls the singer to her and permits him to kiss her hand as a sign of approval. The tenor and the flautist then withdraw, the tenor glaring at the Baron, who acknowledges the look with a gesture of contemptuous indifference.

The hairdresser by this time has completed the Princess's coiffure. She examines the effect in a mirror and then chides the hairdresser for having made her look middle-aged. In great agitation he and his assistants begin changing the coiffure. Valzacchi and Annina now make their way over to the Baron and fawningly offer their services. They are ready to perform any task, they tell him. They will be glad, for example, to report on the activities of his bride-to-be—where she goes, with whom she dines, to whom she writes. At first the Baron tries to ignore the couple but finally tells them they may try their skill by gathering some information about a maid named Mariandel, who is in the service of the Princess von Werdenberg. With that he walks away and turns his attention to the Princess, who has meanwhile dismissed the hairdresser.

At a sign from the Baron the servant steps forward to give the Princess the case containing the silver rose. He is about to open it when the Princess tells him to set it aside for the moment, saying she will look at it later. She promises the Baron to inform Count Octavian at once about carrying the rose to his bride-to-be, then announces it is time for her to go to Mass. Ochs ceremoniously takes his leave, with all the others—the attorney, his three servants, and the two Italians—trooping after him. The major-domo retires, while the footmen close the doors.

Musing alone, the Princess expresses her contempt for the vulgar pomposities of the Baron but soon dismisses these unpleasant thoughts. Gazing again into her mirror, she abandons herself to melancholy reflections on her passing youth in an exquisite refrain ("Kann ich mich auch an ein Mädel erinnern"). She recalls the past when she, a young girl eager for life—much like the Baron's affianced—suddenly found herself bound in wedlock. But that was long ago, and soon they will be referring to her as "the old Princess."

Her train of thought is broken by the entrance of Octavian, dressed in riding habit. He greets the Princess ardently and then expresses concern over her troubled, preoccupied air. When she gently repulses his embraces he excitedly cries that some fatal change has taken place in her heart. In poignant phrases she unburdens her thoughts to him ("Oh sei Er gut, Quinquin"). All things, she tells him, must come to an end. In a tender refrain ("Die Zeit im Grunde"), she sings that time takes its inexorable toll of beauty and that she knows someday he will desert her for someone younger and lovelier. Octavian protests that such a thing can never be. He will love her and her alone forever. The Princess goes on to say that only those who make the most of their happiness when it comes to them, and are prepared to relinquish it when it is over, are spared the pain and grief of regret. At last she quietly tells Octavian that he must go. Perhaps this afternoon he may meet her in the park and ride beside her carriage. Stunned and uncomprehending, Octavian slowly walks out of the room. No sooner has he gone than the Princess cries in remorse and anguish that she allowed him to go without a single kiss.

Distractedly she rings for her four footmen and orders

them to call Octavian back. They return after a moment and report that the Count rode away like a madman and that they shouted after him in vain. Dismissing them, the Princess calls in Mohamed. She gives him the morocco case and tells him to carry it to the Count Rofrano with the message that inside it he will find the silver rose. He will understand, she adds softly. Mohamed quickly leaves. The Princess appears lost in thought as the curtain falls.

Act Two

A room in the home of Herr von Faninal. There are doors to right and left, with a door at the center rear leading into an anteroom. On either side, toward the back, in the rounded corners of the room, are two large fireplaces. It is the day on which the messenger is to bring the silver rose to Sophie. Faninal, about to take leave of his daughter, is loud in his rejoicing. Marianne, looking out of the window, comments excitedly on the new family carriage which is drawing up outside. As Faninal lingers with Sophie his major-domo reminds him that social custom does not permit the father of the bride-to-be to remain in the house when the messenger arrives with the silver rose. Pausing long enough to assure Sophie that when he returns he will be escorting the noble lord of Lerchenau, Faninal hurries away. Sophie, overwhelmed by the thought of being the wife of the great Baron, sings a prayer in which she asks God to make her worthy of so exalted a union ("In dieser feierlichen Stunde"). Marianne, still at the window watching the carriage depart, is in such a state of excitement that Sophie has difficulty concentrating on her prayer.

No sooner has Faninal's carriage gone than shouts of "Rofrano" come up from the street below, and Marianne exclaims that the Count's splendid equipage is approaching. This is too much for Sophie's self-control, and she rushes to the window. She stares in childish awe as the footmen shout Rofrano's name and Marianne describes the Count's magnificent appearance. A moment later the door at the center is flung open and Octavian walks in. He is dressed in a glittering costume of white and silver and in his hand he holds the silver rose. He is followed by his retinue, all in splendid livery.

For a moment Sophie and Octavian, each enchanted by the other's beauty, stand looking at each other without moving. Then follows the ceremony of the *Presentation of the Rose*. With royal grace and dignity Octavian approaches and hands the rose to Sophie. The exquisite theme of the rose is played upon strings, flutes, harps, and celesta. It is reiterated during the ensuing dialogue between Octavian and Sophie, which now begins as Octavian says he is bringing a token of love in behalf of his kinsman the Baron von Lerchenau ("Mir ist die Ehre, widerfahren"). Sophie smells the rose and marvels at its wonderful scent. Octavian explains that a few drops of Persian perfume have been poured upon it. Gazing into each other's eyes, the two sing in passionate phrases of the mysterious enchantment of this moment ("Dahin muss ich zurück"). They sing that the memory of it will last throughout eternity.

Movements among the servants interrupt their brief reverie. Octavian's footman hands the jewel case to Marianne, who takes the rose from Sophie and places it in the case. This she gives to the major-domo, who withdraws with the other servants. Sophie and Octavian seat themselves, while Marianne sits down a little distance away. A graceful waltz theme begins in the orchestra and continues throughout the colloquy that follows.

Sophie observes that she knows all about Octavian, having read of him in *The Mirror of Nobility*. He is seventeen years and two months old, she says, and his given names are Octavian Maria Ehrenreich Bonaventura Fernand Hyacinth. She also knows that he is called Quinquin by his closest friends—including some of the court beauties. With winsome naïveté she tells him how happy she is over the prospect of marriage, adding that she feels sorry for such lonely bachelors as himself. Octavian marvels at her freshness and innocence.

Der Rosenkavalier

Sophie confides more of her views on marriage and then tells Octavian with disarming forthrightness that he is the most gallant and pleasing gentleman she has ever met.

This charming conversation is interrupted by the arrival of Faninal and the Baron. The latter is followed by a coterie of his uncouth servants, who stumble awkwardly into the room. Presented to Sophie, the Baron kisses her hand in a carelessly patronizing manner that makes the girl shrink back in distaste. Octavian fumes in annoyance. Completely ignoring Sophie, Ochs turns to Faninal and remarks over the strange similarity between Octavian and his younger sister, whom he describes to Faninal with a knowing leer. When Sophie fumes over the Baron's lack of manners and makes a reference to his pock-marked face, Marianne simpers that Ochs is a fine figure of a man and a prize catch indeed.

Faninal offers the Baron some old Tokay to drink to the bride's health and the Baron deigns to accept. Turning to Octavian, he observes that occasionally one may show consideration to those of the lower classes, provided one keeps them in their places. The Count acidly compliments him on his superior wisdom. Finally taking notice of Sophie again, Ochs leads her over to a divan and tries to make her sit on his knee. His coarse demonstrations of affection infuriate Sophie, while Octavian looks on in suppressed fury. Vastly amused by the girl's distress, Ochs declares that he prefers a show of spirit in a young filly rather than meek acquiescence. Faninal, looking on, revels in the thought of a Count and a Baron under his roof at one and the same time and wishes, for the benefit of his neighbors, that the walls were made of glass.

Enraged and embarrassed by the Baron's behavior, Sophie finally manages to free herself and leaps to her feet. As the Baron rises and attempts to catch her in his embrace, Octavian, scarcely able to control his rage, crushes the wineglass he holds and hurls the pieces to the floor. Marianne, hurrying to pick up the fragments, exclaims delightedly over the Baron's diverting informalities.

When Sophie, now beside herself with anger, tries to make

the Baron desist, he observes complacently that she will eventually learn how fortunate she is to be the object of his affections. In a mocking waltz refrain he assures her that with him no room is too small, without him the day is a bore ("Mit mir, mit mir, keine Kammer dir zu klein"). With that he tries once more to embrace her, but she violently pushes him away.

Meanwhile the attorney has entered, followed by a clerk carrying a sheaf of papers. Faninal brings them both forward. Seeing the attorney, Ochs immediately goes to him, pausing to suggest to Octavian that he entertain the young lady for the moment. He adds coarsely that he has no objection to a bit of love-making, for the more a young girl knows about it, the better. Indicating to Faninal that he is to follow at the regulation three paces, Ochs strides out of the room. The attorney and clerk follow likewise. A footman closes the side door through which they have left and then goes into the anteroom, leaving the door open.

Octavian hurries over to Sophie and indignantly asks if she actually intends to marry that ruffian. Sophie declares that she will never marry the Baron and begs Octavian to help her. They are momentarily interrupted by an uproar in the anteroom, where two of Lerchenau's servants have caught one of Faninal's maids. Faninal's major-domo rushes in. With Marianne's help he manages to free the girl from the clutches of the servants and takes her away.

With Marianne gone, Sophie more urgently entreats Octavian to help her. Octavian promises to do so but tells her that in order to save them both she must have courage. Sophie is in raptures when Octavian speaks of her and himself together ("Für uns zwei"). In the next moment he takes her in his arms and a beautiful duet ensues ("Mit Ihren Augen voll Thränen"). Sophie sings that she feels safe and happy in his arms because he came in her hour of direst need and saved her from despair. Octavian answers that it is as though they had loved once before in some magic dream and now have met again, never to be parted.

During the closing phrases of the duet Valzacchi and

Annina emerge from the recesses of the two fireplaces in the corners of the room. Stealing up behind the lovers, Annina clutches Sophie's arms while Valzacchi pinions Octavian's hands behind his back. As the two struggle with their captives they scream loudly for Baron Ochs. He comes rushing in. The two Italians free Sophie and Octavian and bow low to the Baron.

Ochs orders Sophie to explain. She stammers some reply. Octavian, advancing defiantly, tries to speak to the Baron. With amused contempt the latter compliments Octavian on his youthful courage, saying that it reminds him of his own mettlesome youth. Even when Octavian finally manages to make him understand that Sophie is determined not to marry him, the Baron refuses to take him seriously. He seizes Sophie's hand and tries to lead her into the other room to sign the marriage contract.

Losing his temper completely, Octavian, his hand on his sword, plants himself in front of the Baron, declaring that he shall not leave the room. Sophie meanwhile frees her hand from the Baron's and takes refuge behind Octavian. Violently denouncing the Baron for his churlishness, Octavian draws his sword. At that, Ochs's courage rapidly oozes away. Putting his fingers to his mouth, he whistles shrilly for his servants. When they come trooping in Ochs grows brave again and blusters that he will not be intimidated by a mere boy. First looking around to make sure that his servants are behind him, he takes a step forward. Octavian rushes at him. The Baron draws his sword, and as he awkwardly tries to defend himself Octavian wounds him slightly in the upper arm.

The servants make a rush for Octavian, but he sends them scampering with a sweep of his sword. Ochs bellows that he has been murdered, while his servants shout for sponges and bandages. Valzacchi and the almoner help Ochs to a chair and take off his coat. Faninal's servants rush in and immediately begin quarreling with the Baron's retinue. Their outcries blend in an agitated chorus. Sophie and Octavian try to give each other courage. When the pandemonium is at its height Faninal bursts in, with the attorney at his heels. Learning from Annina that Sophie and Octavian were surprised in an ardent embrace, Faninal groans in anguish. Wringing his hands, he rushes over to the Baron, roaring to his servants to ride for a doctor. In one breath he laments that the Baron's precious blood is being spilled and in the next he rails at Octavian for his hotheaded attack. The dialogue is punctuated by the Baron's howls of pain.

Octavian courteously tells Faninal that he is sorry for the disturbance but that his own daughter can testify he was not to blame. When Faninal turns furiously on Sophie she calmly tells him that after the Baron's outrageous behavior she refuses to consider him as her future husband. Faninal breaks out into loud lamentation over the terrible scandal that now threatens his house. Spluttering with rage, he shouts to Sophie that she shall marry the Baron. With as much humility as he can muster under the circumstances, he turns to Octavian and requests him to leave at once. Octavian bows, retrieves his hat, which has been badly trampled, and then tries to delay his going long enough to have a word with Sophie.

The doctor, who has meanwhile arrived and examined the Baron's arm, makes it known that the wound is not serious. Sophie, seeing that Octavian is leaving, declares that she will lock herself in her room and starve to death before she will marry the Baron. Faninal growls that he will put her into a carriage by force and pack her off to church. Then, retorts Sophie, she will jump from the coach—or, if she is forced to the altar, she will say "No" instead of "Yes." It is either "Yes" at the altar or the convent, Faninal shouts, and then orders her out of his sight. He refuses to listen to her final plea for forgiveness. The major-domo herds the Faninal servants out of the room. Octavian quickly steps over to Sophie, whispers that she will hear from him later, and then leaves. Marianne bundles Sophie out.

Faninal scurries over to the Baron and embraces him, whereupon Ochs again howls with pain. This throws poor Faninal into even worse confusion. He is so distracted by

Der Rosenkavalier

the thought of Sophie's refusal that he scarcely heeds the Baron's request for wine. Fuming that he will be master in his own house, Faninal stamps out. Soon a footman comes in and serves wine to the Baron, who leans wearily back in his chair.

When Ochs raises the glass to his lips the movement causes a twinge in his arm, which sets him to cursing Octavian and swearing he will have revenge. His threats are comically echoed by his servants, who shake their fists in the direction of the door through which Octavian left. The doctor pours the Baron more wine and he gulps it down. Under the influence of the wine Ochs's humor returns. Ordering the servants to prepare his bed, he downs another glass of wine, then begins humming the refrain of the waltz theme ("Ohne mich"). Its rhythm continues throughout the remainder of the scene.

Annina comes cautiously in and hands Ochs a letter. He glances sharply at it and then orders his servants to withdraw. First he tells Annina to look in his coat pocket for his glasses but suddenly decides not to trust her. He tells her to read the letter. Taking up the waltz refrain, Annina begins reading ("Herr Kavalier! Den morigen Abend hätt i frei"). It is from Mariandel, saying that she will be free tomorrow night. She is very much taken with the Baron and hopes that he has not forgotten her. She awaits an answer.

The Baron, overjoyed, sings that he has all the luck of the Lerchenaus. Musing over the prospect of this delectable conquest, Ochs orders Annina to bring writing materials later to his room, where he will write the hoped-for answer. He completely ignores her obvious hints that a reward is in order for her services. Going out, Annina makes a gesture signifying that she proposes to have her revenge on the Baron for his stinginess. The Baron, one arm in a sling, a wineglass held aloft in the other hand, sings and waltzes about the room in happy anticipation of his meeting with Mariandel. The curtain falls.

Act Three

A large room in an inn. At one side, in a curtained-off alcove, is a bed. At the other side, toward the front, is a door leading into another room. At the back, a fireplace with a mirror above it, a blind window, and a door leading into a corridor. On one side a window looks into the street. Before the fireplace is a table with places for two. There is a large candelabrum on the table, another on a sideboard, and a number of sconces on the walls.

An elaborate pantomime opens the scene. Annina, in mourning dress, is being attended by Valzacchi, who arranges her veil and retouches her make-up. An old woman brings in Octavian, dressed as a girl, and introduces him to Annina and Valzacchi. Octavian lifts his skirt—revealing his riding boots underneath—reaches into his pocket, and brings forth a purse which he throws to Valzacchi. The two Italians, now recognizing Octavian, help him arrange his costume. Five questionable-looking men enter and stand near the door. A clock strikes. Valzacchi, taking out his watch, indicates that the time has come. Octavian and the old woman, who is his "duenna," quickly take their leave. Valzacchi then rehearses the five individuals in popping in and out of various trap doors and wall panels at a given signal. Satisfied with their performance, he sends them to their places and begins lighting some of the candles. A waiter and a serving boy come in to help him. From another part of the inn are heard the strains of a waltz.

Valzacchi opens the door at the back and the Baron enters. One arm is still in a sling. With his good hand he leads in Mariandel. As the Baron looks around, Mariandel runs to the mirror and begins arranging her hair. The innkeeper, followed by several waiters, appears and anxiously inquires if the Baron desires any changes—perhaps a larger room or more candles. But Ochs, already annoyed by the many candles which are being lighted, goes about snuffing as many as he can reach. He listens impatiently to the music and then sharply tells the innkeeper that he did not order an orchestra.

Der Rosenkavalier 345

He is about to have it stopped but suddenly changes his mind and permits the orchestra to continue. As to the waiters, he says, he will not need them—his own servant will take care of his wants. Valzacchi pushes them out of the room. The Baron tells him that he will be well rewarded if he manages to cut down the bill for all this. Bowing and scraping, the Italian leaves.

Mariandel and the Baron sit down at the table and the servant pours wine. Ochs then signals him to leave, but the fellow is so interested in his master's romance that he has to be signaled several times before he obeys. Then, to the accompaniment of the delightful waltz refrains for which the opera is famous, the Baron begins what he thinks will be a most satisfying conquest. The amorous colloquy begins with the phrase Mariandel sings when she refuses to drink any wine ("I' trink kein Wein").

The coy Mariandel keeps the Baron in a fever of uncertainty and impatience. She runs over to the alcove, peeps through the curtains, and exclaims over the size of the bed. When Ochs leads her back to the table and seats her again she looks up at him soulfully and laments that he is promised to another. Assuring her that she may trust him completely, he tells her to look upon him as a highborn gentleman who merely wishes to have a pleasant supper with a pretty girl. Leaning back, Mariandel looks up at him provocatively. Ochs bends over for the first kiss, but as he does so he recalls the resemblance between Mariandel and Octavian. For a moment he almost gives way to terror, then recovers and makes another attempt at a kiss. This time he is interrupted by a head popping out of a trap door in the floor and then disappearing. When the Baron gasps and points to the floor Mariandel innocently asks him what is wrong. Muttering something about being feverish, the Baron mops his brow and gulps down his wine.

The servant enters, and as the door opens the sound of the music from the other part of the tavern floats into the room. As the servant pours more wine and then reluctantly leaves, Mariandel assumes an attitude of deep dejection. The music, she says, makes her very sad. Life is short and fate is cruel, she murmurs. Soon, all too soon, she will die, and the Baron will die, and not a tear will be shed for either of them. Much distressed, the Baron asks her if wine always affects her in this manner. He then suggests that perhaps her bodice is too tight and makes tentative efforts to remedy the situation. Mariandel, however, adroitly rebuffs him.

At that point the Baron, complaining of the heat, takes off his wig. As he looks around for a place to put it faces suddenly leer at him from the walls and the bed curtains. Shaking with fear, Ochs picks up a bell from the table and rings it wildly. The blind window at the back flies open to reveal Annina, standing with arms outstretched to the Baron and crying out that he is her husband. She sweeps into the room, followed by Valzacchi, who pretends to restrain her. The innkeeper and the waiters rush in through the door.

Confronting the Baron, Annina declares that she is his wife and that the law must restore him to her. Pretending to notice Mariandel for the first time, Annina wails that what her friends have been saying is, alas! only too true—this scoundrel already has a *second* innocent maiden in his clutches. Ochs, now convinced he is going mad, groans helplessly as Annina addresses him as her dear "Leopold." The innkeeper and the waiters commiserate loudly with the poor wronged wife. Things are brought to a climax when four small children burst in. Crying, "Papa!" they rush to the Baron, who wrathfully beats them off with a napkin. Octavian finds the opportunity to ask Valzacchi if Faninal has been sent for, and the Italian replies that he will soon be here.

As Ochs bellows orders to clear the room of the maniacal crew that is pestering him, the innkeeper warns him to be careful, for the local police deal harshly with bigamists. The Baron snorts contemptuously at this. Rushing to the window, he yells for police, and shortly a police commissioner and two constables appear. When Ochs haughtily orders the commissioner to drive the rabble out the officer tells him to hold his tongue until he is spoken to. While the commissioner is interrogating the innkeeper the Baron stumbles about look-

Der Rosenkavalier

ing for his wig. The innkeeper explains that the gentleman is the Baron von Lerchenau, but the skeptical commissioner asks if there is anyone else who can identify him. Ochs points to Valzacchi, saying that his "personal secretary" can testify. Valzacchi promptly denies knowing anything.

Mariandel suddenly runs around the room as though trying to escape. The commissioner demands to know who she is. When the Baron tries to pass her off as his bride-to-be the commissioner immediately orders him to disclose her father's name and residence. Helplessly trapped, Ochs says that the girl is Mistress Faninal, daughter of Herr von Faninal.

The words are scarcely out of his mouth when Faninal walks in. The Baron holds his head in his hands and groans. Faninal asks why he has been summoned to rescue his noble son-in-law from a common tavern. While Faninal is answering the commissioner's questions Ochs edges over to Mariandel and tries to hide her behind him. Asked if Faninal is the father of the girl, the Baron says that this man is not Herr von Faninal, but only a cousin. Faninal, however, insists that the Baron is his son-in-law, saying he can still recognize him despite his bald head. Pressed further by the commissioner, Ochs lamely admits that the other gentleman is the young lady's father. Thereupon the commissioner asks Faninal if he still denies that he is the father of the young lady described as his daughter. Noticing Mariandel for the first time, Faninal furiously denies that she is his daughter.

The Baron tries unsuccessfully to bluster his way out. Faninal, in a towering rage, sends for Sophie, who has been waiting outside. When she appears Faninal points to the Baron and bids his daughter look on her future husband—trapped in a low-class tavern with a maiden he was trying to ruin, his morganatic wife, and his four children. When Sophie observes with obvious delight that she never looked upon him as her future husband, Faninal moans in anguish over the disgrace that has fallen upon him. All the servants who have crowded into the room comment in a brief choral phrase on the scandal. They are answered in a hollow echo by those whose heads suddenly appear from wall panels and trap doors.

Losing all control, Faninal rushes at the Baron with upraised fist and then suddenly collapses. Attended by Sophie and the innkeeper, he is carried from the room by footmen. The Baron suddenly finds his wig, puts it on, and assumes some of his accustomed self-confidence. He makes a visible effort to ignore Annina and the four children, who remain in the room.

Nonchalantly taking Mariandel by the arm, the Baron starts to leave, but the commissioner stops him, saying he has more questions to ask. He orders the room cleared, and only Annina and the children remain. The Baron says he will explain things later on and states that he will marry the young lady. Mariandel, however, tears herself away from him and tells the commissioner she has a statement to make to him privately. At a sign from the commissioner the two constables flank the Baron and force him to one side of the room.

Octavian and the commissioner walk over to the curtained alcove. The Count whispers something to the officer which brings a look of mingled surprise and amusement to his face. As the Baron watches in anger and astonishment, Mariandel slips behind the curtains. A moment later her clothes come flying out piece by piece. The commissioner calmly gathers them up, while Octavian shows his head through the opening of the curtains. The Baron, shouting that he must go to the young lady's aid, struggles desperately with the constables.

Suddenly the innkeeper rushes in and announces that the Princess von Werdenberg is coming. With majestic dignity the Princess walks in, followed by her retinue. She looks about her with a faintly distasteful air. Octavian gasps, while Ochs, mopping his brow, deferentially approaches her. Ignoring him for the moment, the Princess speaks to the commissioner, whom she recognizes as a former orderly of her husband, the Field Marshal. Just as she turns questioningly to the Baron he hears a step outside. Hastening to the side door, he stands

Der Rosenkavalier

with his back to it as though trying to prevent someone from entering. Sophie's voice is heard saying she has a message from her father.

Despite Ochs's efforts to keep the door closed, Faninal's servants force it open and Sophie storms in. Octavian, who has meanwhile emerged from the alcove in male attire, whispers to the Princess that this is the girl to whom he brought the rose. Then he dodges back into the alcove. Sophie furiously tells the Baron that she is through with him once and for all. Moreover, she goes on, if he dares come near Faninal's palace he will do so at his own risk. With that she turns on her heel and goes out. The Baron attempts to follow but is restrained by two footmen.

The Princess walks over to him, taps him on the shoulder, and advises him to leave while his reputation as a gentleman is still reasonably intact. Turning to the commissioner, she says, in tones of finality, that the entire affair has been merely a game. Taking the hint, the commissioner bows respectfully and leaves with his two constables. Sophie meanwhile returns. Octavian reappears from behind the curtains, and the Baron, staring at him, now realizes who his Mariandel really was. Gradually the true state of affairs dawns upon him. Your true sportsman, he says, can always appreciate a good joke. He endeavors to make light of matters, saying that, so far as Faninal and Sophie are concerned, he is willing to forgive and forget.

When he asks the Princess's permission to tell Faninal she curtly tells him to leave immediately. More than that, he must renounce his marriage plans. The Baron fumes in helpless anger. At that point the details of the masquerade are revealed to him. Valzacchi comes in and summons his hirelings from their places behind trap doors and panels, while Annina takes off her mourning veil and wipes the make-up from her face.

And now Ochs finds himself confronted by the landlord with a bill in his hand. Behind him is a motley assortment of musicians, waiters, and coachmen. Realizing that he has been cornered, the Baron tries to force his way out but finds himself confronted by Annina, who impudently repeats the refrain he sang when he boasted about having all the luck of the Lerchenaus. In an amusing chorus the landlord and all the others present their claims ("Entschuld'gen Euer Gnaden"). Waiters, musicians, coachmen, and stableboys crowd around him, bawling their demands. Finally, aided by his servant, the Baron fights his way to the door and rushes out, the mob at his heels.

The Princess, Octavian, and Sophie are left alone. Very ill at ease, Octavian tries to explain to the Princess how he came to be involved in the doings at the inn. Sophie, observing his ardent looks, reflects bitterly over the Princess's remark that everything was merely a game. The Count, she sighs, was merely mocking her with his declarations of love. The Princess, wisely realizing the turn which affairs have taken, tells Octavian to go to Sophie. Hesitantly he walks over to her. At first the girl reproaches him for toying with her heart when his own so obviously belongs to the Princess. Octavian fervently assures Sophie that he loves her alone. Though scarcely daring to believe what she hears, Sophie finally is convinced.

Watching the two for a moment in sadness, the Princess approaches Sophie and looks at her intently. When she comments on the girl's distraught look Sophie answers that it is because of her father's humiliation and the Baron's shameful insults. With quiet humor the Princess says that she has a remedy for her father's bruised feelings: She will invite him to ride to his home in her own coach. As for Sophie's own distress, she goes on, Octavian no doubt has the proper cure.

Octavian, overwhelmed by the thought of the Princess's renunciation, can only murmur words of gratitude. Then, in an eloquent phrase of resignation and sorrow, the Princess begins the magnificent trio which is the climax of the opera ("Hab' mir's gelobt, ihn lieb zu haben"). She recalls how she resolved bravely to face the fateful moment when Octavian would give his love to another. Yet, she laments, she did not believe that moment would come so soon. But here they stand—she, alone, and the youth she adored with his new love. And now *they* are all in all to each other. Sophie sings that she should kneel at the Princess's feet in gratitude for the holy joy that has been bestowed upon her. The Princess has given her this youth, yet kept part of him from her. But one thing she knows —she loves him. Octavian wonders if he should dare ask the Princess to explain the riddle of this new enchantment. But perhaps that question is the very one he must not ask. All perplexity vanishes, he sings exultantly, when he looks into Sophie's eyes.

After the fiery climax of the trio the Princess walks slowly from the room. The lovers do not realize that she has gone. Clasped in each other's arms, they pour out their love in passionate phrases ("Ist ein Traum, kann nicht wirklich sein"). As they stand lost in their embrace, the Princess re-enters with Faninal. Faninal approaches Sophie, pats her cheek with paternal affection, and observes philosophically that youth will have its way. Then he and the Princess leave. Sophie and Octavian repeat the refrain they sang a moment ago. As their voices soar to the high notes of its climax, Octavian gathers Sophie in his arms. The theme of the silver rose sounds in the orchestra. Octavian kisses Sophie, and as he does so her handkerchief falls from her hand. The lovers hasten from the room.

For a moment the stage is empty. Then Mohamed, the little turbaned Negro boy, comes in holding a candle. He looks around, finds the handkerchief, holds it up, and then silently trips out to the final, swift phrases of the music. With this artistic and appealing touch the curtain falls.

Salome

by RICHARD STRAUSS
[1864–1949]

Libretto by
HEDWIG LACHMANN

Based on Oscar Wilde's dramatic poem
SALOMÉ

CHARACTERS

Narraboth, a young Syrian captain of the guard	Tenor
A page to Herodias	Contralto
First soldier	Bass
Second soldier	Bass
Jokanaan (John the Baptist)	Baritone
A Cappadocian	Bass
Salome, daughter of Herodias	Soprano
A slave	Soprano
Herod Antipas, Tetrarch of Judea	Tenor
Herodias, his wife	Mezzo-soprano
Five Jews	Four tenors / One bass
First Nazarene	Bass
Second Nazarene	Tenor
Executioner	

Place: The grand terrace in the palace of Herod
Time: About 30 A.D.
First performance: Hofoper, Dresden, December 9, 1905
Original language: German

IN SALOME, Strauss achieved his first important success as a composer of opera. It caused a sensation because of the pathological nature of its subject and the daring harmonic innovations employed in the delineation of subtle psychological reactions. Strongly influenced by Wagner, Strauss uses the technique of the leading motive—identifying the principals of the drama with a characteristic musical phrase—and also the method of superimposing the vocal line on an uninterrupted flow of orchestral accompaniment.

The entire action of *Salome* takes place in one scene. At one side is the entrance to the banquet hall of Herod's palace. Opposite is a massive gateway. In the center of the terrace a barred grating covers the mouth of a large well—the dungeon in which Jokanaan is confined. It is night, and the terrace is flooded with pale moonlight.

First we hear the Salome motive and then the voice of Narraboth, who is talking to the page. The captain looks with burning eyes toward the banquet hall, where Salome is feasting with Herod and his court, and marvels over her beauty. The page warns him not to gaze upon her so ardently, for evil consequences are sure to follow. But the infatuated Narraboth cannot keep his eyes from the Princess. Suddenly from the depths of the well comes the voice of Jokanaan, intoning the Scriptural prophecy, "Nach mir wird Einer kommen der ist stärker als ich [After me cometh One mightier than I]." Several soldiers approach and discuss the prisoner, saying that he is a holy man and a prophet. No one, however, remarks a soldier, can understand the meaning of his strange words.

Presently Salome appears. Restless and troubled, she sings that she can no longer bear the look in Herod's eyes or the brutish revelry of the guests. The cool night air gradually calms her and, gazing up at the moon, she muses softly over its chaste beauty. Jokanaan's voice breaks in on her reverie. Startled, Salome asks the soldiers who cries out in these strange tones, and they reply that it is the prophet. Narraboth approaches and tries to divert her attention by suggesting that she rest in the garden. Meanwhile a slave informs her that Herod wishes her to return to the banquet table, but she angrily declares that she will not go back.

Ignoring Narraboth's plea that she go inside, Salome continues to question the soldiers about the prisoner. She asks them if he is old, and they answer that he is a young man. The Princess listens in tense silence as Jokanaan's grim, foreboding voice is heard again, and then says that she desires to speak to the prophet. One of the soldiers tells her that Herod has said that no one, not even the high priest, is to speak to the prisoner. Completely heedless of his warning, Salome orders the soldiers to bring the prophet before her. She goes over to the well and peers into its black depths. Fiercely she repeats her command, but the trembling soldiers answer that they cannot obey.

Gliding close to Narraboth, she tries to cajole him into granting her request. If he will carry out her wishes, she says in seductive tones, perhaps she will throw him a flower or even smile upon him tomorrow when she passes his post of duty. Helpless under the spell of her tantalizing pleas, Narraboth orders the prophet to be brought forth. There is an orchestral interlude in which the music builds up to the impressive theme of prophecy associated with Jokanaan. The grated cover of the well is thrown back and the prophet emerges, a majestic figure in the rough garb of a pilgrim.

In ringing tones Jokanaan utters strange words of imprecation. Salome, drawing back in awe, asks Narraboth the meaning of his words, but he cannot tell her. Then the prophet bursts forth into a terrible denunciation of Herodias, branding her as the incarnation of evil and depravity, a woman whose sins have infected the very earth itself. Salome is first horrified, then fascinated, and cannot take her eyes from his face. Narraboth desperately pleads with her to leave, but she only answers that she must look more closely on the prophet.

Regarding her with fierce scorn, Jokanaan asks the soldiers who this woman is. Salome tells him that she is the daughter of Herodias. The prophet wrathfully orders her to leave, but Salome, her eyes fixed on his face, sings that his voice is music in her ears. When he exhorts her to go into the wilderness and seek redemption she sings amorously of the beauty of his body. She apostrophizes his hair and his mouth and then voluptuously begs him for a kiss. Narraboth, mad with jealousy, steps between Salome and Jokanaan and kills himself. The Princess does not even look down as he falls. Jokanaan pleads with her to seek the Redeemer on the shores of Galilee and kneel at His feet to ask forgiveness for her sins. Her only answer is a frenzied supplication for a kiss. Thundering that she is cursed, the prophet turns away and descends into the dungeon. When the grating is lowered into place Salome stares into its depths with an expression of ferocious triumph.

Herod and Herodias appear, followed by their drunken, glutted court. The King asks for Salome, his feverish manner betraying his passion for her. Herodias sharply rebukes him for gazing longingly at his stepdaughter. Herod, paying no heed to her words, cries that the moon is like a woman driven mad by desire. Suddenly he slips in a pool of blood and recoils as he sees the body of Narraboth. A soldier informs him that the captain killed himself. Recalling that the Syrian had looked ardently at Salome, he orders the body to be taken away.

As the accompaniment vividly portrays the sound of rushing wind Herod cowers in fear, gasping that mighty wings are beating in the air around him. Herodias, looking at him in cold scorn, remarks that he looks ill. Recovering himself, Herod retorts that it is Salome who has a stricken look. Cajolingly he invites the Princess to eat and drink with him, but she curtly refuses. Herodias gloats over the King's discomfiture at being spurned.

Jokanaan calls out from the dungeon that the appointed hour has come, whereupon Herodias furiously orders the soldiers to quiet him. When Herod protests she taunts him, saying that he is afraid of the prophet, reminding him that he has failed to turn him over to the Jews. The five Jews then approach and ask that Jokanaan be given into their hands. Herod brusquely refuses, saying that the prisoner is a holy man who has seen God. Thereupon the Jews vehemently denounce Jokanaan as a blasphemer, protesting that no one since Elias has seen God. Herod contradicts them, and a long and involved theological argument ensues. It is built up into a strikingly dramatic chorus.

At its climax the voice of Jokanaan breaks through as he prophesies the coming of the Saviour. Two Nazarenes begin to discuss some of the miracles that have been performed by this mysterious leader, one of the most remarkable being the raising of the dead. At this Herod starts in alarm and then excitedly declares that this terrible miracle will be forbidden by royal decree. Jokanaan goes on to foretell the doom of Herodias and the fearful day of reckoning that shall soon dawn for the kings of the earth. Wild with anger, Herodias demands that her accuser be silenced.

Herod, who has been staring intently at Salome, asks her to dance for him. The Queen forbids her to dance, and Salome demurs. The King, however, pleads with her and tries to tempt her by offering to give her anything she asks. Despite the angry protests of Herodias, Salome acquiesces, but first she forces Herod to swear that he will grant her anything she desires. As the ominous theme of the rushing wind again sweeps through the orchestra Herod whimpers that he hears the sound of wings. His mounting fears goad him into frenzy, and he tears the chaplet of roses from his head, shouting that they are burning like a crown of fire. He falls back exhausted. The voice of Jokanaan, repeating his dark prophecy of doom, continues like a relentless undercurrent. Slaves meanwhile prepare Salome for her dance, and then she performs the *Dance of the Seven Veils*.[1]

After its wild climax she stands poised for a moment at the mouth of the dungeon, then flings herself at Herod's feet. In feverish ecstasy he asks her to name her wish. A single note quivers high in the strings as Salome begins speaking. With venomous sweetness she demands the head of Jokanaan on a silver platter.

Herod cries out in unbelieving horror, while Herodias applauds her daughter as her worthy offspring. Frantically Herod offers her his precious gems, his peacocks, the mantle

[1] In some productions this is performed by a dancer instead of by the singer.

of the high priest, the veil of the sanctuary, begging her not to ask for the head of the holy man of God. Salome is obdurate and with savage intensity repeats her request. Shaken by fear and despair, Herod finally sinks back in his chair as if in a faint. Herodias quickly draws the execution ring from his finger and hands it to a soldier, who takes it to the executioner. Herod revives, misses the ring, and wails that its absence bodes terrible misfortune.

Creeping over to the dungeon, Salome watches the executioner descend, then listens intently. When she hears no sound she furiously orders the executioner to strike, cursing him for the delay. Through the gathering darkness the arm of the executioner suddenly can be seen emerging from the well, bearing aloft the platter with the severed head. Seizing it, Salome begins her terrible song of frustrated passion and lust, "Ah! Du wolltest mich nicht deinem Mund küssen lassen!" In life he would not let her kiss his mouth, she cries, but she will kiss it now. The eyes that looked upon her in anger are closed forever, and the tongue that so fiercely denounced her is silent. But she still lives, Salome exults, and then, caressing the head, she again apostrophizes Jokanaan's body.

Herod, stricken with terror at the monstrous sight, turns to leave. Salome murmurs that now at last she has kissed the mouth of the prophet. The kiss had a bitter taste, she muses. In mad exultation she cries out again that she has kissed Jokanaan's mouth, and at that moment a ray of moonlight breaks through the clouds and illumines her. Herod whirls, stares at her in utter horror, and then commands his soldiers to kill her. They crush Salome beneath their shields. The curtain falls.

Tannhäuser

by RICHARD WAGNER
[1813–1883]

Libretto by the Composer

CHARACTERS

Heinrich Tannhäuser, a minstrel knight	*Tenor*
Elisabeth, niece of the Landgraf	*Soprano*
Venus, Goddess of Love	*Soprano*
Hermann, Landgraf of Thuringia	*Bass*
Wolfram von Eschenbach	*Baritone*
Walther von der Vogelweide	*Tenor*
Biterolf — minstrel knights	*Bass*
Heinrich der Schreiber	*Tenor*
Reinmar von Zweter	*Bass*
A young shepherd	*Soprano*
Four noble pages	*Two sopranos and two contraltos*

The Three Graces, sirens, naïads, nymphs, bacchantes, nobles, knights, ladies, and pilgrims

Place: Near Eisenach, in Thuringia, Germany
Time: Early in the thirteenth century
First performance: Dresden, Germany, October 19, 1845
Original language: German

For the basis of this great opera of medieval German legend we must look partly to history, partly to mythology, and partly to Wagner's own rich imagination. The action takes place in Thuringia, where stands the mighty castle of the Wartburg. Near the castle is the hill known sometimes as the Horselberg, sometimes as the Venusberg (Hill of Venus), because, according to legend, it was beneath this hill that the goddess

Tannhäuser

Venus had her abode. Wagner himself visited the castle of the Wartburg, and he took his story from the ancient traditions that centered around this picturesque old-world edifice where, six centuries earlier, the knight minstrels, or minnesingers, were said to have gathered in its great hall for tournaments of song.

The opera revolves around one of these legendary knight minstrels, the passionate, quarrelsome Tannhäuser. Seeking refuge from the griefs of the world, Tannhäuser has left his earthly existence to live under the magic spell of Venus, Goddess of Love. As the opera opens, Tannhäuser has been with Venus a year and a day.

This story of sacred and profane love offered Wagner wonderful opportunities for colorful scenes, rich music, and striking contrasts—as, for example, between the seductive spell of Venus and her supernatural realm and the simple nobility of the fervent band of pilgrims, whose march comes to us again and again in the opera.

The opera opens with the familiar overture, beginning with the solemn *Pilgrim's Chorus*. As it reaches the sensuous melody of the *Venusberg Music*, the curtain rises on the opening scene that takes place in the weird and supernatural grotto in the interior of the Venusberg, where the goddess holds court and preys upon the souls of men.

Act One

[*Scene One*] The Hill of Venus. When the curtains first part they disclose an alluring scene. In the farthest visible background of an apparently endless cave a bluish lake is seen in which naïads are bathing, while sirens are reclining on its banks. In the center are groups of dancing nymphs. Reclining on mounds at the sides are caressing couples, some of whom join the dances of the nymphs in the chorus of the scene. In the foreground Venus is reclining on a couch, surrounded by the Three Graces. Kneeling before her is Tannhäuser. The cave glows with a strange roseate light.

A train of bacchantes rushes from the rear of the cave in a tumultuous dance. They dart wildly through the groups of nymphs and couples, inciting them to the frenzied and voluptuous *Bacchanale*. The dancers suddenly pause and listen to the beautiful singing of the *Chorus of Sirens*, then resume their dance, which rises to the wildest excitement in the famous *Venusberg Music*.

When the frenzy is at its height a sudden weariness comes over the dancers. The couples separate and rest near the entrance of the cave. The bacchantes disappear as a mist gathers and spreads with growing density, gradually enveloping the sleepers. Only a small space in the foreground now remains visible, where Venus, Tannhäuser, and the Three Graces are seen. The Three Graces perform their dance interpretive of the stories of Europa and the White Bull and Leda and the Swan as these scenes loom up in the background. Then they depart, leaving only Venus and Tannhäuser.

Suddenly Tannhäuser raises his head as though starting from a dream. Venus draws him back again, caressingly. She asks the knight what is troubling him, and he replies that he dreams of the life he left on earth. At her insistence he takes up his harp and sings passionately his *Hymn to Venus* ("Dir töne Lob!"). But he sings also that he is weary of the life of the senses which he has been leading and finally begs for freedom from her spell so that he may return to earth, with its mingled pain and pleasure. Angry that her love is praised, yet scorned, she cries that he shall not go. Tannhäuser insists that fate impels his choice.

Venus, with a cry, turns away from him, burying her face in her hands. She seeks gradually to win Tannhäuser's glances again and turns toward him with a seductive smile, singing "Beloved one, come [Geliebter, komm]!" Sirens are again heard singing softly in the distance. Venus once more draws Tannhäuser lovingly to her and tries to charm away his restlessness. With great emotion he takes his harp and once more sings her praises ("Stets soll nur dir") but still begs to be released. Then Venus, in great fury, threatens him. She tells him he will be scorned on earth, an outcast, and that his

Tannhäuser

Christian God will never forgive him. Tannhäuser replies simply that he places his faith in the Virgin Mary. At mention of the name of the Blessed Virgin, the unholy spell is broken. With a cry, Venus shrinks and vanishes. Cymbals crash, and there is complete darkness while the scene changes.

[*Scene Two*] A valley near the Wartburg. Tannhäuser suddenly finds himself in the midst of a peaceful valley, with the sun shining and blue skies above. His life in the Venusberg is over. In the background looms the mighty Wartburg, with a winding mountain path leading down from it. In the foreground is a shrine to the Virgin. From a nearby hill comes the tinkle of sheep bells. On a small rise a young shepherd reclines, playing on his pipe. He sings a pastoral folklike tune to Holda, Goddess of Spring ("Frau Holda kam aus dem Berg hervor").

A company of pilgrims passes in the distance on their journey to Rome, and the *Pilgrim's Chorus* is heard as the wayfarers thread their way down the mountain path. The shepherd, hearing their song, stops his playing and listens reverently. Waving his cap, he calls out to them to breathe a prayer for him when they reach Rome.

All the while Tannhäuser has been standing spellbound, awed at the beauty of the scene. Deeply overcome, he falls to his knees in prayer as the procession passes by the Virgin's shrine and disappears down the mountain road. The shepherd also goes his way, and the sheep bells are heard fainter and fainter in the distance. Tannhäuser remains on his knees, absorbed in fervent prayer. Tears choke his voice. He bows his head to the ground and seems to weep bitterly. Distant bells chime as the chant of the pilgrims dies away.

Then comes a sound of hunting horns, drawing nearer and nearer. A group in hunting dress comes upon the scene. It is Hermann, the Landgraf, with his retinue. In this group is Wolfram, who recognizes his old friend Tannhäuser. Astonished, Tannhäuser rises hastily and bows in silence to the Landgraf, who welcomes his long-lost favorite. Tannhäuser answers their questions vaguely and speaks of having traveled in strange lands. He tries to avoid them, saying he is doomed to roam alone, but they press him to stay. When Wolfram mentions the lovely Princess Elisabeth's name, Tannhäuser stands entranced. Wolfram sings ("Als du im kühnem Sange") that Elisabeth has been grieving for him and his songs ever since he left the Wartburg and has not entered the Hall of Minstrels during his absence. He appeals to Tannhäuser to return. The music of this appeal is especially impressive as the others add their entreaties to Wolfram's. Tannhäuser is deeply touched. He throws himself into Wolfram's arms, greets the minstrels in turn, and bows to the Landgraf, giving his joyful consent to rejoin his old comrades ("Ha, jetzt erkenne ich sie wieder").

Other members of the Landgraf's hunting party come upon the scene. The hunters sound the horns. Tannhäuser then gladly rejoins them as they set off for the Wartburg and the coming song tournament, singing in chorus ("Er kehrt zurück den wir verloren!").

Act Two

The Hall of Minstrels in the Wartburg. Through the spacious opening at the rear we have an open view of the courtyard and the valley below. Elisabeth enters and rapturously greets the hall, overjoyed that Tannhäuser's voice is now to glorify it once again, in the lovely aria "Dich, theure Halle."

As Elisabeth finishes, Tannhäuser is led by Wolfram through the open doorway at the rear, into the hall. For a time he stands leaning against a pillar and then throws himself impetuously at the feet of Elisabeth. In timid confusion, the maiden bids him rise, tells him that this hall is *his* domain, which he has conquered with his songs. Gently Elisabeth asks where he has been. Tannhäuser, slowly rising, pleads that a veil be thrown forever between yesterday and today, for Heaven has wrought a change in his spirit. "I praise the power that wrought it from out my heart's recesses [Ich preise dieses Wunder aus meines Herzen's Tiefe]!" Elisabeth sings. Tannhäuser and Elisabeth are fervently reunited in the duet "Gepriesen sei die Stunde."

Wolfram has remained in the background. He realizes now that his own hopes for Elisabeth are gone. His grave and dignified self-forgetfulness forms a curious contrast to the rapture of Tannhäuser and Elisabeth.

As Tannhäuser and Wolfram leave, the Landgraf makes his appearance, welcoming Elisabeth to the place she has shunned so long and proclaiming her queen of the coming song contest. He tells her that all the nobles will be there, because once again her hand will bestow the victor's wreath.

The court now gathers with much pomp. Four pages announce the arrival of the various groups of guests. The knights, nobles, ladies, and attendants enter and are received by the Landgraf and Elisabeth. This is an inspiring scene of pageantry and ceremony as the music of the *Tannhäuser March* wells up to its tremendous climax. The chorus of knights and nobles sings "Freudig begrüssen wir die edle Halle," joined by the chorus of ladies. The lords and ladies take their places on one side of the great hall of song, the Landgraf and Elisabeth occupying the two seats of honor.

The minstrels now enter, greeting the assembly in stately fashion, and take their places on the opposite side of the hall. The Landgraf rises and announces that Love will be the theme of the song contest and that the hand of Elisabeth herself shall be the prize to the winner ("Gar viel und schön ward hier in dieser Halle").

The contest begins. The four pages collect from each singer a folded slip of paper bearing his name. The slips are placed in a gold cup, which is presented to Elisabeth. She selects one of the papers, hands it to the pages, and in quartet they announce the name. Wolfram is the first chosen. He sings with power and eloquence his *Eulogy of Love* ("Blick' ich umher"). It is a song of placid love for Elisabeth, in which he says he will worship her from afar. He is well applauded by the minstrels and nobles.

During Wolfram's singing Tannhäuser's attitude is one of impatience and scorn. Suddenly his expression turns to exquisite delight. He rises as though dreaming. He seeks the strings of his harp, and an uncanny smile indicates that a strange emotion has control of him. Then he powerfully sweeps the strings, his whole being betraying that he hardly knows where he is. He even seems unaware of Elisabeth as he boastfully sings of sensual passion.

There is general consternation in the assembly. Chaste Elisabeth is startled with conflicting emotions of rapture and anxious surprise. Biterolf—a hot-headed knight—arises quickly and angrily rebukes Tannhäuser, but Tannhäuser, with ever-increasing vehemence, asks Biterolf what *he* knows of such bliss and reiterates his view of love. The nobles, now in great excitement, think he has gone mad. Biterolf draws his sword. The Landgraf, however, calls for order.

Wolfram tries to calm the rising excitement with a second eulogy to love ("O Himmel! Lass' dich jetzt erflehen!"). Tannhäuser, forgetting himself completely, bursts into the *Hymn to Venus* ("Dir Göttin der Liebe"), crying out that he alone among that company of dull mortals has tasted the fullness of love, that Venus alone can teach love. There is general disorder and horror, for they all realize now that Tannhäuser has visited the Venusberg.

The ladies leave the hall in great dismay. Elisabeth, pale and trembling, alone remains. The Landgraf, knights, and minstrels have left their seats and are conferring together. Tannhäuser, standing aloof, remains silent, as though in rapture. The knights and nobles now press toward him angrily with drawn swords, threatening to kill him for his blasphemy. Elisabeth rushes between them, staying their hands, and all stand back in amazement as she shields Tannhäuser. Again they try to close upon the minstrel, and again Elisabeth intervenes, telling them it is not for them to judge him, that he must have his chance to earn heavenly salvation ("Zurück von ihm!"). She pleads that she, who is crushed and wronged, will pray for his soul.

Tannhäuser is now overcome with shame and contrition and, falling to the floor, prays for mercy on his soul. The Landgraf, with great solemnity, steps into their midst and pronounces judgment ("Ein furchtbares Verbrechen ward begangen"). Tannhäuser is banished from the realm. The Landgraf suggests that the knight join a band of pilgrims who are about to leave to seek absolution at Rome, while Elisabeth calls attention to the comforting promise of the *Pilgrim's Chorus*, which echoes up from the valley.

A sudden ray of hope inspires Tannhäuser. He throws himself at Elisabeth's feet, devoutly kisses the hem of her robe, and strides out to join the pilgrim band, calling in exultation, "To Rome!" The chorus of nobles repeats the words, and Elisabeth looks on in despair and pity as the curtain falls.

Act Three

A valley near the Wartburg. It is the same peaceful scene in which Tannhäuser found himself after he had left Venus. Elisabeth has waited hopefully and prayerfully for Tannhäuser's return from his pilgrimage, but in vain. Several months have gone by, and the erring knight has not returned.

Twilight is approaching. Before the shrine to the Virgin, Elisabeth, clothed in white, kneels in prayer. Wolfram approaches from a woodland path and stops as he becomes aware of Elisabeth's presence. He muses on her incessant prayers that Tannhäuser will return forgiven ("Wohl wusst' ich hier sie im Gebet zu finden").

From the distance comes the song of a band of pilgrims. Elisabeth rises eagerly. We hear the beautiful *Pilgrim's Chorus* gradually growing louder as the band of penitents, passing by the shrine, makes its way slowly down through the valley. Elisabeth has been anxiously watching for Tannhäuser among the returning pilgrims, but he is nowhere to be seen. She falls upon her knees once more and prays to the Blessed Virgin that she be set free of this life and that Tannhäuser's sin be forgiven. This is the fervent aria *Elisabeth's Prayer (Elisabeth's Gebet*—"Allmächt'ge Jungfrau").

For a long time she remains kneeling, then slowly rises, as if in a trance. Wolfram approaches to speak to her, but she bids him be silent, and by gesture expresses to him her heartfelt thanks for his faithful love. Her way now leads to heaven, where she has a high purpose to fulfill. She does not want him to accompany or follow her. Slowly ascending the footpath leading toward the Wartburg, she disappears from view. The valley darkens with the approach of night. The faithful Wolfram seats himself at the foot of the hill and begins to finger softly on his harp. As the evening star shines in the distant sky he sings to it, asking that it bless and guide Elisabeth ("O du mein holder Abendstern"). This *Song to the Evening Star* is one of Wagner's loveliest melodies.

In the darkening night a stumbling figure appears in ragged pilgrim dress. It is Tannhäuser. His face is pale and drawn, and he comes with faltering steps, supported by a staff. Wolfram asks how he dares return unforgiven. Tannhäuser declares wildly that he is on his way to the Venusberg again. Wolfram asks in horror if he has not been to Rome. Tannhäuser bitterly answers yes. As Wolfram inquires what took place there, Tannhäuser seats himself in despair. Wolfram is about to sit beside him, but Tannhäuser waves him away, saying that he is accursed. He tells how the Pope had absolved all the other pilgrims but had turned upon him with a grim denunciation. If you have tasted of the forbidden delights of the Venusberg, the Pope had said, then you are doomed forever. Even as the staff I hold in my hand can never burst into bloom, so your soul can never be reborn, nor your sins redeemed. Forsaken by all, Tannhäuser cries, he can find welcome only from Venus. Yes, he is again on his way to the Venusberg. Wolfram tries to stop him in his godless raving.

Light clouds now gradually veil the scene. Tannhäuser calls aloud for Venus. A confusing whirl of dancing forms becomes visible to the strains of the *Venusberg Music* as Venus appears, reclining upon her couch, singing her delirious and seductive melody. He is about to go to her, but Wolfram restrains him and begs him to gain his soul's salvation. The two knights struggle violently. Tannhäuser will not listen to Wolfram's entreaties. Just as Tannhäuser tears himself loose, crying that the heavens are closed to him, Wolfram tells him that salvation is his because an angel prays for him—Elisabeth. Tannhäuser stands spellbound. He repeats the name, "Elisabeth," as his mind turns once more to the true and pure love of this gentle princess. Venus cries out, "Woe! I have lost him [Weh! Mir Verloren]!" and the vision disappears.

The clouds gradually darken, and through them bright torchlights gleam. Then, as the first streaks of dawn begin to glow, a funeral procession winds its way down from the Wartburg into the valley. Pilgrims, followed by the minstrels, bear an open bier on which lies the body of Elisabeth. They are followed by the Landgraf, knights, and nobles, singing that Tannhäuser has been absolved through Elisabeth's love. Wolfram now leads Tannhäuser to the bier of Elisabeth. Sinking down beside it, he cries, "Holy Elisabeth, pray for me!" and dies.

One by one the torches are extinguished and the scene is illumined by the pale, clear morning light. A chorus of young pilgrims enters, singing of the miracle they have seen. With them they have brought the Pope's staff, which has miraculously blossomed with new green leaves—a token of God's forgiveness. As they sing of Tannhäuser's redemption, the curtain falls.

Tosca

by GIACOMO PUCCINI
[1858–1924]

Libretto by
LUIGI ILLICA *and* GIUSEPPE GIACOSA

Based on Victorien Sardou's drama
LA TOSCA

CHARACTERS

Cesare Angelotti, an escaped political prisoner	*Bass*
A Sacristan	*Baritone*
Mario Cavaradossi, a painter	*Tenor*
Floria Tosca, a famous opera singer	*Soprano*
Baron Scarpia, chief of the Roman police	*Baritone*
Spoletta, a police officer	*Tenor*
Sciarrone, a gendarme	*Bass*
A young shepherd	*Bass*
Jailer	*Bass*

Cardinal, the executioner Roberti, judge, clerk, sergeant, infantryman, Swiss Guards, townspeople

Place: Rome
Time: June 1800
First performance: Teatro Constanzi, Rome, January 14, 1900
Original language: Italian

THE STORY of *Tosca* takes place at the time when Rome was torn by fierce political strife between the Bonapartists and the monarchists. In setting to music Sardou's drama of violence, intrigue, and passion, Puccini infused his natural lyricism with powerful dramatic expression.

Act One

The interior of the Church of Sant' Andrea della Valle, in Rome. On one side a grilled gate closes off the entrance to the Attavanti chapel. On the other side stands an easel, partly covered, on which is an uncompleted portrait of a woman, supposedly a Magdalen. Scattered about are painter's implements, and a basket near by.

There is no prelude. After a brief phrase of harsh chords symbolizing Scarpia, chief of police, the curtain rises. Angelotti, unkempt and breathless, and dressed in prison garb, enters in desperate haste. Muttering that he has escaped his pursuers, he steals over to a pillar at which is a shrine to the Madonna, finds a key hidden there by his sister, unlocks the door of the chapel, and disappears inside.

To the accompaniment of a sprightly melody the Sacristan enters, carrying a handful of paintbrushes. He is a rather strange character, afflicted with a nervous jerking of his head and shoulders. Pattering over to the easel, he grumbles about the dirty paintbrushes and expresses surprise that the painter is not there. He looks into the basket, and, finding that the food in it is untouched, he concludes that Cavaradossi will soon return. At the sound of the Angelus the Sacristan kneels and intones a prayer in Latin.

Mario enters and takes up his work at the easel. The Sacristan, staring at the portrait—a beautiful woman with blond hair and blue eyes—exclaims that it is the likeness of the woman who has been praying daily at the shrine of the Madonna. Mario smiles and says that her lovely face inspired him. Laying down his brush, he takes a miniature of Floria Tosca from his pocket. In the beautiful aria "Recondita armonia" he compares the two beauties—Tosca's hair is dark, the Magdalen's blond; Tosca's eyes are black, the other's blue. The Sacristan, in accompanying phrases, expresses pious disapproval over these worldly sentiments. He busies himself awhile with cleaning brushes, notes with sly satisfaction that Mario has not touched his food, then leaves.

As Mario continues painting, Angelotti comes cautiously

out of the chapel and approaches. The painter finally recognizes his friend and cries out in happy surprise. Quickly he locks the door of the church. Angelotti tells him that he has escaped from the prison of Sant' Angelo, and Mario eagerly offers to help him. At that moment Tosca's voice is heard outside. Giving Angelotti the basket of food, Mario pushes him into the chapel, warns him to be quiet, and then opens the door to admit Tosca.

Annoyed at having been kept waiting, she rebuffs Mario's embraces and inquires suspiciously if the beautiful lady of the portrait has been here. Mario denies that he has had any visitors and goes on with his painting. When she asks him to come to her cottage in the evening, he answers with a preoccupied air, which she notes with irritation. She forgets her misgivings, however, in the passionate duet which follows ("Non la sospiri la nostra casetta"). Tosca describes the bliss that she and her lover will share at the cottage, and Mario answers ardently.

Glancing nervously at the chapel, he tells Tosca as gently as possible that she must now leave him to his work. As she prepares to go she looks at the portrait and remarks rather spitefully that the Magdalen is too beautiful. Suddenly recognizing her as the Marchioness Attavanti, Tosca cries out in jealous fury that *there* is the reason for all these furtive movements behind locked doors. A fiery duet ensues as Mario tries to convince her that her suspicions are groundless. She responds amorously as her mood changes, then implores him to make the Magdalen's eyes black like her own, instead of blue. Extorting a promise from Mario to be faithful, she hurries away.

Mario calls Angelotti from the chapel. The fugitive reveals, much to the painter's surprise, that the Marchioness Attavanti is his sister and that she has hidden clothing under the altar to disguise him in his escape from the terrible Scarpia. Mario gives him the key to his villa and tells him of a secret passageway to his cellar, where he will be safe. Taking the bundle of clothing from under the altar, Angelotti is about to leave. Just then several cannon shots are heard, and Mario exclaims that the escape has been discovered. He decides to guide Angelotti to his home.

The Sacristan rushes in and is surprised to find Mario gone. He is followed shortly by a noisy crowd of choirboys and acolytes, to whom he announces that Bonaparte has been defeated. In honor of the event, he continues, there will be a great *Te Deum*, and a new cantata will be sung by Floria Tosca. The boys greet the news with much shouting and singing.

The uproar ceases abruptly as Scarpia enters the church, followed by Spoletta and other police officers. He orders the boys to prepare themselves for the service, then informs the trembling Sacristan that he is on the trail of an escaped prisoner who has been traced to the church. Searching the chapel, he finds a fan bearing the crest of the Marchioness Attavanti. He catches sight of the portrait and exclaims in surprise on recognizing the features of the marchioness. The Sacristan tells him it was painted by Mario Cavaradossi. That name is familiar to Scarpia, for Cavaradossi is under suspicion as a Bonapartist, and is also known to him as Tosca's lover.

A police officer comes from the chapel with the empty basket. The Sacristan babbles stupidly that Cavaradossi did not have the key to the chapel, so could not have eaten his meal there. Scarpia, listening carefully, concludes that it was Angelotti who ate the food and that Cavaradossi is implicated in his escape.

Tosca, prompted by misgivings about Mario's fidelity, returns to the church. Scarpia quickly hides behind a pillar and orders the Sacristan, standing near the easel, not to move. When Tosca asks him about Mario, he mumbles some reply and hurries away. Scarpia quietly approaches and with oily flattery commends her piety. There are some, he continues, who enter the church only to profane it by using it as a lovers' rendezvous. Carelessly holding up the fan, he remarks that some fair lady evidently dropped it in her haste to leave when surprised in a tryst.

Horrified, Tosca sees the Attavanti crest. She tries to hide her jealous fury, but, goaded by Scarpia's insinuations, she finally threatens to have revenge on her rival. Unctuously he reproaches her for giving way to her anger in a holy place. Tosca, weeping with humiliation, now leaves, while Scarpia, pretending to be distressed at her grief, escorts her to the door.

As he returns, Spoletta emerges from a hiding place. Scarpia orders him to follow Tosca and to meet him later at the Farnese Palace to report on her movements. Standing alone in the nave, the wily chief of police gloats over the success of his evil plan. The cardinal enters and the *Te Deum* begins. In a grim obbligato to the chanting, Scarpia sings the soliloquy known as the *Te Deum*, in which he savagely exults over the prospects of a double triumph—Tosca's embraces and Cavaradossi's downfall. The curtain falls.

Act Two

Scarpia's apartment in the Farnese Palace. He is dining alone at a table near a window above the palace courtyard. Nervously he muses that Cavaradossi and Angelotti will soon be swinging from the same gallows. From below comes the sound of music being played at the celebration in honor of General Melas's reported victory over Bonaparte, at which Tosca is to be the soloist. Scarpia rings for Sciarrone, orders him to tell Tosca that Scarpia is expecting her after the cantata, then gives the gendarme a note to take to her. In a dramatic monologue ("Ha più forte sapore") he sings that he scorns the gentler arts of love and finds his pleasure in ruthlessly possessing what he desires.

Spoletta now appears to make his report. Shaking with fear, the officer explains that he and his men searched Cavaradossi's villa but found no trace of Angelotti. Scarpia's fury subsides, however, when Spoletta tells him that he has brought the painter back as a prisoner. He orders Cavaradossi to be led before him, along with the executioner Roberti, a judge, and a clerk.

As Scarpia waits, Tosca's voice, accompanied by the chorus,

is heard in the beginning of the cantata. Mario is brought in, angrily demanding to know why he has been seized. With menacing suavity, Scarpia questions him about Angelotti. When he accuses Mario of hiding the fugitive in his villa, Mario resolutely denies everything. Tosca's voice, soaring over the choir in the stately measures of the cantata, serves as accompaniment to the dialogue of the two men until Scarpia abruptly cuts off the sound by closing the window.

Relentlessly Scarpia questions, but Mario continues to defy him. Tosca, greatly excited, bursts into the room and rushes into her lover's arms. In an aside he warns her not to reveal any information about the villa. Scarpia, springing to his feet, tells Mario that the judge is waiting to hear his confession in an adjoining room—in reality the torture chamber. Mario is led away, followed by Roberti, the judge, the clerk, and Sciarrone. Scarpia calls after Roberti that he is to proceed in the usual way, pending further instructions. Sciarrone, entering the torture chamber last, closes the door behind him, while Spoletta stations himself before the outer door of the room.

Adopting a casual air, Scarpia begins questioning Tosca about the villa. She insists that no one but Mario was there. At that Scarpia calls out to Sciarrone, asking if the witness has made any statement. None, replies the gendarme, whereupon Tosca, unaware that her lover is being tortured, flippantly remarks that this questioning is useless. Scarpia quietly tells her that a truthful answer may save her lover agony. Tosca gasps in horror as he thunders that at this very moment Mario's head is encircled by a spiked band of steel that is being tightened at intervals, bringing the blood spurting from his veins at every denial. A groan from behind the door underscores Scarpia's words.

Tosca makes her way over to the door and calls out to Mario, whose tormented voice is heard cautioning her to keep silent. Wildly she curses Scarpia for his brutality, but he merely compliments her sardonically on her dramatic performance. Suddenly he commands Spoletta to open the door and, as Tosca recoils at the sight of the torture, he harshly repeats his question: "Where is Angelotti?"

Frantically Tosca begs Mario to allow her to speak, but the painter, between his cries of pain, forbids her. As a fearful cry of agony bursts from Mario's lips, Tosca, unable to control herself, gasps out the location of Angelotti's hiding place. Instantly Scarpia orders the torture stopped, and soon Mario, bleeding and unconscious, is brought into the room and placed on a couch. Tosca kneels sobbing at his side. After a few minutes have elapsed he revives and asks weakly if he revealed the secret. As Tosca assures him he did not, Scarpia loudly repeats to Spoletta the words she spoke a moment earlier.

In a torment of pain and fury, Mario curses Tosca for her betrayal. At that moment Sciarrone rushes in with the news that Bonaparte has defeated General Melas at Marengo. A brief but stormy trio ensues ("L'alba vindice appar"). In delirious ecstasy Mario exults over the victory, while Tosca endeavors to calm him. Scarpia pours out his hatred for this defiant rebel and orders him to a cell. Tosca struggles desperately with the guards but is finally pushed aside as Mario is taken away.

Smiling triumphantly, Scarpia sits down at his table, offers Tosca a glass of wine, then resumes his meal. Watching him a moment with loathing and disgust, Tosca asks him his price. Scarpia answers in the great aria "Mi dicon venal." His enemies, he declares, call him corrupt and mercenary. But where a beautiful woman is concerned, he does not stoop to talk in sordid terms of money. Tosca's beauty has so enthralled him that her very hatred has made him resolve to possess her. His price, Scarpia proclaims, coming toward her in passionate excitement, is Tosca herself. As she shrinks from him in unbelieving horror, a roll of drums is heard. In another hour, says Scarpia, after they listen in silence, her lover will die. Tosca pours out her anguish in the magnificent aria "Vissi d'arte." She has always lived only for her art and for love, Tosca laments, harming no one, helping the poor, praying devotedly. And now, in her darkest hour, God has deserted her. Kneeling before Scarpia, she makes a final desperate plea, but he only reiterates his lecherous proposal.

Tosca

Spoletta suddenly rushes in to tell Scarpia that Angelotti killed himself with poison at the moment of capture. Scarpia orders his body hung from the scaffold. "And Cavaradossi?" asks Spoletta. Scarpia turns to Tosca with a questioning look. Crushed with humiliation, she nods her head.

Thereupon Scarpia informs Spoletta that there will be a mock execution. "Just as we did with Palmieri," he says, looking intently at the officer, who, as he leaves, signifies that he understands his meaning. Scarpia agrees to permit Tosca to come to the scene of the execution and inform Cavaradossi of his reprieve. She further inveigles him into giving her a passport for Mario and herself. While he is at his desk writing out the passport, Tosca goes to the table and takes the glass of wine he had poured for her. Carefully she picks up a knife from the table, hiding it behind her as she turns to watch Scarpia. Stamping the passport, he springs to his feet and advances toward Tosca with arms outstretched.

As he tries to embrace her, she plunges the knife into his chest, whispering fiercely, "Here is Tosca's kiss." He dies at her feet. With her eyes on Scarpia's face, she wets a napkin with water from a carafe and washes her fingers. Searching for the passport, she sees it clutched in Scarpia's lifeless hand. A sudden, harsh crescendo sounds in the orchestra as she wrenches it free and hides it in her dress. While the Scarpia motive echoes softly, Tosca places one lighted candle at the right of Scarpia's head and another at the left, takes a crucifix from the wall and lays it on his breast. She steals from the room and the curtain falls.

Act Three

The roof of the prison castle of Sant' Angelo. On a table at the left stands a lantern, and next to it is the prison register book. On one wall is a crucifix with a lamp beneath. At the right is a trap door. It is just before daybreak on the morning of Cavaradossi's supposed execution. No one is on the scene. After a quiet prelude, sheep bells tinkle in the distance and we hear the plaintive song of a shepherd. It dies away as church bells ring for matins.

The jailer enters through the trap door and seats himself at the table. Soon Cavaradossi is brought in by a sergeant and an infantryman, who leave after the sergeant signs the register. Mario requests permission to write a farewell letter and offers the jailer a ring in return for the favor.

As he writes, the theme of the first-act love duet sweeps through the orchestra. Laying down his pen, he recalls his blissful past with Tosca in the poignant aria "E lucevan le stelle." Overwhelmed by despair, he breaks into sobs, burying his face in his hands. Tosca is brought in, and the two are left alone. Excitedly she shows him the passport. When Mario sees Scarpia's signature, he looks darkly at Tosca. In a fiery aria ("Il tuo sangue o il mio amore volea") she relates how she killed Scarpia, staining her hands with his blood. Mario takes her hands in his and comforts her in an ardent refrain ("O dolci mani").

Tosca then explains that the firing squad will use blank cartridges and that he must pretend to fall dead when the soldiers fire. There is a final duet as they sing of the happiness of the future, concluding with poignant, unaccompanied phrases as Spoletta appears with the firing squad.

Cavaradossi is led to the wall. Smilingly he refuses a blindfold. Tosca withdraws some distance away and faces him. The firing squad is lined up, and Spoletta raises his sword. Tosca covers her ears with her hands. The sword descends, there is a burst of fire, and Mario falls. The sergeant steps forward to administer the *coup de grâce,* but Spoletta stops him. After covering the body, the officer and soldiers leave.

Tosca cautiously approaches, warning Mario not to move. Making sure that the soldiers have gone, she calls his name, first softly, then more desperately when he does not answer. She flings back the cover, sees that he is dead, and falls over his body with a terrible cry. Suddenly angry shouts are heard below, and in a moment Spoletta and Sciarrone clamber hastily through the trap door. The officer flings himself on Tosca, shouting that she will pay for Scarpia's murder. She violently hurls him back. Crying, "Scarpia, avanti a Dio!" ("Scarpia, we meet before God!"), she throws herself over the parapet. The curtain falls.

La Traviata

by GIUSEPPE VERDI
[1813–1901]

Libretto by
FRANCESCO MARIA PIAVE

Based on Dumas's play
LA DAME AUX CAMÉLIAS (CAMILLE)

CHARACTERS

Violetta Valery, a courtesan	*Soprano*
Dr. Grenvil, Violetta's physician	*Bass*
Marquis d'Obigny, a nobleman	*Bass*
Flora Bervoix, friend of Violetta	*Mezzo-soprano*
Baron Douphol, rival of Alfredo	*Baritone*
Gastone, Viscount of Letorieres	*Tenor*
Alfredo Germont, lover of Violetta	*Tenor*
Annina, Violetta's maid	*Mezzo-soprano*
Giorgio Germont, father of Alfredo	*Baritone*

Salon guests, masqueraders, dancers, and servants

Place: In and near Paris
Time: About 1700
First performance: La Fenice Theater, Venice, March 6, 1853
Original language: Italian

LA TRAVIATA is the story of the tragic romance of Violetta Valery, a beautiful courtesan of Paris, and Alfredo Germont, a sincere and poetic young man of a respectable provincial family.

Verdi wrote *La Traviata* in 1853 while at work on another opera, *Il Trovatore*. Although Verdi usually devoted about four months to the composition of an opera, he completed *La*

Traviata in four weeks. Its first performance was a complete failure. It was performed in modern costume, an innovation which aroused the distaste of the audience. The leading tenor was hoarse. The soprano cast as Violetta was a fat prima donna, and when Dr. Grenvil announced in the last act that the heroine was dying of consumption, the audience howled with laughter.

La Traviata was next presented about a year later, the period of the opera being put back from 1850 to 1700 and costumed accordingly. The performance was an outstanding success, and since then *La Traviata* has been a favorite of opera lovers.

There is a short prelude dominated by two themes. The first is associated with Violetta's fatal illness and death and is heard again in the introduction to the fourth act. The second is the haunting, impassioned melody of Violetta's parting from Alfredo near the close of Act Two.

Act One

The richly furnished drawing room of Violetta Valery in Paris. The music reflects an atmosphere of festivity, for the pleasure-loving Violetta is giving another of the brilliant parties which have made her famous in Parisian society. About the room are several tables lavishly laden with food and drink.

Although afflicted with a grave illness, Violetta is determined to ignore the precarious state of her health in a ceaseless round of enjoyment. We first see her seated on a sofa, talking to Dr. Grenvil and several friends. Guests begin to arrive, among them Marquis d'Obigny, Flora, Violetta's closest friend, and Baron Douphol. Musical dialogue follows in which Violetta vivaciously welcomes her guests, and they inquire solicitously if she really has the health and strength for revelry. Violetta replies that she lives for pleasure alone, that Pleasure is the only physician who can heal her.

At that moment Gastone, Viscount of Letorieres, enters with Alfredo Germont, who is presented to Violetta as one of her latest admirers and who, in fact, is deeply in love with her. She receives him graciously, yet with a trace of coquetry, then invites her guests to be seated at one of the tables. She herself sits between Alfredo and Gastone. The latter tells her of Alfredo's infatuation, but Violetta discourages any sentiments other than friendship. Baron Douphol, Violetta's jealous admirer (later revealed as Alfredo's bitter rival), sings in an aside to Flora that he instinctively dislikes Alfredo.

There is a round of toasts, and Alfredo is prevailed upon to sing a drinking song. Other guests crowd into the drawing room to listen as he begins the famous "Libiamo, libiamo, ne' lieti calici." It is a catchy refrain in waltz time praising the joys of youth, love, and wine. Alfredo's eyes are on Violetta as he sings, and she joyously takes up the melody in response. Then the entire chorus joins in to bring the song to a rousing conclusion.

Violetta now invites her guests to dance and rises to lead them to the ballroom. Suddenly she sways and appears on the verge of fainting. There is a flurry of alarm, but Violetta explains that it is only a dizzy spell. She assures her guests that she will join them shortly. Alfredo remains with her, deeply concerned. "These nightly revels," he warns, "will one day be fatal." He implores her to be more mindful of her health, expressing a wish that he might always be near to take care of her. Violetta laughingly tries to brush aside his solicitous attentions.

Then in a tender and moving melody, "Un di felice," Alfredo tells Violetta of the first day he saw her. For more than a year, he sings, he has been hopelessly in love. Violetta, now realizing that he is passionately sincere in his avowals, is profoundly moved and replies that she is unworthy of such great love.

"I have only friendship to offer," Violetta tells him. "I live for love and liberty and use my friends only to serve my pleasure. If you do not care to be one of them, forget me."

La Traviata

Alfredo's declaration of love and Violetta's insistence on her own unworthiness are united in a beautiful duet. Although Alfredo persists in his love, he finally promises to say no more about it and turns to leave the room. Violetta calls him back, takes a flower from her breast, and tells him he may see her when it fades. Rapturously Alfredo takes the flower and kisses Violetta's hand.

The guests, weary of dancing and merrymaking, drift back into the drawing room to thank Violetta for the good time they have had and assure her they are always ready to be her companions in gaiety. Alfredo and the guests depart and Violetta is left alone.

In a recitative she meditates on the happenings of the night. She thinks of Alfredo's deep and abiding love in contrast to the empty flattery of her fair-weather friends. She ponders the choice between a life of quiet happiness with him and her own hectic, meaningless existence. Then she begins the tender, expressive aria, "Ah, fors'è lui che l'anima solinga ne' tumulti." It is a confession to herself that she has at last learned the meaning of real love. Overwhelmed by the thought, Violetta stands pensively.

In another instant her mood changes. "Folie, folie [What folly]," she sings as she is stung by the realization that such love can never be, that her loneliness and helplessness make Paris a vast, empty desert in which she is condemned to live and die. These thoughts are sung in a short recitative. Then Violetta bursts into the dazzling aria, "Sempre libera degg'io folleggiare di gioja in gioja." The scintillating coloratura passages reflect Violetta's determination to abandon herself solely to pleasure. She will forget Alfredo's love by pursuing new joys, each wilder and fiercer than the last.

Suddenly her song is interrupted by the sound of Alfredo's voice outside. He repeats the passionate melody in which he declared his love earlier in the act. Violetta stands as if hypnotized, then bursts forth again into the glittering phrases of her aria. This brilliant climax brings the first act to a close.

Act Two

A room on the ground floor of a country home near Paris.[1] After a short orchestral introduction Alfredo enters, attired in hunting costume. Putting away his gun, he sings in recitative about the idyllic happiness of his life with Violetta. He rejoices that she so willingly gave up the gaiety and excitement of Paris, where she had reigned as a social queen, to be with him in the seclusion of the country. In a melodious aria Alfredo recalls how Violetta tamed his wild and youthful passions and revealed to him the calm depths of mature love ("De' miei bollenti spiriti"). Her devotion has been a source of unbelievable joy and inspiration.

His thoughts are interrupted by the entrance of Annina, Violetta's maid, obviously in a state of agitation. In response to Alfredo's questions, Annina says she has just returned from Paris, where, on Violetta's orders, she has sold some of her mistress's personal possessions to pay the heavy household expenses. Unwillingly the maid reveals that two thousand louis are still needed. Shocked and startled by this state of affairs, Alfredo announces that he will go to Paris at once to raise the money. He sends Annina away with a warning not to reveal to Violetta the purpose of his journey.

In a florid and dramatic aria Alfredo voices his humiliation and remorse for having lived like a drone on Violetta's money. He bitterly reproaches himself for his thoughtlessness, swears he will make amends before another day dawns, then rushes distractedly from the room.

Violetta enters, looking for Alfredo. Annina informs her that he has gone to Paris for a day. A servant hands Violetta a letter, which she reads with an amused smile. It is an invitation to a ball from Flora Bervoix, Violetta's former Parisian companion. Violetta carelessly tosses the letter aside with the comment that Flora will look for her in vain.

Now a dignified, elderly gentleman is shown into the room.

[1] The opera was first written in three acts, and this was Scene One of Act Two.

He introduces himself as Alfredo's father and brusquely accuses Violetta of luring his son to ruin. Angered by the elder Germont's charge, Violetta starts to leave, then turns and sits down. She denies that Alfredo is lavishing his money on her and hands her visitor a legal paper prepared for the sale of her possessions. Germont, although somewhat abashed, points out that her past still casts a shadow over her life and Alfredo's. Violetta replies that her deep love for Alfredo has blotted out her past sins.

Germont's attitude softens. With dignity and restraint he tells Violetta that he has come to ask her to make a great sacrifice. Violetta, suddenly fear-stricken, faces Germont, saying she foresees the end of her happiness. Germont sings the aria in which he reveals that his daughter's plans for marriage are threatened by the scandal of Alfredo's intimate friendship with Violetta. She replies that she is willing to give up Alfredo until after his sister's wedding. Germont insists that it must be forever. In an intensely dramatic aria, Violetta protests that giving up Alfredo is impossible ("Non sapete quale affetto"). She is already beset by illness, and separation from the man she loves will only hasten her doom. The only other alternative, she cries, is death.

In an effort to induce Violetta to release his son, Germont now resorts to a different strategy. He reminds her that when time has destroyed her youth and beauty Alfredo's love will be destroyed with them. The years will thus bring nothing but sorrow and regret. She will find her own happiness, Germont adds, only in the happiness she can bring to both his children by her great renunciation.

The somber, minor key of the music underscores Violetta's anguish as she realizes the hopelessness of the situation. Weeping, she asks Germont to tell his daughter that for the sake of her future happiness Violetta's heart has been broken. Now she awaits the father's command. Germont says she must tell Alfredo that she no longer loves him. Violetta warns that Alfredo will not believe her, and if she attempts to leave him he will follow her. Then she thinks of a plan. She tells Germont that his son will be restored to him but that the separation will break Alfredo's heart too. Shaken and distressed by the bitterness of the sacrifice he has demanded of the lovers, Germont asks Violetta how he can repay her for her noble act.

Only death can end her agony, Violetta sings. Her remaining hope is that Alfredo will not curse her memory but will understand that she has made this supreme sacrifice for his sake alone. Brokenhearted, she bids Germont farewell, while he goes into the garden to await his son.

Violetta sits down to write a letter to Alfredo, but no sooner has she sealed it than he himself enters. She attempts to hide the letter, and Alfredo is momentarily puzzled by her confusion. He tells Violetta that he has received a stern note from his father, who is expected to arrive any moment. Unaware, of course, of the scene between Violetta and the elder Germont, Alfredo attempts to reassure her by saying that when his father sees her he, too, will love her. She counsels him first to meet his father alone. She will wait in the garden during the interview and later plead with Germont in her own way. Scarcely able to conceal her despair, Violetta asks Alfredo again and again to say that he loves her. Alfredo ardently replies, mystified by her tears. Then regaining control of herself, she bids him farewell to the intensely passionate music of the theme previously heard in the prelude of the opera.

Alfredo is left alone. He reflects on Violetta's devotion, then picks up a book and tries to read. Nervous and impatient, he puts it quickly aside. The servant enters hastily to tell him that Violetta and her maid have taken a coach for Paris. Alfredo assumes that she has gone to arrange for the sale of her possessions, a contingency which he thinks Annina will prevent. A messenger enters with a letter for Alfredo. He tears it open and staggers as he reads Violetta's message of farewell. With a tortured cry he turns to go and finds himself in the arms of his father. Sinking down at the table, Alfredo buries his face in his hands in utter despair.

In the great aria, "Di Provenza il mar," Germont, in majestic, sweeping phrases, recalls Alfredo's happy childhood in Provence by the sea. Gently he implores his son to return home, where he can find solace for his grief in the sympathy and kindness of his family.

Suddenly a dark suspicion crosses Alfredo's mind, rousing him to jealous fury. He is certain that Baron Douphol has persuaded Violetta to betray him. In vain his father pleads with him to forget Violetta and return home. As Germont's entreaties rise to a dramatic climax, Alfredo discovers Flora's invitation, which is still lying on the table. This confirms his suspicions and he furiously swears vengeance. Alfredo rushes madly from the stage, followed by his father.

ACT THREE

The luxurious mansion of Flora Bervoix in Paris.[2] Another gay party is in progress. Prominent on the scene are a gaming table and another large table set with refreshments and decorated with flowers. As in the first act, the music is lively and festive.

Flora, Marquis d'Obigny, Dr. Grenvil, and other guests engage in musical dialogue. The hostess promises her friends a night of brilliant revelry, then announces that Violetta and Alfredo are expected. The Marquis, however, informs her that the lovers are separated and that if Violetta appears it will be with Baron Douphol, not Alfredo. The others are incredulous. Just then some of the masqueraders come in.

First we hear a delightful chorus of women gypsies. Some have wands and others tambourines with which they beat time as they sing. They invite the guests to hold out their hands so that they may have their palms read. One group reads Flora's hand and tells her there is a rival in the offing. Others of the chorus read the palm of the Marquis. They laughingly inform him that no one will ever accuse him of being constant in his love affairs. In sprightly music Flora and the Marquis indulge in a bit of banter. Flora brands

[2] Originally Scene Two of Act Two.

D'Obigny a gay deceiver, while he in mock seriousness swears he is true to her alone. Then both join the gypsies in a carefree song.

The music takes on a new rhythm as Viscount Gastone and others make a colorful entrance as Spanish matadors and picadors. They sing the tale of a brave young picador whose ladylove promised him her hand only if he succeeded in killing five bulls in one day. This feat the daring young man accomplished and so proved his love. Everyone joins in a chorus of joyous revelry, while the gypsies beat time with their tambourines and the picadors with their staves, creating a stirring rhythmic effect.

At the end of the number Alfredo enters and is hailed by the gathering. Flora inquires about Violetta. He curtly answers that he is not concerned, then strides over to the gaming table to join the others at cards. A moment later Violetta enters on the arm of Baron Douphol. Flora welcomes her and thanks the Baron for bringing Violetta back to her friends. In an aside Douphol tells Violetta that Alfredo is present and grimly warns her not to speak to him. In a poignant musical phrase, which is repeated several times later in this scene, Violetta expresses foreboding and anxiety over the inevitable meeting of Alfredo and Douphol.

Taking Violetta aside, Flora asks her what has happened. Alfredo, winning consistently at the gaming table, sings with contemptuous indifference that whoever is unlucky in love is lucky at cards. He pointedly announces that he intends to retire to the country again with his winnings, to lavish them on someone who once shared his life there but has temporarily deserted him. Violetta gasps at the remark while Gastone begs Alfredo to spare her feelings. Angrily the Baron starts to address Alfredo. Violetta, in an aside to the Baron, threatens to leave him if he causes trouble. Alfredo disdainfully recognizes the Baron. With suave malice Douphol compliments Alfredo on his luck, then offers to play him at cards. Alfredo coolly accepts the challenge. The premonitory theme is again heard as Violetta voices her fear of the outcome of this contest.

Douphol stakes one hundred louis. Alfredo wins. They double the stakes and again Alfredo wins. The tension mounts as the guests discuss Alfredo's luck, while Flora comments that the night promises to be an expensive one for the Baron. The situation is saved by a servant's announcement that supper is served. The guests withdraw to the banquet room. For the third time we hear the theme of Violetta's apprehension and distress. Alfredo and Douphol face each other alone. Alfredo asks his adversary if he wishes to continue the game, but the Baron replies that he will take his revenge later. Alfredo scornfully offers to meet the Baron at any game he chooses.

The stage is momentarily empty. Suddenly Violetta re-enters, greatly excited. She has asked Alfredo to come to her but fears that his hatred will make this interview useless. Alfredo appears and the two unhappy lovers are face to face. Violetta implores him to leave, warning him of the Baron's jealousy. Alfredo retorts that he and the Baron are mortal enemies and taunts her with the threat that he may kill Douphol. In vain Violetta tries to convince Alfredo that her anxiety is for him alone and again beseeches him to leave. Alfredo merely jeers at her terror and says he will leave only if she promises to go with him. Frantic with despair, Violetta answers that a fatal promise forces her to refuse his request. With mounting fury Alfredo demands to know who exacted the promise. In a desperate lie Violetta answers that it was Douphol and that she made the promise because she is in love with the Baron.

Raging, Alfredo rushes to the doors, throws them open, and calls in the guests. As they excitedly crowd around him he points to Violetta and hurls his accusations. He tells them that she attempted to buy his love by lavishing her possessions on him. He blindly accepted because of his real love for her. Now that he has unmasked her infamous scheming, he calls on the guests to witness that he is paying her back in full. Mad with anger, he hurls the purse containing his winnings at the feet of Violetta, who faints in the arms of Flora and Dr. Grenvil.

In a thrilling, dramatic chorus, Violetta's friends denounce Alfredo's brutal insults and angrily order him to leave. The elder Germont, who entered just as Alfredo was finishing his tirade, now steps forward. He vehemently reproaches Alfredo and renounces him as his son. Alfredo cringes at his father's words and in a tense aside voices his remorse for his shameless conduct.

Then begins the magnificent closing chorus of the act, in which all join. Flora, Gastone, the Marquis, Germont, and the others attempt to console Violetta, who is slowly reviving. Baron Douphol, burning for revenge, challenges Alfredo to a duel. Alfredo himself, in humiliation and despair, cries out that he has forever lost the one he loves. Over the music of the chorus Violetta sings to Alfredo—softly at first, then with passionate intensity. Someday, she says sorrowfully, he will know how great her sacrifice has been and how deeply he has wronged her. Despite the dark tragedy of their misunderstanding, she will love him forever. As the chorus ends in a tremendous flood of sound, Germont slowly leads Alfredo away, followed by the Baron. Flora and Dr. Grenvil support Violetta as she leaves. The remaining guests slowly depart and the curtain falls.

Act Four

Violetta's modest apartment in Paris.[3] Ravaged by illness, Violetta lies asleep on her bed, at the side of which stands a table with a decanter, a glass, and several vials of medicine. Annina, the maid, is drowsing by the fireplace. The windows are shuttered and a night lamp is burning. The orchestral introduction softly intones the theme of Violetta's illness and impending death.

Violetta awakens, calls to Annina, asks for a glass of water, then learns that it is seven o'clock in the morning. She asks Annina to open the shutters. As the maid does so, she sees Dr. Grenvil approaching below. Violetta tries to rise but falls

[3] Originally Act Three.

back exhausted. As she is helped to her feet by Annina, Dr. Grenvil enters and they both assist her to a nearby sofa. With pathetic gratitude Violetta welcomes the faithful doctor, who asks if she is feeling better. She answers that though she is weak her mind is at peace. She has found solace and spiritual strength in prayer. When she informs Grenvil that she has slept soundly, he cheerfully assures her that recovery is not far off. With a sad smile Violetta feigns to accept this professional consolation. As the doctor leaves he answers Annina's whispered question with the grim truth: Violetta's death is only a matter of hours.

Annina turns back to her mistress with forced cheerfulness, bidding her have courage. Violetta says she hears sounds of revelry in the streets, whereupon Annina reminds her that it is carnival time. Musing on the poor unfortunates who are doubtless among the pleasure-mad throng, Violetta asks Annina how much money is left. When Annina tells her that twenty louis remain, Violetta directs the maid to keep ten for herself and distribute the other ten among the needy in the streets. She assures Annina that whatever money is left will be sufficient for her needs, then asks her to find out if a letter has arrived.

When Annina leaves, Violetta takes a letter from her bosom and reads it aloud in a hollow voice as the orchestra softly plays the music of the love theme. It is a message from the elder Germont: Alfredo and the Baron fought a duel—the Baron was wounded but is recovering. Alfredo has gone abroad, but Germont has revealed to him the meaning of Violetta's great sacrifice. Soon Alfredo will come to beg her forgiveness. Germont bids her have faith in a happier future. Violetta stops reading and the tender theme in the orchestra dies out incompleted.

Despairingly Violetta sings that she has waited in vain. She looks at her reflection in a mirror and is horrified at the change illness has made in her features. Despite Dr. Grenvil's reassuring words she realizes that the weakness which seizes her is fatal. Then Violetta begins the tragic and moving aria in which she bids farewell to the world ("Addio! del passato"). Her cherished hopes are shattered—friendless and utterly alone, she awaits a grave which shall be unmarked by cross or flower.

As the last note dies away like a sigh, a bacchanalian chorus of revelers outside harshly breaks in on Violetta's mood of sorrow and resignation. In ironic contrast the merrymakers sing lustily in praise of the fine, fat bull which is traditionally led to slaughter to provide the carnival feast. The revelers finally move on. Suddenly Annina enters, scarcely able to suppress her excitement. Hesitantly she asks Violetta to remain calm because a wonderful surprise is in store. In feverish suspense Violetta asks if it is Alfredo. Annina nods. The door is flung open and in another moment the lovers are in each other's arms, pouring out their love and longing in an ecstatic burst of song.

The music gradually grows quieter, and then follows the famous duet, "Parigi, o cara." Alfredo tenderly sings of how he will take Violetta to the country, far away from Paris, to restore her to health and happiness. Alfredo's rapturous promises revive Violetta and she echoes the melody as she rejoices over the end of her sorrow. In tranquil simplicity the duet comes to a close. Violetta asks Alfredo to go to church with her so that they may give thanks for their reunion. Suddenly she falters, and Alfredo is alarmed at her pallor. It is nothing, Violetta says reassuringly, only the shock of supreme joy after so much sorrow. With a desperate effort Violetta fights off her weakness, tries to put on a dress Annina hands her, but collapses helplessly. Panic-stricken, Alfredo orders Annina to get the doctor. Violetta instructs the maid to say that Alfredo has returned and that now she wants to live. When Annina leaves, Violetta, with calm resignation, tells Alfredo that if his return cannot restore her to health, nothing on earth can save her.

Suddenly the thought of dying so young spurs her to anguished protest against her fate. Frantically Alfredo attempts to give Violetta courage, and their voices again unite in a dramatic duet. At its climax Violetta sinks back upon the bed —now within a few moments of the end. Annina, Dr. Grenvil, and the elder Germont rush in. Alfredo's father has come to beg Violetta's forgiveness and give his consent to the marriage of the lovers. Stricken with remorse as he realizes it is all too late, he reproaches himself for having wronged Violetta.

For a parting gift Violetta gives Alfredo a miniature of herself. Alfredo cries out that she must not die; and his father joins him in an expression of agonized grief. Violetta gently continues, bidding Alfredo to give the miniature to the maiden he may someday marry. It will be a token of Violetta's prayers for them. There follows a short but strikingly melodic quintet in which the persons in this tragic scene express their individual sorrow. ("Cara, sublime vittima"). It is suddenly interrupted as Violetta, with that false strength which sometimes comes just before the end, sings deliriously that her pain is gone and life is returning. The love theme soars high and clear in the orchestra. With a final cry of ecstasy Violetta falls back, lifeless. The others express their profound grief. Dr. Grenvil, feeling Violetta's pulse, signifies that all is over. The final curtain falls.

Tristan und Isolde

by RICHARD WAGNER
[1813–1883]

Libretto by the Composer

Based on the medieval legend of
TRISTAN AND ISOLDA

CHARACTERS

A young sailor	*Tenor*
Isolde, a princess of Ireland	*Soprano*
Brangäne, lady in waiting to Isolde	*Mezzo-soprano*
Tristan, a knight of Cornwall	*Tenor*
Kurvenal, henchman to Tristan	*Baritone*
Melot, courtier to King Marke	*Tenor*
King Marke of Cornwall	*Bass*
A shepherd	*Tenor*
A helmsman	*Baritone*

Knights, soldiers, attendants, sailors

Place: Aboard a ship, Cornwall, and Brittany
Time: A medieval period
First performance: Royal Court Theater, Munich, June 10, 1865
Original language: German

IN 1857 WAGNER resolved to discontinue temporarily his work on *Der Ring des Nibelungen* and forthwith halted the composition of *Siegfried*. He turned to the writing of *Tristan und Isolde*, plans for which had been occupying his mind since about 1854. The score was completed in 1859, but six years elapsed before this great masterpiece was given its première. After repeated postponements it was performed under

Tristan und Isolde

the baton of the brilliant conductor, Hans von Bülow, before young King Ludwig of Bavaria, Wagner's patron, and an audience of notables. Although the advanced musical ideas of *Tristan* were generally beyond the grasp of the public hearing it for the first time, the opera was enthusiastically applauded. Primarily it represented an artistic triumph rather than a popular success.

The introduction eloquently states several underlying musical motives of the opera. It begins with the themes of confession of love and desire, then moves on to the love-glance motive. Gathering intensity, the music sweeps on, through the themes of the love drink, the death potion, and the magic casket, to the motive symbolizing the longing of the lovers for the release of death. The first theme is again interwoven as the music builds up to a tremendous climax, after which it subsides to a meditative restatement of the love-suffering-longing motive.

Act One

The deck of the ship in which Tristan is bringing Isolde from Ireland to be the bride of his uncle, King Marke of Cornwall. We see a royal pavilion erected near the bow of the ship. It is decorated with luxurious tapestries and enclosed at the rear with great hangings. At one side is a couch, on which Isolde is reclining. Her face is dark with anger and dejection. Brangäne, standing near an opening of the curtain, is looking toward the sea.

From the lookout's post high up on the mast comes the voice of a sailor singing a rollicking chantey about an Irish maid he left behind. The words strike Isolde's ears like a taunt, and she rises from the couch with an exclamation of annoyance at this fancied insult. Impatiently she asks Brangäne how far they have journeyed. When the lady in waiting replies that the ship will land in Cornwall by evening Isolde abandons herself to bitter reflection. She, daughter of a line of mighty sorcerers who could command the elements, has contented herself with brewing magic potions to heal her bitterest enemy. In a burst of rage she calls on the wind and waves to destroy the ship and all who sail in it. Brangäne, much distressed, tries to calm her mistress's anger. Isolde cries out that she is suffocating and orders Brangäne to draw aside the hangings.

A large part of the main deck now becomes visible. Sailors are busy at their tasks; men-at-arms are seated about. Lost in thought, Tristan stands alone, looking out over the water. Kurvenal sits near him. The lookout's voice is again heard as he sings his chantey with its characteristic sea motive. Isolde glares at Tristan, scornfully remarking that this fabulous hero —he who has only death in his heart—lacks the courage to face her. The somber death motive gives menace to her words. She tells Brangäne to inform Tristan that she wishes to see him— and it is a command, not a request.

As the sea motive sounds out in a strong rhythmic beat from the orchestra, Brangäne timorously approaches Tristan, who is startled from his reverie by a warning word from Kurvenal. Brangäne delivers her message. Tristan courteously answers that when the ship lands he will be proud to fulfill his duty and escort Isolde to King Marke. He adds that, at the moment, he cannot leave the helm. Kurvenal brashly interrupts to observe that the knight Tristan is not a man to be ordered about by a woman. He sings a sturdy refrain ("Herr Morold zog zu Meere her"), in which he jeeringly relates how Morold, the Irish lord who was to wed Isolde, tried to collect taxes from Cornwall. For his pains the brave Tristan cut off his head and sent it back to Ireland. The sailors lustily repeat the refrain.

Angrily Brangäne leaves, while Tristan tries to restrain his henchman. Closing the curtains behind her, Brangäne re-enters the pavilion and tells Isolde of Tristan's refusal and Kurvenal's insult. In fury Isolde recalls the fateful events in Ireland. Tristan, badly wounded in the fight with Morold, came to Ireland to be healed by Isolde's magic arts. He called himself Tantris, but Isolde soon found out his real identity.

Tristan und Isolde

She noted that a piece was missing from the edge of Tristan's sword and that a broken fragment of steel taken from the head of Morold exactly fitted into the sword blade. Thereupon Isolde came sword in hand to the stricken Tristan, resolved to kill him in revenge. But the knight looked into her eyes and left her powerless to kill. Isolde restored the knight to health and sent him home to Cornwall. This great hero repaid her kindness, Isolde continues sardonically, by returning to claim her as the bride of his graybeard uncle, King Marke. Savagely Isolde reproaches herself for her weakness in showing mercy to Tristan.

Brangäne tries to calm and console Isolde by pointing out that as King Marke's bride she will be Queen of a great realm. Isolde betrays her real feelings when she speaks of the torment of living near Tristan in unrequited love. The loyal but naïve Brangäne, assuming that Isolde is concerned about the success of her marriage, hastily assures her that the magic potions provided by Isolde's mother will make marital happiness certain.

Isolde, obsessed with thoughts of revenge and death, orders Brangäne to bring the casket containing her mother's preparations. She takes from it a vial of poison and tells Brangäne that this is the only magic potion she desires. The maid is horror-stricken. Meanwhile there is a great stir on deck as the sailors prepare the ship for landing. Kurvenal strides into the pavilion and tells Isolde that his liege lord bids her make ready to greet King Marke. Isolde coldly replies that before Tristan may lead her to the King he must first seek her forgiveness for his overbearing conduct. Kurvenal grimly promises to inform Tristan accordingly.

In rising desperation Isolde thinks of suicide. She fervently embraces Brangäne, pauses in sudden resolve, then commands Brangäne to prepare the poison cup. Tristan, she intones, will drink with her the cup of atonement. When Brangäne tries to dissuade her Isolde answers with angry sarcasm. Truly, she says, her mother has provided her with helpful libations. One above all will give surcease from deepest pain—the death potion. With brooding intensity Isolde sings the death motive.

As she orders Brangäne to prepare the drink Kurvenal enters to announce Tristan.

The Tristan motive thunders in the orchestra. Quietly the knight steps into the pavilion, greeting Isolde with the words, "Begehrt, Herrin, was ihr wünscht [Noble lady, what is your wish]?" In answer, Isolde observes harshly that the noble Tristan has evidently forgotten the chief tenets of knighthood—to make amends for wrongs he has done and to seek forgiveness of his enemies. She reminds him that the blood feud between them has not yet been erased. Furiously she condemns Tristan for his wanton murder of Morold and swears she will yet have revenge.

With great dignity Tristan offers her his sword. In cold contempt Isolde observes that King Marke would hardly welcome as his bride the murderess of his most trusted knight. Then, pretending to cast aside thoughts of revenge, she asks Tristan to drink the cup of peace with her. The chorus of sailors breaks in sharply. With an impatient gesture Isolde commands Brangäne to hand her the drink. Tristan softly voices his premonition of the fate that awaits both him and Isolde in the cup.

Isolde proffers the beaker, saying scornfully that Tristan may now tell his lord that he has drunk of the cup of friendship with this fair bride who saved his life. Confused and shaken, Tristan excitedly shouts an order to the sailors, then takes the cup. With a ringing phrase of despair and resignation he drinks. Isolde watches for a moment, then tears the cup from his hands, drains it, and flings it away. They stand transfixed as the love theme begins whispering in the orchestra. As the music rises in intensity they gaze at each other in unbelieving wonder. With passionate outcries they rush into each other's arms. From another part of the ship comes a chorus of sailors hailing King Marke. Brangäne, watching the lovers, laments her fateful ruse of substituting the love potion for the drink of death. Oblivious to everything, Isolde and Tristan pour out their love for each other.

While all the men on board acclaim King Marke in a thunderous chorus, Tristan stares uncomprehendingly toward the

Tristan und Isolde

shore. Brangäne quickly places the regal mantle over Isolde's shoulders. In sudden terror Isolde asks her, "Ha! welcher Trank [Ah, what was the potion]?" When Brangäne answers that it was the love drink, Tristan and Isolde cry out in mingled ecstasy and despair. The curtain falls.

Act Two

The garden of King Marke's palace in Cornwall. The brief introduction is dominated by the tense, agitated theme of anticipation. It is night. A torch burns at the entrance of Isolde's apartments, off a balcony at the rear. The horns of King Marke's hunting party sound in the distance. Brangäne gazes apprehensively toward the forest, then back at the doorway. Isolde enters hurriedly. Lost in rapture, she sings of her impatience to be in Tristan's arms. Brangäne, haunted by fear and remorse over her deed, vainly tries to bring Isolde to her senses. She warns that Melot, though posing as a friend, is planning some treachery and that this hunting expedition is part of his evil plan. But Isolde derides her fears and commands her to extinguish the torch as a signal for Tristan to approach. When Brangäne protests, lamenting bitterly over mixing the love potion, Isolde sings that destiny has brought her and Tristan together. Impetuously she throws the torch to the ground as the theme of anticipation sweeps through the orchestra. Brangäne, disturbed and uneasy, mounts an outer flight of steps to a turret where she may watch and warn the lovers of the return of King Marke and his huntsmen.

Isolde looks eagerly beyond the ramparts and hopefully waves her scarf, the symbolical scarf motive accompanying her movements. The music grows wilder and she sees Tristan and signals him in fervid excitement. At its climax Tristan rushes in. They embrace in utter ecstasy and sing in exultant tones of the miracle of their love. The storm of their passionate utterances gradually subsides. Tristan slowly leads Isolde to a grassy slope. Gazing into each other's eyes, they sing the magnificent love duet, "O sink hernieder, Nacht der Liebe."

When they pause Brangäne's warning voice floats from the tower ("Habet Acht"). It is lost again as Tristan and Isolde continue their duet. In the intensity of their passion they cry for death, so that they may be forever united beyond the reach of the world.

The flood of love music stops suddenly at its height. A harsh chord crashes in the orchestra. Brangäne screams in terror. Kurvenal runs in shouting a warning to Tristan. Then King Marke and his huntsmen, led by Melot, stride in. Brangäne hurries to Isolde's side. Tristan springs up and stands before her, shielding her form with his cloak. For a long moment no one moves or speaks, while in the orchestra the motives of love's transfiguration and the coming of day mingle softly.

Tristan is the first to break the silence, murmuring, "Der öde Tag—zum letzen Mal [Wretched dawn—for the last time]!" Melot smugly exults that his ruse has successfully trapped the lovers. King Marke turns on Tristan with a flood of bitter reproach for betraying his friendship and trust. In helpless bewilderment he asks why fate has dealt him this cruel blow. To that question, Tristan says dolorously, there is no answer. He asks Isolde if she is prepared to follow him into the land of night to which he now must go. When Isolde answers in the affirmative Melot cries out that he will avenge this final insult to the King. Drawing his sword, he challenges Tristan, who accepts with cold contempt. He hurls himself at Melot, then deliberately allows his adversary to wound him. Kurvenal and Isolde rush to him as he sinks to the ground, while King Marke restrains the treacherous Melot. The King Marke motive thunders forth as the curtain falls.

Act Three

The rocky courtyard of Tristan's castle, Kareol, in Brittany. At the rear is a watch tower commanding a view of a broad waste of ocean. Before the curtain rises there is a brief prelude in which the motive of suffering and longing is combined with the rising wail of the desolation theme.

Tristan und Isolde

Tristan, gravely wounded, lies motionless on a couch. Kurvenal is at his side, watching him closely. From beyond the ramparts comes the plaintive and melancholy sound of a shepherd's pipe. Soon the young shepherd appears and inquires if Tristan still sleeps. Were he to awake, Kurvenal answers sadly, it would be only to die. He bids the shepherd watch closely for any sign of a ship on the horizon, and directs him to change his sad piping to a merry tune, should a vessel heave in sight.

Tristan revives, and in answer to his confused questions Kurvenal explains how they made their way to Tristan's castle —that after the duel he carried his master to the ship which brought them home. Here in his homeland, Kurvenal assures him, his wounds will quickly heal. But Tristan now sinks into delirium, calling wildly for Isolde and raving against the light of day, which he associates with his doom.

When he again becomes quiet Kurvenal goes on to tell him that he has dispatched a servant to Cornwall to bring Isolde, so that she who once before had restored Tristan to health may do so again. In poignant phrases Tristan expresses his gratitude for Kurvenal's loyalty, having shared with him joy and sorrow and even betrayal. One thing only this loyal friend cannot share—the fearful pain of love in his heart. In his feverish excitement Tristan imagines that Isolde's ship is approaching.

He tries to rise but falls back exhausted. Listening to the shepherd's mournful piping, he murmurs that he had heard this dirge long ago at the death of his mother and father and that its refrain is interwoven with his own fate. Again the madness of pain overcomes him, and in a spasm of anguish he curses the love potion. Frenziedly crying out that the ship is approaching, he implores Kurvenal to go to the rampart. As Kurvenal, deeply distressed, tries to calm him, the shepherd's piping changes to a gay and sprightly tune. Kurvenal springs to the rampart and joyously describes the approach of the ship. Tristan orders him to meet Isolde.

In a paroxysm of ecstasy and pain Tristan raises himself, rips away his bandages, and struggles to his feet. Isolde appears, calling his name, as the motive of love's longing soars up in a tremendous crescendo. Tristan sinks into her arms. There, tenderly breathing her name, he dies. Isolde, stunned, kneels beside his body. Bitterly she laments that death has robbed her of the bliss of this reunion. She collapses, fainting, at Tristan's side.

Kurvenal, who has been watching horror-stricken, is roused by the shepherd's warning that another vessel is coming. Looking seaward, Kurvenal recognizes it as King Marke's ship. Hurriedly he and the shepherd attempt to barricade the gate at the entrance to the courtyard. In another moment there is a confusion of sounds and the clashing of swords from below the rampart. Brangäne is heard calling for Isolde. Melot rushes up, and Kurvenal kills him with a blow. When King Marke and his followers storm the barricade Kurvenal attacks them furiously. While they are fighting, Brangäne makes her way to Isolde. Soon Kurvenal, fatally wounded, staggers over to Tristan's couch and falls dead. King Marke gazes down on the scene, murmuring brokenly, "Todt denn Alles—Alles todt [Now all—all are dead]."

Isolde revives. Brangäne explains to her that she had confessed mixing the love potion and that when King Marke heard her story he came in all haste to Brittany to forgive Isolde. In grief-stricken tones the King adds that he had absolved Tristan of all blame and was prepared to give him Isolde as his bride. But death alone has triumphed, he cries out in sorrow and despair.

With her eyes fixed on Tristan's face, Isolde begins her magnificent and heart-rending song of farewell, the *Liebestod* ("Mild und leise wie er lächelt"). As her voice soars in the exaltation of approaching death, the themes of bliss, parting, and transfiguration surge through the orchestra to an overwhelming climax. Isolde sinks upon Tristan's body—the lovers reunited at last in death. King Marke raises his hands in blessing over the dead. The music dies away high in the strings. The curtain falls.

Il Trovatore

by GIUSEPPE VERDI
[1813–1901]

Libretto by
SALVATORE CAMMARANO

Based on Antonio García Gutiérrez's play
EL TROVADOR

CHARACTERS

Ferrando, captain of the palace guard and henchman of Count di Luna	*Bass*
Inez, companion to Leonora	*Soprano*
Leonora, a titled lady-in-waiting to the Queen in a court of Aragon	*Soprano*
Count di Luna, a nobleman in the same court	*Baritone*
Manrico, the troubador, an officer in the service of the Prince of Biscay, and brother of Count di Luna	*Tenor*
Azucena, a gypsy woman	*Mezzo-soprano*
Ruiz, an officer in the service of Manrico	*Tenor*

Soldiers in the service of Count di Luna and Manrico, guards, gypsies, a messenger, a jailer, nuns, palace attendants

Place: Aragon and Biscay, in Spain
Time: Fifteenth century
First performance: Teatro Apollo, Rome, January 19, 1853
Original language: Italian

IL TROVATORE, Verdi's seventeenth opera, was composed in what has been termed his "second period" (1851–53), during which he also wrote *Rigoletto* and *La Traviata*. These operas firmly established his position as the greatest of Italian operatic composers. *Il Trovatore* has enjoyed uninterrupted success from the day of its première, and its melodies are perhaps more widely known than those of any other opera.

Act One
(The Duel)

[*Scene One*] A chamber adjoining the apartments of Count di Luna in Aliaferia Palace. Soldiers are on guard, while a group of di Luna's servants wait outside the chamber door to be assigned to their duties. Ferrando warns the servants to remain awake and watchful, for the count may return at any moment from his nightly vigil under the window of his ladylove, Leonora. The officer reveals that the count is much perturbed over the recent appearance of a rival on the scene—a certain troubador. This information, however, fails to interest the weary servants, who request Ferrando to help them keep awake by telling the story of Garcia, brother of Count di Luna. As the retainers and soldiers gather round, Ferrando begins his narrative ("Di due figli vivea"), which reveals events prior to the time of the opera.

One day long ago the nurse to the younger of two children of Count di Luna (the present count's father) found a gypsy woman bending over the baby's bed. The screams of the nurse brought the servants, who drove the gypsy away despite her protests that she had come only to read the child's horoscope. The child, however, fell victim to a wasting illness as the result of a spell cast upon him by the gypsy, who was later captured and burned at the stake for her sorcery. The gypsy's daughter, burning for revenge, stole the count's other child and hurled him upon the flames that were consuming her mother. Although there was no witness to the terrible deed, so Ferrando's story goes, the charred bones of a child were found in the ashes. The grief-stricken count clung until his death to the conviction that his child was still alive. As he lay dying he charged his older son (the present Count di Luna) to devote his life to the search for his brother.

Il Trovatore

In foreboding tones Ferrando goes on to say that the tortured spirit of the gypsy haunts the castle to this day in various shapes. In fact, one of the servants who struck the gypsy on her way to the stake had died in a state of madness that night as the clock struck twelve, the result of being haunted by her spirit in the form of an owl. A bell strikes midnight, and the listeners curse the witch. Servants and soldiers then resume their places of duty, and the curtain falls.

[Scene Two] In the garden of the Aliaferia Palace. It is night. Inez, entering the garden with Leonora, reminds her that she is awaited by the queen. Leonora, however, can think only of her mysterious admirer. She tells Inez that she first saw the knight at a tournament, where he appeared in black armor, with a shield that bore no identifying device. He vanquished all his opponents in the lists, and Leonora placed the victor's crown upon his brow. But with the outbreak of civil war in the land, the knight vanished as suddenly as he had come. In a melodious aria ("Tacea la notte placida") Leonora relates the sequel to the story—how the knight, now in the role of an ardent troubador, has returned to sing passionate serenades beneath her window. In rapturous phrases Leonora declares her love for him. Inez expresses the hope that Leonora's love will not be in vain. The two voices blend in the closing phrases of the song as the women enter the palace.

Count di Luna now steps out of the shadows, gazes up at Leonora's window, and sings of his love in fervent phrases. Just as he is ascending the staircase to the palace he hears the notes of a harp and exclaims in fury that it is the troubador. The voice of Manrico is heard in a brief but lyrical serenade ("Deserto sulla terra"). Leonora hurries out of the palace and stands for a moment on the staircase, peering into the gloom of the garden. She sees the count muffled in his cloak. Mistaking him for Manrico, she rushes into his arms with a passionate cry.

At that moment she hears Manrico's angry exclamation, "Infida [Faithless one]!" As she gasps out "Qual voce [That voice]!" a ray of moonlight reveals the visored knight standing before her. A fiery trio now ensues. Freeing herself from the count's embrace, Leonora kneels before Manrico and in confusion and despair implores him to believe that her ardent words were meant for him. He gently reassures her, while the count furiously demands that his rival identify himself. In answer, Manrico raises his visor. The count rages at the impudence of this henchman of Urgel of Biscay, archenemy of Aragon, in daring to cross the boundaries of the kingdom. Manrico coolly taunts di Luna and defies him to call out his guards. When Leonora tries to intercede, the count, in a stormy refrain ("Di geloso amor sprezzato"), swears he will have Manrico's life and reproaches Leonora for her deception. Manrico continues to defy him, while Leonora resigns herself to death for the sake of her love. After the tremendous climax of the trio the two adversaries draw swords and rush away to fight. Leonora swoons. The curtain falls.

Act Two
(The Gypsy)

[*Scene One*] A gypsy camp in the mountains of Biscay. Azucena is huddled before a fire. On a cot near by is Manrico, wrapped in his cloak, his helmet put aside. He is holding his sword, gazing at it thoughtfully. As the dawn grows brighter the gypsies begin to move about. The men go to their forges, take up their hammers, and swing them in rhythm as they break into the stirring *Anvil Chorus* ("Chi del gitano i giorni abbella?"). They pause in their work to ask the women to bring wine, and then the chorus takes up the lusty song in praise of women, wine, and the carefree life of a gypsy.

The mood of the scene changes with dramatic swiftness as Azucena begins the great aria "Stride la vampa." Obsessed by the terrible memory of her mother's execution, she sings of how the victim was dragged to the pyre and how her screams of pain mingled with the jeers of the vengeful throng. The gypsies, who have gathered around Azucena, try to console

Il Trovatore

her. Oblivious to their attentions, she turns to Manrico and fiercely commands him to avenge her ("Mi vendica"). Manrico is mystified at her insistence on revenge. One of the gypsies now reminds his companions that they must be on their way to forage for food in the neighboring villages. They all leave the camp to the strains of the *Anvil Chorus*.

Manrico bids Azucena continue her story. Grimly the gypsy says that her mother was burned at the very spot on which Manrico is now standing. With an exclamation of horror he moves away. In somber tones Azucena tells how she tried vainly to reach her mother's side as the brutal guards drove her to the stake. Through the smoke and flames came the dying cry for vengeance, and that cry has haunted Azucena day and night. Desperately resolved to avenge her mother, she stole the younger child of the old Count di Luna and carried him to the pyre. The child's cries momentarily aroused her pity. But then the fearful vision of her mother's agony began to torment her, Azucena sings in tense, whispered tones. Her voice gradually rises to a wild crescendo as she relates how she hurled the baby into the flames, only to discover that in her madness and confusion she had sacrificed her own child, whom she had brought to the scene of the execution. Azucena's voice dies away in a brooding, tragic phrase as she sinks to the ground spent with fury and despair.

When Manrico shakes off the sinister spell of Azucena's story, he tries to unravel the mystery of his own birth. Now aware that the gypsy had destroyed her only child, he reasons that she is not his mother. When he asks whose son he really is, Azucena insists excitedly that he is her son. She reminds him that she has given him a mother's love—that she rescued him from the battlefield of Petilla, where he had lain half dead from wounds, and nursed him back to health.

Manrico recalls how he, sole survivor of his company, had faced the hated Count di Luna's men and had been badly wounded. Why, then, Azucena asks vindictively, had he spared the life of this treacherous enemy in the duel over Leonora. Manrico replies that some mysterious impulse had stayed his sword at di Luna's throat. In an impressive air

("Mal reggendo all'aspro assalto") he sings that when the count lay at his mercy a strange voice warned him not to kill. In vengeful fury Azucena exhorts Manrico to strike down his foe mercilessly, should they meet again. Manrico's voice blends dramatically with hers as he vows to plunge his dagger into di Luna's heart at their next encounter.

A horn call is heard in the distance. Manrico sounds an answer, and in a moment a messenger appears with a letter from his henchman, Ruiz. Manrico reads that Castellor fortress has fallen to them and that he has been ordered to take over its defenses. But the letter contains other startling news. Leonora, having heard the false report that Manrico has been killed in battle, has abandoned the world and is preparing to enter a convent this very day.

In great excitement Manrico tells Azucena that he must leave immediately. Feverishly the gypsy implores him not to go, but Manrico brushes aside her entreaties, saying that nothing can part him from Leonora. Their colloquy ends in a dramatic and powerful refrain. Manrico finally tears himself from Azucena's grasp and rushes away. The curtain falls.

[*Scene Two*]   Outside a convent near Castellor fortress. It is night. Count di Luna, Ferrando, and a company of their men stealthily approach. In recitative, di Luna tells Ferrando that his burning passion for Leonora has driven him to this desperate attempt to carry her away from the convent by force. He expresses his tormenting love for her in a fervent aria ("Il balen del suo sorriso").

As the count finishes his song a bell tolls. Ferrando explains that it is the signal for the ceremony at which Leonora will become a nun. The count plans to intercept Leonora before she can take her holy vows and orders Ferrando and the men to conceal themselves. In a hushed chorus the men assure their leader that his orders will be carried out. In another impassioned aria ("Per me ora fatale") he again declares his resolve to possess Leonora. As di Luna and his men withdraw to places of concealment, their voices die away in tense, rhythmic phrases.

From within the convent come the voices of the nuns chanting of Leonora's renunciation. The sustained, solemn notes float above the staccato phrases sung by the count and his followers in a continuation of their chorus. Again the voices fade away, and all is silence. Chords sound softly in the strings as Leonora enters with Inez and a group of women attendants. Inez laments the parting from her mistress, who endeavors to comfort her. In a brief but exalted refrain Leonora commends herself to God. Suddenly the count strides forward crying that she is destined only for the altar of marriage. As Leonora and the other women exclaim in shocked surprise, Manrico enters.

Leonora rushes into his arms, singing that she scarcely dares believe that Manrico is standing before her ("E deggio e posso crederlo?"). Her refrain introduces the brilliant chorus of the act. While her ecstatic tones soar high over the ensemble, Manrico and di Luna pour out their hatred for each other and prepare to fight. The nuns sing that heaven has sent Manrico at this moment to save Leonora. Ferrando and his men warn Manrico that he is tempting fate by opposing the count. Soon Ruiz and Manrico's men rush in, and a fierce encounter ensues. Manrico fights his way to Leonora's side while his men force the count and his adherents to retreat. The nuns make their way to the shelter of the convent. As the chorus rises to a great crescendo the curtain falls.

ACT THREE
(The Gypsy's Son)

[Scene One] The camp of Count di Luna, whose tent is seen at one side. In the background can be seen the ramparts of Castellor, to which Manrico has taken Leonora. The count is now besieging the fortress, and his soldiers are busily preparing for an attack. Ferrando addresses them briefly, assuring them of rich booty if they take Castellor. The soldiers answer in a spirited chorus ("Squilli, echeggi la tromba") in which they sing of their eagerness for combat and the glorious fruits of victory. Their voices fade into the distance as they march away.

Count di Luna emerges from his tent and gazes at Castellor. Bitterly he muses that Leonora is there in the embraces of his hated rival. In a burst of fury he swears revenge, then passionately sings Leonora's name. Ferrando comes rushing in with the news that the guards have seized a gypsy prowling about the outskirts of the camp. She is suspected of being a spy. Azucena is dragged in by the guards, who roughly urge her on as she pleads for mercy. The count orders her to be released and begins questioning her. Asked where her home is, Azucena replies that, after the manner of gypsies, her home is wherever she happens to be. She has lately come from Biscay, she adds, which brings an exclamation of surprise from both the count and Ferrando.

In a moving refrain ("Giorno poveri vivea") Azucena recalls her life in Biscay with her son, who was her only joy. But he disappeared, she continues, and since that day she has wandered everywhere in search of him. Ferrando, who has been watching her closely, remarks that he notes a strange familiarity about her features. Count di Luna asks the gypsy if she remembers that some fifteen years ago the child of a nobleman was stolen and carried off into the mountains of Biscay. Azucena, startled, asks di Luna if he was that child. The count replies that the baby was his brother. When the count persists in his questioning, Azucena vehemently denies that she knows anything about the theft of the child. Ferrando, noting her rising terror, declares that she is the sorceress who hurled the count's brother into the flames. Angrily di Luna orders the guards to seize her. When Azucena, distractedly calling for help, cries out "O Manrico, o figlio mio [O Manrico, my son]!" di Luna fiercely exults that now he has the mother of his rival at his mercy.

Azucena implores her tormentors to let death put an end to her misery. Suddenly she turns on di Luna and in a fierce whisper warns him that an angry God will strike him down for this injustice. The voices of Azucena, di Luna, Ferrando, and the guards blend dramatically. Azucena reiterates her warning, the count ordains death for the sorceress, and Ferrando and the guards consign her to the eternal fires of hell. At the conclusion of the chorus the guards drag the gypsy away. The curtain falls.

[Scene Two] A chamber in the castle of Castellor. At the rear is a balcony, beyond which can be seen the tents of di Luna's camp. It is the day set for the marriage of Leonora and Manrico. Leonora, however, is restless and apprehensive over the impending attack of the count's forces. In an effort to reassure her, Manrico sings the beautiful aria "Ah si, ben mio," in which he promises that even if he should die on the battlefield he will be faithful to her beyond the grave. The sound of organ music drifts from the chapel of the castle. Leonora and Manrico pledge their eternal love to each other in a brief but eloquent duet ("L'onda de' suoni mistici").

Their idyll is interrupted as Ruiz bursts into the room and excitedly bids Manrico look toward di Luna's camp. There, he says, the gypsy woman is being led in chains to the stake. Manrico reels in horror, then turns to Leonora and gasps that the gypsy is his mother. Recovering himself, he orders Ruiz to prepare his men for an attack upon the camp. As Ruiz leaves, Manrico begins the famous aria "Di quella pira," one of the most dramatic numbers in the opera. In ringing tones he vows to save his mother from a fiery death. Fervently he bids Leonora adieu, declaring that he cannot forsake his mother now. Leonora heartbrokenly sings farewell.

Ruiz and the soldiers enter, armed and ready for battle. In a powerful chorus they pledge themselves to follow Manrico to the rescue of his mother. He and the soldiers rush away to the blaring of trumpets as the curtain falls.

Act Four
(The Torture)

[Scene One] At the battlements of the Aliaferia Palace. A prison tower with barred windows rises at one side. It is night.

Manrico and Azucena are imprisoned in the tower, having been brought there after Manrico's unsuccessful attempt to rescue his mother. Not only were Manrico and his followers defeated by di Luna, but Castellor itself was stormed and taken. Leonora and Ruiz fled to the safety of the mountains, but Leonora has returned to Aliaferia in a desperate effort to save Manrico.

As the curtain rises Leonora and Ruiz, their faces hidden in their cloaks, cautiously approach the ramparts of the castle. Leonora dismisses Ruiz. On her right hand Leonora wears a ring containing poison. She gazes at it for a moment, murmuring that this guardian will protect her from all harm. Raising her eyes to the tower, she muses in recitative about her imprisoned lover. Then in a tender and passionate aria ("D'amor sull'ali rosee") Leonora voices the hope that Manrico will be sustained by the assurance of her love for him.

At the end of her song a bell tolls ominously. From within the castle come the voices of men chanting a *Miserere* for the doomed prisoner, introducing one of the most famous ensemble numbers in all opera. To the accompaniment of softly throbbing chords in the orchestra, Leonora expresses her terror and despair in broken, sobbing phrases. Then from the tower comes the voice of the troubador in the sweeping phrases of the great aria "Ah! che la morte ognora." He frets that death is too slow in bringing him release, and bids farewell to Leonora. The voices of the lovers rise above the chanting of the chorus as, unseen by each other, they pour out their devotion.

After the ensemble surges to a tremendous climax, Leonora sings a fervid refrain ("Tu vedrai che amore in terra") in which she resolves to make one final attempt to save her lover. She then withdraws as the count appears with several attendants. He indicates the spot where Manrico is to be beheaded and his mother burned at the stake. When the attendants leave, di Luna laments that he has been unable to find any trace of Leonora.

Thereupon Leonora steps out of the shadows and stands before him. A stormy musical dialogue follows. The count

Il Trovatore

answers Leonora's anguished pleas for Manrico's life with violent refusals. When she kneels abjectly before him, di Luna cries out that his only desire is to prolong his rival's torment. Half mad with despair, Leonora finally promises the count that she will be his if he will grant Manrico's freedom. She asks only that she be permitted to go to Manrico and tell him that he has been spared.

Before the count can reply, a guard appears. As di Luna turns to speak to him Leonora swiftly raises the ring to her lips and swallows the poison concealed under the jewel. In low tones she murmurs that the count will claim only her cold and lifeless body. When di Luna turns back to her, saying he will spare Manrico's life, Leonora sings in feverish exaltation ("Vivrà! Contende il giubilo"). The count, mistaking her ardor and excitement, sings triumphantly that his heart's desire at last has been granted. The two voices join in ecstatic phrases at the climax of the scene. Leonora and the count hurry into the tower. The curtain falls.

[*Scene Two*] The dungeon in the prison tower. Azucena lies on a pallet, with Manrico at her side. They try to comfort each other. Azucena exults that she will yet escape her captors because death will claim her before she can be led to the stake. Then, as the theme of her "Stride la vampa" aria echoes in the orchestra, Azucena is seized by the tormenting recollection of her mother's death. She rises in wild terror from her pallet as she relives the scene. Shaken and exhausted, she sinks into Manrico's arms.

Gently he bids her seek comfort in sleep. Azucena sings a plaintive refrain which introduces the tender duet "Ai nostri monti," popularly known as "Home to our mountains." She and Manrico envision a happy return to their homeland. With Manrico kneeling beside her, Azucena gradually falls asleep. The music softly dies away.

Without warning, the door of the dungeon opens and Leonora steps inside. The lovers rush into each other's arms with exclamations of rapture. Tearing herself from Manrico's embrace, Leonora frantically implores him to leave at once.

He refuses to go without her. Leonora's agitated demeanor arouses Manrico's suspicions, and he demands to know at what price she has obtained his freedom. Before she can answer he furiously denounces her for having made an unholy bargain with di Luna. Heedless of her protests, he bitterly reproaches her for her faithlessness. Azucena's voice is interwoven with their angry phrases as in her dreams she again sings of returning home to her beloved mountains.

Leonora collapses at Manrico's feet as the poison begins to take effect. In blind anger he orders her to leave, but when he sees the agony in her face he takes her in his arms and distractedly beseeches her to speak. Leonora gasps that she has taken poison and that death is near. In a torment of remorse and grief, Manrico implores her forgiveness.

Count di Luna enters. Seeing Leonora in Manrico's arms, he cries out in fury. Leonora bids farewell to Manrico, who brokenly repeats his entreaties to be forgiven. The count rages that he will have revenge on both for this ultimate deception. With a last cry of farewell, Leonora dies in the arms of Manrico.

The count now orders the guards to lead Manrico to his execution. His parting words, "Ah, madre, addio [Ah, Mother, farewell]!" rouse Azucena. Dazed and bewildered, she rises and staggers toward the window, calling for her son. In ferocious triumph the count thunders that Manrico is dying on the scaffold. With that Azucena turns on the count and reveals her terrible secret—Manrico was his brother ("Egli era tuo fratello"). Exultantly she sings that her mother is revenged at last. She falls unconscious as Count di Luna cries out in horror and despair. The curtain falls.

Die Zauberflöte
(The Magic Flute)

by WOLFGANG AMADEUS MOZART
[1756–1791]

Libretto by

EMMANUEL SCHIKANEDER and JOHANN GEORG METZLER (GIESECKE)

Based on Liebeskind's oriental story
LULU, ODER DIE ZAUBERFLÖTE

CHARACTERS

Tamino, an Egyptian prince	*Tenor*
Three Ladies, attendants of the Queen of Night	*Two sopranos / Mezzo-soprano*
Papageno, a birdcatcher	*Baritone*
The Queen of Night	*Soprano*
Monostatos, a Moorish slave in the palace of Sarastro	*Tenor*
Pamina, daughter of the Queen of Night	*Soprano*
Three Genii	*Soprano / Mezzo-soprano / Contralto*
A priest, Speaker of the Temple of Isis	*Baritone*
Sarastro, High Priest of the Temple of Isis	*Bass*
First priest	*Tenor*
Second priest	*Baritone*
Two Men in Armor	*Tenor / Baritone*
Old Woman, later Papagena	*Soprano*

Priests of the temple, attendants, slaves

Place: In and near the Temple of Isis in Egypt
Time: About the period of Rameses I
First performance: Theater auf der Wieden, Vienna, September 30, 1791
Original language: German

DIE ZAUBERFLÖTE, written by Mozart at the age of thirty-five, not long before his death, is considered by many to be his finest opera. In it he combined simple German folk tunes and classic operatic writing with brilliant effect. The plot is a curious hodgepodge of political satire, the symbolism of Freemasonry, and naïve humor, set against an Egyptian background.

The Temple of Isis, more or less the focal point of the action, represents Freemasonry. Sarastro is its High Priest. Pamina, typifying the Austrian people, finds refuge in the temple from her wicked mother, the Queen of Night, said to have been identified with the Empress Maria Theresa, who was actively opposed to Freemasonry. Prince Tamino is presumably symbolic of the Emperor Joseph II, who was comparatively liberal in his attitude toward the order. The trials by fire and water imposed on Pamina and Tamino, the conflict between light and darkness, and the ultimate triumph of good over evil are all inherent in the Masonic philosophy.

The brilliant overture is an established favorite in the concert repertoire. Prominent in it is a series of impressive chords sounded three times in groups of three, said to be symbolic of the knocking at the door of the temple as part of the Masonic rites of initiation. They will be heard again during the temple scene.

Act One

[*Scene One*] A wild rocky pass near the Temple of Isis. Prince Tamino, dressed in Japanese hunting costume and carrying a bow but no arrows, rushes down the pass.[1] He is being pursued by a ravenous snake. Tamino implores the gods to deliver him from the fangs of this monster, then falls fainting to the ground. Just as the serpent is about to attack him

[1] In most productions Tamino is dressed in a modified Greek costume. Also, he sometimes appears with one arrow left. This he shoots at the serpent but misses.

Die Zauberflöte

the temple doors open and the Three Ladies rush to his aid. They kill the snake with their silver spears. In a melodious trio they rejoice that they have saved Tamino ("Sie ist vollbracht, die Heldenthat"). They gaze fondly down at Tamino and comment on his handsome looks. Their Queen must be informed at once, they finally decide. An amusing colloquy follows, in which each of the Three Ladies urges the other to hasten to the Queen while offering to stand guard over the stricken youth. As none of the three makes a move, they resign themselves to leaving together and ardently bid the unconscious Tamino farewell.

After they re-enter the temple Tamino revives, looks wildly about, and is startled to see the serpent dead at his feet. As he wonders where he is he hears someone approaching down the pass. Tamino quickly conceals himself behind some trees. From the orchestra comes a sprightly refrain, punctuated by a flutelike phrase of five ascending notes. Soon Papageno appears. He is dressed in a fantastic, brightly colored bird costume, and on his back is a large cage containing birds. He carries a pipe of Pan, on which he plays his whimsical five-note call. Without further ado he sings a gay ditty ("Der Vogelfänger bin ich ja"). He explains that he sets his traps, blows on his pipe, and the birds come flocking round. In a second verse he muses on how pleasant it would be if he could set his traps for pretty maidens.

With a final flourish on his pipe he starts for the temple. Tamino intercepts him, and dialogue ensues in which each questions the other. Tamino asks Papageno who he is. A man like himself, Papageno replies. In turn, Tamino reveals that he is a prince of a far-off country, then asks Papageno who reigns here. The birdcatcher answers that he knows nothing about this country. His business, he says, is to catch birds for the Queen of Night, in payment for which the Three Ladies bring him food and drink. Tamino exclaims excitedly over mention of the Queen.

Papageno, frightened and suspicious of Tamino's manner, tries to hide his fear by warning that he has the strength of a giant when aroused. Tamino, thinking that perhaps Papageno is one of the Queen's mystic entourage, asks him if he killed the snake. Thereupon Papageno—first making certain that the snake is dead—boasts that he strangled the monster with his bare hands.

At this point the Three Ladies appear and overhear Papageno's lurid bit of fiction. Sternly they tell him that today he is to have only water instead of wine to drink and a stone instead of bread. One of the Ladies fastens a padlock to his mouth and informs him that it is his punishment for lying. Turning to Tamino, they explain that it was they who saved him from the serpent. They hand him a portrait of the daughter of the Queen of Night. The three then leave, taking Papageno along.

Gazing at the portrait, Tamino, in a tender aria ("Dies Bildnis ist bezaubernd schön"), sings that if he could but find this lovely creature he would ardently declare his love and then she would be his forever. At the finish of the aria the Three Ladies appear to tell Tamino that the Queen of Night has decided to grant his wish. If he is as brave as he is comely, the Queen has told her attendants, he is worthy of the task of saving her daughter. The Three Ladies then reveal that the Queen's daughter is being held captive by a wicked sorcerer. As Tamino eagerly urges the Ladies to guide him to the sorcerer's lair there is a crash of thunder and the Queen of Night stands before him.

In recitative the Queen tells Tamino that he need have no fear because he is pure in heart. In a moving aria ("Zum leiden bin ich auserkoren") she relates how her daughter was carried off by the sorcerer. Dramatically she imposes on Tamino the task of rescuing the girl. As the thunder crashes again the Queen and the Three Ladies vanish.

Tamino, astounded, wonders if he has been dreaming. He is about to leave when Papageno enters. Dolefully he points to his padlock and hums in lieu of speech. Tamino says he can do nothing for him. Thereupon the Three Ladies appear, saying the Queen has ordered Papageno to be freed. They remove the padlock and warn him not to do any more lying. A

Die Zauberflöte

quintet follows ("Dies Schloss soll deine Warnung sein"), in which they moralize over the evils of lying. The Ladies hand Tamino a golden flute, saying that it will give him power over human emotions and move the hardest heart to love.

Papageno is informed that he is to accompany Tamino to the palace of Sarastro. In terror Papageno protests, saying that this fiend will have him plucked, fried, and tossed to his hounds. The Ladies assure the birdcatcher that the Prince will protect him. The Prince can go to the devil, Papageno retorts, pointing out that Tamino might decide to desert him. At that the Ladies hand him a set of chimes with a warning that no one but himself must play upon them. In a brief but charming ensemble ("Silberglöckchen") the Ladies, Tamino, and Papageno sing that the chimes, if rung when danger threatens, will dispel all harm. When Tamino and Papageno ask who is to lead them to Sarastro's palace the Ladies tell them that three wise and fair youths will act as their protectors. The quintet is concluded as all sing farewell. The curtain falls.

[*Scene Two*] An elaborate Egyptian room in Sarastro's palace. Monostatos suddenly appears, dragging in Pamina.[2] He threatens her with death, but she ignores her own plight and laments that her mother will die of grief. Monostatos orders other slaves to chain the girl. Resisting his advances, she then falls fainting on a couch. The Moor, on leaving, encounters Papageno, who has wandered into the palace quite by accident. An amusing duet follows ("Hu! das ist der Teufel sicherlich!"). Each is terror-stricken at the sight of the other, and they both beg each other for mercy. Panic-stricken, they finally dash off in opposite directions.

As Pamina revives, Papageno reappears. Approaching Pamina, he addresses her (in dialogue) as the daughter of the Queen of Night and tells her he is Papageno. Just to make sure that she is the Queen's daughter he compares her with the portrait given him by Tamino.

---

[2] In some performances three slaves first reveal in dialogue, before Monostatos actually enters, that Pamina is his captive.

When Pamina asks Papageno where he got the portrait he tells her about Tamino. He's a fellow who calls himself a prince, the birdcatcher says. He was given the portrait by the Queen and commanded to rescue her daughter. No sooner did he see the portrait than he fell in love with the original, Papageno goes on, and he will be here shortly to save her. Pamina says they must hurry because Sarastro will soon be home from the hunt. Papageno observes that he knows only too well what will happen to them if they are caught. The fact that Papageno has her portrait convinces Pamina that the birdcatcher is not one of Sarastro's minions. And besides, she says, she knows by looking at Papageno's face that he has a kind heart. "A kind heart, yes," Papageno agrees sadly, "but no Papagena to appreciate it." Now follows a beautiful duet ("Bei Männern, welche Liebe fühlen"), in which Pamina and Papageno sing of the magic power of love.

[*Scene Three*] A sacred grove with three massive doorways, above which are inscribed, respectively, *Temple of Wisdom, Temple of Reason,* and *Temple of Nature.* Tamino is led in by the Three Genii, each carrying silver palm branches. In a trio ("Zum Ziele führt dich diese Bahn") they bid him go forward to victory, remembering always that he must be firm, patient, and silent. He asks them if he will now be able to rescue Pamina. In answer they repeat their exhortation, "Be firm, patient, and silent." Manliness will bring him victory, they proclaim as they leave.

Tamino tries to enter the Temples of Reason and Nature, but each time he is turned away by a warning voice from within. Finally, in answer to his knock at the Temple of Wisdom, a venerable priest appears. When the priest asks Tamino why he has come he replies that he seeks revenge upon the tyrant Sarastro, whose cruelty has caused a woman to suffer. "Could Sarastro but reveal to you his true purpose!" the priest exclaims. "Is he not the thief who tore Pamina from her mother's arms?" Tamino cries. The priest bids him be calm and in a phrase of great dignity tells him that only when he is inspired by friendship and love may he enter the temple to be united with Pamina.

Within the temple voices chant softly that Tamino will soon see Pamina and that she still lives unharmed. Joyfully thanking the gods for guiding him to the temple, he puts the magic flute to his lips and begins playing. But when Pamina, contrary to his expectations, does not appear, Tamino frets in disappointment. Again and again he plays his flute and calls her name. Suddenly, from the distance he hears the five-note tune of Papageno's Panpipe. Excitedly he sings that perhaps Papageno has found Pamina, then rushes off.

No sooner has he disappeared than Pamina and Papageno hurry in from the opposite direction. They are being pursued by Monostatos. In a duet ("Schnelle Füsse, rascher Muth") they reassure themselves that they will elude their pursuer. Could they but find Tamino, they sing, all would be well. When Pamina cries out his name Papageno says he will send forth a call on his Panpipe. His notes are immediately answered by a flute in the distance. Joyously Pamina and Papageno exclaim that now they can hasten to Tamino's side.

But Monostatos, mockingly repeating the last phrase of their duet—"Nur geschwinde, nur geschwinde [Hasten, hasten]!"—leaps into their path and bars their way. Exultantly he sings that he has them in his power at last, then calls to his slaves to put the fugitives in chains. Thereupon Papageno remembers the chimes and begins playing a delightfully rhythmic refrain. Instantly under the spell of the music, Monostatos and his slaves begin dancing in droll fashion as they happily sing in chorus ("Das klingt so herrlich"). Like automatons, Monostatos and his crew dance harmlessly away to Papageno's music.

Gratefully Pamina and Papageno sing of the magic power of the chimes. Then from the distance a chorus is heard hailing Sarastro. Trembling, Papageno asks Pamina what they are to say to the High Priest. Pamina resolves to speak only the truth. Sarastro enters in a majestic procession, accompanied by priests, attendants, and slaves. In a stirring chorus ("Es lebe Sarastro") they acclaim him as their mentor and idol.

Falling to her knees before him, Pamina confesses that although she had long planned to seek her freedom her real reason for fleeing was to escape the attentions of Monostatos. In a stately melody ("Steh' auf, erheitre dich, Liebe") Sarastro answers. Gravely he tells her that though he cannot compel her to love he cannot grant her freedom.

When Pamina pleads to be freed for her mother's sake, Sarastro angrily replies that he dare not return her to this woman, for she is wicked and false. Monostatos now appears, leading in Tamino. Tamino and Pamina rush ecstatically into each other's arms, but Monostatos roughly parts them. Fawning before Sarastro, the Moor lies that Tamino and his companion, the birdcatcher, tried to abduct Pamina from the palace. But he, brave fellow that he is, prevented it, Monostatos goes on, hinting modestly that some sort of reward no doubt is in order. Sarastro dryly agrees. The reward, he announces, will be seventy-seven lashes. Monostatos is led away, loudly protesting. The chorus hails the justice of the great Sarastro's decision.

Sarastro orders Pamina and Tamino to be veiled, led into the Temple of the Ordeal, and prepared for the sacred ceremonies. Papageno, also veiled, is led off with Tamino, while Sarastro conducts Pamina to the door of the temple. A mighty chorus in praise of virtue and justice concludes the act.

Act Two

[*Scene One*] A palm grove dominated by a tall obelisk. To the grave measures of the *March of the Priests*, Sarastro and the priests enter and arrange themselves in a circle. In dialogue Sarastro announces that Prince Tamino waits at the northern gate of the temple. He seeks to pierce his veil of darkness so that he may see the light. The solemn chords heard in the overture sound forth. Sarastro informs the priests that the gods have destined Pamina and Tamino for each other, and for this reason he took Pamina from her mother, who was bent on destroying the temple. Tamino himself shall

Die Zauberflöte 421

now aid in thwarting her evil designs. Sarastro orders Pamina and Tamino to be brought to the temple porch.

As the Speaker leaves and the other priests gather around Sarastro he sings the impressive aria, "O Isis und Osiris," invoking the blessings of the gods on the novitiates. Solemnly echoing his words, the priests follow him out of the temple. The curtain falls.

[*Scene Two*]   Before the temple. Two priests lead in Tamino and Papageno, remove their veils, then withdraw. In dialogue Tamino and his companion discuss this stage of their initiation. The priests return shortly to question them. Tamino says that he is prepared for the ordeal. Papageno asserts that he is mainly concerned with getting enough to eat and drink —and perhaps a loving wife into the bargain. The priests inform him that Sarastro will provide him with a feathered companion. He may look upon her during these trials, one priest says, but he must not speak to her. To Tamino the priests likewise say that he may see Pamina, but they impose silence. As the two prepare to leave they sing a brief duet ("Bewahret euch vor Weibertücken"), warning of women's wiles.

Papageno complains about the darkness, but Tamino counsels forbearance. Suddenly the Three Ladies appear, lighting their way with torches. A spirited quintet ensues ("Wie! Ihr an diesem Schreckort!"). The Three Ladies try to persuade Tamino and Papageno to flee with them to the Queen of Night by describing the dire fate in store for them if they remain in the palace of Sarastro. Tamino warns Papageno not to listen to them, declaring that the brave man will not be swerved from his purpose by idle chatter.

Within the temple the priests thunder in angry chorus that the sacred precincts have been profaned by the presence of women. They consign the interlopers to hell, whereupon the Three Ladies sink into the earth with cries of lamentation. Papageno grovels in fear. The Speaker and the two priests then reappear and, in dialogue, commend Tamino for resisting temptation. He and Papageno are again veiled and led away. The curtain falls.

[*Scene Three*] The garden of Sarastro's palace. Pamina is seen sleeping. Monostatos creeps in, gazes fondly upon the Princess, and then sings an amorous lament ("Alles fühlt der Liebe Freuden"). Everybody in the world except himself, he sighs, has someone to love. He decides that he will make love while he can to this radiant beauty. But as he approaches Pamina there is a flash of lightning and a loud clap of thunder, and the Queen of Night appears. Pamina awakes and calls to her mother. Monostatos slinks away.

The Queen asks Pamina what has happened to Tamino. He is to become one of the elect of the temple, Pamina tells her. The Queen fumes that now she can never regain her daughter. When Pamina implores her mother to take her away the Queen exclaims that she is powerless, for she no longer possesses the "sevenfold shield of the sun." Pamina's father, at his death, gave the shield to Sarastro, who wears it now. The Queen hands Pamina a dagger, imperiously commanding her to kill Sarastro and bring back the shield.

As Pamina recoils in horror the Queen begins the brilliant aria "Der Hölle Rache kocht in meinem Herzen." Furiously the Queen orders Pamina to slay Sarastro, threatening to disown her if she disobeys. At the end of the aria the Queen vanishes, leaving Pamina staring fearfully at the dagger in her hand. Monostatos re-enters, takes away her dagger, and tells her that the only way she can save her mother and herself is by agreeing to love him. Pamina flatly refuses. In fury Monostatos raises the dagger. At that instant Sarastro strides in and drives the Moor off.

Tearfully Pamina implores Sarastro not to punish her mother. Sarastro replies that if Tamino proves worthy in his trials all will be well with Pamina and her mother. He then sings the magnificent aria, "In diesem heil'gen Hallen." In the sacred temple, Sarastro declares, the hand of brotherly love guides the erring one and the foe finds forgiveness. As Sarastro leaves the curtain falls.

Die Zauberflöte 423

[*Scene Four*[a]] A great hall. Tamino and Papageno are led in by the Speaker and two priests to undergo a further trial, the test of silence. When Papageno complains that he is thirsty an old crone brings him a cup of water. The talkative Papageno cannot resist the temptation to chat with the Old Woman. Thereupon ensues an amusing dialogue during which, to Papageno's dismay, she declares that she is his sweetheart. Finally telling her his name, he asks hers. Just as she is about to answer there is a roll of thunder. She disappears.

The Three Genii now enter. They bring in a table laden with food and drink, then give Tamino his flute and Papageno his chimes. In a charming trio ("Seid uns zum zweitenmal willkommen") they remind the novices that the flute and bells will protect them. They urge the two to refresh themselves. With a warning to maintain silence, the Genii disappear.

Papageno promptly devotes his entire attention to the food, while Tamino plays his flute. Pamina enters and eagerly greets him. Sadly Tamino shakes his head and with a gesture bids her leave. Pamina voices her despair at his apparent indifference in a moving aria ("Ach, ich fühl's, es ist verschwunden"). When Tamino still remains mute Pamina disconsolately leaves.

Three blasts of the trumpet now summon Tamino and Papageno to the crypt beneath the temple for further trials. The birdcatcher, unwilling to leave the table, is dragged off by Tamino. The curtain falls.

[*Scene Five*] The inner shrine of the sacred order in the crypt beneath the temple. Sarastro and the priests enter and sing the impressive chorus, "O Isis und Osiris." They invoke the gods and hail the approaching climax of Tamino's ordeal. After the chorus Tamino and Pamina, veiled, are led in. Sarastro bids them say their final farewells because Tamino still must undergo two more stern trials.

[a] Sometimes the opera is played in three acts instead of two, and this scene becomes Scene One of Act Three. In other three-act versions Scene Five becomes the opening scene of the third act.

A dramatic trio ensues ("Soll ich dich, Theurer, nicht mehr sehn?"). Pamina voices her fear of dangers ahead, but Sarastro assures her that she will see her lover again. Tamino resolutely declares that he will bow to the will of the gods. Sarastro and the priests depart as Tamino and Pamina are led off in opposite directions.

When all are gone Papageno enters, calling in frightened tones for Tamino.[4] Thoroughly bewildered, the birdcatcher is confronted by the Speaker, who sternly tells him that because of his unworthiness he shall never know the bliss of the chosen ones. Papageno replies that his sole desire at the moment is a glass of wine. In the next moment a glass is placed in his hands.

Papageno drinks deeply and then, accompanying himself on his chimes, sings a delightful song ("Ein Mädchen oder Weibchen wünscht Papageno sich"). If he had either a maiden or a wife, he sings, he would be her devoted slave.

No sooner has he finished his song than in comes the Old Woman to whom he had spoken previously. Before his startled eyes she turns into a young girl, his birdlike counterpart. "Papagena!" he cries. Just as he is about to embrace her the Speaker enters and bars his way, saying he is not yet worthy. The priest drags Papagena away, while Papageno follows, protesting loudly. The curtain falls.

[*Scene Six*] A palm garden near the temple. The Three Genii enter and sing a hymn to the sun ("Bald prangt, den Morgen zu verkünden"). As they sing they see Pamina approaching. Mad with grief over being parted from Tamino, she prepares to stab herself with the dagger given her by her mother (having retrieved it meanwhile from Monostatos). The Three Genii intervene just in time. They assure her that she will soon see her lover and offer to lead her to him. As she expresses her gratitude her voice blends with theirs in a melodious quartet ("Zwei Herzen, die von Liebe brennen"). The Genii and Pamina then leave. The curtain falls.

[4] Sometimes this is played as a separate scene.

Die Zauberflöte

[*Scene Seven*] Two rocky caves with grilled gates. Behind one gate a fire glows; behind the other water is visible. Between the gates is a great doorway before which stand two men in black armor. During a brief but somber prelude Tamino is brought in by the priests. The two armored men, singing in powerful octaves, proclaim that he who treads this stern path must be purified by fire, water, air and earth ("Der, welcher wandert diese Strasse").

As Tamino is about to enter he hears Pamina calling. A short trio ensues ("Ja! das ist Paminens Stimme!"). Tamino rejoices over the prospect of meeting Pamina, while the Men in Armor declare that she has proved herself worthy of him. When she is brought in she rushes into Tamino's arms. Then, clasping hands, the lovers prepare for the trial by fire and water. Pamina bids Tamino play the magic flute, which, she now reveals, was carved long ago by her father. The Two Men in Armor now join the pair in an exultant quartet hailing the magic power of the flute ("Ihr wandelt durch des Tones Macht").

To the accompaniment of a stately march Tamino and Pamina walk safely through the fire and water, Tamino playing his flute. As they finish the tests the temple gates swing open and the two enter. From within come the voices of the priests hailing the redeemed couple ("Triumph! du edles Paar!"). As Sarastro and the priests conduct them to the inner shrine the curtain falls.

[*Scene Eight*] A garden. Papageno comes in, plays on his Panpipe, and disconsolately calls for Papagena. He sings a doleful song ("Weibchen! Täubchen, meine Schöne!"), lamenting that he is the most wretched man on the face of the earth. Taking a rope from his belt, he prepares to hang himself, at the count of three, from a nearby tree. Slowly counting, "One—two—two and a half," he manages to postpone the hanging long enough to permit the Three Genii to come on the scene and dissuade him altogether. When he wails that nothing can soothe his aching heart, they suggest that he play his chimes. This he does eagerly, singing "Klinget, Glöckchen, klinget!" He implores the bells to work their magic and bring his sweetheart to his side. Meanwhile the Three Genii, unnoticed by Papageno, bring forth Papagena, then tell the birdcatcher to turn and look. In transports of joy he greets his mate at last, and a delightful love duet follows. The birdlike creatures sing of their future happiness as man and wife. First there will be a little Papageno, then a little Papagena. Then another little Papageno, and so on ad infinitum. The duet closes with the pair happily chattering each other's name.

[*Scene Nine*] A dark and gloomy spot not far from the temple. The Queen of Night, the Three Ladies, and Monostatos approach, determined to make one last assault on the temple and carry off Pamina. But as they are about to put their plans into effect there is a blaze of lightning and a tremendous crash of thunder. The five people representing the thwarted forces of evil sink into the earth. In a descending musical phrase they voice their last despairing cry: "We are plunged into eternal night."

A brief musical interlude follows, during which the scene becomes bathed in a brilliant light, bringing into view Sarastro, the priests, Tamino, Pamina, and a great host of temple adherents. Sarastro, sole possessor of the "sevenfold shield of the sun," proclaims in a short recitative that light has conquered darkness. The entire assemblage then breaks out into a mighty chorus ("Heil sei euch Geweihten!"). As it rises to a glorious climax the curtain falls.

PART II

HOW TO ENJOY AN OPERA

To ENJOY ANYTHING, you must first understand it. As for opera, there are at least three main avenues to understanding even before you see a performance: reading the story, studying the libretto, hearing the music—either on records or in an instrumental transcription. Reading the story is really of first importance. It is the essential framework for the music, and no appreciation of an opera is complete if the story is confused and unclear to the listener.

At the outset, you should be warned that many opera plots are weak and illogical. Some are full of obscure symbolism (Debussy's *Pelléas et Mélisande*), some wholly in the realm of legend (Wagner's *Der Ring des Nibelungen*), some—particularly those of the modern school—are as puzzling as a non-objective painting (Thomson's *Four Saints in Three Acts*, which consists mostly of unintelligible words, or intelligible words that seem to have no relation to each other). But an opera must begin somewhere, and you will find, when you later listen to the music, that the composer has clothed the plot with meaning, excitement and drama.

Learning about opera need not stop with simply reading the stories themselves. In fact, the more you know about opera and its relation to other forms of culture the more you will enjoy it. Books that have been written about it cover every phase of the subject—there are biographies of composers, analyses of music, critical essays on individual operas, translations of lyrics and explanation of plots, stories by and about famous operatic personalities. This kind of reading will help you relate opera to its own time. To life, in other words. Know who the artist is, what he thinks and where he stands in relation to the world about him—and you know his work.

Probably the ideal way to study an actual opera before seeing it performed is to follow the musical score while listening either to a radio broadcast or to recordings. That, of course, presupposes a knowledge of music. If you live in one of the larger cities, it is likely that operatic scores and libretti are available at libraries, as well as recordings of operas and facilities for listening to them. Recordings and radio broadcasts make it possible for anyone interested in opera today to familiarize himself not only with the important choruses and arias of an opera but with the entire work. Moreover, with abridged versions of certain operas now being performed for television, it is possible to *see* a work as well.

If it happens that the score is too difficult for you to follow, then the most important requisite is the libretto. Admittedly, standard translations of operas do not always make particularly interesting reading, but at least they provide some idea of what the story is about. In the main, grand opera translations are stiff and stilted, for it is next to impossible to render into understandable vernacular the poetic, flowing phrases constructed primarily for singing. Operas of the *verismo* school—*Cavalleria Rusticana, La Bohème, Louise, Pagliacci*—come off better in translation because emotions and sentiments are more realistically expressed. Wagnerian translations are generally ponderous and highly involved, due to the difficulty of translating the complicated prose which the composer created to suit his dramatic requirements. The full effect of Wagner's surging cadences and resounding alliterations can be appreciated only by those who understand German.

But in the absence of a detailed paraphrase of the lyrics of an opera, it will generally pay you to labor through a libretto in order to know what the plot is really about. In the

How to Enjoy an Opera

love duet between Elsa and Lohengrin in the third act of *Lohengrin*, for example, dark and somber chords suddenly interrupt the flood of glorious love music. The real meaning of this change of mood will be utterly lost on the listener unless he knows that at this point Elsa asks the forbidden question—Lohengrin's name. In *Traviata*, Violetta's abrupt change from the tender, reflective mood of the "Ah, fors'è lui" to the abandon of the "Sempre libera" will mean little to anyone who does not know that it symbolizes a gesture of repudiation and despair—Violetta thrusts aside her thoughts of Alfredo's love and resolves to abandon herself to the life of gaiety she knows will doom her.

Familiarity with the lyrics will also help you to recognize and understand the leitmotif, or leading motive. This is a way of "spotting" a character musically, and is used extensively by such composers as Weber, Wagner and Bizet. Wagner is its chief exponent. If, in listening to the *Ring* operas, for example, you learn to associate the utterances of the characters with certain motives as they are stated in the orchestra, the various elements of music and drama gradually fall into proper perspective in relation to the plot. After repeated hearings of Wagnerian operas, you may find that the composer's closely integrated system of leitmotif makes reference to the libretto unnecessary. Likewise, in *Carmen* the dramatic Fate motive associated with the gypsy becomes more eloquent and forceful at each hearing.

In many instances the enjoyment of opera can begin, not with the rise of the curtain, but with the first bars of the overture. Not every operatic overture, it is true, is written with a serious purpose. Early composers usually assumed that the audience would talk before the curtain went up, and they contented themselves with writing inconsequential music that merely served as a background for conversation. In writing *Salome* and *Elektra*, Richard Strauss eliminated the overture altogether, on the theory that the abrupt rise of the curtain would instantly capture the attention of the audience. It does—as you will learn when you see these operas.

Certain other composers, however, have designed their

overtures to state the important themes of their operas and to establish the proper emotional mood. Thus the overtures to *Le Nozze di Figaro*, *Die Meistersinger*, *The Bartered Bride*, or the Leonore overtures of *Fidelio* fully prepare the listener for what he is about to see and hear on the stage.

One of the important things about understanding and enjoying opera is the recognition of certain irreconcilable differences between it and the spoken drama. To these differences the opera-goer must learn to adjust himself. There is the view that opera is merely the stepchild of the arts—a sort of mongrel offspring of ballet, music and drama. Granted that it is not a pure art form, familiarity with it will soon lead you to realize that it is a highly complicated and specialized form of expression.

Opera rarely approaches the detached realism of drama. A play can be intellectual—in the manner of Shaw, Ibsen or T. S. Eliot, let us say—and still retain enough of an extrovert element, so to speak, to carry its subtleties over the footlights. But opera must remain emotional because music is emotional. No one in real life, for instance, would pause to express his feelings in the lengthy soliloquies which are sometimes the high point of operatic performances. Yet the magnificent soliloquies of Gerard in *Andrea Chénier*, or of Hans Sachs in *Die Meistersinger*, or of Iago in *Otello* do not seem long-winded or out of place. They are profound and to the point because the music frees emotional expression from the confines of mere speech.

If it seems to you that opera singers move in slow motion and with unnecessary formality of gesture, remember that they must synchronize with the orchestral accompaniment not only vocally but physically. When a performer sings a long phrase on a single word, his gestures must be timed accordingly. Correctly synchronized, the gestures will not seem awkward. Operatic acting is difficult, and only the most accomplished and versatile performers can make it convincing. Over and above all else is the singing, which imposes certain limitations on movement and gesture and makes strenuous physical demands on the performer. Artists singing the leading roles in *Tristan und Isolde*, for example, have been known to lose as much as five pounds during a performance.

When opera is viewed within the scope of its own possibilities and limitations, it becomes endlessly fascinating. It offers comedy, tragedy, pageantry and romance in a repertoire that is almost inexhaustible. In *American Opera and Its Composers*, Edward Ellsworth Hipsher says: "In the Bibliothèque Nationale in Paris are the scores of 28,000 operas; yet of this prodigious number, less than 200 are found in the standard repertoire of the great opera houses of the world." Even if no one ever writes another opera, there is still a vast storehouse of lyric wealth available.

Opera is unusual in its appeal to both old and young alike, and with its gods and goddesses, its kings and queens and clowns, has a special appeal for children. As the eminent basso, Ezio Pinza, once said: "Children are born with a subtle sense of fantasy. If one plays along with it, opera is just their meat." They approach opera with simple directness—a god is a god, a witch is a witch, a dragon is a dragon. They wisely leave to their elders any musical problems involving such characters.

In *The Child and His Music*, Hazel G. Kinscella and Elizabeth M. Tierney suggest that "an ideal introduction to opera is a study of *Hänsel und Gretel*. The plot is plausible and picturesque, the stage action simple and pleasantly melodic. An informal performance can be done in the schoolroom without scenery, costumes or stage accessories."

Another opera recommended is one by Benjamin Britten—*Let's Make an Opera*. During its first scene children of an imaginary household talk about opera and then decide to write and produce one themselves. This they do. "Many small operatic scenes," say Kinscella and Tierney, "can be staged in schoolrooms in much the same way as Britten's work. They may be based on actual world events, local history, favorite selections from child literature, legends or folk tales. All that is needed is a simple story in which something actually happens. Children may select appropriate music from familiar songs and recordings."

What children like in operatic music covers a surprisingly wide range. On the basis of actual experimentation and study, here is a sampling: Music from Reginald de Koven's *Robin Hood;* the Children's Chorus from Act I of *Carmen;* the contest scene from the last act of *Die Meistersinger;* Polka and Fugue from Weinberger's *Schwanda;* Entrance of the Gods into Valhalla, from Wagner's *Rheingold.* Favorite recordings in the modern vein include Prokofief's *Peter and the Wolf* and Douglas Moore's *The Emperor's New Clothes* (based on the Hans Christian Andersen tale). The child who is thus led into the world of opera is bound to develop intelligent standards of taste as he grows up.

You will find that many people are inclined to accept traditional opinions about operas—that *Traviata, Trovatore* and *Aïda* are barrel-organ music, that *Lucia di Lammermoor* is an opera for twittering coloraturas. Some of these notions have prevailed for a long time and are the result either of the most casual acquaintance with opera or no familiarity at all. When you completely understand opera, your perspective changes.

Once you have heard enough opera to make comparisons and to formulate your own standard of values, stick to your own opinions. You have a perfect right to prefer to listen to the music of Mozart's *Zauberflöte* on the radio or recordings rather than see it on the stage, if you think the plot interferes with your enjoyment of the music. On the other hand, once you know the plot framework upon which the music revolves, and accept it for what it is, you will almost certainly be better able to appreciate the performance.

There are many kinds of operas, and no one who has developed any discrimination is going to like all of them—just as no one likes all of the novels he reads, the paintings he sees, or the lectures he hears. But the most certain route to wider appreciation of music and opera is surely through increased knowledge. To enjoy the true depth and beauty of

How to Enjoy an Opera

opera, you must consciously develop your understanding of the form.

The section of this book called "A Brief History of Opera" is a starting point. In its brief analyses of periods and types of operatic music, and in its discussions of aims and purposes of composers and librettists, you will be able gradually to orient yourself. Before you listen to an opera—indeed, even before you read the libretto or the story in brief—it will be wise to find out when it was written and by whom. Knowing even a little about the period and the composer may give the opera itself deeper meaning and considerably enhance your appreciation.

Just as knowing the background of an opera will make it more interesting, so familiarity with the music will add to your enjoyment. Before you go to a performance or before listening to an opera broadcast, take time to listen to recordings of the music that are available. No one can catch all of the nuances of great music at first hearing, and even the person who is somewhat familiar with only the important arias has thus prepared himself for new pleasures when he hears the music in its complete operatic setting.

Sincere people are often puzzled and sometimes antagonized when they go to an opera and are bored or disappointed, simply because they haven't bothered first to acquire even a little knowledge about it. There is an unfortunate number of such people, and one is always tempted to remind them that the little effort it takes to understand the fundamentals of opera is a small price to pay for the pleasure they seek. To enjoy any activity, you must know something about the forms and rules. You can't expect to enjoy a baseball game if you can't tell a foul ball from a double play. The pleasures of great literature come only after a long and difficult apprenticeship in the art of reading. Appreciation of a painting presupposes some familiarity with that art form, though pictorial representation is so much a part of our daily lives that we often forget that taste in art is acquired.

Certainly all pleasure arising in the arts demands of the participant some background, some foundation in education.

Opera, principally because it is a complicated art form difficult to produce, is somewhat more removed from common experience than other arts. But obstacles that may have interfered with wide public appreciation in the past have been greatly reduced in recent years by the perfection of techniques of television, radio broadcasting and recording. Today the difficulties that remain are easily surmounted by anyone interested enough to make the effort, and with constantly increasing opportunities to hear and see opera, the rewards are greater than ever before.

When you have the knowledge and understanding properly to enjoy opera, it is for you to decide the way you enjoy it most. Can you attend a performance and lose yourself in the make-believe of the stage while absorbing the music? Then do so. Do you prefer the complete performance via radio—or an abridged version via television—having read the story earlier? Many others do too. Do you want only the recordings of outstanding excerpts? Or recordings of complete operas? Let no one tell you one is better than the other or replaces the other. You are the judge. Your enjoyment is a personal thing, and with understanding, your pleasure is secure.

PART III

A BRIEF HISTORY OF OPERA

OPERA was born in Italy at the end of the sixteenth century. Actually, the influences that led to its birth are rooted in antiquity. Centuries ago, when actors declaimed the mighty dramas of Sophocles, Aeschylus, and other tragic poets of Greece, they were sometimes accompanied by stringed and wind instruments. An integral part of the play was the chorus, which chanted a commentary on the action of the drama. It was inevitable, of course, that music and drama should eventually serve each other, but several centuries went by before musical minds achieved that happy combination.

We shall see in this brief history that the development of opera as we know it today involves a process of revolution and evolution that has been going on for more than three hundred years. Opera grew out of a revolt against the highly complicated polyphonic writing of the sixteenth century. The "rebellion" was accomplished near the beginning of the seventeenth century in Italy by Jacopo Peri in his opera *Dafne*, in which single-voiced recitative replaced the contrapuntal madrigal style, with its five, six, or even seven separate vocal parts. The influence of this rebellion, spreading northward from Italy through Europe, motivated—or at least vitalized— other forces, which then began moving in parallel direction.

In England, during the reigns of James I and Charles I in the early years of the seventeenth century, the court masques —elaborate allegorical presentations declaimed, mimed, and danced to the accompaniment of incidental music—led to the development of the recitative. In 1617 the London-born

Italian, Nicolo Laniere, set to music a masque written by Ben Jonson. The influence of this work, however, was temporary, and the real progenitor of opera in England is acknowledged to be Henry Purcell, whose work appeared some decades later.

As for Germany, the first signs of Italy's musical invasion appeared at Dresden about 1627. Heinrich Schütz, a German who had studied at Venice, composed an opera on the libretto of *Dafne,* which Peri had used. As might be expected, it was in the Italian style and—as was true in England—this first German effort at opera had only a temporary influence. It served, however, to put operatic forces in motion.

In France the story was different. Because of their peculiar sensitivity to drama, the French did not take readily to Italian opera, in which vocal elements were emphasized at the expense of dramatic principles. They prided themselves on a preference for French techniques, in which plot and action were given a more important place. True French opera was developed in the mid-seventeenth century by Jean Baptiste Lully, ironically enough, a Florentine, and under the aegis of the renowned *Académie Royale de Musique,* founded under the patronage of Louis XIV. France resisted Italian influence until the time of the Revolution.

By the end of the seventeenth century Italian opera was flourishing in England and Germany—and imitated in France, but not at the cost of dramatic principles. Singers from Italy traveled all over the continent and to England, popularizing Italian opera and style of performance. It was the "golden age" of singers, for opera, under the influence of such composers as Alessandro Scarlatti, was written primarily for exhibition of the voice and with little thought to dramatic entertainment. Sometimes known as the "oratorio era," because operas were virtually concert performances with the singers in costume, it extended, roughly, from the production of Scarlatti's *Pompeo* in Naples, in 1684, to the presentation of Gluck's *Orfeo ed Euridice* in 1762.

With *Orfeo* came the second revolution in opera. By balancing musical and dramatic values, Gluck took it out of the category of costumed oratorio and gave it a new significance. It is interesting to note that the lines of Italian and French influence converged in Gluck's operas. His later works molded the pattern of French grand opera, which had been in the process of development under Lully and Rameau.

After Gluck, the progress of opera was profoundly affected by the newly born Romantic movement and the political changes wrought by the French Revolution. These cultural and social upheavals ushered in the era of opera that pulsed with the new spirit of romanticism and nationalism—the names of Mozart, Beethoven, Meyerbeer, Rossini, Donizetti, and Weber glittered in the operatic firmament. Then, at the climax of the Romantic epoch, the cycle of operatic revolution began again with Wagner and Verdi. As in the case of Gluck, it was a matter of cutting through artificiality and superficiality to essential musical and dramatic values.

Russia was left more or less untouched by operatic changes and trends until the latter part of the eighteenth century, when Italian opera was introduced in Moscow and St. Petersburg. The nineteenth century saw a return to native music, and the beginning of Russian opera is generally dated from the production of Michail Glinka's *A Life for the Czar* in 1836. The spirit of nationalism that first showed itself in Glinka's opera was fostered by the composers known as "The Five"—Alexander Borodin, Mily Balakirev, César Cui, Modest Moussorgsky, and Nikolai Rimsky-Korsakov. Pre-eminently nationalistic, they resisted Italian influence and gave their works native flavor through the infusion of the melodies and rhythms of Russian folk songs.

The epoch of the third revolution extends from the end of the nineteenth century into our own time. Opera turned from romanticism to *verismo*—realism—and then went through impressionism and objectivism to modern experimental forms.

The development of opera as an art form should be viewed —like that of any other art form—against the broader background of civilization itself. Certain important events in the history of human progress influenced its growth and change from time to time. The Renaissance, for example—one of the milestones of civilization—set in motion certain artistic forces which brought opera into being. The Renaissance began in 1453, when the Turks captured Constantinople. For eleven centuries the city had been the seat of eastern Christianity, and there a coterie of great Greek scholars had brought the arts and sciences to a fine flowering. When Constantinople became the capital of the Ottoman Empire, these artists, scientists, and philosophers scattered to different parts of the world. The closest place of safety was Italy, and it was there that most of these distinguished refugees fled. Thus it was that Italy became the cradle of the Renaissance.

The Renaissance brought immediately to Italy a revival of the classic learning of the Greeks and Romans in all the arts but one—music. It was a relatively easy matter to return to the simplicity and directness of classical antiquity in the other arts, because they had lain neglected during the Middle Ages and presented no obstacle to outside influence. Music, however, had grown and developed to high stature, and actually medieval influence carried over a century and a half into the Renaissance. The revolt in music, as we have noted, was a revolt against the complicated polyphony of the day, as exemplified by the church music of Palestrina and the madrigalists.

In Florence, more than a hundred years after the dawn of the Renaissance, there lived a group of musical scholars who were devotees of the art of ancient Greece. This group included Jacopo Peri, Vincenzo Galilei (the father of Galileo, the astronomer), and Giulio Caccini, and they had as their patron Count Giovanni Bardi, a wealthy Florentine nobleman. The Bardists, as they were sometimes called, sought to re-create the power and splendor of the Greek drama and to heighten its effect with musical accompaniment.

Restless, radical thinkers—like all men of the Renaissance—they revolted against the involved polyphonic writing that had become the high musical art of the sixteenth century. Determined to give music the same elemental and powerful simplicity of the Greek drama, the Bardists went to the other extreme—from the intricate, multivoiced structure of the madrigal to the single vocal line. That was recitative, and recitative was the beginning of opera.

The first work written in the revolutionary style of the accompanied recitative was Peri's *Dafne,* produced for a private audience in 1597. It may be said to be the first opera ever put on a stage. Peri's *Euridice,* written in collaboration with Caccini, was *publicly* produced in 1600, and this is generally recognized as the date of the birth of opera. *Euridice* was in five acts, each concluding with a chorus, and the dialogue was in the form of accompanied recitative. There was also an aria, introduced by an instrumental passage.

Mention should be made here of a work which is sometimes considered an important forerunner of opera. That is *Amfiparnasso,* written in 1594 by Orazio Vecchi, a composer of madrigals and church music and one of the great masters of the polyphonic period. It is a musical setting of a Comedy of Masks—the *commedia dell' arte*—and is written in five-part madrigal form, with three acts and fourteen scenes. *Amfiparnasso* was *not* acted, only sung. It is interesting to note that the work was produced in New York City as recently as 1933.

There were other forms of music in the thirteenth, fourteenth, and fifteenth centuries which had the seed of opera in them. Secular and religious composers injected certain drama qualities into their music, as did the *trouvères* (poet-musicians) of northern France and the players in the mystery and miracle plays of England.

Opera, as "invented" by the Florentines, won the favor of the musical world, and *Dafne* and *Euridice* long served as models for other composers. In the hands of composers like Claudio Monteverdi, who wrote *Ariadne* and *Orfeo,* and Pietro Francesco Cavalli, a Venetian with some forty operas to his credit, opera made significant strides. Monteverdi revolutionized music by establishing the tonal system and contributed to the development of the recitative by giving it a more flexible accompaniment. Among Cavalli's important contributions was the introduction of the comic character into opera, a popularizing influence which took opera out of its sphere of austere classicism and brought it closer to the people. This innovation of Cavalli's appeared in his *Doriclea*, produced in 1645.

Monteverdi and Cavalli not only widened the emotional and dramatic scope of opera but its orchestral requirements as well. They scored their works for larger orchestras and introduced melodic passages to break up the continuous recitatives. It is interesting to note that even at this stage the irresistible impulse for melody showed itself, despite the rules of severe simplicity that governed the recitative. In the works of Monteverdi and Cavalli, for example, there appeared long melodious passages on a single vowel, devices which were later to be used with spectacular effect by Scarlatti and Händel.

As opera gradually won popular attention, there was an increasing demand for public performance. In 1637 the first public opera house was opened in Venice. Up to that time opera audiences had been small in size and aristocratic by nature. By 1700 there were no fewer than eleven opera houses in that city, then renowned as Italy's operatic capital. There, and in other opera houses which were built in the principal cities of Italy, was offered an extensive repertoire of works by Monteverdi, Pietro Cavalli, Marc Antonio Cesti, Giacomo Carissimi, and other early composers.

The late seventeenth century saw a surprising development in opera. Whereas the inventors of opera had disdained melody, composers now began developing melodies of the most formalized sort. The emphasis shifted from simple and direct dramatic utterance, and opera became a medium for sheer vocal display. The principal reason was that Italy, fountainhead of opera, produced the best singers—performers with tremendous vocal resources and magnificent tone quality. There is little doubt that singing as an art, though later developed throughout the world, was cradled in Italy in the seventeenth and eighteenth centuries. Opera was written mainly to give these singers a chance to show off. The logical medium for vocal prowess was, of course, the long sustained passages, and thus the aria was born. Eventually it developed into a rigid pattern: a first section, a contrasting middle section, and then a recapitulation of the first section. Opera finally degenerated into a succession of arias and choruses at the sacrifice of intelligible plot and dramatic content.

Typical of this trend in operatic writing were the works of Alessandro Scarlatti (1659–1725), composer of some one hundred and fifteen operas, who is regarded as the true founder of Italian opera. With Scarlatti, vocal display came first; for the most part, simple musical accompaniment would suffice. He added an orchestral embellishment to the aria in the form of an introduction, an interlude, and a postlude. Scarlatti set a style for operatic composition that remained in vogue for nearly a century. It is known as *opera seria*.

While opera was flowering in Italy, a native type of this art form was springing up in France and Germany. In France, opera grew out of the ballet, which had as its chief exponent Jean Baptiste Lully (1632–1687), a Florentine who became court composer to the king of France. He is considered the founder of true French opera, and his *Les Fêtes de l'Amour et de Bacchus*, produced in 1672, is an important operatic milestone. Lully was the first to introduce brasses into the orchestra. He did opera a particularly good turn by pruning away the florid, meaningless arias of the Scarlatti school. Putting the plot in its proper perspective and emphasizing scenic values, Lully gave French opera the individuality that has characterized it ever since. After Lully came Jean Philippe Rameau, a famous French organist and composer. He enriched opera musically by giving it greater harmonic variety and fuller orchestral background.

The rise of opera in Germany was largely under Italian influence, and practically every German court had its Italian opera company, or one functioning under Italian direction. A native form of opera, called the *singspiel (songplay)*, however, flourished in the folk theaters of small communities. Simply defined, *singspiel* is a musical play in which the vocal interludes are connected by spoken dialogue. In its general pattern it is analogous to English *ballad opera*, Italian *opera buffa*, and French *opéra bouffe*. These four forms, incidentally, all had their origin in the medieval miracle and mystery plays of the fifteenth century. *Singspiel* reappeared later in a highly refined form in works of Beethoven and Mozart, while composers such as Pergolesi, Donizetti, and Rossini brought *opera buffa* to a peak of perfection. *Opéra bouffe* of France developed into the form later known as *opéra comique*, of which *Carmen* and *Faust* are typical examples. *Ballad opera* of England projected its influence into the late nineteenth-century operas of Gilbert and Sullivan.

True national opera was nurtured in North Germany, particularly in Hamburg, where the first German opera house was opened in 1678. One of its initial attractions was the première of what may be considered the first native German opera, *Adam und Eva*, by Johann Theile (1646–1724). Two popular composers who contributed to the musical and dramatic progress of opera during this era—although they wrote in the Italian idiom—were Reinhart Keiser and Johann Adolph Hasse, both with about one hundred operas apiece to their credit. The foremost composer of the day was Georg Friedrich Händel (1685–1759). He wrote several operas in Germany, but reached the peak of his brilliant career in London, where he completely dominated the operatic scene. Händel was an exponent of the formalized *opera seria* developed by Scarlatti, with its emphasis on the aria as a vehicle for vocal display. The Scarlatti-Händel period, in fact, can be called the epoch of the aria. It was also the era of the *castrati*, adult male sopranos and contraltos whose brilliant vocalization made them the pampered stars of the operatic stage.

In England, before the advent of Händel, opera had achieved no particular importance. Henry Purcell (1658–1695), one of the most gifted of the seventeenth-century English composers, had written *Dido and Aeneas* and *Dioclesian*, both of which showed extraordinary promise. Purcell's tragically early death at the age of thirty-seven virtually changed England's operatic history. With no truly English champion, opera remained under the influence of Händel and the Italian school. Eventually there was a reaction to the stilted Italianate style. It came in the form of ballad opera, typified by Gay's *The Beggar's Opera*, produced in 1728. Curiously enough, the music for this opera, which achieved tremendous popularity, was composed by John Pepusch, a German expatriate. After the success of *The Beggar's Opera* scores of other ballad operas were composed, establishing a traditional English form which persisted through the works of Gilbert and Sullivan. Prominent among later composers identified with opera in England were Michael William Balfe, who wrote *The Bohemian Girl*, William Vincent Wallace, composer of *Maritana*, and Henry Rowley Bishop, composer of *Clari*, which contains one of the world's best-known songs, "Home, Sweet Home."

By the time the eighteenth century dawned, opera had progressed through an artistic cycle and was ripe for rebellion. The refreshing inventiveness and spontaneity of the Florentines had long ago given way to highly stylized and conventional forms. Composers were practically under an obligation to write a certain number of arias for each singer so that each artist could strut to his heart's content. There was even a standardization of libretti, oddly reminiscent of the standardization of the aria in the preceding century. Whenever a composer wanted a libretto he would simply apply to Pietro Metastasio, an Italian poet who was the foremost librettist of the period. Some of his texts were set to music as many as thirty or forty times by various composers. The effect of this assembly-line technique may well be imagined.

This was the state of affairs when Gluck and Mozart appeared on the scene and altered opera's destiny. Christoph Willibald, Ritter von Gluck (1714–1787), who had become one of Germany's greatest composers in the Italian style, was the first to break with tradition. In middle life he suddenly discarded the accepted forms as the result of contacts with the musical life of Paris and Vienna. His *Orfeo ed Euridice* (1762) marks the beginning of his rebellion, as we noted earlier. It expressed his conviction that opera must have dramatic coherence and that the music must serve the plot, not merely a singer's ego. In his insistence on dramatic values, Gluck was going back to the sound ideals of the Florentines, as did later great performers of opera—Verdi, Wagner, and Debussy.

When *Orfeo* was rather coolly received in Vienna, Gluck went to Paris, where, under the patronage of Marie Antoinette, he launched a campaign in behalf of his new ideas. He promptly ran head-on into the musical reactionaries, who roared long and loudly against the iconoclast. The musical world was divided into two camps. Champions of the operatic status quo were led by Nicola Piccinni, a leading composer of conventional opera. They opened violent attacks on the "radical" Gluck, and the epic feud between the Gluckists and the Piccinnists was on. Some accounts say that the war became so bitter that it reached the stage of physical violence. At any rate, the situation finally came to a climax in 1779, when the directors of the Paris Opéra commissioned both Gluck and Piccinni to write an opera based on *Iphigénie en Tauride*. Gluck's version won by popular acclaim and his triumph marked the beginning of a new epoch in opera.

Although Gluck infused opera with new life and meaning, it remained essentially in the tradition of Peri and Scarlatti, as far as subject matter was concerned. The first to break out of this pattern was Wolfgang Amadeus Mozart (1756-1791). He turned from the lofty Olympian themes of antiquity to contemporary life for his plots, endowing his characters with natural human emotions. Although strongly influenced by the Italian school, Mozart, like Gluck, avoided showy vocalization and made his music conform to the vital dramatic elements in the plot. He wrote some of his operas in Italian simply because that language was the most musically adaptable to his purposes. The new musical and dramatic concepts expressed in *Don Giovanni*, *Le Nozze di Figaro*, and *Die Zauberflöte* make those operas symbolic of one of the most significant periods in operatic history. *Die Zauberflöte* had the innovation of spoken dialogue, and in this respect it classed as a glorified example of *singspiel*.

Mozart represents not only the dawn of the Romantic period in opera but reflects the new spirit of enlightenment that was awakening in Europe at the time. It was the spirit

Rousseau was talking about when he preached nature and the individual man. It was expressed in the dramas of Beaumarchais when he favored the middle class at the expense of the nobility.

In addition to the reforms of Gluck and Mozart, another purging influence on opera during the eighteenth century was *opera buffa*. This form of lyric drama gradually became identified with between-the-acts diversions presented at performances of *opera seria*. Gradually acquiring a status of its own, *opera buffa* relied for its effects largely upon a comic plot of a contemporary or topical nature. It was therefore free of many of the restrictions of conventional opera, and was fertile soil for satiric characterization. Important composers of the eighteenth and nineteenth centuries turned to *opera buffa* and its naturalistic approach to life because it offered greater dramatic and musical freedom. Some examples of *opera buffa* at its best are Giovanni Pergolesi's *La Serva Padrona*, Mozart's *Così Fan Tutte*, Donizetti's *Don Pasquale*, and Rossini's *Il Barbiere di Siviglia*. It should be mentioned that another Italian composer, Giovanni Paisiello, wrote another *Il Barbiere di Siviglia* some decades before Rossini, and it ranks high on the list of *opera buffa*. Paisiello, who wrote more than one hundred operas, had a tremendous vogue in Italy during the eighteenth century.

The Romantic movement found eloquent expression in *Fidelio*, by Ludwig van Beethoven (1770–1827). Although it is grounded in the classic tradition, it has revolutionary fire and spirit. Like Mozart, Beethoven used spoken dialogue, thus carrying on the tradition of the *singspiel*. The emotional intensity of the Romantic movement was heightened by the social upheavals that stirred Europe at the end of the eighteenth century and the beginning of the nineteenth. Artistic revolt against classicism, the newly awakened spirit of chivalry and adventure, the preoccupation with the picturesque—all these manifestations were akin to the revolutionary mood which found its outlet in the Napoleonic wars. Romanticism and revolution virtually merged into one dynamic force that affected human destiny and the arts alike. In opera it found its expression in the passionate and heroic themes of works by Cherubini, Spontini, Auber, Rossini, Meyerbeer, Halévy, and Weber. They were concerned with human problems and aspirations, and delineated them against backgrounds of spectacular pageantry.

Operatic works reflecting the spirit of this exciting epoch won varying degrees of permanence in repertoire. Maria Luigi Cherubini, distinguished Italian composer who became head of the Paris Conservatoire, won considerable fame with *Les Deux Journées* and *Faniska*. Gasparo Spontini, also an Italian, and an important figure in the German operatic world of the time, was highly successful with *La Vestale*, *Fernando Cortez*, and *Agnes von Hohenstaufen*, the last-mentioned more or less after the style of Weber. The French school, with its emphasis on dramatic verities, was prominently represented. François Fromental Elie Halévy scored a great success with *La Juive*, and the opera has survived in repertoire. Others of importance include Etienne Nicolas Mehul (*Joseph*), Daniel François Esprit Auber (*Masaniello, Fra Diavolo*), and François Adrien Boieldieu (*Le Calife de Bagdad, Jean de Paris, La Dame Blanche*). The last-mentioned opera contains the famous song "Robin Adair." The works of both Auber and Boieldieu were favorites with American audiences of the early nineteenth century.

Head and shoulders above these composers, however, was Giacomo Meyerbeer (Jakob Liebmann Beer) (1791–1864), who seemed to concentrate in his works the dominant German, Italian, and French influences of the early Romantic era. Meyerbeer typifies the penchant of the Romanticists for pageantry, melodrama, and themes of high tragedy. He won such tremendous successes with *L'Africaine, Les Huguenots*, and *Robert le Diable* that he became the undisputed monarch of the operatic kingdom.

In Italy the new Romantic influence was reflected in the works of the foremost composers of the period—Gioachino Antonio Rossini (1792–1868), Vincenzo Bellini, and Gaetano Donizetti. While they carried on the tradition of the Italian school, with its emphasis on vocal virtuosity, they responded to the contemporary spirit in their versatility of plot treatment. The most brilliant spokesman for Romanticism in Italy was Rossini. One of his important operatic innovations was doing away with the thinly accompanied *secco* (dry) recitative peculiar to *opera buffa*. Rossini embellished these explanatory interludes with fuller orchestral accompaniment, which avoided monotony and made for smoother transition. In his last opera, *Guillaume Tell*, written under the influence of the French school, Rossini departed radically from his earlier style. This opera, with its melodrama and pageantry, has a serious revolutionary theme that is in sharp contrast to the satiric mood of his other works.

When composers turned away from the abstractions of classicism, they demanded more theatrical realism in their libretti. The need for sounder and more cogent libretto writing was amply supplied by the French dramatist Eugène Scribe. As prolific as Metastasio before him, Scribe was an expert in stagecraft and extraordinarily inventive in the matter of plot mechanics. It was said of him that, at a moment's notice, he could write lines or create a scene that would not only meet the needs of the plot but fit perfectly into the pattern of the music as well. Scribe wrote libretti for Meyerbeer, Halévy, Auber, Cherubini, Gounod, Donizetti, and Verdi. At this period, also, opera underwent a change not only musically and dramatically but scenically. The classic background of the abode of the gods was discarded in favor of realistic settings which accurately portrayed the locale of the plot.

In general, composers of the early nineteenth century advanced opera by developing several types from earlier forms. Thus, out of the *opera buffa*, the ingenious French devised a more elaborate form called *opéra comique*, in which comedy was made to serve the larger aims of drama. It is characterized by variety of subject matter, interludes of spoken dialogue, and versatility of musical and dramatic treatment. The *singspiel* of Germany blossomed into *romantic opera* under Weber's influence, while the old *opera seria*, embellished by Spontini and Meyerbeer with vivid stage display and orchestral coloring, became *grand opera*.

The Romantic epoch was vitalized by the spirit of nationalism that spread through Europe during the nineteenth century. The acknowledged master of the movement in music was Carl Maria von Weber, who represents the high tide of German nationalism. Thoroughly Germanic in spirit and concept, his operas are full of romantic fervor and melodrama. *Der Freischütz*, produced in 1821, took Germany by storm, and from then on Weber superseded all other operatic composers in public favor. He was one of the most powerful influences of the nineteenth century.

Although somewhat overshadowed by Weber, other composers reflected the new Germanic spirit in operas that were widely popular during the period. Chief among these were Heinrich Marschner, a close friend of Weber, whose *Hans Heiling* was long a favorite. Ludwig Spohr, not only a composer but a great violinist and conductor, wrote *Zemire und Azor* and *Jessonda*. Spohr was an associate of Richard Wagner and produced *Der Fliegende Holländer*. Gustav Albert Lortzing delighted German audiences with his light operas such as *Zar und Zimmermann* and *Der Wildschütz*.

The nationalistic spirit gradually spread through eastern Europe and found voice in the operas of Czechoslovakia, Poland, Hungary, and Russia. Bedřich Smetana caught the vigor and exuberance of his people in *The Bartered Bride*, which became the Czech national opera. In Poland there was Stanislaw Moniuszko, whose *Halka* was the first Polish opera. The pioneer of national opera in Hungary was Ferencz Erkel, with operas such as *Hunyády Laszlo* and *Bank Bán*.

In Russia the Romantic era was marked by stirrings of revolt. Nationalism came to life as the people turned on their oppressors, threw aside the restraints of provincial existence, and became aware of a world outside Russia's borders. Such works as *Russalka*, by Alexander Dargomijsky (1813–1869), and *Russlan and Ludmilla* and *A Life for the Czar*, by Michail Glinka (1804–1857), heralded musical nationalism. Operas which further developed it include *Eugen Onegin*, by Peter Ilyitch Tschaikowsky (1840–1893), *Prince Igor*, by Alexander Borodin (1834–1887), *Le Coq d'Or*, by Nikolai Rimsky-Korsakov (1844–1908), and *Boris Godunof* by Modest Moussorgsky (1835–1881).

Meanwhile there appeared on the operatic scene two composers who brought the Romantic movement to the pinnacle of its expression and who shaped the future of opera. They are Giuseppe Verdi (1813–1901) and Richard Wagner (1813–1883), both of whom instituted the most significant reforms in operatic composition since the time of Gluck and Mozart.

Although Verdi's earlier operas adhered to the conventional Italian style, his lyric gift and instinct for dramatic values infused Italian opera with a strong quality of realism and restored the balance of music and plot. As Verdi progressed in his career, the conventional arias of his earlier works gave way to a more continuous melodic line, which was given more prominent orchestral support. His final works, *Otello* and *Falstaff*, represent the welding of music and drama in a technique that closely approaches that of Wagner.

"Wagner," says Ernest Newman in his *Wagner As Man and Artist*, "was one of those dynamically charged personalities after whose passing the world can never be the same as it was before he came—one of the tiny group of men to whom it is given to bestride an old world and a new, but to sunder them by a gulf that becomes ever more and more impassable; one of the very few who are able so to fill the veins of a whole civilization with a new principle of vitality that the tingle of it is felt not only by the rarer but by the commonest of spirits—some new principle from which, whether a man like it or not, he will find it impossible to escape."

The operatic craftsmanship and musical nationalism of the early Romanticists paved the way for the greatest genius in the history of opera. In his early days he had absorbed the influences of such composers as Spontini, Cherubini, Auber, and Meyerbeer, and he raised the German nationalism of Weber to a high plane of development. It is in his later works

—the *Ring* operas, *Die Meistersinger*, *Tristan und Isolde*, and *Parsifal*—that he reached his goal. That was the creation of a revolutionary form of opera—the music-drama. He replaced the traditional operatic aria and connecting recitative with an "endless chain" of musical speech which is an integral part of a complex orchestral accompaniment.

Wagner also perfected the leitmotif, or leading motive. This device is a melodic or harmonic figure associated with a dramatic situation, a particular person, or a motivating thought. Where earlier composers, such as Weber, used the leitmotif merely as a musical label to identify a character or an idea, Wagner altered the structure of the motif itself to conform to the progress of the drama. It should be pointed out here, however, that Wagner was a musician first and dramatist second. As creator of his own plots, he fashioned the drama to fit the music, not the music to fit the drama. Wagner symbolizes the next great operatic reform after the Florentines: drama and music are components of an artistic whole, with each created to serve the purpose of the other.

After Verdi and Wagner brought the Romantic era to a brilliant climax, a new influence began to make itself felt in the economic and cultural life of the people. The great strides made by science and industry during the last decades of the nineteenth century ushered in the era of Materialism. Interest was centered in the struggle of man for material benefits, and in the arts this preoccupation with the individual led to a naturalistic portrayal of the details of human existence.

In opera there was, naturally, a period of transition, marked by the works of composers under the influence of Wagner. He, of course, had many imitators, few of whom were successful. Engelbert Humperdinck (1854–1921) used the rudiments of music-drama technique with pleasing effect in *Hänsel und Gretel*. Arrigo Boïto (1842–1918) and Amilcare Ponchielli (1834–1886) were among the first in Italy to adapt advanced musical ideas, and are considered by some as founders of modern Italian opera. Boïto applied certain Wagnerian techniques to his fantastic and beautiful *Mefistofele*, a setting of the Faust legend, while Ponchielli's *La*

Gioconda shows the modern influence in its richness of orchestration, bringing the accompaniment on a plane of equal importance with the voice.

The impact of Wagnerian ideas on composers like Georges Bizet (1838–1875) and Camille Saint-Saëns (1835–1921) was very evident. Bizet's *Carmen*, in fact, at first was frowned on by the French as being too Wagnerian, while Saint-Saëns's *Samson et Dalila* was kept from the stage of the Paris Opéra for a number of years for the same reason. Charles Gounod (1818–1893), another composer of the transition period, reveals in his emphasis on lyrical elements more of the Verdian influence. To the transition group may be added the names of Ambroise Thomas (1811–1896) and Jules Massenet (1842–1912).

Materialism somewhat dimmed the emotional glow which had pervaded opera during the Romantic era, but the lyric stage lost none of its power. Realism gave the drama more impact, the music more incisiveness. The effect of preoccupation with the individual and his problems is well illustrated by *Louise*, by Gustave Charpentier. Although set against a romantic background—like *Carmen*—it is a realistic and sometimes uncompromising picture of lower levels of Parisian life.

In Italy the new realism found voice in the *verismo* school of composers—Leoncavallo, Mascagni, Giordano, Wolf-Ferrari, and Puccini. Though in most cases the plots were starkly realistic, the Italians, with their natural impulse of melody, clothed the expressions of violent emotions in rich trappings of harmony.

After the turn of the century, composers seemed to turn to a more symphonic style, with the vocal line serving as an accompaniment. The music served to express subtle moods and psychological reactions rather than sentiment or emotion. In that respect opera turned toward Impressionism, which had first made its influence felt in painting. Among the first to use this newer technique was Richard Strauss. Operas such as *Salome* and *Elektra* show projections of Wagnerian techniques to which he added certain dramatic and musical concepts of his own, while the psychological problems posed in these operas reveal traces of the Impressionistic influence. In that period Strauss reflected a preoccupation with the erotic and the pathological, as did composers such as Alban Berg and Franz Schreker. But Strauss broke out of the pattern with *Rosenkavalier,* which brims over with a lusty, extrovert spirit and exuberant melody.

One of the most remarkable operas of the twentieth century is Claude Debussy's *Pelléas et Mélisande.* In its use of the leitmotif it is Wagnerian; in its psychological nuances and subtle delineation of moods it is Impressionistic. At the same time *Pelléas* marks another return to the Florentines in the perfection of its blending of music and drama.

Taken as a whole, European operatic composition of the twentieth century reveals several trends. Some composers show the influence of Wagnerian reform, under which they have developed distinct styles of their own. In this category may be named such men as Italo Montemezzi (*L'Amore dei Tre Re*), Ildebrando Pizzetti (*Fra Gherardo*), Ottorino Respighi (*La Campana Sommersa*). Later twentieth-century composers forged into experimental fields with interesting results. A trend toward absolute objectivity is revealed in *Christoph Colomb,* by Paul Claudel and Darius Milhaud, in which stage action is supplemented by movie projection. Men like Arnold Schoenberg (*Die glückliche Hand*) and Alban Berg (*Wozzeck*) turned to atonality in music and expressionism in plot. Others whose innovations have attracted attention include Paul Hindemith (*Neues vom Tage*), Jaromir Weinberger (*Schwanda*), Ernest Krenek (*Jonny spielt auf*), Kurt Weill (*Dreigroschenoper*), and Dmitri Shostakovitch (*Lady Macbeth Mtsenskago Uyezda—Lady Macbeth of Mtsensk District*). One interesting trend in European opera is in the direction of the old forms, as though opera, in the fourth century of its existence, were completing a full circle. A notable example of this is Strauss's *Ariadne auf Naxos,* which interestingly combined elements of Florentine technique, *opera buffa,* and *opera seria.*

The development of opera in America was shaped—as it was in Europe—by economic and cultural trends. The harsh struggle for existence in the pioneer days left little opportunity for the amenities of civilization. Yet, with the gradual establishment of communities, the desire for entertainment and relaxation asserted itself, and the theater of the day met the demands of the public with importations of English ballad operas, which were long in vogue. The popularity of ballad operas, however, aroused the ire of some of the sterner citizens, who protested that the "strolling Comedians" presenting these entertainments were "propagating vice and immorality." These moral objections, in fact, led indirectly to the use of the term "opera house" for the first time in America, in August 1787. It was applied to the Southwark Theater, in Philadelphia, by the way of removing the taint that clung to the professional title of "theater," with all that it implied in the form of worldly entertainment.

During the colonial period there were interesting attempts at native opera, among which may be mentioned *Flora; or, Hob in the Well* (1735), usually cited as the first performance of native opera in America; *Tammany; or, The Indian Chief* (1794), an opera on an Indian subject by James Hewitt; *Edwin and Angelina* (1796), by the French-born Victor Pelissier, and *The Saw Mill; or, A Yankee Trick* (1824), by Micah Hawkins. The popularity of musical attractions may be gauged by the fact that the Hallam family, an American theatrical troupe, was active from about 1735 until 1800 with a repertoire of some two hundred operas and musical plays.

There were, so to speak, operatic repercussions of the French Revolution in this country which were felt principally in New Orleans. Many musical artists who fled the war in Europe made their way to that city, with the result that it became the center of French drama and opera, and its audiences were among the first to see the *opéra comique* works of Boieldieu and Auber. In the 1830s operas by these composers were given in abridged form in New York by artists who came northward from New Orleans. Called an "American Paris," New Orleans was an operatic center rivaling New York and Philadelphia in the eighteenth century and during the early part of the nineteenth. It was virtually a French provincial city in which were reproduced the cultural life of Paris and, as for opera, it remained a completely French institution.

Operatic history in New Orleans centered in the Théâtre d'Orléans, built in 1813. Destroyed by fire and rebuilt four years later, it was known as the finest theater in America. For close to half a century it provided operatic performances on a level of professional excellence that almost approached that of the foremost European lyric theaters. The repertoire was the standard one of the period and included—besides Boieldieu and Auber, mentioned previously—works of Halévy, Meyerbeer, Verdi, Rossini, Spontini, and Mozart. New Orleans opera was important for its influence on opera in Philadelphia and New York, by virtue of the fact that experienced artists from the Théâtre d'Orléans gave performances in those cities. It was not until the mid-nineteenth century, when New York became the mecca for foreign artists, that New Orleans lost its place as the operatic capital of America.

Opera benefited by the fact that the invention of the steamship more closely linked Europe and America. Original opera companies were imported from Europe and there was an influx of European musical personalities into this country. Many arrived under encouragement from Lorenzo da Ponte, Mozart's famous librettist, who had come to America at the beginning of the century. In 1825 the famous Manuel Garcia operatic troupe arrived to inaugurate the first season of grand opera in New York.

It is an interesting fact that a desire for opera in English manifested itself in America in the eighteenth century. Edward Ellsworth Hipsher, in his *American Opera and Its Composers*, states: "From that eventful February 8, 1735, when the opera of *Flora; or, Hob in the Well* was produced at Charleston, South Carolina . . . till the end of the century, Opera in English held undisputed sway." The preference was so strong that attempts made toward the end of the century to introduce French opera outside of New Orleans met with little success. In 1793 a New York company was presenting an entire repertoire of operas in English.

The cause of opera in the vernacular, however, suffered a

serious blow with the arrival of Garcia's troupe, one member of which was his daughter, who, as Marie Malibran, was to become one of the greatest singers of the day. Garcia and his colleagues represented the best in Italian operatic art, which was then at high tide in Europe. They quickly built up a following and threatened the supremacy of opera in English. In the 1830s, however, there were performances in English of such operas as *Fidelio, Sonnambula,* and *Robert le Diable.* Another interesting phase of the battle of opera was introduced with the establishment in New York of the Italian Opera House by da Ponte. One of the first opera houses, *per se,* in America, it was supported by subscribers in the manner of later organizations of that kind, and the operas were performed by noted Italian singers. In competition with it, however, was a company giving operas in English. After a two-year period of intense rivalry, the English company emerged triumphant. Balfe's *Bohemian Girl,* introduced to American audiences in 1840, is said to have inspired the Philadelphian William Henry Fry to write *Leonora,* which is considered the first real American *grand opera.* Another important composer of this period was George F. Bristow, who wrote the grand opera *Rip Van Winkle,* presented in New York in 1855. Both composers are important in American operatic history for their championship of American music.

During the middle of the nineteenth century the influx of foreign singers gradually crowded singers of English opera from the stage, leaving the field to French, Italian, and German performers. Then came the epoch of the "star system," when the opera-going public clamored to hear the fabulous performances of such artists as Patti, Sembrich, Malibran, and Nilsson. In the face of their vocal accomplishments, the language in which they sang was a matter of indifference to their listeners. The custom of opera in foreign tongue firmly established itself, and opera in English lost ground it has never regained.

Opera moved westward with the tide of territorial expansion. During the 1850s Chicago became an operatic center of the Middle West, with English and Italian companies playing there. During the Gold Rush days opera invaded San Francisco, and affluent patrons heard some of the famous stars such as Jenny Lind, Patti, and Malibran in performances of standard operas. It was the fantastic era of sudden wealth, when the society that followed on the heels of lusty prospectors demanded spectacular entertainment and enthusiastically acclaimed even as "high-brow" a form as opera. Opera lovers whose pockets were literally bulging with new-found wealth sometimes threw chunks of raw gold on the stage as tokens of appreciation of an operatic favorite. A colorful chapter in the history of the Gold Rush days was the famous Central City Opera House, Central City, Colorado, built in 1878. Opera troupes from the East, on their way to the Coast, stopped there to give performances that were applauded to the echo by bearded miners and resplendently attired patrons. Some of the greatest dramatic actors of the day, including Sarah Bernhardt and Tommaso Salvini, played at the Opera House during its nine-month season. When the boom passed, the glory and glitter faded, but the Opera House has survived to the present day as an important cultural institution.

Industrial and economic development after the Civil War established a wealthy society which was able to support opera in its most lavish form. Opera houses were built in all the larger cities—Philadelphia, Boston, Cleveland, Cincinnati, St. Louis—and opera became an important part of society life. The present Metropolitan Opera House was opened in 1883, and in ensuing years European artists came to this country in greater numbers than ever before. In 1884, Leopold Damrosch organized a season of Wagnerian operas, and the repertoire was repeated yearly until 1891. During this period, representing the high tide of German opera in America, Anton Seidl, who had been Wagner's assistant at Bayreuth, conducted the first American performances of *Die Meistersinger, Tristan und Isolde,* and the *Ring*.

Although foreign operas were consistently popular in all parts of the country during the nineteenth century, native American opera was in continuous existence. Pioneer composers such as Hewitt, Hawkins, Fry, and Bristow had their successors in men like Charles Wakefield Cadman (*Shanewis*), Frederick Shepherd Converse (*The Pipe of Desire*—presented at the Metropolitan in 1910, the first American opera by a native composer to be given there), Walter Damrosch (*Cyrano de Bergerac*), Reginald de Koven (*Robin Hood, Canterbury Pilgrims*), Victor Herbert (*Natoma*), and Horatio Parker (*Mona*).

Conspicuous among contemporary American grand-opera composers are Deems Taylor (*The King's Henchman, Peter Ibbetson*), Louis Gruenberg (*Emperor Jones*) and Howard Hanson (*Merry Mount*). These works were regarded as having made important musical and dramatic contributions to the progress of opera, and their initial presentations—in the early Thirties in this country—were acclaimed. They have not, however, established a place for themselves in grand-opera repertoire.

Virtually the only grand opera, presented in America during that period, which has lasted in repertoire is *Wozzeck*, by the Viennese composer Alban Berg. It had premières in Philadelphia and New York in 1931. *Wozzeck* is a grim tragedy of murder and madness, set to an unorthodox combination of traditional and modern music. Some consider it an operatic milestone as important as *Pelléas et Mélisande;* others dismiss it as sheer insanity. Yet it has enduring power as a new operatic form.

The depression and the social upheaval that swept America during the first half of the Thirties were reflected in opera just as they were in the drama. Playwrights and composers turned to stark realism, to the harsh realities of hunger, poverty and frustration. To match such dramas as *One Third of a Nation* or *Class of '29*, there was Marc Blitzstein's opera, *The Cradle Will Rock*. The plot centers around the efforts of steel workers to organize a union. The opera had its première in New York on June 15, 1937, under hectic circumstances. Because of its political overtones it was banned at the last moment from a WPA theater on Broadway. Producers scurried around, found another vacant theater, and there the opera was performed without scenery or costumes. Blitzstein himself played the score, sitting at a piano on the stage. One New York critic compared the work, in its realistic approach to social problems of the day, to Charpentier's *Louise*.

An opera in an entirely different vein was produced at about the same period. This was *Porgy and Bess*, by George Gershwin. It had its première in Boston, September 30, 1935. *Porgy and Bess* is rich in folklore of the South, and Gershwin planned it as a *native* American opera. Critics consider it a hybrid—somewhere between opera and musical comedy. Hybrid or otherwise, it has been performed time and again by singing companies throughout the country.

The period of the Thirties also marks the emergence of a composer who gave opera freshness and renewed vitality. That composer is Gian-Carlo Menotti, Italian by birth, American by adoption. The first of his works was *Amelia Goes to the Ball*, expertly written in the old *opera buffa* style. He followed that with *The Old Maid and the Thief*, in the same vein. Then came *The Medium*, in a quite different, modern style, with spiritualism as its theme. Following these, Menotti wrote *The Consul*, which is really in the pattern of grand opera. Its theme is the tragedy of the displaced person and his struggle to cope with a world that is cynically indifferent to his fate. Here Menotti makes effective use of *singspiel*, simple melody, traditional aria forms and modern dissonances.

Among the latest of Menotti's operatic works is *Amahl and the Night Visitors*, the first opera expressly written for television. It had its television première on Christmas Eve, 1951, and has since been performed by opera companies. From the première of *Amelia Goes to the Ball*, in 1937, to that of *Amahl* in 1951 is a span of 14 years, a period in which Menotti made a lasting contribution to the cause of opera in America.

The matter-of-fact realism of operatic works of the Thirties seems to have paved the way for a return to the *verismo* school of writing. Composed mostly in the modern idiom, opera today sticks more or less to facts and spurns romantic flights of fancy. When it is not harshly realistic it is satiric. *Il Prigioniero*, for example, a one-act opera by Luigi Dellapiccola (1947), has for its theme the torture of a political

A Brief History of Opera

prisoner. *L'Apostrophe*, a comic opera by Jean Françaix (1950), is based on one of Balzac's *Droll Stories*. *Trouble in Tahiti*, by Leonard Bernstein, is in the American jazz idiom. *The Trial*, (*Der Prozess*), a full-length opera by Gottfried von Einem, is based on a novel by Franz Kafka. It depicts one man's struggle against totalitarian despotism, which finally destroys him.

In the forefront of present-day operatic composers is England's Benjamin Britten. He has contributed two grand operas (*Peter Grimes, Billy Budd*), a chamber opera (*The Rape of Lucretia*) and an *opera buffa* (*Albert Herring*). Although not yet securely in opera repertoire, they are performed from time to time in this country. One of the most important premières in recent years in America was that of *The Rake's Progress* by Igor Stravinsky. It was first presented at the Metropolitan (in English) on February 14, 1953. It opened in this country to mixed reviews and while at first it was acclaimed by the public, it gradually lost favor and although still in the repertoire it is rarely given. At any rate all of the above, since they are in English, do help to keep alive the healthy controversy over opera in that language.

One organization that lends weight to the argument for opera in English is the New England Opera Theatre—or NEOT, as it is known in Boston, where the company puts on its performances. Under the direction of Boris Goldovsky, NEOT presents restudied versions of classic and modern operas in English. Goldovsky has introduced such unconventional methods as having singers turn their backs to the conductor during rehearsals—so they will not get into the habit of staring into the pit during performances, instead of acting. He has the actors analyze their actions offstage to find out what motivates their entrances on cue.

The NEOT chooses for performance little-known operas like Mozart's early satire on opera, *La Finta Giardiniera* (written when he was 12), presented as *The Merry Masquerade*. The company's repertoire also includes Mozart's *Idomeneo* and Rossini's *The Turk in Italy*.

On the basis of what has already been presented on television, this camera-medium is certain to loom large in the future of opera. The possibilities—as with the presentation of dramas—are limitless. Already, standard operas adapted for television presentation in English include *Madama Butterfly, Pique Dame, Pagliacci, Carmen, Il Tabarro, Gianni Schicchi, Macbeth, The Marriage of Figaro, The Taming of the Shrew, Pelléas et Mélisande* and *Salome*. Obviously, this is only a beginning. The future of opera on television is in the hands of those producers who have the necessary taste, talent and imagination to exploit its possibilities.

In opera, as in human history, "the Past is Prologue." The techniques of the Florentines and the achievements of later creators and "reformers"—Monteverdi, Lully, Gluck, Mozart, Verdi and Wagner—comprise a treasure house of operatic theory and principle from which composers of today draw their inspiration. We have seen how the tide of lyricism, gathering force in 1600, swept northward from Italy into Europe and England, thrust eastward into Russia, and surged westward into the New World. In the three and a half centuries of opera's existence it has left its mark on the culture of virtually every country of the globe.

Opera has gained a permanent place in America's culture. There are no fewer than six major opera companies in the United States today, as well as a great many smaller organizations that give performances ranging from the oldest and most conservative repertoire to the newest experimental forms. Still to be reckoned with is the impact of television on opera. There, in the making, may well be a new chapter in operatic history.

SELECTED READING GUIDE

American Opera and Its Composers, Edward Ellsworth Hipsher. Philadelphia. Theo. Presser Company.
> Beginnings of opera in America, American composers and their operas.

Miniature History of Opera, Percy Scholes. London. Oxford University Press.
> Carefully selected highlights of opera history in a brief but scholarly survey.

Opera, Edward J. Dent. New York. Penguin Books.
> History plus comment on enjoyment of opera, ballet in opera, operatic singing and acting, and opera in English.

Our American Music, (3rd ed.), John Tasker Howard. New York. Thomas Y. Crowell.
> Opera in relation to general musical developments in America. Discusses important American composers.

The Life of Richard Wagner (4 vols.), Ernest Newman. New York. Alfred A. Knopf.
> This biography is not only the story of the composer's life and works, but virtually a history of the era in which he lived.

The Opera and Its Future in America, Herbert Graf. New York. Norton.
> Reviews European history of opera, then turns to American scene, discussing opera in relation to social and cultural trends.

The Perfect Wagnerite, George Bernard Shaw. New York. Brentano's.
> Provocative essays on the philosophy of *Der Ring des Nibelungen.*

A Short History of Opera (2 vols.), Donald Jay Grout. New York. Columbia University Press.
> A history of opera from its sources to modern times, for layman or music scholar.

The Opera Reader, compiled and edited by Louis Biancolli. New York. McGraw-Hill.
> A chatty, informative discussion of operas and composers.

Opéra Comique, Martin Cooper. London. M. Parrish.

> Traces origins of *opéra comique*, analyzes its style and explains how it differs from grand opera and operetta.

French Grand Opera, William Loran Crosten. Kings Crown Press.

> Discusses the role of French composers in the development of opera and their contributions to its progress.

Walt Whitman and Opera, Robert D. Faner. University of Pennsylvania Press.

> A discussion of opera and its relation to poetry. The great American poet Whitman was intensely interested in opera from the standpoint of musical speech.

The Tales of Hoffmann, A Study of the Film, Monk Gibbon. London. Saturn Press.

> An interesting and vivid account of how Offenbach's opera was made into a full-length film, a spectacular example of how opera can be adapted to the medium of the screen.

Opera for the People, Herbert Graf. University of Minnesota Press.

> Opera and its problems as viewed by one of today's leading operatic stage directors.

Makers of Opera, Kathleen O'Donnell Hoover. New York. H. Bittner.

> A discussion of how operas came into being.

A Front Seat at the Opera, George Marek. Allen, Towne and Heath.

> "Close-ups" of performers and performances.

Behind the Gold Curtain, Mary E. Peltz. New York. Farrar, Straus and Company.

> Backstage at the Metropolitan.

Opera Production for Amateurs, Harold Smethhurst. London. Turnstile Press.

Problems of Opera Production, Walter W. Volbach. Texas Christian University Press.

The Rise of English Opera, Eric W. White. Philosophical Library, New York.

The International Cyclopedia of Music and Musicians, Oscar Thompson. New York. Dodd.

> A reference book by an eminent scholar and musicologist.

Selected Reading Guide

The Victor Book of Operas, Louis Biancolli and Robert Bagar. New York. Simon and Schuster.
> This includes a discography.

The Complete Book of 20th Century Music, David Ewen. Prentice-Hall, Inc. New York.
> Brief but authoritative analyses of musical compositions written since 1900 (including operas), biographies of composers, critical evaluations.

The Child and His Music, Hazel Gertrude Kinscella and Elizabeth M. Tierney. University Publishing Company. Lincoln, New York, Dallas, Kansas City.
> Contains practical suggestions on how to introduce children to opera and how to stimulate their interest in it.

The Magic World of Music, Olga Samaroff Stokowski. W. W. Norton and Company, New York.
> A book that explains opera and its origins in terms of a delightful fantasy.

Accents on Opera, Boris Goldovsky. Farrar, Straus & Young. New York.
> Brief essays and analyses of operatic plots and musical themes, with musical notations.

Milton Cross' Encyclopedia of the Great Composers and Their Music. New York. Doubleday & Company.
> While this is concerned primarily with composers of all types of music there are numerous references to operatic works. There is such information as the date of the première and a brief analysis of the plot as well as discussion of the music.

SELECTED OPERA RECORDINGS*

Thanks to the spectacular development of recording techniques, you can bring the music of grand opera into your home and enjoy it at your leisure. Today, the repertoire of recorded opera includes practically every major work performed on operatic stages throughout the world. Below is a list of *complete* recordings of the thirty-six operas described in this book with the exception of *Tannhäuser* and *Siegfried*, which are currently available only in excerpts and which are so indicated in the listings.

Excerpts of other operas are similarly available in recorded form. Record catalogues list overtures, choruses, ensembles and arias, with individual performers.

AÏDA:
    Angel 3525-C/L—Orch. and Cho. of La Scala, cond. by Serafin. Callas, Gobbi, Tucker, Barbieri.
    Cetra 1262—Orch. and Cho. of Radio Italiano, cond. by Questa. Curtis-Verna, Pirazzini, Corelli, Guelfi, Neri, Zerbini.
    Cetra 1228—Orch. and Cho. of Radio Italiano, cond. by Gui. Mancini, Filippeschi, Simionato, Panerai, Neri, Massaria.
    London A-4345; **OSA-1313**—Vienna Phil. Orch., cond. by Von Karajan. Tebaldi, Bergonzi, Simionato, Corena, MacNeil.
    Victor LM 6122—Orch. and Cho. of Rome Opera House, cond. by Perlea. Milanov, Bjoerling, Warren, Christoff, Barbieri.
    Victor LM 6132—NBC Symphony Orch., cond. by Toscanini. Robert Shaw Chorale. Nelli, Stich-Randall, Tucker, Gustavson, Valdengo.

*This list is complete to February, 1961.
Those record numbers listed in boldface type are stereophonic recordings.

Selected Opera Recordings

UN BALLO IN MASCHERA:
Angel 3557-C/L—Orch. and Cho. of La Scala, cond. by Votto. Callas, Di Stefano, Gobbi, Barbieri.
Cetra 1250—Orch. and Cho. of Radio Italiano, cond. by Questa. Tagliavini, Tassinari, Valdengo, Curtis-Verna.
Victor LM-6112—NBC Symphony Orch., cond. by Toscanini. Robert Shaw Chorale. Haskins, Nelli, Turner, Peerce, Merrill.

IL BARBIERE DI SIVIGLIA:
Angel 3559-C/L; S-3559-C/L—Philharmonia Orch. and Cho., cond. by Galliera. Callas, Gobbi, Alva.
Capitol GCR-7138—Orch. & Cho. of Milan Symphony, cond. by Serafin. De Los Angeles, Bechi, Rossi-Lemeni.
Cetra 1211—Orch. and Cho. of Radio Italiano, cond. by Previtali. Simionato, Broilo, Infantino, Taddei, Badioli, Cassinelli.
London A-4327—Orch. and Cho. of Maggio Musicale Fiorentino, cond. by Erede. Bastianini, Simionato, Corena, Siepi.
Pathé DTX-185/7—Orch. and Cho. of Paris Opéra-Comique, cond. by Gressier. Berton, Dens, Giraudeau, Depraz, Lovano.
Victor LM-6143; LSC-6143—Orch. and Cho. of Metropolitan Opera, cond. by Liensdorf. Merrill, Peters, Valletti, Tozzi.

LA BOHÈME:
Angel 3560-B/L—Orch. and Cho. of La Scala, cond. by Votto. Callas, Di Stefano, Moffo.
Cetra 1237—Orch. and Cho. of Radio Italiano, cond. by Santini. Tagliavini, Taddei, Latinucci, Siepi, Zorgniotti, Carteri, Ramella, Benzi.
Columbia M2L-401—Orch. and Cho. of Teatro di San Carlo, cond. by Molinari-Pradelli. Stella, Poggi.
Columbia SL-101—Orch. and Cho. of Metropolitan Opera, cond. by Antonicelli. Tucker, Sayão, Baccaloni.
London A-4236; OSA-1208—Orch. and Cho. of L'accademia di Santa Cecilia, Rome, cond. by Serafin. Tebaldi, Bergonzi, Bastianini, Siepi, Corena.
Victor LM-6006—NBC Symphony Orch., cond. by Toscanini. Albanese, Peerce, McKnight.
Victor LM-6042—Orch. and Cho. of RCA Victor, cond. by Beecham. Columbus Boychoir. Amara, De Los Angeles, Merrill, Bjoerling, Corena, Tozzi.

BORIS GODOUNOV:
Capitol GDR-7164—French National Radio Orch., cond. by Dobrowen. Russian Cho. of Paris. Christoff, Borg, Gedda.
London A-4317—Orch. and Cho. of National Opera House, Belgrade, cond. by Baranovich. Changolovich, Sesardich, Jankovich, Miladinovich.
Period 554—Bolshoi Theatre Orch., cond. by Golovanov. Pirogov, Slatogorova, Kruglikova.

CARMEN:
>   Capitol GCR-7207; **SGCR-7207**—Orch. and Cho. of French National Radio, cond. by Beecham. Petits Chanteurs de Versailles. De Los Angeles, Gedda, Blanc.
>   Epic SC-6035; **BSC-106**—Orch. and Cho. of Concert de Paris, cond. by Le Conte. St. Nicholas Children's Choir. Rubio, Simoneau, Alarie, Rehfuss.
>   London A-4304—Orch. and Cho. of Paris Opéra-Comique, cond. by Wolff. Juyol, de Luca.
>   Victor LM-6102—RCA Victor Orch., cond. by Reiner. Robert Shaw Chorale. Albanese, Stevens, Peerce, Merrill.

CAVALLERIA RUSTICANA:
>   Angel 3509-3S/L—Orch. and Cho. of La Scala, cond. by Serafin. Callas, Di Stefano.
>   Angel 3528-C/L (with *Pagliacci*)—Orch. and Cho. of La Scala, cond. by Serafin. Callas, Di Stefano.
>   Cetra 1233—Orch. of Cetra-Turin, cond. by Basile. Simionato, Cadoni, Braschi, Tagliabue, Pellegrino.
>   Cetra 1238 (with *Pagliacci*)—Orch. of Cetra-Turin, cond. by Basile. Simionato, Cadoni, Braschi, Tagliabue, Pellegrino.
>   Columbia SL-124 (with *Pagliacci*)—Orch. and Cho. of Metropolitan Opera, cond. by Cleva. Harshaw, Tucker, Guarrera.
>   Electrola 80474/5S—Orch. and Cho. of La Scala, cond. by Mascagni. Gigli, Bruna-Rasa, Bechi.
>   London A-4216—Orch. and Cho. of Milan, cond. by Ghione. Del Monaco, Nicolai, Protti.
>   London A-4323 (with *Pagliacci*)—Orch. and Cho. of Milan, cond. by Ghione. Del Monaco, Nicolai, Protti.
>   London A-4240; **OSA-1213**—Orch. and Cho. of L'accademia di Santa Cecilia, Rome, cond. by Serafin. Simionato, Del Monaco, MacNeil.
>   Period SHO-317—Lombard Prom. Cho. and Orch., cond. by Falco. Soloists.
>   Victor LM-6059; **LSC-6059**—Orch. and Cho. of Maggio Musicale Fiorentino, cond. by Erede. Tebaldi, Bjoerling, Bastianini.
>   Victor LM-6106 (with *Pagliacci*)—RCA Victor Orch., cond. by Cellini. Robert Shaw Chorale. Milanov, Bjoerling, Merrill.

COSI FAN TUTTE:
>   Angel 3522-C/L—Philharmonia Orch. and Cho., cond. by Von Karajan. Schwarzkopf, Merriman, Simoneau.
>   Columbia SL-122—Orch. and Cho. of Metropolitan Opera, cond. by Stiedry. Steber, Tucker, Peters.
>   London A-4318; **OSA-1312**—Vienna Phil. Orch., cond. by Böhm. Vienna State Opera Cho. Della Casa, Dermota, Ludwig, Loose, Kunz, Schöffler.

Selected Opera Recordings

DON GIOVANNI:
Angel 3605-D/L; **S-3605-D/L**—Philharmonia Orch. and Cho., cond. by Giulini. Wächter, Taddei, Schwarzkopf, Sutherland.
Cetra 1253—Radio, Televisione Italiana Symph. Orch. of Turin, cond. by Rudolf. Taddei, Curtis-Verna, Valletti, Tajo, Ribetti, Susca, Gavazzi.
Deutsche Grammophon DGM-302; **7302**—Berlin Radio Symphony Orch., cond. by Ericsay. Fischer-Dieskau, Jurinac, Stader, Seefried, Häfliger.
Epic SC-6010—Vienna Symphony Orch., cond. by Moralt. Vienna Chamber Choir. London, Zadek, Simoneau.
London A-4406; **OSA-1401**—Vienna Phil. Orch., cond. by Krips. Vienna State Opera Cho. Siepi, Corena, Dermota, Della Casa, Gueden, Boehme.
Pathé DTX-218/21—Paris Consv. Orch. and Cho., cond. by Rosbaud. Moffo, Gedda, Danco, Stich-Randall.
Victor LM-6410; **LSC-6410**—Vienna Philharmonic Orch., cond. by Leinsdorf. Siepi, Nilsson, Price, Valletti, Corena, Ratti.

FAUST:
Capitol GDR-7154; **SGDR-7154**—Orch. and Cho. of Théâtre National de l'Opéra, cond. by Cluytens. Gedda, Christoff, De Los Angeles, Berton.
Columbia SL-112—Orch. and Cho. of Metropolitan Opera, cond. by Cleva. Steber, Conley, Siepi.

LA FORZA DEL DESTINO:
Angel 3531-C/L—Orch. and Cho. of La Scala, cond. by Serafin. Callas, Tucker, Nicolai, Tagliabue, Rossi-Lemeni, Capecchi.
Cetra 1236—Orch. and Cho. of Radio Italiano, cond. by Marinuzzi. Dominici, Caniglia, Tagliabue, Masini, Stignani, Pasero, Meletti.
London A-4408; **OSA-1405**—Orch. and Cho. of L'accademia di Santa Cecilia, Rome, cond. by Molinari-Pradelli. Del Monaco, Tebaldi, Bastianini, Siepi, Simionato, Bergonzi.
Victor LM-6406; **LSC-6406**—Orch. and Cho. of L'accademia di Santa Cecilia, Rome, cond. by Previtali. Milanov, Elias, Di Stefano, Warren, Tozzi.

GIANNI SCHICCHI:
Capitol GAR-7179; **SGAR-7179**—Rome Opera Orch., cond. by Santini. Gobbi, De Los Angeles.
Cetra 50028—Orch. and Cho. of Radio Italiano, cond. by Simonetto. Rapisardi, Dubbini, Savio, Taddei.

HANSEL UND GRETEL:
Angel 3506-B/L—Philharmonia Orch., cond. by Von Karajan. Schwarzkopf, Felbermayer.
Columbia SL-102—Metropolitan Opera Orch., cond. by Rudolf. Stevens, Conner, Brownlee, Votipka, Turner.

LOHENGRIN:

Decca DX-131—Orch. and Cho. of Bavarian Radio, cond. by Jochum. Fehenberger, Kupper.

London A-4502—Orch. and Cho. of Bayreuth Festival, cond. by Keilberth. Steber, Varnay, Windgassen.

LUCIA DI LAMMERMOOR:

Angel 3601-B/L; **S-3601-B/L**—Philharmonia Orch. and Cho., cond. by Serafin. Callas, Elkins, Tagliavini.

Cetra 1205—Orch. and Cho. of Radio Italiano, cond. by Tansini. Manacchini, Pagliughi, Malipiero, Giovagnoli, Neroni.

Columbia SL-127—Orch. and Cho. of Metropolitan Opera, cond. by Cleva. Pons, Tucker, Guarrera.

Mercury OL-2-108; **SR-2-9008**—Orch. and Cho. of La Scala, cond. by Sanzogno. Scotto, Di Stefano, Bastianini.

Victor LM-6055; **LSC-6141**—Rome Opera House Orch., cond. by Leinsdorf. Peters, Peerce, Tozzi.

MADAMA BUTTERFLY:

Angel 3523-C/L—Orch. and Cho. of La Scala, cond. by Von Karajan. Callas, Gedda.

Angel GRB-4000—Orch. and Cho. of Rome Opera House, cond. by De Fabritiis. Dal Monte, Gigli, Palombini, Basiola.

Capitol GCR-7137—Rome Opera House Orch., cond. by Gavazzeni. De Los Angeles, Di Stefano, Gobbi.

Cetra 1248—Orch. and Cho. of Radio Italiano, cond. by Questa. Petrella, Tagliavini, Tadei.

Columbia SL-104—Orch. and Cho. of Metropolitan Opera, cond. by Rudolf. Tucker, Steber.

Electrola 80481/2—Rome Opera House Orch., cond. by De Fabritiis. Dal Monte, Gigli, Palombini, Basiola.

London A-4337; **OSA-1314**—Orch. and Cho. of L'accademia di Santa Cecilia, Rome, cond. by Serafin. Tebaldi, Del Monaco, Bergonzi.

Pathé DTX-225/7—Orch. of National Opéra-Comique, cond. by Th. Wolff. Angelici, Lance, Collard, Giovanetti.

Victor LM-6135; **LSC-6135**—Orch. and Cho. of Rome Opera House, cond. by Leinsdorf. Moffo, Elias, Valletti.

DIE MEISTERSINGER:

Angel 3572-E/L—Berlin Philharmonic Orch., cond. by Kempe. Hoffgen, Schock.

Electrola 90275/9—Bayreuth Festival Orch., cond. by Von Karajan. Edelmann, Schwarzkopf, Hopf, Kunz, Malaniuk.

London A-4601—Vienna Philharmonic Orch., cond. by Knappertsbusch. Vienna State Opera Chorus. Schöffler, Gueden.

MIGNON:

London A-4309—Belgian National Orch., cond. by Sebastian. Brussels Cho. Moizan, Micheau, De Luca.

Selected Opera Recordings

SALOME:
  London A-4217—Vienna Philharmonic Orch., cond. by Krauss. Goltz, Patzak.
  Oceanic 302—Dresden State Opera Orch., cond. by Keilberth. Goltz.

TANNHÄUSER:
  Angel 35844; S-35844—Orch. and Male Chorus of German State Opera, Berlin, cond. by Konwitschny. Grümmer, Frick. (excerpts)
  Decca 9928—various orchs. and conductors. Rysanek, Windgassen, Waechter, Greindl. (excerpts)

TOSCA:
  Angel 3508-B/L—Orch. and Cho. of La Scala, cond. by de Sabata. Callas, Di Stefano, Gobbi.
  Cetra 1230—Orch. and Cho. of Radio Italiano, cond. by Molinari-Pradelli. Guerrini, Poggi, Silveri, Emanuel, Badlioli, Benzi, Coda, Biellesi.
  Cetra 1261—Turin Symphony Orch. and Cho., cond. by Basile. Tagliavini, Frazzoni, Guelfi.
  Columbia M2L-402—Orch. and Cho. of Teatro di San Carlo di Napoli, cond. by Serafin. Stella, Poggi, Taddei.
  London A-4235; OSA-1210—Orch. and Cho. of L'accademia di Santa Cecilia, Rome, cond. by Molinari-Pradelli. Tebaldi, Del Monaco, London.
  Victor LM-6052—Orch. and Cho. of Rome Opera House, cond. by Leinsdorf. Bjoerling, Milanov, Warren, Corena, Carlin, Monreale, Catalani.
  Victor LSC-6052—Orch. and Cho. of Rome Opera House, cond. by Leinsdorf. Bjoerling, Milanov, Warren, Carlin, Monreale, Catalani.

LA TRAVIATA:
  Angel 3545-B/L—Orch. and Cho. of La Scala, cond. by Serafin. Stella, Di Stefano, Gobbi.
  Capitol GCR-7221; SGCR-7221—Orch. and Cho. of Rome Opera House, cond. by Serafin. De Los Angeles, Del Monte, Sereni.
  Cetra 1246—Orch. and Cho. of Radio Italiano, cond. by Santini. Callas, Albanese.
  London A-4314—Orch. and Cho. of L'accademia di Santa Cecilia, Rome, cond. by Molinari-Pradelli. Tebaldi, Poggi.
  Victor LM-6003—Orch. and Cho. of NBC Symphony, cond. by Toscanini. Albanese, Merrill, Peerce.
  Victor LM-6040—Orch. and Cho. of Rome Opera House, cond. by Monteux. Carteri, Valletti, Warren.

TRISTAN UND ISOLDE:
  Angel 3588-E/L—Philharmonia Orch., cond. by Furtwängler. Flagstad, Fischer-Dieskau, Thebom, Schock.

IL TROVATORE:

Angel 3554-5-S/L—Orch. and Cho. of La Scala, cond. by Von Karajan. Callas, Di Stefano.

Cetra 1226—Orch. and Cho. of Radio Italiano, cond. by Previtali. Mancini, Pirazzini, Sciutti, Lauri Volpi, Tagliabue, Cololla.

London A-4326; **OSA-1304**—Suisse Romande Orch., cond. by Erede. Tebaldi, Del Monaco, Simionato, Tozzi.

Victor LM-6008—RCA Victor Orch., cond. by Cellini. Robert Shaw Chorale. Milanov, Bjoerling, Warren.

Victor LM-6150; **LSC-6150**—Orch. and Cho. of Rome Opera House, cond. by Basile. Price, Elias, Tucker, Warren, Tozzi.

DIE ZAUBERFLÖTE:

Decca DX-134—RIAS Chorus, Symphony Orch., cond. by Fricsay. Fischer-Dieskau, Streich, Greindl, Häfliger, Stader, Borg.

Electrola 80471/3S—Berlin Philharmonic Orch., cond. by Beecham. Strienz, Roswaenge, Lemnitz, Berger, Hüsch.

London A-4319—Vienna Philharmonic Orch., cond. by Böhm. Vienna State Opera Chorus. Gueden, Simoneau, Schöffler, Loose, Lipp, Boehme.

Index

Opera titles are set in SMALL CAPITALS; titles of arias, duets, ensembles, and instrumental numbers in *italics*.

Abendlich glühend, 208
Abendlich strahlt, 298
Abends, will ich schlafen, 165
Académie Royale, 436
Ach, ich fühl's, 423
Adalgisa, 222ff.
ADAM UND EVA, 442
Addio! del passato, 389-90
Addio fiorito asil, 197
Addio, O dolce, 55
Addio, senza rancor, 54
Adelia, 10
Adieu, Mignon, 218
AFRICAINE, L', 446
AGNES VON HOHENSTAUFEN, 446
Aha! da streicht schon, 209
Ah! che la morte, 410
Ah! chi mi dice, 116
Ah! del Tebro, 228
Ah! Du wolltest mich, 357
Ah, fors'è lui, 381
Ah, Mimì, tu più, 56
Ah, per sempre, 141
Ah si, ben mio, 409
Ah! si, fa core, 226
AIDA, 1 (*story*); 432
Ai nostri monti, 411
Ainsi que la brise, 131
Alberich, 290ff.
Alcalde, 139ff.
Alcindoro, 51ff.
Alerte! Alerte!, 138
Al fato dan legge, 104
Alfio, 94ff.
Alfredo Germont, 378ff.
Alisa, 183ff.

All' idea di quel, 31
Allmächt'ge Jungfrau, 365
Almaviva, Count, 25ff. (IL BARBIERE DI SIVIGLIA); 233ff. (LE NOZZE DI FIGARO)
Almaviva, Countess, 233ff.
ALMAVIVA, OSSIA L'INUTILE PRECAUZIONE, 25
Ambrosius, 33ff.
Amelia, 12 (*footnote*)
American opera, 452
American Opera and Its Composers, 454
A merveille!, 216 (*footnote*)
AMFIPARNASSO, 439
Amfortas, 266ff.
Amfortas! Die Wunde!, 274
Amneris, 2ff.
Amonasro, 3ff.
AMORE DEI TRE RE, L', 452
Amore o grillo, 193
Am stillen Herd, 202
ANDREA CHENIER, 430
Annina, 334ff. (ROSENKAVALIER); 382ff. (TRAVIATA)
Antonio, 238
Anvil Chorus, 404
Aprite un po' quegl', 242
Ardon gl'incensi, 189
ARIADNE AUF NAXOS, 452
Arturo Bucklaw, Lord, 185ff.
A terra!—si, nel livido, 255
Auber, Daniel, 10, 446, 447, 449, 453, 454
A un dottor della, 35

469

470 INDEX

AURELIAN IN PALMYRA, 27 (footnote)
AURELIANO IN PALMIRA, 27
Avant de quitter, 130
Ave Maria (OTELLO), 256
Azucena, 404ff.

Bacchanale (TANNHAUSER), 360
Balakirev, Mily, 437
Balcony Scene (LOHENGRIN), 174
Bald prangt, 424
Balfe, Michael William, 443, 455
Ballad opera, 442
Ballatella, 261
BALLO IN MASCHERA, UN, 10 (story); 139
BANK BAN, 448
Barbarina, 234ff.
BARBER OF SEVILLE, THE, 25 (story); 232, 445
Barbier, Jules, 128, 212
BARBIERE DI SIVIGLIA, IL, 59 (story); 232, 445
Barcarolle (UN BALLO IN MASCHERA), 16
Bardi, Count Giovanni, 438
Bardists, 438
Baron Douphol, 379ff.
BARTERED BRIDE, THE, 448
Bartolo, Dr., 27ff. (IL BARBIERE DI SIVIGLIA); 233ff. (LE NOZZE DI FIGARO); 242 (footnote)
Batti, batti, 120
Beaumarchais, 25, 232, 445
Beckmesser, 201ff.
Beethoven, Ludwig van, 437, 442
BEGGAR'S OPERA, THE, 442
Bei Männern, 418
Bellini, Vincenzo, 222, 446
Benoit, 46ff.
Berceuse (MIGNON), 219
Berg, Alban, 457
Bertha, 33ff.
Betto di Signa, 156

Bishop, Henry R., 443
Biterolf, 364
Bizet, Georges, 76, 451
Blick' ich umher, 363
Blühendes Lebens, 321
BOHEME, LA, 42 (story); 428
BOHEMIAN GIRL, THE, 443, 455
Boieldieu, François, 446, 453
Boïto, Arrigo, 245, 249, 450
Bonzo, 193, 194
BORIS GODUNOF, 60 (story); 449
Borodin, Alexander, 437, 449
Borsa, 280ff.
Boyars, 62 (footnote)
Brangäne, 393ff.
Brindisi (CAVALLERIA), 100; (OTELLO), 247
Bristow, George F., 455-56
Brother Melitone, 145ff.
Brüderchen, komm tanz', 162
Brünnhilde, 302ff.
Buoso Donati, 156ff.

Caccini, Giulio, 438
Cadman, Charles W., 457
CALIFE DE BAGDAD, LE, 446
Cammarano, Salvatore, 183, 401
CAMPANA SOMMERSA, LA, 452
Canio, 260ff.
CANTERBURY PILGRIMS, 457
Carissimi, Giacomo, 440
CARMEN, 76 (story); 429, 451
Caro nome, 284
Carré, Michel, 128, 212
Cassio, 246ff.
Casta Diva, 224
CAVALLERIA RUSTICANA, 94 (story); 259, 428
Cavalli, Pietro, 439-40
Celeste Aïda, 2
Cesare Angelotti, 369ff.
Cesti, Marc Antonio, 440
Champagne Aria, 119
Charpentier, Gustave, 451

INDEX

Che gelida manina, 48
Chernikofsky, 73
Cherubini, Maria Luigi, 446, 447, 449
Cherubino, 234ff.
Che soave zeffretto, 241
Chi del gitano, 404
Children's Prayer (HANSEL UND GRETEL), 162, 165, 168
Chi mi frena, 187
Chi vide mai a bimbo, 196
Chorus of Sirens, 360
Chorus of the Bells, 261
Chorus of the Swords, 131
CHRISTOPH COLOMB, 452
Cio-cio-san, 193
CLARI, 443
Claudel, Paul, 452
CLEMENZA DI TITO, LA, 102
Clotilda, 226ff.
Colline, 44ff.
Col sangue sol, 152
Come scoglio, 105
Commendatore Don Pedro, 115ff.
Connais-tu le pays?, 214
Converse, Frederick S., 457
COQ D'OR, LE, 449
Coronation Scene, 61 (*footnote*)
Cortigiani, vil razza, 286
COSI FAN TUTTE, 102 (*story*); 445
Count Ceprano, 280ff.
Countess Ceprano, 280
Court masques, 435
Credo, 249
Credo in un Dio, 248
Crudel! perchè, finora, 240
Crust Waltz, 167
Crust Witch, 164
Cui, César, 437
Curra, 140
CYRANO DE BERGERAC, 457
CYRUS IN BABYLON, 27 (*footnote*)

Czar Feodor, 61

DAFNE, 435, 439
Dafür ist man kein, 333
Dalla sua pace, 119
Dalle stanze, ove Lucia, 189
DAME BLANCHE, LA, 446
D'amor sull'ali rosee, 410
Damrosch, Leopold, 456
Damrosch, Walter, 457
Dance of the Seven Veils, 356
Da Ponte, Lorenzo, 102, 232, 460
Dargomijsky, Alexander, 448
Das schöne Fest, 202
Das süsse Lied verhallt, 178
David, 200ff.
Debussy, Claude, 452
Deh non parlare, 283
Deh vieni (Serenata), 122
Deh vieni, non tardar, 243
De Koven, Reginald, 457
De l'enfer qui vient, 131
Dell' aura tua, 223
De' miei bollenti, 382
Der Hölle Rache, 422
Der Irrnis und der, 276
Der kleine Sandmann, 165
Der kleine Taumann, 165
Der Vogelfänger bin ich, 415
Desdemona, 246ff.
Deserto sulla terra, 403
De son coeur, 220
Despina, 104ff.
DEUX JOURNEES, LES, 446
Dewman, 162ff.
Dich, theure Halle, 362
DIDO AND AENEAS, 442
Di due figli vivea, 402
Die Knusperhexe!, 164
Dies Bildnis ist, 416
Die Zeit im Grunde, 336
Di Luna, Count, 402ff.
Dimitri the Pretender, 61ff.
Din, don, suona vespero, 261

DIOCLESIAN, 442
Dio! mi potevi, 252
Dio ti giocondi, 252
Di Provenza il mar, 384
Di quella pira, 409
Di rigori armato, 332
Dir töne Lob, 360
Di' tu se fidele, 16
Don Alfonso, 103ff.
Don Alonzo, 38, 39
Don Alvaro, 140ff.
Don Basilio, 30ff. (IL BARBIERE DI SIVIGLIA); 233ff. (LE NOZZE DI FIGARO); 242 (*footnote*)
Don Carlo di Vargas, 142ff.
Don Curzio, 240
DON GIOVANNI, 114 (*story*); 444
Don Giovanni Minuet, 120
Donizetti, Gaetano, 183, 442, 445, 446, 447
Don José, 78ff.
Don Juan, 114
Donna Anna, 115ff.
Donna Elvira, 117ff.
Donne mie, 110
Donner, 293ff.
Don Ottavio, 116ff.
Don Ottavio! son morta!, 119
DON PASQUALE, 445
Dorabella, 103ff.
DORICLEA, 440
Dostig ya, 68
Dove sono, 241
Dovunque al mondo, 192
DREIGROSCHENOPER, 452
Dresden Amen, 266
Du bist der Lenz, 302
Duke of Mantua, 280ff.
Du Locle, Camille, 1, 2
Du trugest zu ihm, 172

E' Amore un ladroncello, 110
Ecco ridente, 27
Edgardo, 12ff. (UN BALLO IN MASCHERA); 184ff. (LUCIA DI LAMMERMOOR)
EDWIN AND ANGELINA, 453
Egli è salvo!, 149
Ein Mädchen oder, 424
Ein Männlein steht, 164
Einsam in Trüben Tagen, 171
Ein Schwert verhiess, 301
El Dancairo, 84ff.
ELEKTRA, 329, 429, 451
Elisabeth, 362ff.
Elisabeth's Prayer, 365
ELISABETTA, REGINA D'INGHILTERRA, 27
Elle ne croyait pas, 220
El Remendado, 84ff.
Elsa of Brabant, 171ff., 429
Elsa's Dream, 171
E lucevan le stelle, 376
Emilia, 250ff.
EMPEROR JONES, 457
Enfin ma colère, 90
Enrico, Lord, 184ff.
En vain j'interroge, 129
En vain pour éviter, 88
Era la notte, 251
Erda, 297ff.
Eri tu che macchiavi, 21
Erkel, Ferencz, 448
Escamillo, 83ff.
E scherzo od e follia, 16
Euch Lüften, die mein, 174
Euch wird es leicht, 210
EUGEN ONEGIN, 448
Eulogy of Love, 363
EURIDICE (Peri), 439
Eva Pogner, 200ff.
Even bravest heart, 130

Fafner, 293ff.
Faites-lui mes aveux, 132
FALSTAFF, 449
Fanget an!, 203

INDEX

Faninal, 337ff.
FANISKA, 446
Fasolt, 293ff.
Father Guardiano, 145ff.
FAUST, 128
Feodor, 61ff.
FERNANDO CORTEZ, 446
Ferrando, 103ff. (COSI FAN TUTTE); 402 (IL TROVATORE)
FIDELIO, 445, 455
Figaro, 28ff. (IL BARBIERE DI SIVIGLIA); 233ff. (LE NOZZE DI FIGARO); 242 (footnote)
Figaro trilogy, 25, 233
Finch' han (*Champagne Aria*), 119
Fiordiligi, 103ff.
Fiorello, 27ff.
Firenze è come, 158
Five, The, 437
Flavio, 223
FLIEGENDE HOLLANDER, DER, 448
Flora Bervoix, 379ff.
FLORA; OR, HOB IN THE WELL, 453, 454
Florentines, 438, 439, 443, 452, 460
Flower Song (CARMEN), 86
Forest Murmurs (*Waldweben*), 312
Forge Song, 311
Fortunati affetti, 34
FORZA DEL DESTINO, LA, 139
Forzano, Gioachino, 155
Fountain (Garden) Scene (BORIS GODUNOF), 70 (footnote)
FRA DIAVOLO, 446
FRA GHERARDO, 452
Fra gliamplessi, 111
Fra poco a me, 190
Frasquita, 83ff.
Frau Holda kam, 361
Fredda ed immobile, 36
Frédéric, 215ff.

Frederick Telramund, 170ff.
Freia, 293ff.
FREISCHUTZ, DER, 448
Fricka, 292ff.
Froh, 293ff.
Fry, William Henry, 455, 456
Fuggiam gli ardori, 7
Fuggi, crudele, 116
Fugitif et tremblant, 213
Fu la sorte dell' armi, 5

Galilei, Vincenzo, 438
Garcia, Manuel, 27 (footnote); 454
Gastone, Viscount of Letorieres, 380ff.
Gertrude, 163ff.
Gherardino, 157
Ghislanzoni, Antonio, 1
Giacosa, Giuseppe, 42, 191, 368
Già i sacerdoti, 9
Gia nella notta densa, 248
GIANNI SCHICCHI, 155
Giarno, 213ff.
Gibichungs, 320
Giesecke, 413
Gilbert, W. S., 442, 443
Gilda, 282ff.
GIOCONDA, LA, 451
Giordano, Umberto, 451
Giorgio Germont, 383ff.
Giorno poveri vivea, 408
Giovanna, 283ff.
Giusto cielo! rispondete, 190
Givi i sdravstvuy, 64
Glinka, Michail, 437, 448
Gloire immortelle, 136
Gloria all' Egitto, 5
Glory and love, 136
Gluck, Christoph Willibald von, 436, 443, 444, 445, 449
GLUCKLICHE HAND, DIE, 452
Gluck-Piccinni feud, 444
Good Friday Spell, 277

474 INDEX

Goro, 192ff.
GOTTERDAMMERUNG, DIE, 318 (story); 291
Gott grüss euch, 170
Gounod, Charles, 128, 447, 451
Grand opera, 448, 455
Grand (Triumphal) March (AIDA), 5
Grenvil, Dr., 379ff.
Gretel, 162ff.
Grigory, 62ff.
Gruenberg, Louis, 457
Grüss Gott, mein Junker, 207
Guccio, 159
Guglielmo, 103ff.
GUILLAUME TELL, 447
Gunther, 320ff.
Gurnemanz, 266ff.
GUSTAVUS III, OU LE BAL MASQUE, 10
Gut'n Abend, Meister, 204
Gutrune, 320ff.

Habanera, 79, 83
Habet Acht, 398
Hab' mir's gelobt, 350
Hagen, 320ff.
Halévy, Jacques, 446, 447, 454
Halévy, Ludovic, 76
HALKA, 448
Hallam family, 453
Halte là, qui va là?, 85
Händel, Georg Friedrich, 442ff.
Hänsel, 162ff.
HANSEL UND GRETEL, 161 (story); 95, 450
HANS HEILING, 448
Hanson, Howard, 457
Hans Sachs, 200ff.
Ha più forte sapore, 372
Hasse, Johann Adolph, 442
Hawkins, Micah, 453, 456
Heil dir, Elsa, 176
Herald (LOHENGRIN), 175ff.

Herbert, Victor, 457
Herod Antipas, 353ff.
Herodias, 355ff.
Herr Morold zog zu, 394
Herzeleide, 269ff.
Hewitt, James, 453, 456
Hier sitz' ich, 322
Hindemith, Paul, 452
Hipsher, Edward E., 454
Hofmannsthal, Hugo von, 328
Hojotoho!, 303
Home, Sweet Home, 443
Home to our mountains, 411
Hopp, Galopp, 167
Horn Call, 312
HUGUENOTS, LES, 446
Humperdinck, Engelbert, 161, 450
Hunding, 300ff.
HUNYADY LASZLO, 448
Hymn to Venus, 360, 364

Iago, 246ff.; 430
Ich sah das Kind, 273
I DUE LITIGANTI, 126 (footnote)
Ieri son salita, 194
Il balen del suo, 406
Il était un Roi, 133
Illica, Luigi, 42, 191, 368
Il mio tesoro, 124, 126 (footnote)
Il pallor funesto, 186
IL TABARRO, 155
Il tuo sangue, 376
IL TURCO IN ITALIA, 26
Im fernem Land, 180
Immolation Scene, 327
Inaffia l'ugola!, 247
In diesem heil'gen, 422
Inez, 403ff.
Infami loro, 99
In mia man alfin, 229
Innocent Fool, 272ff.
Intermezzo (CAVALLERIA), 100
In uomini, 104

INDEX

IPHIGENIE EN TAURIDE, 444
Isis und Osiris, 423
I' trink kein Wein, 345

JEAN DE PARIS, 446
Je connais un pauvre, 217
Je crois entendre, 217
Je dis que rien, 89
Je ris de me voir, 133
Jerum! Jerum!, 205
JESSONDA, 448
Je suis heureuse!, 220
Je suis Titania, 213, 219, 220
Jewel Song, 133
Jokanaan, 353ff.
JONNY SPIELT AUF, 452
JOSEPH, 446
JUIVE, LA, 446

Kack tomitelno, 69
Kack vo gorode (Kazan), 65
Kann ich mich auch, 336
Kate Pinkerton, 197
Keiser, Reinhart, 442
Khrushchof, 72
King Henry, 170ff.
King Marke, 393ff.
King of Egypt, 2ff.
King of Thule, 133
KING'S HENCHMAN, THE, 457
Kirchenchor, 200
Klingsor, 267ff.
Knusper, knusper, Knäuschen, 166
Knusperwalzer, 167
König's Gebet, 173
Krenek, Ernest, 452
Kundry, 267ff.
Kurvenal, 394ff.

La calunnia, 33
Lachmann, Hedwig, 352
Là ci darem, 118
La donna è mobile, 287

LADY MACBETH OF MTSENK DISTRICT, 452
LADY MACBETH MTSENKAGO UYEZDA, 452
Laërtes, 213ff.
La fleur que tu m'avais, 86
Laisse-moi contempler, 134
La mia Dorabella, 103
L'amour est un oiseau, 79
Landgraf Hermann, 361ff.
Laniere, Nicolo, 436
Largo al factotum, 28
La rivedro nell'estasi, 12
Lauretta mia, 160
La vendetta, 234
Lavitsky, 73
Leb' wohl, du kühnes, 306
Légères hirondelles, 215
Leitmotif, 450
Leoncavallo, Ruggiero, 259, 451
Leonora, 402ff.
LEONORA, 455
Leporello, 115ff.
LES FETES DE L'AMOUR, 441
Lesson scene, 38
Les tringles (Chanson Bohème), 83
Let me gaze, 134
Letter Duet (LE NOZZE DI FIGARO), 241
Leuchtende Liebe!, 317
Le veau d'or, 130
L'ho perduta, 242
Libiamo, libiamo, 380
Liebestod, 400
LIFE FOR THE CZAR, A, 437, 448
Lindoro, 30ff.
Lodovico, 253ff.
Loge, 293ff.
LOHENGRIN, 169 (*story*); 429
Lola, 95ff.
Lortzing, Gustav Albert, 448
Lothario, 213ff.
LOUISE, 428, 451

476 — INDEX

LOVE OF THREE KINGS, THE, 452
LUCIA DI LAMMERMOOR, 183 (*story*); 432
Lully, Jean Baptiste, 436, 441

Ma dall' arido, 18
MADAMA BUTTERFLY, 191
Madamina, 117
Madre, pietosa Vergine, 145
Mad Scene (LUCIA DI LAMMERMOOR), 188
Magdalene, 200ff.
MAGIC FLUTE, THE, 413
Mal reggendo, 406
Ma mère, je la vois, 80
Mamma Lucia, 96ff.
MANON LESCAUT, 42
Manrico, 403ff.
Marcellina, 234ff. (LE NOZZE DI FIGARO); 242 (*footnote*)
Marcello, 43ff.
March of the Priests, 420
Marguerite, 129ff.
MARIAGE DE FIGARO, LE, 25, 232
Mariandel, 331ff.
Marianne Leitmetzer, 337ff.
Marina Mnishek, 69ff.
Mario Cavaradossi, 369ff.
MARITANA, 443
Marquis d'Obigny, 379ff.
Marquis of Calatrava, 140ff.
MARRIAGE OF FIGARO, THE, 232 (*story*); 25
Marschallin, Princess von Werdenberg, 329ff.
Marschner, Heinrich, 448
Marullo, 281ff.
MASANIELLO, 446
Mascagni, Pietro, 94, 259, 451
Ma se m'è forza, 23
Masetto, 117ff.
MASKED BALL, THE, 10
Mask Trio, 120
Massenet, Jules, 451

Meco all'altar, 224
MEFISTOFELE, 450
Mehul, Etienne, 446
Meilhac, Henri, 76
Mein Herr und Gott, 173
MEISTERSINGER, DIE, 199 (*story*); 430, 450, 456
Melot, 398ff.
Menasci, Guido, 94
Me pellegrina, 141
Méphistophélès, 129ff.
Me protegge, 224
Mercedes, 83ff.
MERE COUPABLE, LA, 25
Mérimée, Prosper, 76
MERRY MOUNT, 457
Mesyatz yedet, 72
Metastasio, Pietro, 443
Metzler, Johann (Giesecke), 413
Me voici dans son, 217
Meyerbeer, Giacomo, 446, 448, 449, 454
Micaela, 78ff.
Mi chiamano Mimi, 48
Mi dicon venal, 374
MIGNON, 212
Mild und leise, 400
Milhaud, Darius, 452
Mime, 294ff.
Mime hiess ein, 326
Mimi, 47ff.
Mira o Norma, 228
Miserere, 410
Missail, 64ff.
Mit Ihren Augen voll, 340
Mitiukha, 62
Mit mir, mit mir, 340
Mi tradi, 117 (*footnote*)
Mohamed, 330ff.
MONA, 457
Moniuszko, Stanislaw, 448
Monostatos, 419ff.
Montano, 246ff.
Montemezzi, Italo, 452

INDEX

Monterone, Count, 281ff.
Monteverdi, Claudio, 439, 460
Morales, 77
Morgenlich leuchtend, 210
Moussorgsky, Modest, 60, 437, 449
Mozart, Wolfgang Amadeus, 102, 114, 232, 413, 437, 442, 443, 445, 460
  COSI FAN TUTTE, 102
  DON GIOVANNI, 114
  NOZZE DI FIGARO, LE, 232
  ZAUBERFLOTE, DIE, 413
Musetta, 43ff.

Narraboth, 353ff.
NATOMA, 457
Nedda, 261ff.
NEUES VOM TAGE, 452
Newman, Ernest, 449
Nibelheim, 294
Non la sospiri, 370
Non mi dir, 126
Non più andrai, 236
Non sapete quale, 383
Non siate ritrosi, 105
Non so più cosa son, 234
NORMA, 222
Normanno, 184ff.
Norns, 318-19
Nothung! Nothung!, 311
Notte e giorno, 115
Nous avons, 84
NOZZE DI FIGARO, LE, 232 (*story*); 126 (*footnote*); 430, 444
Nun sei bedankt, 172
Nur eine Waffe taugt, 278

O che bel sole, 261
Ochs, Baron, 331ff.
O Columbina, il tenero, 263
Octavian, 330ff.
Odnajdi v vetcherniy, 74
O du mein holder, 366

Ohne mich, 343
Oh, quanti occhi fisi, 194
Oh, tu che in seno, 147
O mio babbino, 158
O nuit, étends sur eux, 134
Opéra bouffe, 441-42
Opera buffa, 445, 447, 452
Opéra-Comique, 76, 453
Opera seria, 445, 447, 452
Ora e per sempre, 253
ORFEO ED EURIDICE, 436, 443
Oroveso, 223ff.
Ortrud, 171ff.
Oscar, 12 (*footnote*)
O sink hernieder, 397
O soave fanciulla, 49
OTELLO, 245 (*story*); 449
O terra addio, 9
Oui, je veux par, 214
O wunden-wundervoller, 267

Pace, pace mio Dio!, 153
PAGLIACCI, 259 (*story*); 94, 428
Pagliaccio non son, 264
Paisiello, Giovanni, 26, 445
Pamina, 414ff.; 417 (*footnote*)
Papagena, 418ff.
Papageno, 415ff.
Parigi, o cara, 390
Pari siamo, 282
Parker, Horatio, 557
Parmi veder le lagrime, 285
Parpignol, 50ff.
PARSIFAL, 265 (*story*); 161, 169, 450
Pauvre enfant!, 218
Pelissier, Victor, 453
PELLEAS ET MELISANDE, 452, 457
Peppe, 261ff.
Pepusch, John, 443
Pergolesi, Giovanni, 445
Perigourdine, 281
Peri, Jacopo, 438, 439
Per me ora fatale, 406

INDEX

Per pietà, ben mio, 109
Per poco fra le, 187
Per te d'immenso, 187
PETER IBBETSON, 457
Peter the broommaker, 163ff.
Philine, 213ff.
Piave, Francesco, 139, 279, 378
Piccinni, Nicola, 444
Piccolo Iddio, 198
Pilgrim's Chorus, 361, 365
Pimen, 62ff.
Pinellino, 159
Pinkerton, Lieutenant, 192ff.
PIPE OF DESIRE, THE, 457
PIQUE-DAME, 460
Pizzetti, Ildebrando, 452
Pogner, 201ff.
Pogner's Address, 202
Pollione, 222ff.
Polonaise, 71 (BORIS GODUNOF); 219 (MIGNON)
POMPEO, 436
Ponchielli, Amilcare, 450
Porgi amor, 236
PORGY AND BESS, 458
Possente, Phtha, 4
Preislied, 210
Presentation of the Rose, 338
Preziosilla, 142ff.
PRINCE IGOR, 449
Prince Yamadori, 195
Prize Song, 210
Prologue (PAGLIACCI), 260
Protegga (*Mask Trio*), 120
Protshay moy sin (*Farewell of Boris*), 74
Puccini, Giacomo, 42, 155, 191, 368, 451
   BOHEME, LA, 42
   GIANNI SCHICCHI, 155
   MADAMA BUTTERFLY, 191
   TOSCA, 368
Purcell, Henry, 436, 442
Pushkin, Aleksandr, 60

Quando me'n vo'soletta (*Valse*), 51
Quando rapita in estasi, 185
Queen of the Night, 416ff.
Questa o quella, 280
Quest' è una ragna, 253

Radames, 1ff.
Raimondo, 184ff.
Rameau, Jean Philippe, 441
Ramfis, 2ff.
Rangoni, 70ff.
Rataplan (LA FORZA DEL DESTINO), 151
Recondita armonia, 369
Re dell' abisso, 14
Regina Coeli, 97
Regnava nel silenzio, 184
Renaissance, 438ff.
Renato, 12ff.
Respighi, Ottorino, 452
RHEINGOLD, DAS, 290 (*story*); 432
Rhinemaidens, 292ff.
Riccardo, 11ff.
Ride of the Valkyries, 291, 305, 322
Ridi, Pagliaccio, 260, 263
RIGOLETTO, 279 (*story*); 401
Rimsky-Korsakov, Nikolai, 61, 449
RING DES NIBELUNGEN, DER, 290 (*story*); 392, 427, 450, 456
Rinuccio, 156ff.
RIP VAN WINKLE, 155
Ritorna vincitor, 3
Robert le Diable, 446, 455
Robin Adair, 446
ROBIN HOOD, 457
Roderigo, 246ff.
Rodolpho, 43ff.
Romani, Felice, 222
Romantic opera, 444ff.
ROSENKAVALIER, DER, 328 (*story*); 452

INDEX

Rosina, 28ff., 232
Rossini, Gioachino Antonio, 25, 232, 437, 442, 445, 446, 454
Rousseau, 445
Ruiz, 406ff.
RUSSALKA, 448
RUSSLAN AND LUDMILLA, 448

Sacristan, 369ff.
Saint-Saëns, Camille, 451
Salce! Salce!, 256
SALOME, 352 (*story*); 95, 329, 429, 451
Salut! demeure, 132
SAMSON ET DALILA, 451
Samuele, 11ff.
Sandman, 165
Santuzza, 95ff.
Saper vorreste, 23
Sarastro, 417ff.
SAW MILL, THE, 453
Scarlatti, Alessandro, 436, 441ff.
Scarpia, 370ff.
Schaunard, 44ff.
Schikaneder, Emmanuel, 413
Schläfst du, Hagen, 323
Schoenberg, Arnold, 452
Schreker, Franz, 452
Schütz, Heinrich, 436
SCHWANDA, 452
Sciarrone, 372ff.
Scorrendo uniti remota, 285
Scribe, Eugène, 447
Scuoti quella fronda, 196
Sdyes moya golubka, 71
Se a caso madama, 233
Secco recitative, 447
Secondate, aurette, 108
Seguidilla, 82 (CARMEN); 142 (LA FORZA DEL DESTINO)
Seidl, Anton, 456
Se il mio nome, 30
Seit er von dir, 322
Seit Ewigkeiten harre, 274

Selig, wie die Sonne, 209
Sempre libera, 381, 429
Senti cor mio, 116
SERVA PADRONA, LA, 445
Se vuol ballare, 234, 237
Sextet (LUCIA DI LAMMERMOOR), 187
SHANEWIS, 457
Sharpless, 192ff.
Shchelkalof, 64ff.
Shostakovitch, Dmitri, 452
Shuisky, 64ff.
Siciliana, 95
Si corre dal notaio, 158
Siebel, 130ff.
Siegfried, 307ff.
SIEGFRIED, 308 (*story*); 392
Siegfried's Funeral March, 326
Siegfried's Rhine Journey, 319
Siegmund, 300ff.
Siegmund, sieh' auf, 304
Sieh, Evechen!, 208
SIGISMONDO, 26
Si le bonheur, 135
Silvano, 14, 15
Silvio, 262ff.
Simone, 156
Simpleton, 72
Sinfonia (LA FORZA DEL DESTINO), 140
Singspiel, 441, 444, 445
Si, pel ciel, 251
Si puo? Signore!, 260
Si tu m'aimes, 91
Sleale! Il segreto, 149
Smanie implacabili, 104
Smetana, Bedřich, 448
SO DO THEY ALL, 102
Soffriva nel pianto, 186
Soldiers' Chorus, 135, 136
Solenne in quest'ora, 148
Somma, Antonio, 10
Song of the Flea, 67 (*footnote*)
Song of the Golden Calf, 130

INDEX

Song of the Rat, 130
Song to the Evening Star, 366
SONNAMBULA, LA, 455
Sono andati?, 58
Son Pereda, son ricco, 144
Sophie von Faninal, 337ff.
Sparafucile, 282ff.
Spargi d'amaro pianto, 189
Spinelloccio, 158
Spinning Wheel Song (FAUST), 135
Spohr, Ludwig, 448
Spoletta, 375ff.
Spontini, Gasparo, 446, 448, 449, 454
Sterbini, Cesare, 25
Strauss, Richard, 328, 352, 429, 451
   ROSENKAVALIER, DER, 328
   SALOME, 352
Stride la vampa, 404, 411
Struggi, o Re, 6
Styrienne (MIGNON), 217
Sullivan, Sir Arthur, 442, 443
SUOR ANGELICA, 155
Susanna, 233ff.
Suzuki, 192ff.

Tacea la notte, 403
Tamino, 414ff.
TAMMANY; OR, THE INDIAN CHIEF, 453
T'amo ripetilo!, 284
T'amo, si t'amo, 24
TANNHAUSER, 358 (story)
Tannhäuser March, 363
Targioni-Tozzetti, Giovanni, 94
Taylor, Deems, 457
Te Deum (TOSCA), 371, 372
Teneri figli, 227
Theile, Johann, 442
Thomas, Ambroise, 212, 451
Three Genii (DIE ZAUBERFLOTE), 423ff.

Three Ladies (DIE ZAUBERFLOTE), 415ff.
Tituel, 268ff.
Tommaso, 11ff.
Tonio, 260ff.
Toreador Song, 84, 91, 93
TOSCA, 368
Trabuco, 142ff.
Tradito, schernito, 110
Transformation Scene (PARSIFAL), 269-70
TRAVIATA, LA, 378 (story); 432
Treulich geführt, 178
TRISTAN UND ISOLDE, 392 (story); 209, 450, 456
Trouvères, 439
TROVATORE, IL, 401 (story); 378, 432
Tschaikowsky, Peter Ilyitch, 449
Tu che a Dio, 190
Tu qui Santuzza, 98
Turiddu, 95ff.
Tutte le feste, 286
TWILIGHT OF THE GODS, 318
Two Men in Armor, 425

Ulrica, 13ff.
UNA COSA RARA, 126 (footnote)
Una donna, 108
Un' aura amorosa, 106
Una voce poco fa, 32
Un bel di, 195
Un di felice, 380
Un di, se ben rammento, 287
Un nido di memorie, 260
Un rat plus poltron, 130

VAIN PRECAUTION, THE, 29
Valentin, 130ff.
Valkyries, 299ff.
Valzacchi, 334ff.
Varlaam, 64ff.
Vecchia zimarra, 57
Vedrai carino, 123

INDEX

Vedrò mentr'io sospiro, 240
Venite inginocchiatevi, 237
Venusberg Music, 359, 366
Venus (TANNHAUSER), 359
Verachtet mir die, 211
Verdi, Giuseppe, 1, 10, 139, 245, 279, 378, 401, 437, 447, 449, 450, 451, 454, 460
  AIDA, 1
  BALLO IN MASCHERA, UN, 10
  FORZA DEL DESTINO, LA, 139
  OTELLO, 245
  RIGOLETTO, 279
  TRAVIATA, LA, 378
  TROVATORE, IL, 401
Vergine degli angeli, La, 146
Verismo, 329, 430, 437, 451
Verranno a te, 185
VESTALE, LA, 446
Vesti la giubba, 262
Via resti servita, 234
Viene la sera, 194
Viens! la libre vie, 215
Vin ou bière, 130
Violetta Valery, 379ff.
Vissi d'arte, 374
Viva il vino, 100
Voi, che sapete, 237
Voi dovrete fare, 101
Voi lo sapete, 97
Volta la terra, 13
Von Kuchen und Torten, 166
Vous qui faites, 136

Wach' auf, es nahet, 210
Wagner, 130-31 (FAUST)
Wagner As Man and Artist, 449
Wagner, Richard, 169, 199, 265, 290, 353, 358, 392, 448, 449, 450, 451, 460
  GOTTERDAMMERUNG, DIE, 318
  LOHENGRIN, 169
  MEISTERSINGER, DIE, 199
  PARSIFAL, 265

  RHEINGOLD, DAS, 290
  RING DES NIBELUNGEN, DER, 290
  SIEGFRIED, 307
  TANNHAUSER, 358
  TRISTAN UND ISOLDE, 392
  WALKURE, DIE, 299
Wahn! Wahn!, 207
Walhalla, 293ff.
WALKURE, DIE, 299 (*story*); 291, 292, 307, 316, 318
Wallace, William Vincent, 443
Wälse, 300ff.
Wälsungs, 300ff.
Walther von Stolzing, 200ff.
Waltraute's Narrative, 322
Wanderer, 309ff.
Weber, Carl Maria von, 437, 446, 447, 448
Wedding Chorus (LOHENGRIN), 178
Wehwalt, 301
Weibchen! Täubchen!, 425
Weiche, Wotan, weiche, 297
Weill, Kurt, 452
Weinberger, Jaromir, 452
Wenn die Not, 162
Wette, Adelheid, 161
When need is direst, 162, 168
Wie duftet doch, 204
Wie Du warst!, 330
Wie Sonne lauter, 327
WILDSCHUTZ, DER, 448
Wilhelm, 313ff.
Willow Song, 256
Winterstürme wichen, 302
Witches' Ride, The, 164
Wohl wusst' ich, 365
Wolf-Ferrari, Ermano, 451
Wolfram von Eschenbach, 265, 361ff.
Woman is fickle, 287
Wotan, 292ff.
WOZZECK, 452

Xenia, 67ff.

Yesho odno, 62

ZAR UND ZIMMERMANN, 448
ZAUBERFLÖTE, DIE, 413 (story); 102, 444
ZEMIRE UND AZOR, 448

Zerlina, 117ff.
Zum Leiden bin ich, 416
Zum letzten Liebesmahle, 270
Zu neuen Thaten, 319
Zuniga, 78ff.
Zurück von ihm, 364
Zwangvolle Plage!, 308